Nigel Hawthorne
on Stage

Nigel Hawthorne
on Stage

KATHLEEN RILEY

UNIVERSITY OF HERTFORDSHIRE PRESS

First published in Great Britain in 2004 by
University of Hertfordshire Press
Learning and Information Services
University of Hertfordshire
College Lane
Hatfield
Hertfordshire AL10 9AB

British Library Cataloguing in Publication Data
A catalogue record for this book is available from the British Library

ISBN 1-902806-29-8 hardback

Design by Whiteing Design Partnership, Hemel Hempstead HP2 7SN
Cover design by John Robertshaw, Harpenden AL5 2JB
Printed in Great Britain by Antony Rowe Ltd, Chippenham SN14 6LH

For my parents,
Jean and Frank,

and in memory of
Sir Nigel Hawthorne
(1929-2001)

Contents

List of Illustrations

Acknowledgements

My greatest debt is to Nigel Hawthorne for authorising this history of his theatre career and making time for me in person, on the telephone, and in writing despite both his commitment to completing his own book and his precarious health once cancer rudely took hold. He was a joy to interview, articulate, thoughtful and blessed with an excellent memory and strong powers of analysis, and he was kindness itself. When I began work on the book I never imagined that he would not be around to see the finished product and, like everyone who loved Nigel the man and admired his gifts as an actor, I miss him terribly.

I am enormously grateful to three other very special people who have been, and are, true friends and allies. Nigel's partner Trevor Bentham gave his blessing to my project just as readily as Nigel. His personal memories and insights, and his critical eye, have been invaluable, in addition to which he allowed me access to Nigel's earliest diaries, photographs and other memorabilia. Trevor's unfailing support and enthusiasm and, above all, his friendship have meant a tremendous amount to me. Thelma Holt, Nigel's close friend for forty years, has been another staunch supporter and made herself available time and again in an extremely hectic schedule. She was always willing to share with me her memories of Nigel from their early days together in the West End up until their *King Lear,* and she has provided a wonderfully intimate and loving portrait of Nigel in her foreword. Without Percy Tucker, fountain of all knowledge about South African theatre, the first two chapters of this book could not have been written. Percy continually pointed me in the right direction with my research into the companies of Brian Brooke and Leonard Schach, and nothing was ever too much trouble for him. In chasing up elusive production facts and chronological details, he spent hours consulting his vast personal records and trawling through theatre collections in Pretoria and Grahamstown. He supplied several photographs and countless press cuttings, and prevailed upon a number of Nigel's South African friends and colleagues to send me their memories. His energy, patience and care were limitless.

I am grateful to all those who gave so generously of their time to speak to me about Nigel. They include Alan Bennett, Samuel Goldwyn Jnr, Joyce Grant, Nicholas Hytner, Jonathan Lynn, Sheridan Morley, Peter Nichols and Hiroyuki Sanada. My thanks must also go to Sweetpea Slight, Malcolm

Taylor, Keisuke Asada and Rorri Feinstein for their help with contact information and arranging interviews. I would like to thank Shirley Firth, Michael McGovern and Helen Robinson for their written contributions and supporting material. I owe a special debt to Shaun Sutton who not only sent me many pages of facts and reminiscences about Nigel's first professional jobs in South Africa and England, but also put at my disposal a wealth of photographs, programmes and reviews. Those who responded to my enquiries by letter or e-mail include Jane Alexander, Douglas Gresham, Sir Alec Guinness, Clive Hirschorn, Richard Ingrams, the Rt. Hon. Lord Jenkins of Hillhead and James Roose-Evans.

In the course of my research for this book I received courteous and efficient assistance from numerous libraries, museums, theatres, archivists and theatre scholars. I would like to record my sincere gratitude to the following individuals and institutions: Richard Mangan of the Mander and Mitchenson Theatre Collection; the Shakespeare Centre Library and the Shakespeare Institute Library, Stratford-upon-Avon; the National Theatre Archive; the British Film Institute Library; the National Sound Archive; the British Library; Doug Hindmarch of Sheffield Local Studies Library; Dr Richard Foulkes of Leicester University; Northamptonshire Record Office; John Willmer, Archivist of the Connaught Theatre, Worthing; Ros Westwood, Derbyshire Museums Manager; the Goethe Institut Library, London; the State Library of New South Wales; the National Library of Australia; Lesley Hart, Head Librarian of the Manuscripts and Archives Department, University of Cape Town; Jeremy Fogg of the National English Literary Museum, Grahamstown; Susan Cole, Theatre Administrator, and Patrick Curtis, Production Manager, of the Little Theatre, Cape Town; Professor Temple Hauptfleisch of Stellenbosch University; Tim Meier, Secretary of the Hancher Auditorium, University of Iowa; and the Citadel Theatre, Edmonton, Alberta. Most of all I wish to thank the knowledgeable and dedicated staff of the Study Room at the Theatre Museum in London and, particularly, Janet Birkett for her tireless, prompt, and accurate attention to my endless queries. I am grateful to Liane Froneman for the generous loan of three hard-to-find books which provided the basis of my South African research.

I thank the Right Reverend Christopher Herbert, Bishop of St Albans, for permission to quote from the beautiful address he gave at Nigel's funeral, and Sacha Newley, whose splendid portrait of Nigel as George III is reproduced on the cover.

I am indebted to Bill Forster of the University of Hertfordshire Press for his professionalism and care and for his confidence in, and enthusiasm for, what is an unusual biography. I am also most grateful to Stephanie Grainger of the University's Drama Department for her helpful and pertinent suggestions, and to Jane Housham for her very thorough and efficient editorial work.

Last but certainly not least I wish to thank my parents to whom this book is dedicated. As well as lending very practical assistance in the considerable task of proof-reading, they have encouraged and sustained me in this great labour of love through their own unstinting love and their belief in me and the worthiness of my undertaking.

Foreword

BY THELMA HOLT

When I was asked to write the foreword to this book, I hesitated. So many of us know Nigel Hawthorne the great actor and mourn his passing, but for me Nigel Hawthorne the man was just as important, and had a considerable effect on my life both professionally and personally. I can merely reminisce about someone it was very easy to love and to share some very happy memories. As a young man he had a great sense of fun, but he was also very reserved and did not show his playfulness until he was comfortable in your company. He also had an unerring ability to sniff out tensions and subtext, a must in a fine actor.

The *Yentl* in our relationship was the No. 31 London bus, but our memories of the event differed considerably. We had both been cast in William Saroyan's double bill *Across the Board on Tomorrow Morning* and *Talking to You*. At the tea break on the first day of rehearsal, we discovered that we both lived on opposite sides of the same road in Swiss Cottage, North London. He suggested that we should take the 31 together. On all the occasions when this story has been related his version was that I asked him, 'The 31 what?', to which he replied, 'The 31 bus.' He claimed that my rejoinder was, 'Oh, one of those big red things. What an adventure!' The love affair was on.

When Nick Hytner was putting together the celebration of Nigel's life, destined for the National's Olivier Theatre in 2002, I was spoilt for choice on Nigel stories, many of which I have cherished for forty years. It was Nigel who bought me my first pair of jeans and nearly gave me pneumonia, making me sit for ten minutes in the freezing English Channel in the middle of November in order to stop them looking 'so new, Thellie'. It was he who showed me how to grow an avocado, taught me to say quite unspeakable things in Afrikaans, and nurtured in me a talent I never knew I had. As a young man he was very attractive and regiments of women fell hopelessly in love with him. One of my duties was to let these ladies down as lightly as possible.

One such besotted fan followed us round on an eight-week tour, until he thought he was going batty. Frankly I too was getting bored with playing gooseberry. When he could stand it no longer he endured a conversation with her, which he thought would put an end to it. She was sufficiently resourceful that she had engineered staying in the same boarding house. Alack a day, next morning there she was at breakfast, a bit pink around the eyes, but otherwise as large as life and twice as determined. Nigel suffered a minor panic attack, and refused to come into the breakfast room. I could see that this was getting too complicated and so plotted with Nigel what I might do to persuade this lady to give up her quest. We were in Nottingham that week and I suggested he spend the day in Newstead Abbey, the seat of the Byrons. That good lord too had problems with ladies, and on the whole handled them much worse than Nigel ever did. This trip would take the whole day and when he came back he should come to the theatre in case I had failed.

He greeted this with enormous enthusiasm, and in a moment of euphoria declared that if we got away with it he would buy me the best curry in town. I was successful in my endeavours, and even took the rejected suitor to the railway station and waved her goodbye. I waited to share my success with him, and true to form he was delighted. When the curtain came down he fulfilled his promise and swept me off to the Taj Mahal. In the middle of the meal I said that I was grateful for the promised dinner, but that a word of thanks would not go amiss. A long pause (a Nigel pause) followed. He then said, 'I am terribly grateful and I would have said so, but then I realised that my gratitude fades into insignificance compared to your job satisfaction. You are obviously quite delighted with yourself. What are you going to find to do tomorrow?' Many years later when casting *The Clandestine Marriage,* we had a similar situation with Nigel's inability to disappoint. For a cast of eighteen he saw well over a hundred actors, and we discovered when we came to contracting people that he appeared to have promised roles to everyone he had seen. I had an awful lot of letters to write.

It was not all fun with Nigel. We talked late into the night about the pain he felt for South Africa and the deep love he had for his country, a love that never left him. It was he who arranged for me to spend six months in Johannesburg in a Peter Shaffer play, *The Private Ear and the Public Eye,* a visit that induced in me the birth of a political conscience. I have Nigel to thank for that. We knew each other's family, and Nigel was there for me when the father-in-law I greatly loved died. Nigel wrote me a letter of celebration, not condolence. He wrote about the golden days when we first knew each other and reminded me of a couple of funny things that my father-in-law had done. It was very different from the letters one receives or indeed writes on such occasions. It seemed so effortlessly graceful. I knew it had not been effortless, and I knew that much time and trouble had been taken in the writing of it. Some years later, he lost a dear friend, and the letter I wrote to him was almost a replica of the one he had written to me. I could think of no words better than his own.

After *The Clandestine Marriage,* we did not work again together until *King Lear,* his last performance on stage. I have a very deep affection for Yukio Ninagawa, the play's director, and to bring these two together was for me a complete and total joy. The day they met they were both attempting to be very grown-up. Nigel was very smart in a blazer and tie and Ninagawa was inevitably in designer black from head to toe. Ten minutes after they met, in spite of the fact that neither could speak the other's language, they were roaring with laughter. This *King Lear* was a co-production with the RSC, and we lived in a glorious fool's paradise in Japan, where we rehearsed and gave our first performances. Everything seemed to be perfection. Nigel embraced Japan, its people and culture wholeheartedly, and they returned the compliment.

He had previously met Hiroyuki Sanada after a performance in which Sanada had played Hamlet, directed by Ninagawa. I remember well their encounter in the Barbican car park. Nigel congratulated him on his performance and said, 'Why don't you play the Fool?', which is exactly what came to pass, to the delight of all of us. Nigel came home to London and landed with a bump. We did not please the critics, but this did not stop our audiences voting with their hands and voting loudly. His was a great Lear, albeit a very unexpected one. After that notoriously difficult opening scene of the play, we found that this was no declaiming king, but a frightened and disintegrating old man, hanging on to his dignity with what little strength he could muster.

He was there for me in my youth when I needed a shoulder to lean on and I hope I was there for him. We enjoyed having secrets and we had quite a few. I want to keep it that way until we meet again. I speak often to his partner, Trevor, who made their years together such joyous ones for Nigel and which Nigel spoke of many, many times when we were alone. I do not feel that Nigel has gone very far and when I do things of which he would disapprove (and there are many), I can hear him, see him shaking his head, wagging his finger. Much as he will welcome me where he is, he could do with a bit of a pause before I join him. Nevertheless, I have absolutely no doubt what his first words will be. He will simply beam at me and say, 'I've had an idea. Why don't we …'. I hope we don't need to make the books balance in heaven.

London, 2003

Prologue

Journeying Home

*If it be now, 'tis not
to come; if it be not to come, it will be now; if it be not
now, yet it will come: the readiness is all.*

(*Hamlet*, V.ii.220-24)

Although Sir Nigel Hawthorne achieved his international reputation through the media of television and film, the greater part of his career was spent in the theatre. The volume and variety of his stage work were formidable and encompassed everything from weekly repertory to the Royal Shakespeare Company, distinguishing him as a performer of unusual substance and protean range. He created roles in highly controversial plays by revolutionary writers like Edward Bond and John Osborne, and gave risk-taking and unexpected interpretations of canonical roles, most notably in *King Lear*. His climactic stage role in Alan Bennett's *The Madness of George III,* which he repeated on film, is his secure monument. The vast catalogue of actors with whom he worked on stage includes such diverse talents as Sir Ralph Richardson and Japanese actor Hiroyuki Sanada.

Nigel's progression in theatre, however, was a most unorthodox one in comparison with the other actor knights of his own and preceding generations. He did not issue from a theatrical dynasty and was not obviously endowed with the stuff of which actors are made. As a young actor he had to contend with his father's obdurate disapproval as well as his own crippling shyness and insecurity. He did not attend one of the major drama schools. Nor had he any immediate background in the England in which, in 1951, he chose to live and work and in which he ultimately achieved enormous success. Instead, his ambition to become an actor was conceived in early apartheid South Africa where dynamic artistic expression was often frustrated by profound social inequity, governmental philistinism, and the still prevalent colonial sense of cultural inferiority. Lacking the theatrical pedigree of a Gielgud or the innate panache and certitude of an Olivier, Nigel was closer in temperament to Kenneth Tynan's description of Alec Guinness as 'the humble Houdini'[1] who knows the combination to a part and has no need of ostentatious pyrotechnics.

Owing partly to his atypical beginnings, and the unpredictable nature of the route he subsequently followed in theatre, Nigel has featured seldom, and only peripherally, in theatre histories of the latter half of the twentieth century. This is a serious omission in view of his eventual eminence in the acting profession and the extent to which his work was directly affected by many of the definitive events, movements and personalities of this chapter of British theatre history. His first decade as a professional actor also saw his involvement in an important period of South Africa's theatrical evolution, a golden age dominated by the companies of Brian Brooke and Leonard Schach, between the end of the Second World War and the birth of an assertively indigenous dramaturgy that attended South Africa's increasing cultural isolation in the early 1960s. My purpose, therefore, is twofold: to redress this omission, and to present a new appraisal of post-war theatre by focusing on the personal journey of one of Britain's finest and most respected actors.

I have composed the book in three parts or acts. The first examines the developmental phases of Nigel's career; the circumstances of his professional formation are closely documented in order to explain the influence exerted by certain individuals and theatre companies on Nigel's evolving style and philosophy. Act Two explores the distinctive qualities of the mature actor, and the affirmation of his unique gifts and artistic principles. These later chapters, which concentrate on specific performances, constitute a case study of his theatrical methodology, having particular regard to his dissection of the text; his research into and preparation for a role; and his interaction, during the creative process of building a character, with writers, directors and fellow actors. Linking the first two sections is a short chapter on Nigel's occasional forays into playwriting and directing. The third act comprises three chronologies: first, a comprehensive record of Nigel's amateur and professional stage work from 1947 to 2000, with details of each production; secondly, a less exhaustive list of his film and television appearances; and finally, a table of theatrical events and premieres in Britain which coincided with his half century as a professional stage actor.

There are two recurrent themes in the story of Nigel Hawthorne's life in the theatre. The first of these is encapsulated in a line from *Hamlet*, 'the readiness is all'. In newspaper profiles and chat-show interviews of recent times, and in the numerous obituaries that followed his death, Nigel was uniformly, and somewhat erroneously, portrayed as a late starter. The first twenty-five years of his career were plagued by a sequence of rejections and disappointments and a mounting urgency to have his aspirations vindicated. Because he never fitted naturally into the mould of a juvenile lead, major success and recognition eluded him until the arrival of middle age. It is a popular misconception, however, that Nigel's role as Sir Humphrey Appleby in the television comedy series *Yes, Minister* was the decisive break that ended years of obscurity and dormancy. Of much greater consequence to his growth as an actor were several turning points that occurred in the theatre. As my chronology of his stage work demonstrates, before he achieved television stardom in the 1980s he was continually improving and plying his craft, and in some renowned quarters. His television and film work was not something separate from his achievements in the theatre, but stemmed directly from a strengthening confidence and credibility on stage.

In the 1950s Nigel was playing solid though largely conventional character roles within the South African and English repertory systems. At the beginning of the 1960s he was introduced to the school of Method acting by the American director Arthur Storch and shortly after joined, on the brink of its lively decline, Joan Littlewood's Theatre Workshop at Stratford East, where he found himself in an alien and exhilarating world of improvisation and collective creation. This was the crucial *peripeteia* of his career; he became a 'thinking clown' with a dangerous, anarchic streak. While working with the radical Littlewood, his most influential teacher, he was discovered by William Gaskill and soon began an equally instructive, if less liberating, association with the English Stage Company at the Royal Court in the wake of its first and legendary 'angry' decade. There, in the late 60s and early 70s, he helped to present some of the most original and provocative new writing within contemporary British theatre, including the last play to be banned by the Lord Chamberlain. The next major turning point in this progression occurred in 1973 when Nigel took over the lead in Christopher Hampton's *The Philanthropist*. His complete identification with the part of the diffident and vacillating bachelor don Philip was the catalyst to what became a defining quality of his artistry on stage and film, the exposure of his vulnerabilities. In the last two decades of his life Nigel performed leading parts in the West End and on Broadway, and belatedly made his mark on the principal institutions of Britain's theatre establishment, the National Theatre and the Royal Shakespeare Company. This was by no means a steady ascent, but, rather, an eccentric progress determined by erratic fortunes and singular talents.

The second theme in this story emerges from an examination of Nigel's maturing notion of the actor's assignment and is a motif central to much of ancient Greek epic and drama, that of *nostos* (a journey home). As with all good performers, Nigel's primary impulse and preoccupation were always to take his audience on a journey of exploration into the human condition. At its most successful this journey, which achieves its greatest immediacy in the theatre, is a homeward odyssey as both actor and spectator venture outside themselves into the experience of another character, time, or place, and return to the familiar enriched or enlivened by their shared discovery. In undertaking this voyage of discovery Nigel brought to bear the gifts of the seasoned storyteller as well as an emotional truthfulness, a burning imagination and intelligence, and a penetrating insight into the character he portrayed.

Nigel's stature as an actor and the scale of his achievements were reflected in the generous responses to my requests for interviews of those who worked closely with him. People such as Thelma Holt, Alan Bennett, Peter Nichols, Jonathan Lynn, Joyce Grant, Shaun Sutton, Samuel Goldwyn Jnr, Nicholas Hytner and Hiroyuki Sanada have spoken or written willingly, and at length, in praise of a greatly admired and respected actor and a much-loved friend. My research of Nigel's early South African stage career enjoyed some fortuitous information coups assisted, above all, by the unflagging enthusiasm of the magnanimous helper I discovered in Percy Tucker. My personal interviews with Nigel provided most valuable guides to the manner in which he developed his stagecraft and fashioned performances, as well as to his thoughts, general and specific, about the profession he served, and his perspective of the changes in theatre over the last five decades.

I grew up watching Nigel Hawthorne in *Yes, Minister* and *Yes, Prime Minister*, enthralled by his comic timing, verbal dexterity and the subtlety of his characterisation. At the same time I zealously sought out his other performances on television and film, for example his beautifully crafted roles in *The Knowledge, Edward and Mrs Simpson, The Barchester Chronicles* and *Mapp and Lucia*, and began looking into his past work in the theatre. I first saw him on stage in *The Madness of George III* at the National in 1993. I had not long left school and the play was a revelatory and transforming experience for me. The combination of Alan Bennett's writing and Nigel Hawthorne's acting inspired in me a deep passion for theatre. A year later I had the chance to see him again on the London stage in his own West End production of *The Clandestine Marriage*. On both occasions I wrote to him and received prompt and friendly replies.

In January 2000 I flew from Sydney expressly to see Nigel's *Lear* at Stratford. I had written to him a few months earlier asking whether, during my visit, I could interview him about *The Madness of George III* and *King Lear*, as I was then engaged in research on the parallels between these texts and Euripides' *Herakles* and Seneca's *Hercules Furens*. Nigel invited me backstage after the performance and two days later at his RSC digs we met to discuss his work on the mad kings. At the conclusion of a long and wonderfully enlightening conversation, I plucked up courage to ask his permission to write an authorised history of his theatrical work, an idea I had been formulating since seeing him in *The Madness of George III*. That he so readily and graciously gave his consent to the project continues to amaze me, especially as I was only twenty-five years old, had never written a book, and was shortly to embark on a D.Phil. in Classics at Oxford. In the two years that followed I enjoyed his full support and active co-operation in my task. My long-standing admiration for him as a truly magnificent actor grew into a deep affection for a person of exceptional warmth, humour and quiet dignity, who was both the gentlest and the bravest of men.

Not long after *King Lear* closed Nigel was diagnosed with pancreatic cancer. He underwent surgery, made an excellent recovery, and for a time resumed work. The following year in early spring he suffered a relapse. I last saw him on a beautiful summer's day at his home in Hertfordshire. He had just emerged from an intensive period of chemotherapy and had received a second 'all-clear' from his oncologist; but the reprieve proved only temporary. Nigel died of a heart attack on 26 December 2001, exhausted by his heroic eighteen-month battle against an unappeasable enemy. He died at home with Trevor Bentham, his beloved partner of twenty-two years, at his side. During the final four months of his life I had been in regular contact with Trevor and was aware of the many painful setbacks Nigel had sustained in the course of his treatment. Nevertheless his death was unexpected. He had been determined not to surrender to illness, but like his last stage character King Lear, 'to crawl towards death'. He remained cheerful and positive, in spite of his pain, unaccustomed frailty and the unpleasant nature of his treatment, and he believed he would get better.

It is a huge sadness to me that Nigel did not survive to see the book finished. The pleasant hours I spent in his company, revisiting a rich and remarkable life in the theatre, were a special experience and one I would not have missed for anything.

While the following history is not a traditional biography, it does recount a very substantial and, of course, inseparable part of its subject's life story, and does not falsely or arbitrarily impose a distinction between his private and professional selves. What I have sought to provide, however, is a detailed and historically integral account of the actor's performance work, to complement the personal narrative of his posthumously published memoirs. At its centre is an inspiring and human story of what Nigel himself called 'a struggle for dignity and justification'. Thus, an analysis of this uncompromising career inevitably reveals not only the talent, but also the courage, tenacity and resilience which were essential to its formation. The actor's journey home is reflected in the achievement.

Notes to Prologue

1   *Harper's Bazaar,* 1952: 'Olivier […] ransacks the vaults of a part with a blowlamp, crowbar, and gunpowder; Guinness is the nocturnal burglar, the humble Houdini who knows the combination.'

ACT ONE:

The Journey

(1929 – 1974)

'The poet's soul was with me at that time,
Sweet meditations, the still overflow
Of happiness and truth. A thousand hopes
Were mine, a thousand tender dreams, of which
No few have since been realised, and some
Do yet remain, hopes for my future life.

(William Wordsworth, *The Prelude*
[Text of 1805], Book VI, ll. 55-60)

Chapter 1

London Calling

'Does no other profession occur to you, which a young man of your figure and address could take up easily, and see the world to advantage in?' asked the manager. 'No', said Nicholas, shaking his head. 'Why, then I'll tell you one,' said Mr Crummles, throwing his pipe into the fire, and raising his voice. 'The Stage!' 'The Stage!' cried Nicholas, in a voice almost as loud. 'The theatrical profession,' said Mr Vincent Crummles.

(Charles Dickens, *Nicholas Nickleby*)

On 26 February 2000, five weeks short of the combined milestones of his seventy-first birthday and his half-century as a professional actor, Sir Nigel Hawthorne gave his last performance on stage. The play was *King Lear* and the venue the Royal Shakespeare Theatre at Stratford-upon-Avon. Newly knighted and appearing with the world famous Royal Shakespeare Company in the Bard's hallowed birthplace, millennial successor to the superlative role in dramatic literature and recipient of backstage plaudits from British and European royalty, he seemed to have firmly in his grasp all the conventional trappings of the great classical actor. Yet, in spite of these prestigious circumstances and his own gilt-edged credentials, Nigel's interpretation of Lear had defied convention and forsworn an awesome theatrical inheritance, thereby completing the unique pattern of his professional progress. He had chosen to do something daring and difficult rather than safe, mirroring his original decision to become an actor. It should have been his finest moment but was blighted by a conservative backlash from the critics. Nevertheless, it was a final demonstration of the integrity, imagination and pertinacity that had shaped an eventful career from its unlikely beginnings.

Nigel Barnard Hawthorne was born in Coventry on Friday 5 April 1929, the second child and elder son of Dr Charles Hawthorne, a local general practitioner, and his much younger wife Rosemary Rice. His father had served in France during the First World War as a captain in the Royal Army Medical Corps and now ran his own practice. He was a man who appreciated order and discipline, a formidable parent, autocratic and temperamental but capable of great charm, musical in a vigorous and rather bellicose fashion, and with a definite eye for the ladies.

> *Dad was old enough, I suppose, by the time I really got to know him, to have been my grandfather. He was someone we were rather fearful of because he was very strong and he demanded his role as a Victorian father. [...] I think that my relationship with my mother was a good deal closer than that I had with my father. She told me once that she had never been in love with him, but she believed he would make a good father for her children.*[1]

Nigel's more passive and forbearing mother came from a family of pioneering feminists and progressive educationalists. Elizabeth Garrett Anderson (1836-1917), the first British woman to qualify as a doctor, and her younger sister Millicent Garrett Fawcett (1847-1929), President of the National Union of Women's Suffrage Societies, were second cousins. In 1893 Rosemary's aunt and uncle, Amy and Jack Badley, founded the co-educational Bedales School in Hampshire as a radical and liberal alternative to the muscular Christianity of Arnold's Rugby. Then, as now, the school placed a strong emphasis on art, theatre and music. Its first art mistress was Nigel's adored grandmother Elsie Rice, a graduate of the Royal Female School of Art and a gifted painter and botanist.

When Nigel was just three years and four months old the family, which also included his older sister Sheila and infant twin brother and sister John and Janette, immigrated to Cape Town where Dr Hawthorne had bought a house and practice. The voyage from Liverpool took two weeks. They left behind a pallid and receding English summer and arrived on the threshold of a glorious Southern Hemisphere spring, with the exotic flora of the Dark Continent emerging into full splendour. The family initially set up home in the centre of town, under the shadow of Table Mountain and opposite the Company Gardens onto which opens the South African Museum, National Arts Gallery and St George's Cathedral. Later they built a new house nestled into the rugged rock-face in the middle of Barley Bay, a smaller inlet beyond Camps Bay.

Like many English expatriates the Hawthornes made little accommodation culturally to their new environment. The verandas around their second house were a concession to the Western Cape's Mediterranean climate, but their furnishings, habits and loyalties remained typical of the mother country.

> *The Cape was a very, very English place because it was still part of the Empire then. The people seemed to want to remain English and certainly the*

lives that my parents led were very English. We shot bolt upright when 'God Save the King' was played and there were Union Jacks everywhere. It was all really, obviously, a colonial part of Britain, but was still very much part of Britain.[2]

In one respect, however, the family did unconsciously assimilate. Without being at all affluent, their new life was an extremely privileged one. They had exchanged a modest Midlands existence for the sort of easy, insular lifestyle taken for granted by white South Africans and sustained by entrenched inequality.

In the months leading up to the outbreak of the Second World War the question of South Africa's possible involvement, and to which side it owed support, hung precariously in the balance, as many Afrikaners were not only staunchly anti-British but also aggressively pro-Nazi. But on 6 September 1939 South Africa, guided by the wisdom of General Jan Smuts, formally pledged its allegiance to the Allied cause by declaring war on Germany. Troop ships were farewelled and welcomed, the coast was blacked out, and air-raid shelters constructed, but for the most part the war did not drastically alter the day-to-day lives of the civilian population. The Hawthorne children continued to enjoy a comfortable colonial upbringing in their coastal idyll, far removed from the privation and constant peril facing millions across Europe. Fresh food and sea air were plentiful, rationing was slowly introduced but was not severe, and the horrors of the Holocaust and the Blitz were experienced only through filtered newsreel footage.

All during the war I spent the most wonderful childhood. When other children were, of course, deprived and being bombed and things, we didn't see any of that. So, if you like, it was a wonderful opening to a life, and a very healthy one because one was getting all that fresh air and the swimming and the mountain-climbing and everything.[3]

Their good fortune in being at such a distance from events in the homeland they could scarcely remember was chillingly brought home to their parents when, on 14 November 1940, Coventry suffered one of the most devastating bombing raids of the Blitz. Three-quarters of the city centre was razed to the ground, hundreds were killed, thousands injured and left homeless, and the medieval cathedral, in which Charles and Rosemary Hawthorne had been married and their four children baptised, was gutted.

The serenity and wholesomeness of Nigel's childhood were marred by a growing and, to him at the time, inexplicable inner unhappiness as he became acutely inhibited, introspective and withdrawn. The onset of his awkwardness and feeling of isolation coincided with his entry into the Christian Brothers' College in Green Point. He had previously attended St Cyprian's, idyllically situated on the mountain in Oranjezicht. Named after Cyprian of Carthage, the first African to be canonised, this was a girls' school but boys were admitted in kindergarten. Here Nigel, aged five, made his acting debut, doubling the roles of Michael Darling and the crocodile in an open-air staging of J.M. Barrie's *Peter Pan.* Two years later he was enrolled in St George's Grammar School, the oldest private school in South Africa and attached to the Cathedral, where he was rudely introduced to corporal punishment and the rigours of learning Afrikaans, the country's second language. When the family moved out of town to the Camps Bay area it became necessary to find schools for the children that were closer to their new home. Although the Hawthornes were not Catholic, the Christian Brothers' College on the slopes of Signal Hill was chosen for Nigel. The Brothers subscribed to a policy of intimidation, employing predominantly the strap but just as effectively a waspish and lacerating tongue, in teaching a rigidly circumscribed curriculum which favoured mathematics and science. They were past masters at instilling in their youthful charges a heightened, and in some instances lifelong, sense of guilt. Nigel quickly learnt that the College demanded strict conformity and was no refuge for the sensitive boy:

> *This was not a particularly happy experience for me and I think that at one time I would have been really quite brainy, quite academic, but it was sort of knocked out of me. I was very fearful of the Brothers. They were very aggressive. I think that this outward growing child eventually started to grow inward. I didn't really know who I was, what I was, or where I was. I was spotty and skinny and I really felt that I didn't exist as a being.*[4]

He had inherited his grandmother's artistic talent, though their styles were markedly different. In contrast to her very detailed and carefully executed watercolours and floral studies, Nigel produced lively and wonderfully observed caricatures. His father kept old copies of *Punch* at home and, as quite a small boy, Nigel could name every one of the periodical's artists from the 1920s and 30s. He earned the wrath of his teachers by covering his school books with their exaggerated likenesses. Never was his facility for drawing encouraged at school.

There was respite from the regularity of beatings and the drudgery of algebra and other abstruse subjects for which Nigel displayed scant aptitude in the transient excitement generated by the College's annual show. More often than not this was chosen from the works of Gilbert and Sullivan and produced by Brother Price, a young man with an infectious enthusiasm and a love of music. Like many of the younger boys whose voices had not yet broken, Nigel was usually assigned to the chorus. To his shame, in *The Pirates of Penzance* he was dressed and instructed to disport himself as one of a giggling group of pretty and flirtatious maidens. Performing in drag was an indignity he loathed and to which in his professional career he only twice submitted and with deep distaste. At least in *HMS Pinafore* in 1941 he was consoled by being part of a manly chorus of sailors.

Libretto of *HMS Pinafore* bearing Nigel's twelve-year-old signature. Christian Brothers' College, Cape Town. *(Courtesy of Ron Pinn)*

Around the same time he made his Shakespearean debut, taking part in a dramatic reading of *Richard II*. He was allowed to play the King only in Act IV, scene i, the deposition scene, as the other major scenes were allotted to other boys. At the moment when Richard dashes a mirror to the ground as a symbol of his loss of identity and cries, 'For there it is, crack'd in a hundred shivers', the wooden property Nigel had been given to simulate the looking-glass bounced from the designated place into the wings. He gamely pointed to where it had landed and said the line. There was a stirring from the auditorium; the coveted part was unceremoniously taken away from him and given to another pupil.

In his final year of school he had a momentary taste of stardom when the boy playing the Pirate King in a revival of *The Pirates of Penzance* fell ill and Nigel was called upon, at a few hours' notice, to step into the breach. This was the first occasion on which his improvisatory flair surfaced. With insufficient time to become word-perfect, he forgot the second verse of his solo and, without missing a beat, sang a reprise of the first. The nerves and apprehension he felt before going on stage evaporated as soon as the curtain rose. He counted this single performance as the one real triumph of his school years. His involvement, on even a limited scale, in these productions was a curiously exhilarating experience for an otherwise painfully shy lad who sometimes doubted his own existence.

Nigel also began to dabble in theatre outside school during his Matriculation year, performing in a series of one-act plays of a repertory nature staged by the vicar's wife in the parish hall of St Peter's in Camps Bay. He had earlier been drawn to St Peter's for a very different reason. Having mistaken his sexual confusion and apparent incongruity with the world around him for a Messianic destiny, he became for part of his adolescence fervently religious; he was confirmed by the Bishop, served as a minister of the Eucharist, and persuaded himself that he had a vocation to the priesthood. Eventually, as he slowly started to come to terms with his homosexuality and was made aware of the human fallibility of the priest, he grew disenchanted with the inability of the Church to supply the answers he earnestly sought and realised that he had mistaken his calling. Acting helped to fill the void created by his estrangement from the Church and, more than anything, it provided a temporary sanctuary from his complex self. But he had not as yet conceived any notion of forging a future from his enjoyment of theatre, beyond his immediate desire for escape.

I've no idea why I wanted to act, except it was a chance not to be me. I thought it would be a relief to hide behind strange characters. Some people act to parade their vanities and others to hide from themselves – that was me. I was a nothing as a young man. Although I had a quirkish instinct for making people laugh, I'm not extrovert enough to be a natural comedian. I used to observe, which meant I could stand right outside life and not exist. In a roomful of people I'd be too shy to reply if someone spoke to me. It wasn't until I was middle-aged I realised that to be good at this job you have to open yourself up and let the audience see what you are.[5]

During the war years in Cape Town there was very little in the way of professional live theatre to fire the imagination of a budding actor. English-language professional theatre was sluggish in establishing itself, and the already established Afrikaans-language professional companies, pioneered by Paul de Groot, the Hanekoms and André Huguenet, concentrated their efforts on remote tours and their productions were never a mainstream form of entertainment (although in 1947 Huguenet gave an unforgettable and widely lauded performance as Hamlet in an Afrikaans translation). The monopolist and commercially driven syndicate African Consolidated Theatres (ACT), which owned all the theatres in the country, was obliged under its contracts with the film distribution companies to screen films virtually fifty-two weeks a year. Stage presentations were intermittently incorporated into the programmes of cinemas (or bioscopes as they were called) that could suitably accommodate live performance, but these rather half-hearted bids for prestige and variety usually incurred financial loss. Occasionally straight plays of quality were staged but, in general, ACT preferred light entertainment such as musicals and pantomimes. Theatre was largely, therefore, an amateur concern, centred in schools and later in universities and repertory societies. Overseas touring companies were popular attractions before the war and local talent was often neglected in favour of imported stars. When hostilities began and the practice of importing performers became impossible, it seemed that even the minimal professional theatre activity there was would cease. Yet, since the mid 1930s, events in Europe had indirectly created in South Africa a greater than ever demand for local professional theatre. The influx of German-Jewish refugees, intent on making and supporting theatre, had a positive impact on the country's attitudes to drama; to Johannesburg, Leonard Schach records, they brought 'the theatre of social conscience',[6] while to Cape Town they introduced the concept of serious and conscientious theatre patronage.

What principally saved wartime South Africa from a famine of professional theatre was the emergence of dedicated and energetic actress-managements, including the partnerships of Gwen Ffrangcon-Davies and Marda Vanne, Nan Munro and Margaret Inglis, and René Ahrenson and Cecilia

Sonnenberg. The companies headed by these enterprising women mounted productions in the empty theatres on the ACT circuit and laid the foundations of a renascent South African theatre. The best-known company, and the one with the most impressive and varied repertoire, was that of English actress Gwen Ffrangcon-Davies and her on- and off-stage partner, Vanne, who was born in Pretoria. In April 1940 the pair arrived in South Africa from Britain and remained there for the duration of the war. They originally assembled a company of bilingual actors and undertook two extensive tours of the country, travelling in a special railway carriage which doubled as their home. The plays they presented were *Twelfth Night* and Barrie's *Quality Street.* Other tours of Shakespearean and contemporary classics followed. In 1945 sixteen-year-old Nigel saw the Ffrangcon-Davies-Vanne production of *The Merry Wives of Windsor* in which Wensley Pithey appeared as Falstaff. After the war Pithey established himself in England as a character actor on stage and screen, frequently playing portly authority figures, and in the late 1970s he gave a splendid performance as Winston Churchill in the television series *Edward and Mrs Simpson,* in which Nigel with brilliant accuracy portrayed the King's friend and legal adviser Walter Monkton.

Ffrangcon-Davies, who had played Juliet to John Gielgud's Romeo in London in 1924, was one of the earliest and most abiding influences on Nigel. Back in Britain forty years later the two formed a close and delightfully out-of-the-ordinary friendship that lasted until her death at the age of 101.

She was a great friend. I don't know how it happened and you can't really explain that. I grew up with her in a way because I'd seen her when I was a young boy. It was during the war. She used to come out to South Africa and tour. And it wasn't until she was ninety-four that I got to know her and went to stay with her. Trevor and I went to stay at her home in Essex. She took to phoning me up three and four times a week and wouldn't let me off the hook. She just said, 'You're my friend now and that's what you are for life.' And whether I was in New York or South Africa or wherever I was, I always had to ring her at least once a week to see how she was and she wouldn't hear otherwise. I loved her and it was the most odd relationship.

Her approach to acting was something I very much understood. She had huge dedication and huge technical knowledge, even though her eyesight was so terrible. She remembered things, she remembered acres of Shakespeare from her youth. She did poetry recitals with me on BBC radio just from memory, because she couldn't see to read. So she was a real influence, and a very, very precious person to me.

We got very close indeed and I saw her just a couple of days before she died. I went and sat by her bed and she took my hand and she said, 'Do you know, you and I have had a very special relationship and I wouldn't have missed it for anything.'

Despite the excellent work of Gwen Ffrangcon-Davies and other actress-managers, in the mid 1940s Cape Town still lacked a vibrant and focal theatre scene in which aspiring actors and eager audiences could engage. On the home front, with the exception of his like-minded grandmother who had joined the family in South Africa, Nigel received even less encouragement in his new-found interest in the stage. His father in particular opposed any idea of play-acting as a serious or worthwhile occupation. Quite apart from his very reasonable concern that his son's extra-curricular involvement in theatre might interfere with his studies, Charles Hawthorne's animosity stemmed from a deeper anxiety.

He really didn't understand about plays at all, had no liking for them. He used to call them 'dressing-up'. It was a sort of sissy side that he didn't want any part of, or want his children to be part of. And so to see one of his own sons moving in that direction I think rather horrified him.[7]

In later life Nigel recognised the key to his difficult relationship with his father in a passage from John Betjeman's autobiographical verse cycle *Summoned by Bells* (1960). Betjeman was a poet with whom Nigel had a particular affinity and whose eccentricity and flirtatiousness and his humorous use of the language of the nursery, reminded him of his father.

> *'Catch hold,' my father said,*
> *'Catch hold like this!'*
> *Trying to teach me how to*
> *   carpenter.*
> *'Not that way, boy! When will*
> *   you ever learn?'*
> *I dug the chisel deep into my*
> *   hand.*
> *'Shoot!' said my father, helping*
> *   with my gun*
> *And aiming at the rabbit -*
> *'Quick, boy, fire!'*
> *But I had not released the safety*
> *   catch.*
> *I was a poet. That was why I*
> *   failed.*

The adolescent Nigel was not entirely bereft of inspiration in his artistic pursuits. He was, in fact, surrounded by theatre in its broadest, most vital sense. Leonard Schach, who within the next decade would help to revolutionise Cape Town's professional theatre, wrote at the opening of his personal history of theatre in the old South Africa: 'Everything about Southern Africa is theatrical and dramatic,' adding that 'if the Greeks had colonised the Cape, they would have fashioned here a theatre far outstripping the glories of Epidaurus and Syracuse.'[8] Schach was referring to the country's inherent drama and majesty, its unique geography and geology, and the rich cultural mix of its inhabitants. The theatrical landscape of the Cape Peninsula, with its imposing backdrop of mountains presiding over vast stretches of sea, was something to which Nigel, although English-born, felt profoundly connected. He had a special affinity with the dominant Table Mountain, which for him remained an always comforting symbol of wonder and uncomplicated joy.

Nigel left the Christian Brothers at the end of 1946 with little sense of direction. Like many school leavers, he did not yet know what he wanted to do with his life or where his talents lay. At his father's suggestion he went for an interview at Southern Insurance, whose offices were located in the same building as Dr Hawthorne's consulting rooms, and was offered the position of junior clerk in the firm's Motor Department. His duties were to answer customer enquiries and process third-party insurance claims. He was by no means ideally suited to the job as he had no interest or expertise in cars and did not even learn to drive until he was fifty.

Meanwhile his enthusiasm for acting had not waned and in July 1947, no doubt partly as an antidote to the oppressively pedestrian nature of his work, he became a member of the Cape Town Repertory Theatre Society. The first occasion on which he performed with the Rep was a Members' Evening in September, when he participated in a dramatic reading of Sean O'Casey's *Juno and the Paycock* at the University of Cape Town's Little Theatre. As a result of his reading of the part of Johnnie Boyle, which he thought very poor, he was asked by the director Rosalie van der Gucht to walk on in her student production of *The Merchant of Venice*. At one matinée he was given the chance to play Tubal: 'I was very excited, and although probably a very insecure and uncertain Tubal, it seemed to go without a hitch.' The first full-scale Rep production in which Nigel appeared was James Bridie's *Tobias and the Angel*, directed by Joyce Burch and again staged at the Little Theatre. He played a trio of parts – the bandit, Sam and Asmoday – and, in the words of the critic for the *Cape Argus*, 'trebled competently'.[9] He afterwards wrote of the production:

The play was a great success. Mr Bateman [critic for the Cape Argus] had a kind word (literally) to say about me. A lovely production – an imaginative use of lighting, lovely costumes and settings and excellent performances from Tobias, the Angel, Sara, Tobit and Anna.

J. O. [Johanna Oliver who played Sara] was my first stage flame, and used to sit on my lap while waiting for her cue.

In the play I was 'adequate'.

```
REPERTORY  THEATRE  SOCIETY

P. O. Box 2179    CAPE TOWN


                    15th July, 1947.

Mr N. B. Hawthorne,

Dear Sir/Madam,

                I acknowledge with much pleasure
receipt of Form of Application for Membership duly
completed by you, together with your remittance of

            £   1  :   1  :  -

being your Subscription up to 31st Mar.194 8.  At
the last meeting of the Executive Committee you
were elected a member of this Society.

                Herewith I enclose your Membership
Card which, on presentation at the booking-office,
entitles you to two seats for the price of one at
all Repertory Theatre Society and University pro-
ductions. Notices of these productions and of other
meetings and functions of the Society will be posted
to you from time to time.

                Thanking you for your response to
our Invitation, and hoping that you will derive much
pleasure from your association with us,

                I remain,

                Yours faithfully,



                HON. SECRETARY.
```

Letter acknowledging membership of Cape Town Repertory Theatre Society.

Nigel persevered in motor insurance for a year before finally deciding to give in his notice and make the transition to university in the hope of improving his prospects. He enrolled at the University of Cape Town in a Bachelor of Arts degree with a diploma in broadcasting, majoring in English and Afrikaans. University opened up a whole new world of self-determination and self-discovery for him. It was a welcome change from the regulation of school and the tedium of his desk job and allowed him a break from paternal strictures as he was able to stay with his grandmother in Rondebosch to be nearer the campus. University also reunited Nigel with his former Christian Brothers' classmate, the impish and extremely likeable Jobie Stewart who was studying Drama. They became inseparable companions, sharing a keen sense of the absurd, and under Jobie's influence Nigel gravitated more and more towards the Speech-Training and Drama Department and its familiar and enviably well-equipped Little Theatre at the top end of Government Avenue.

The Drama Department of the University of Cape Town, which today on its web page proudly lists Nigel among its distinguished alumni, was the first university faculty of drama to be established in the English-speaking world and, according to Leonard Schach, 'the Little can justly be said to have laid the foundations of South African theatre.'[10] The Little was the brainchild of the University's Professor of Music, W. H. Bell, who in 1931 converted an old chemistry laboratory into an experimental and rehearsal theatre space in the hope 'that experiments in production and "décor" may be carried out somewhat akin to those already brought to such interesting issues, not only in the great State-subsidised theatres of the Continent, but in many Little Theatres in England, America, Canada and elsewhere.'[11] His success was such that two years later he was granted approval to enlarge the auditorium to its current proportions. This unpretentious and purpose-built theatre, which for two and a half years was Nigel's second home, provided an unrivalled training ground for the country's future professional actors, directors and designers, and, in presenting to a high standard the work of writers from Euripides to Samuel Beckett, they 'made the Cape Town audience an informed and perceptive one.'[12] In the forties the Head of Drama was the legendary Rosalie van der Gucht who had trained at London's Central School of Speech and Drama and was largely responsible for the quality and renown of the Little's productions.

Through his association with the Speech-Training and Drama Department, Nigel became part of a close-knit group of seven friends that, along with Jobie Stewart, included Anthony Holbery, Cecil Jubber, Helen Houghton, Peter Lamsden and Meryl O'Keeffe. Helen Houghton (now Dr Helen Robinson) performed with Nigel in a number of student productions and remembers him as a wonderful mimic, who, aided and abetted by Anthony Holbery and the irrepressible Jobie, would execute a parody of their three lecturers in the Drama Department:

Pre-empting the Peter Sellers/Monty Python style, it was a very in-joke but hilarious. Nigel usually played our Head of Department (Rosalie van der

Gucht) but he had variations. They did it regularly at parties and elsewhere but only once did Rosalie walk in and catch them at it. There were other scenarios too, often involving a limekiln and heavy German accents — definitely post-World War II. We were very much children of our time, but all of us rather eccentric and sometimes over the top. We must have been what is known today as a 'challenging' group. […]

There are so many memories of the fun we had as students — and the disappointments when we were passed over — lunches at the Orange Hue café over the road on a very small allowance for most of us, hitching a lift along the highway from Varsity in Rondebosch to the Little Theatre precinct in town — very few students had their own cars at that time and none of us had one. We walked a lot and it kept us fit.

Nigel's formal theatre training was minimal and unstructured as he was still ostensibly studying literature and broadcasting, but he happily allowed himself to be co-opted into his friends' drama classes and attended lessons in movement, voice-production and verse-speaking. There was also an improvisation class conducted by Leonard Schach during which the ambitious group gave a lively rendering of *The Rake's Progress*. The first play in which Nigel appeared at the University was an English Department production of *Twelfth Night*, playing one of the smallest roles in the Shakespearean canon, that of Curio, an attendant to Duke Orsino. He was then chosen for the minor parts of Sir Charles Marlow and a yokel in the Speech-Training and Drama Department's staging of Goldsmith's *She Stoops to Conquer*. Although it was early days, he already suspected that he was not destined to be a shining juvenile lead. However, he did distinguish himself in slightly offbeat roles and his skills as a character actor and comedian were shown to good effect in the title role of *St Simeon Stylites*, a Dramatic Society production of F. Sladen-Smith's one-act play written in 1926. *The Cape Argus* reported: '*St Simeon Stylites*, in which the anchorite is discovered at the top of his 60-foot pillar, was excellent philosophical fooling, and Nigel Hawthorne gave a strikingly sympathetic performance in the name part.'[13] Nigel himself dubbed St Simeon 'my most successful rôle to date'.

At the end of Nigel's first year at University it was announced that Leonard Schach would shortly be returning to Cape Town from a lengthy foreign tour of national theatres, having accomplished the astonishing feat of securing the rights to produce Tennessee Williams's *The Glass Menagerie* in South Africa. The play was scheduled to premiere at the Little Theatre and, intent on being considered for parts in this historic production, Nigel and his fellow student thespians devoted their summer holidays to preparing a programme of one-

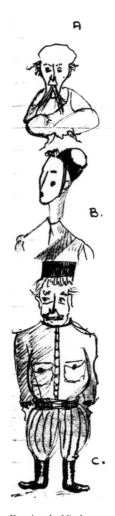

A

B.

C.

Drawings by Nigel
of himself as:
A. St Simeon in
St Simeon Stylites;
B. Puppet-Master
in *Puppet Show;*
C. Stepan Stepanovitch
in *The Proposal.*

(From his diary)

act plays which they planned to direct and perform. Ten of them formed a small company called The Players and rehearsed their programme furiously over several weeks. They arranged publicity and sponsorship, took charge of costumes, lighting and décor, and hired as their venue the old Bathing Pavilion at Muizenberg (since demolished and rebuilt quite differently). Three performances were given on 17, 18 and 19 February 1949 and all the proceeds were donated to the Israeli Relief Fund. The four short plays they presented were *St Simeon Stylites,* Alice Gerstenberg's *Overtones,* Sidney Box's *Puppet Show* and Chekhov's *The Proposal.* Nigel reprised his performance as St Simeon of the previous year, played the Puppet-Master in *Puppet Show,* and Stepan Stepanovitch in *The Proposal,* and made his directorial debut with *Puppet Show.* He gave, Helen Robinson recollects, 'an excellent performance – very funny as St Simeon and as my father in the Chekhov. He had, even at that age, a gravelly voice, which he used so well that he was often cast as an older character.' Also discernible in the nineteen-year-old Nigel was a fine talent for eccentric comedy which he later ascribed to an adopted ethnic tradition of humour: 'I had Jewish friends in Cape Town and worked in a Jewish community. That's where I sourced my emotion because there was always that un-English humour and warmth.'

While the formation of The Players, Helen Robinson maintains, arose from the group's 'desire to act as much as possible and to learn to direct', the immediate objective was to attract the right sort of attention. Leaving nothing to chance, they invited Leonard Schach to their opening night, hoping that their show of initiative and versatility would ensure them an audition for *The Glass Menagerie.* Schach was certainly impressed with what he saw, but the only member of the youthful company to whom he offered a part in the much-anticipated production was Jobie Stewart. Jobie's character in *The Glass Menagerie* was Tom Wingfield, a would-be poet who yearns for adventure, while Nigel's function was humble indeed, namely one third of the stage-management team. This was the first serious rejection he suffered and he did not easily recover from the disappointment. It was not that he begrudged his friend such a rare opportunity, but he envied Jobie's confidence and the speed with which his ambitions were being realised.

Many years later Leonard Schach recalled:

One of the most endearing memories of my life in the theatre was the evening the young stage manager of The Glass Menagerie *politely and shyly asked me for a lift home after a late rehearsal. It appeared that he lived close to my home. The bus had already departed and it was raining heavily.*

Conversation at first was rather desultory. Then the student suddenly asked me accusingly, 'Can I ask you why you cast Jobie Stewart in the play? And you never gave any of us the chance to audition?'

There was nothing arrogant in this outburst. His expression, rather, was one of anguished disappointment and frustration.

I improvised my answer. 'Of course you may,' I replied, 'but do try not to ask that sort of question if you decide to make the theatre your profession. Jobie is a typical juvenile lead; you are not. You are a character actor. Your turn will come with middle age. Do try not to be too impatient.'

I don't think Nigel Hawthorne was satisfied or convinced.

Schach's retelling of this incident might have been, not unreasonably, influenced by a disposition to credit himself with the shrewd judgement which subsequent events would have vindicated.

In July 1949 the University of Cape Town Dramatic Society entered the Cape Peninsula District Drama Festival of the Federation of Amateur Theatrical Societies of Southern Africa with a production of Hjalmar Bergman's Scandinavian fantasy *Mr Sleeman is Coming* (a play later directed for television by Ingmar Bergman). The Chairman of the Dramatic Society, Arnold Pearce, who at that time was strongly influenced by Schach, directed the play and his cast consisted of Nigel, Cecil Jubber, Edna Jacobson, Pamela Lewis and Helen Houghton. For the first time Nigel played a young romantic lead as Walter, The Hunter, giving a very delicate and moving interpretation. Over three nights at the Labia Theatre in Cape Town eight amateur dramatic societies contended for a place in the finals. *Mr Sleeman* was presented on the third night of competition and was the single play chosen to represent the Western Province at the Eleventh Annual National Festival in Benoni on 30 July. The *Cape Times* reported:

The Hunter in *Mr Sleeman is Coming* (1949), with Helen Houghton. *(Anne Fischer/Courtesy of Helen Robinson [née Houghton])*

> *The adjudicators said that the winning play was the most popular play during the preliminary contests and was the best to represent a dramatic organization at a national festival. It was a good play as a piece of writing, was full of charm and appeal, and it had been staged with enterprise and imagination by the producer.*
>
> *Three of the five young players in the piece had to impersonate elderly people, and this had been done very beautifully, especially by Cecil Jubber in the part of old Mr Sleeman.*[14]

The very next day, 8 July, obviously spurred on by this victory, Nigel began to keep a diary-cum-scrapbook documenting his theatrical activities. In this, along with the programmes and press cuttings he meticulously preserved and annotated, are his detailed descriptions, written in blue fountain pen, of all aspects of the Rep and student productions on which he worked and of his own and others' performances. The margins and available spaces of the now yellowed pages are filled with the colourful caricatures he drew of characters and sets. There is something intensely moving in seeing his neat and youthful handwriting and in the optimism, excitement and earnestness he vividly conveys. What the diary reveals is a young man passionate about acting and about the mechanics and magic of theatre. The first entry, written in the nostalgic vein of a seasoned performer, records his theatrical baptism and his affection for the Little Theatre:

I can remember the first time I went on the Little Theatre stage; I remember being awe-struck by all the gadgets in the flies, and feeling a strong sense of pride in being on it. It seems so strange now, although it is less than two years ago, that I should have ever felt anything but at home there. One grows very attached to a stage, and I have rehearsed there and acted there so many times now, that I think I know every hole in the canvas on the floor.

In high spirits the *Mr Sleeman* company travelled by train to Benoni in the Transvaal where they were to perform at the Town Hall. On the morning of their big night Nigel received a telegram (still preserved in his diary) from his proud mother: 'Wishing you a happy performance and success tonight from all.' Among the four adjudicators were professionals Leonard Schach and Elizabeth Sneddon. University of Cape Town tied for first place with the Port Elizabeth Musical and Dramatic Society, making them the first society from the Cape Province to be awarded the Breytenbach Trophy for the best production. But on their return to Cape Town their success, for a time, went unrecognised by their peers. A disgruntled Nigel penned a letter to the Editor of *Varsity,* the University's newspaper, deploring that publication's meagre coverage of the Dramatic Society's work. His comments appeared under the sub-heading 'Nigel Asks For More':

Dear Sir,

May I suggest that your newspaper devote a little more attention to the activities of the University Dramatic Society? During the past two years, I can remember only a meagre paragraph on the production Happy as Larry, *produced in 1948, and a photograph from Mr Leonard Schach's very successful production of* Cockpit *early this year.*

Not nearly enough students realise that they have their own theatre which has every facility and is acoustically perfect. The theatre should be packed out every night by students, instead of which there is merely a sprinkling of them. The question of money cannot enter into it at all, as the extremely reasonable price of 1/6 is charged and is considerably less than the average price paid for a cinema seat. The standard of production, too, is on the whole very laudable. Why is it then that the productions are not supported?

Again, last month the Dramatic Society succeeded in winning the Provincial Festival of FATSSA with Arnold Pearce's production of Mr Sleeman is Coming. *When I opened my* Varsity *this morning I expected to find a glowing account of this achievement, but there wasn't a word about it.*

As a result of winning the Provincial Festival, Mr Sleeman is Coming *was sent to compete at the National Festival, held this year at Benoni; it tied for first place! Not only is it the first time that the University Dramatic Society has entered, but it is the first time the Festival has been won by Cape Town.*

Varsity *is bought by the majority of students, and it is only right that they should know much more about the activities of their own Dramatic Society. It is up to your newspaper to solve this problem. Christopher Fry's new comedy* The Lady's Not for Burning, *which was a great success in London recently, is to be presented in September, and incidentally, it is the first full-length play to be produced in the Little Theatre by a student. I sincerely hope that by your encouragement there will be a larger percentage of students in the auditorium than ever before.*

Nigel Hawthorne[15]

In the very same issue of *Varsity* the oversights Nigel had complained of were promptly corrected in an article entitled 'Laurels to Dramatic Society'. A detailed account of the Society's victory in Benoni was provided and accompanied by a photograph of the director and players which had appeared in the *Cape Argus*. The acting and production of *Mr Sleeman* were acclaimed 'imaginative, theatrical and thoroughly competent [...] and a tribute to the high standard of work at the Little Theatre.' The article closed with a ringing endorsement of the Little's recent achievements:

One wonders whether the student body itself is fully aware of the Little Theatre, the work of their fellow-students there and the hours of enjoyment available to them throughout the year. Productions during 1949 have included The Glass Menagerie, The Match Girls, Cockpit *and* The Fan *– a record of which the University can be justly proud. [...]*

In October the Society is to produce the current West End success, Christopher Fry's The Lady's Not For Burning, *and the student body should support Cecil Jubber and his cast and give some evidence of their satisfaction in the success of their own students in this National Festival.*

The production of Bridget Boland's *Cockpit* to which Hawthorne referred in his letter to *Varsity* had opened at the Little Theatre on 3 May 1949 and supplied its director, Leonard Schach, with a name for the company he founded a year later. Set during the Allied advance on Berlin in a disused German theatre which is now under British and American control and functioning as a clearing house for an international group of displaced persons awaiting repatriation, the play is about how the suspected outbreak of bubonic plague briefly unites the disparate and warring band of exiles as they restore the theatre to life and stage a performance by an opera singer fortuitously in their midst. It was later adapted to the screen as *The Lost People,* starring Dennis Price, Richard Attenborough and Siobhan McKenna. *Cockpit* was a great triumph for the Dramatic Society; Ivor Jones of the *Cape Times* declared it 'Quite the most exciting thing which has happened in the Cape Town theatre in the last few years […] and for players so young their achievement might well be envied by more experienced (and more professional) groups.'[16] Nigel featured as Barnes, a British NCO, and attracted excellent notices. 'Different types and personalities are carefully portrayed,' said Ivor Jones, 'outstanding being the laconic sergeant of Nigel Hawthorne.'[17] Nigel was struck by the professionalism and camaraderie of the large student ensemble as well as the tremendous impact of the play on its audience. He wrote in his diary:

A wonderful production and my first big part at the Little Theatre. The press and public were most enthusiastic. It was, as Ivor Jones says, an 'exciting production'. Guns were let off. People jumped up in the audience – made their entrances through the double doors at the back of the theatre.

Most of the cast grew beards, and before the play covered the visible parts of their bodies with dust. The same treatment had been given to the clothes. Some of the cast were very glad to get into baths at the end of the extended run to take it all off, and become normal people again. We could have run for months, but we had to attend lectures during the day and it proved too much of a strain.

Later that year Nigel starred as the young soldier Tegeus-Chromis in Christopher Fry's one-act romantic comedy *A Phoenix Too Frequent,* a modern verse adaptation of the episode of 'The Widow of Ephesus' in Petronius' *Satyricon,* which the Drama Department staged as part of a Season of Comedy at the Little. The production, directed by Leonard Schach, was reviewed as far afield as Johannesburg and gave Nigel some desirable publicity: 'One remained conscious, alas, that it was very much a students' effort, although

Tegeus-Chromis in *A Phoenix Too Frequent* (1949), with June Range. *(Anne Fischer/ Courtesy of Trevor Bentham)*

Nigel Hawthorne showed flashes of the brilliance which so often marks his work.' He had based his characterisation on a drawing of Tegeus-Chromis executed by the English artist and cartoonist Ronald Searle, which Nigel had fortuitously discovered in a shop. Searle, who began his career as a cartoonist for *The Cambridge Daily News* and became famous for his St Trinian's cartoons and as illustrator for the theatre column of *Punch,* greatly influenced Nigel's developing style as a caricaturist.

After their memorable experience in *Cockpit,* Nigel and Jobie Stewart were determined to act at every available opportunity and to create opportunities for themselves. Along with other members of the *Cockpit* cast, they approached Leonard Schach, more than ten years their senior, to direct them in Arthur Laurents's anti-war play *Home of the Brave.* Schach admired their resourcefulness and choice of vehicle, and on 4 April 1950 the newly formed Cockpit Players presented *Home of the Brave* at Cape Town's Labia Theatre. The company was paid a small fee, giving it something approximating to professional status.

With its candid exploration of anti-Semitism and combat trauma, the play was both challenging and exciting to perform. It opens in 1944 inside the hospital of a military base in the South Pacific where a young Jewish GI, 'Coney', is suffering from psychosomatic paralysis after being part of an engineering outfit's perilous mission to a Japanese-held island. His doctor uses narcosynthesis to rehabilitate him and much of the first of the play's two acts is a visualisation of what Coney is prompted to remember of events on the island, culminating crucially in the killing of his one faithful companion after a period of extended abuse. Nigel played the part of Coney's ill-fated best friend, the 'Arizona hayseed' Finch, proclaimed by one critic 'a triumph of sustained American accent'. The *Cape Times* praised all aspects of the production and especially the four central performances:

> Suspense and emotional pull figure largely in the acting, and I was amazed to find Mr Schach's youthful players giving such effective performances, although the majority of them had exhibited a feeling for drama in Cockpit, one of 1949's theatre triumphs in Cape Town. Here let me say that [...] last night's cast outstripped their previous achievement and frequently brought tears to the eyes of at least one member of the audience. [...] Nigel Hawthorne really convinced me that he was the brazen GI to the life.[18]

Finch (far left) in *Home of the Brave* (1950), Nigel's last amateur performance. *(Anne Fischer/ Courtesy of Percy Tucker)*

In the audience that night was Brian Brooke, the urbane actor-manager of Cape Town's only permanent repertory company which was now in its fourth year. Born in the North-Eastern Transvaal and educated at Grahamstown, Brooke arrived in England before the war and, with no stage experience, worked his way up through the country's repertory system, emerging as a successful leading man. When war broke out he joined the British Army and served as Company Commander and Staff Officer in the Normandy Landings. As part of the Army of Occupation in Germany at the end of the war he employed his spare time in organising and performing in theatrical entertainments for the troops. At the same time he conceived the idea of a permanent repertory company for South Africa. On his demobilisation he returned to Cape Town and, against the advice of colleagues and also in defiance of both the ACT's monopoly of theatre ownership and the post-war shortage of professional actors, he assembled a company modelled on the British provincial theatres where he had learnt his trade. The company's leading lady was Brooke's wife Petrina Fry, the daughter of London theatrical manager and director Reginald Fry. Although diminutive in stature, she was possessed of an undeniable stage presence. She had recently given a compelling performance at the Hofmeyr as Catherine Sloper in *The Heiress,* displaying admirably her understated and remarkably instinctive style.

On the strength of Nigel's performance in *Home of the Brave,* and possibly also his appearance with The Players at the Muizenberg Pavilion (since this was the venue of the Brian Brooke Company's earliest productions), Brooke offered him a place in his Company, effective immediately. Nigel had less than a year to go before completing his degree but his official studies had long since become a subsidiary concern and acting his first priority. The chance to turn professional could not, he felt, be missed. There was no longer any doubt in his mind as to the career he wanted and he did not regret his premature departure from university, but he had to negotiate his father's predictable wrath and bitter disappointment. Charles Hawthorne had, at one stage, fostered hopes of Nigel following in his footsteps or else entering either the Diplomatic Corps or the Civil Service, and for his elder son now to abandon his studies and more acceptable prospects and enlist in so puerile and uncertain a profession as acting, to attempt to earn a living from 'dressing-up', seemed wilfully irresponsible. His indignation was very probably compounded by his tacit awareness of Nigel's homosexuality and an undisguised abhorrence of theatrical types, whom he branded effete and unnatural. Ironically, he had himself been a member of the famous Cambridge Footlights while reading medicine at Clare College and was even elected Musical Director on the Footlights Committee for 1904 and 1905.

In those years C. B. Hawthorne featured prominently in the casts of the revues *The New Dean* and *Paying the Piper* (or *A Tale of Old Cambridge*). He also penned an operetta. But he never regarded dramatics as a dignified or grown-up activity, least of all a respectable form of employment. As a consequence, Nigel confirmed, 'this began a sort of breach between him and me which we were never able to fill.'[19] Father and son had in common a stubborn pride, and from early on their relationship was characterised by little openly declared warmth or empathy. Nigel knew that a lot of the time his father barely tolerated him, and he, in his turn, used his father's lack of faith in him as an incentive to succeed and thus prove him wrong. Sadly, Charles Hawthorne did not live to see the remarkable vindication of his son's errant ambition, but as one who set great store by honours he would have taken immense pride in Nigel's knighthood.

On 5 April 1950, his twenty-first birthday, Nigel presented himself at the Hofmeyr Theatre, the unprepossessing upper-storey home of the Brian Brooke Company in Adderley Street, the main thoroughfare of Cape Town. The theatre, he recalled, was in fact 'a Dutch Reformed Church hall. It didn't have a raked auditorium. It had a very, very tiny stage and only two dressing rooms. So it was very modest and not soundproof. When the southeaster, which was the prevailing wind, blew it rattled the windows and made it rather difficult to be heard.' With the Church as landlord, rehearsals and set changing on Sunday were prohibited. The Company was currently in financial difficulty and Nigel was taken on as assistant stage manager at just three pounds a week with only a vague promise of smaller parts when required. A further cause for despondency was the formulaic quality of plays in commercial weekly repertory which, after the progressive student productions at the Little, was less than stimulating. It was not an encouraging beginning but, with his father expecting him either to fail or to outgrow this foolish phase, there was no turning back. Once again Nigel found himself casting envious glances at friends like Jobie Stewart and Anthony Holbery whose first professional engagements were rather more illustrious:

The only other professional theatre in the country in those days was the newly formed National Theatre and they were doing a production of Hassan *by James Elroy Flecker, which was being directed by Basil Dean who was a rather formidable English director. And a lot of my friends had gone into that.*

Nigel's entry into the Brian Brooke Company was preceded by that of a young English couple, Shaun Sutton and Barbara (Ba) Leslie. Sutton, who later became Head of Drama at BBC Television, had made his first theatre appearance at the age of six, walking on in *Julius Caesar* in a festival production for the famous actor-manager Sir Frank Benson. At the conclusion of his war service in the Royal Navy Destroyers he was employed as Stage Director of Anthony Hawtrey's repertory companies in Buxton, Croydon and Eastbourne, during which time he met and married actress Barbara Leslie. In 1950 the Suttons were offered a joint contract to join Brian Brooke's company in Cape Town, an opportunity they looked upon as a paid holiday. On the journey to South Africa they were accompanied by two other new Brooke employees, Andrew Broughton and Barbara Walter. The Company was thus becoming quite British in composition.

Nigel's professional acting debut arrived sooner than he anticipated with the added bonus that it was a leading part. Two days before the opening of the Company's latest production, Edward Percy's thriller *The Shop at Sly Corner,* its director and star, Englishman Gabriel Toyne, a drunken and volatile bully, fired the juvenile actor playing Archie Fellowes and the role went to Nigel. Despite the short notice he seized the opportunity with alacrity and earned the critics' approval for his performance as the unscrupulous shop assistant who blackmails his employer, an antique dealer with a criminal past, for both his money and his daughter. 'A clever study of a Dickensian blackmailer' and 'his Cockney [was] admirably within the sound of Bow Bells' were among the notices he received. Shaun Sutton, however, thought Nigel embraced the sneering villainy of the character with too much relish: 'I must confess that he wasn't very good. Knowing the Nigel of later days, it is hard to believe that he *overplayed* in it, but he did. It was, in fact, the only time that we ever saw Nigel less than good in a part.' Nevertheless, Nigel was rewarded with an increased workload if not a dramatic rise in salary:

> *I was on three pounds a week at the Brian Brooke Company, so it was very, very little. Then they put me up to four pounds by taking me on as the publicity manager as well. So I was doing all the advertising and interviews as well as playing leading roles and doing stage management. That was my lot and it was a hell of a lot.*

The Shop at Sly Corner was followed by productions of Arthur Macrae's comedy *Travellers' Joy* and Noel Langley and Robert Morley's sprawling, difficult play *Edward, My Son,* in each of which Nigel had a cameo role, impersonating, as he often would, a character of mature years. Sutton recounts that during the run of *Traveller's Joy* Nigel befriended him and his wife Ba:

Publicity Portrait 1950. *(Anne Fischer/ Courtesy of Little Theatre, Cape Town)*

We were a few years older than him, and I think we brought him support and good company and confidence. We took to going out for a modest drink after the performance, and he began to show us the countryside round Cape Town. We had a memorably good day climbing up Table Mountain, not the sheer front, but up one of the gullies on the side of the mountain, called the Apostles. We picked Nigel up at his house in Camps Bay and started up the mountain together. Nigel's dog came halfway, looked up at the steep climb ahead, shook its head and went home. We took food and a grill up with

Nigel on Table Mountain above Camps Bay, Cape Town. *(Courtesy of Shaun Sutton)*

us and had sausages at the top. The views on the way up, over Camps Bay, were stunning, and from the top, looking over the edge of the Table, they were unique.

We found that we shared the same sense of humour and of the ridiculous. Our first impression of Nigel was that he was really rather shy and naïve about life and the theatre. His father was a doctor in Cape Town and we both felt that he disapproved of Nigel going into the theatre. However well we got to know Nigel, we were never invited into his home at Camps Bay and we assumed that as actors we might not be welcome.

Although nothing categorical was ever said, it was obvious to Sutton that he had been brought over to Cape Town to replace Gabriel Toyne, whose behaviour had become increasingly erratic and a source of appalled merriment to the younger members of the Company:

I had known Gabriel slightly before the war, but only as an expert swordsman. It did not take me long to realise that he was a very moderate director, one of those who 'played' at being a director, with a lot of stock phrases and thoughts. But not a man to really work at a production.

There was a particular disaster during Edward, My Son *that delighted all three of us [the Suttons and Nigel]. Gabriel Toyne played the headmaster in Scene Four of the play, a headmaster whom Edward's father had come to 'buy off' after some misdemeanour. One matinée day Gabriel just didn't arrive and arrangements were quickly made for another actor to play the part, script in hand. Someone, I think it was Brian [Brooke], went before the curtain at the end of Scene Three and announced that 'Owing to the indisposition of Mr Gabriel Toyne, the part of the headmaster would be played by ….' At that moment Gabriel, who had been asleep in the back row of the stalls after a heavy lunch, leapt down the aisle shouting 'I'm here, I'm here.' There followed a strong argument in the dressing room with Gabriel insisting that he went on, and Brian insisting that he didn't. Shortly after this Gabriel returned to England. This was a theatrical absurdity that none of us had experienced before, and I must admit that we all enjoyed it disgracefully.*

In June the Company embarked on a tour of the Union and Southern Rhodesia with *Edward My Son* and *Travellers' Joy*, opening in Johannesburg at His Majesty's Theatre. *Edward My Son* was poorly received and *Travellers' Joy* only partially successful. The plays were running at a loss and, although Brooke played down the failure in the press, blaming the moderate houses on the Durban 'July' (a society horse-racing event) and the Korean situation,[20] it was decided to scrap the double bill and hastily rehearse two more suitable vehicles. As substitutes Shaun Sutton suggested Noël Coward's *Present Laughter* and Philip King's *See How They Run*, both of which he had previously directed. While Nigel played the small part of Fred, Gary Essendine's valet, in *Present Laughter*, his performance as the perplexed curate, Arthur Humphrey, in *See How They Run* turned out to be his greatest critical success with the Company. He was consistently singled out for his talent for physical comedy: in Port Elizabeth he was described as 'a delight as he draped himself across the sofa, or tripped backwards and forwards', and the *Rhodesia Herald* noted, 'Nigel Hawthorne as the Rev. Arthur Humphrey, had a relatively small part, but he played it splendidly. His facial expressions as the shy young parson were perfect.'[21] Sutton remembers that even then it was evident Nigel was blessed with superior comedic reflexes and an innate ability to improvise:

Early in the run of this under-rehearsed comedy [See How They Run], *Ba and Nigel, who had a number of comedy scenes together, got themselves into a rare tangle. The bewildered curate asked Ba for a glass of milk. She rushed off to get it and returned a moment later, crossed the huge Johannesburg stage, and extended her hand to Nigel with the line, 'Here's your milk, sir.'*

But only her hand, she had forgotten to bring the milk. Nigel was equal to the situation. He took the phantom glass from Ba's hand, drank from it thirstily, said, 'That was delicious' and handed nothing back to Ba. It got such a huge laugh we kept it in for future performances.

The Rev. Arthur Humphrey in *See How They Run* (1950), with (l. to r.) Michael Marais, Brian Brooke, Shaun Sutton and Brenda Walter. *(Anne Fischer/ Courtesy of Shaun Sutton)*

After a disappointing and disrupted start the tour proved a popular and critical success, and, as well as being a highly enjoyable experience, Sutton believes it was for Nigel akin to a rite of passage:

Ba, Nigel and I had some great trips round Bulawayo, where Rhodes is buried up in the Matapo Hills, curious round-topped hills of granite. Ba and I laboured up to the top of one to see an unlimited view of bush all round. Nigel suddenly appeared on an adjoining one, and we conversed affably in the middle of nowhere. I remember thinking that we were miles away from the sea in any direction, something quite impossible in England.

I think Brian and Petrina were amused by our passionate interest in the whole panorama of beautiful country, but it was all new to us. Exploring it also cemented a strong friendship with Nigel that lasted until he died.

One thing the tour had done for him, we both noticed, was it had matured him, professionally and personally, especially his success in See How They Run. *He came back to Cape Town more confident and assured.*

Ba and Shaun Sutton, South Africa. *(Courtesy of Shaun Sutton)*

Back in Cape Town the Company staged at the Hofmeyr productions of *Rain,* an adaptation of Somerset Maugham's short story 'Sadie Thompson' (with, its director Shaun Sutton recalls, 'real rain pouring down at the back of the set and probably bringing wet rot throughout the building'), the Ben Travers farce *Thark,* and Edgar Wallace's thriller *The Case of the Frightened Lady,* in which Nigel scored a leading part as the neurotic and homicidal last survivor of a long aristocratic line. This last production received mixed reviews but the *Cape Argus* reported, 'Full credit must go [...] to Nigel Hawthorne for his portrayal of the young Lord Lebanon, a difficult role played with sureness and mature judgment.'[22] Next, having played a minor role in the touring production of *Present Laughter,* Nigel 'slipped eccentrically into the part of the flamboyant playwright done before by Michael Marais'[23] in Petrina Fry's revival of Coward's comedy. He confessed in his diary that 'Roland Maule was a part I'd always wanted to play, and still regard it as one of my favourites.' Unfortunately the production, though very successful, was rushed through in order to make way for the Company's Christmas attraction, Brandon Thomas's *Charley's Aunt*, written in 1892 and perpetually performed. Nigel played the love-sick undergraduate Charley Wykeham which he deemed 'surely one of the dreariest parts ever written in a farce.'

The first production of the new year was Charlotte Hastings's strange play *Bonaventure*, directed by Petrina Fry's mother Mary Byron. The play is set in a convent on the Norfolk coast in the middle of a flood. Among those taking shelter in the convent are two prison officials and, in their custody, a young woman under sentence of death for the murder of her brother. The plot revolves around the efforts of Sister Mary Bonaventure to prove the condemned girl's innocence and force a confession from the real murderer. Nigel contributed 'a notable character study'[24] as Willy Pentridge, a simple-minded but physically very strong local boy whom the convent employs to carry out odd jobs. It was a performance of which he was justly proud as his diary solemnly reveals:

> *Perhaps the best thing I've done so far, and really right up my street. The pathos in some of my scenes was a little obvious, perhaps, but theatrically speaking it was most effective.*
>
> *The play slips in the last act, from an unusual thriller to a common or garden detective story. It's a great pity as the general theme is most unusual.*

The Brian Brooke Company offered Nigel plenty of work and a regular income and he was steadily acquiring useful skills and experience doing what he most enjoyed. But after a while he began to feel dissatisfied and restless and to formulate plans of a future beyond Cape Town:

> *The Brian Brooke Company and the National Theatre drew on the youth of the country that wanted to become involved in the theatre and outside that there was no other opportunity. I think that I found in those early days a tremendous draw towards England, largely because the work I was doing was very often boulevard comedies or farces. Occasionally you'd get a drama or a melodrama but it was very much in the repertory form and the quality of the work was not very good. We did the best we could, but we were really just recycling the same people. And so I was sort of itching to get away. [...] It seemed as though one was almost trapped, that there was no escape, there was nowhere else to go. You either were there or you didn't work. So the lure of England was constantly in my head.*

He was scornful not only of the mediocrity of the commercial repertoire but also of what he perceived as the unprofessional and indecorous habits of some of the local performers: 'Actors there, and then, behaved very badly. They drank, they swore, they farted, because they knew they wouldn't be kicked out of the company: there were so few people who could replace them. I got very toffee-nosed about this and said I wouldn't stay.'[25]

Other factors too contributed to Nigel's malaise and his sense of being trapped. The general election of 1948 had brought to power the Afrikaner National Party led by D. F. Malan and the concept of apartheid was swiftly converted into a major political programme. Apartheid added structure to the racial segregation and white domination that already existed in South Africa in areas such as land ownership, the legal system and the distribution of wealth, and that had begun as far back as the mid-seventeenth century with the Dutch East India Company's establishment of a provisioning station on the Cape. Growing up in Cape Town in the 1930s and 40s, Nigel was used to the presence of a succession of black servants at home. The classrooms, lecture halls and theatres he inhabited were almost exclusively the preserve of the white community. What had been unofficial policy before 1948 now became more sinister and comprehensive with the introduction of legislation, like the Prohibition of Mixed Marriages Act in 1949 and the Bantu Authorities Act in 1951, which effectively removed black people's citizenship. For most middle-class white South Africans life continued comfortably and in much the same way as before, but the repressive legislation and ingrained philistinism of the Nationalist government generated anger and discontent among liberal-thinking whites, especially those within the arts who were committed to free creative expression. It was, however, all too easy for such people to become immune to the climate of injustice. To prevent this, many took the line of least resistance by leaving the country and some, like the actress Janet Suzman, initiated active campaigns abroad against the apartheid system.

In determining his own departure, a more pressing and personal reason than South Africa's political transformation was Nigel's inner turmoil:

I was an unhappy child and an unhappy young man. To be perfectly honest, I was absolutely unrequited in every aspect of my life. You have to learn to love yourself just a little before anyone else will accept you as you wish to be accepted.[26]

He was not at all relaxed about his homosexuality and suffered increasing discomfiture when confronted with even the most benign enquiry from his relatives as to why he still did not have a girlfriend. In the theatre world he had found a relatively safe and sympathetic environment in which to try to fathom, or at least escape, his maladjustment. Ian McKellen has remarked: 'The reason that a disproportionate amount of actors are gay is that they discover a job in which they can present their self-confidence in a disguise.'[27] For Nigel, and other young men like him, acting was a matter of disguising what he was:

> *I was able to bury myself and not have to be me. It was an escape really. I was a very self-conscious young man, very shy and awkward. I was quite good at getting under the skin of people and finding odd things people did and putting them into a performance.*[28]

He could also identify with the contradictions fundamental to John Gielgud's definition of acting as 'half shame, half glory. Shame at exhibiting yourself, glory when you can forget yourself.'[29] The impossibility of confiding his distress to his parents intensified his desire to leave South Africa and, as he confessed, 'running away to England when I was twenty-one was again not facing up to my sexuality.'[30] He was, moreover, desperately lonely and the idea of seeking professional and emotional fulfilment far from the scrutiny of his family had definite appeal.

Nigel later recollected that he was encouraged in his escape plans by his friends the Suttons whom he consulted over lunch at the Hawthorne family home. According to Shaun Sutton, however, this lunch did not take place. He and Ba returned to England for Christmas and rejoined Anthony Hawtrey's Company in Buxton, Derbyshire, where, he says, some weeks into the season he received a telegram from Nigel which read, 'Have saved the fare. Any chance of a job in your rep?' In either case, on 8 March 1951, after eleven months at the Hofmeyr Theatre, Nigel gave his final performance as part of the Brian Brooke Company in Lillian Hellman's *The Little Foxes* and prepared to set sail for Britain. In his diary, beside an autographed programme of *The Little Foxes,* he has written:

> *My last performance at the Hofmeyr – and very few regrets. I'm far too anxious to pack my trunks and climb the gangway of the* Arundel Castle. *I will always be grateful for the experience I have received at the Brookes', but am still most thankful to leave the tiny stage and inadequate dressing rooms.*

Poignantly, beneath a small pen drawing of the *Arundel Castle,* he has pasted in his diary a picture postcard of the Shakespeare Memorial

Nigel with Brian Brooke Company members Diane Bester, Gyneth Erskine, Nick Van Doesburgh and Barbara Leslie aboard *Stirling Castle. (Courtesy of Shaun Sutton)*

Theatre in Stratford-upon-Avon, and in the top right-hand corner of this has written 'GOAL?'

Nigel was not a solitary fugitive:

> *About six or seven of us were of an equal mind, a like mind, and we all decided to come away together – not necessarily on the same boat or anything like that, but we left. And there was an outcry in the local paper, saying, 'What is it about the young talent that we have that we are unable to keep them and they are all planning to go to England?' And I was part of that contingent that escaped. That was the only future.*

The other hopefuls were Jobie Stewart, Anthony Holbery, Hilda Kriseman, Noelle Ahrenson and Pamela Lewis. The portraits of all six appeared in the *Cape Argus* of 15 March 1951 around the heading 'Seeking Fame in Europe' and the accompanying report sounded a note of anguished reproach:

> *Is South Africa a good country to get out of? I should hate to think so, but the traffic between the Union and Britain is tending to become almost one-way, in spite of shipping advertisements in English papers urging Britons to come to South Africa during the Festival of Britain.*

41

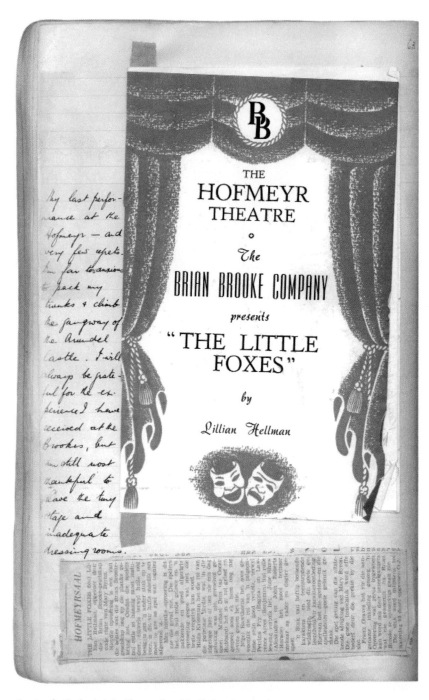

My last perfor-
mance at the
Hofmeyr — and
very few upsets.
Im far too anxious
to pack my
trunks & climb
the gangway of
the Arundel
Castle. I will
always be grate-
ful for the ex-
perience I have
received at the
Brookes, but
am still most
thankful to
leave the tiny
stage and
inadequate
dressing rooms.

B
B

THE
HOFMEYR
THEATRE

The
BRIAN BROOKE COMPANY

presents

"THE LITTLE
FOXES"

by

Lillian Hellman

Leaving for England. A double page from Nigel's diary/scrapbook

80 | 64

Will try meet Nigel's boat train Waterloo if not phone Shepherds Bush 5044 love Ba and Shaun

THE CAPE ARGUS, THURSDAY, MARCH 15, 1951

TALK...

at the TAVERN of the SEAS

St. George's Street, Thursday.

IS South Africa a good country to get out of? I should hate to think so, but the traffic between the Union and Britain is tending to become almost one-way, in spite of shipping advertisements in English papers urging Britons to "come to South Africa during the Festival of Britain."

During the past few months I have written about settlers in the Union who have become so unsettled that they preferred to face again the austerity of Britain rather than enjoy the plenty of South Africa.

Only last week I heard of a skilled carpenter who, after two and a half years here, was returning to Britain with his family. But as an antidote to this a charming American tradesman came to tell me that he was working for a Government department on Robben Island and loved the life there. I envy him his contentment.

IN AVALANCHE

I have also recorded the frequent departures of our ballet ...ancers for abroad and, happily, ...heir almost unfailing ability to ...nd work with the best ballet ...mpanies.

But this week I have to report ... exodus which must be a seri... blow to indigenous theatre.

Starting tomorrow and continu...g for the next fortnight six ...ented, experienced and valuable ...ung actors and actresses and ...e male ballet-dancer are leaving ...uth Africa to make their names ... Europe. Whether they return ...ere will be determined by their ...ilure or success.

The tragedy is that, to make their careers on the lines they have themselves chosen, South Africa is no use to them except as an early training-ground.

'T is true 't is pity;
And pity 't is 't is true.

The ballet dancer who is leaving is Lionel Luyt, veteran of the early days of the Cape Town Ballet Club, and the stage players, whose portraits you will find on this page, are: Hilda Kriseman, Noelle Ahrenson, Pamela Lewis, Nigel Hawthorne, Jobie Stewart and Anthony Holbery.

They will all be missed.

P.B.

Seeking fame in Europe

(Top, left to right) Nigel Hawthorne, Noelle Ahrenson, Hilda Kriseman, Jobie Stewart. (Bottom) Anthony Holbery, Pamela Lewis.

(See opening paragraphs.)

ARUNDEL CASTLE

We have all made a very great decision. Sailed for England on 6th April 1951, to arrive at Southampton on April 20th.

And to add to the gloomy picture half a dozen of the best young players in the country—Hilda Kriseman, Noelle Ahrenson, Jobie Stewart, Anthony Holbery, Pamela Lewis and Nigel Hawthorne have packed their bags and gone to Britain, leaving our theatre with only a handful of young hopefuls.

P.B. in the "OUTSPAN"

GOAL?

Shakespeare Memorial Theatre, Stratford-upon-Avon

> *During the past few months I have written about settlers in the Union who have become so unsettled that they preferred to face again the austerity of Britain rather than enjoy the plenty of South Africa. [...]*
>
> *This week I have to report an exodus which must be a serious blow to indigenous theatre.*
>
> *Starting tomorrow and continuing for the next fortnight six talented, experienced and valuable young actors and actresses and one male ballet-dancer are leaving South Africa to make their names in Europe. Whether they return here will be determined by their failure or success.*
>
> *The tragedy is that, to make their careers on the lines they have themselves chosen, South Africa is no use to them except as an early training-ground.*
> > *'t is true 't is pity;*
> > *And pity 't is 't is true. [...]*
> *They will all be missed.*

With only twelve pounds to his name after paying his passage, Nigel boarded RMS *Arundel Castle* on 6 April 1951 for the fortnight's journey to Southampton. Before his departure he had called upon Ivor Jones, the world-weary and somewhat bibulous drama critic for the *Cape Times,* who had always reviewed Nigel's amateur and professional performances generously but who on this occasion did his best to deflate the ambitious young actor with the Parthian shot, 'See you back in six months, dear boy.' Jones's condescension and his cruel certainty that Nigel would fail served merely to stiffen the latter's resolve. It was, in fact, not six months but a full six years before he returned to South Africa's shores.

Nigel arrived in England on 20 April. It was the year of the Festival of Britain, a grand exposition showcasing British industry, architecture, art and culture, with the main exhibits on the South Bank and a Festival fairground in Battersea Park. The Festival had been dubbed 'a tonic to the nation'; its organisers and Clement Atlee's Labour government wanted to offer a much-needed diversion to Britons who, six years after Victory in Europe had been declared, were still coping on a daily basis with rationing, food queues, fuel shortages and bomb-damaged urban landscapes. The engineered optimism of the Festival did not conceal or ameliorate for Nigel the grey post-war reality awaiting him, the cold, damp weather and insipid skies. As he sat on the boat train, contemplating his unsettled future and the magnitude of his adventurous undertaking, his first sight of London was of rows of houses of squalid sameness and smoky, cluttered scenes reminiscent of the world of Ealing comedies and T. S. Eliot's 'Preludes'. He already ached for the paradise from which he had fled.

At Waterloo Station he was considerably cheered by the sight of Ba and Shaun Sutton who were there to greet him, and by the news that Shaun had arranged an interview for him with Anthony Hawtrey at the Embassy Theatre in Swiss Cottage. Hawtrey was the son of the celebrated Edwardian actor-manager Sir Charles Hawtrey, who had mentored Noël Coward when the latter was a precocious child actor. He had followed his father into theatre as a producer and, although engaged in weekly rep, his companies in Buxton, Croydon and at the Embassy in North London produced work of an exceptionally high standard. On Sutton's recommendation, Hawtrey hired Nigel for his Company's sixth summer season at Buxton's Playhouse. For seven pounds a week Nigel was to combine the duties of assistant stage manager with those of juvenile character actor. In his diary he writes elatedly and, at the same time, philosophically about his first engagement:

I am of course extremely thrilled that I've been so lucky – the stage management side I'm not keen on naturally, but it's a means to an end, of that I'm certain. It's weekly rep, hard work and not much sleep, but a season in Buxton should give me a great deal of experience. Anyhow, it's my first job in England!

Underneath this entry he has pasted a black-and-white studio portrait of himself with the inscription 'Nigel Hawthorne, Juvenile Character Actor, London April 24th 1951.'

The new season commenced in May. In the intervening weeks, having found himself digs in South Kensington, Nigel expended his limited resources in avidly sampling nearly everything West End theatre had to offer. This intensive period was like an extended masterclass for the neophyte. From his seat in the gods he watched enthralled the glamorous and revered stage stars whom he had previously only read about, studying their techniques with a keenly critical eye:

When I got to England the first thing I did was to go absolutely mad and see every play. I was only in England for three weeks before I went up to Buxton and I saw two plays a day through all that time. I was insatiable, I just went to everything, and saw a lot of heroes and heroines. There were also a lot of disappointments. Things like [Christopher Fry's adaptation of Anouilh's] Ring Round the Moon *I remember with Paul Scofield as a young actor, and I was very struck by how mannered people were, particularly Scofield and people like that who seemed to have an odd way of speaking, almost a sort of self-consciousness. And I remember saying at the time, 'Why can't they just talk to each other, why do they have to put on a voice?' And it's something that has obviously been part of my approach to theatre ever since, a more honest approach rather than a demonstration of one's talent. I didn't ever feel that I wanted to get up and say, 'Oh, I can do this and I can do that, and watch my dexterity here!'*

At twenty-two and with a year's professional experience behind him, Nigel was beginning to assess seriously his assets and shortcomings as an actor and to determine his niche in this variable profession. From the start he had a clear purpose in mind:

I just wanted to be accurate; I wanted to find a point as near what it should be as I could. And so I came unstuck quite often because there were a lot of people doing a lot more than I did to attract attention and very often getting attention. But I had always believed, particularly in drama, that if I could get as near the truth as possible, that that was the way to go about it. Although in comedy I could be extreme, and in Hornchurch rep, for example, in the lavatory there was a sign which said: 'Twinkle, twinkle little star, / Nigel Hawthorne's gone too far.' I remember that being put up by some wag.

He also held firm opinions about the veterans of his craft, which were influenced by his disapproval of fustian attitudes and declamation and his inchoate creed grounded in the principles of honesty and subtlety:

Heroes in those days were people like Alastair Sim – unlikely people – and Guinness. And the most likely of all was Laurence Olivier. I used to think he was the cat's whiskers. When I saw him in the film of Henry V, *that's really what began my admiration for him. And I'd seen him in* Wuthering Heights *and a lot of the Hollywood pictures which he was later very disdainful about. He made them so that he could make some money in order to run a company back in London. But you saw the ease with which he rode the waves and it was something that I knew I would never be able to emulate. I was never that sort of person; I didn't have that virtuosity. But I suppose I thought that I had a very good sense of humour and I thought I had an honesty and, if I could combine the two, that comedy would be like tragedy and tragedy would be a bit like comedy, and so I could find a way of operating within that little framework, which is really what I've stuck to.*
But Olivier had feet of clay eventually for me and I lost my faith. I went right off and saw all the wheels going round.

I didn't think Gielgud was a good actor. Gielgud had a most mellifluous voice and a wonderful technique and a great understanding of verse. But it really wasn't until he got into films like The Charge of the Light Brigade *where he was absent-minded and funny that I started to like him, but it was long into his career. And all the classics and everything was a great turn-off for me.*

But there were other actors, and very often they weren't stars, they were just ordinary actors, who did simple things which used to amaze me. They were so accurate and so unexpected, and they weren't done for effect, they were done because the actor was clever enough to be able to find a path through. There were actors of whom I used to think, 'Well, I can do that, I'm sure I can do it as well as that. Why don't they give me a chance?'

I think a lot of the time I was so itching to get going and even though I did admire people, very often I could be very sharply critical. Not of Alastair Sim because there was nothing he did that I could find in my heart to criticise. He was able to register such absurd pain and suppress emotion and hysteria. A very, very, very gifted man.

Since the demise of provincial repertory, Buxton's Playhouse Theatre has had an unremarkable afterlife as a discothèque and bingo hall, but in the late 1940s and early 1950s it was the bustling, well-patronised summer home of the Anthony Hawtrey Company. Nigel's first month at Buxton was spent entirely behind the scenes as assistant stage manager, the lowliest of beings in the stringent hierarchy of weekly rep, whose job description was general dogsbody and whipping boy. He was not naturally adept at stage managerial tasks – his imagination and creativity always outshone his practical skills – and he struggled to meet the seemingly endless demands made on him by his ill-tempered immediate superior, Brian Whittle, and members of the Company.

His first acting assignment was as the High Church and highly strung curate, Ronald Hawes, in an adaptation of Agatha Christie's *Murder at the Vicarage* which opened on 4 June. Two weeks later there appeared in the *Buxton Advertiser and Herald* a small write-up of Nigel's arrival, the first mention of him in the British press:

It took South African Nigel Hawthorne just three days to get his first theatrical engagement in this country. He arrived just in time to get 'booked' by Anthony Hawtrey for the summer repertory season at the Playhouse.

'It was a lucky break,' he says, 'for I came to England without a job lined up for me.'

> *In South Africa he was with a touring company for a year and during that time met Shaun Sutton, the Playhouse producer.*
>
> *In* Bonaventure *at the Playhouse next week, Mr Hawthorne will be playing Willie, the village half-wit, a role he played in South Africa.*[31]

Above the piece, in the centre of the page, is a photograph of Nigel in sports jacket and rather florid cravat, an improbable and uneasy symbol of rakish sophistication.

The season was directed exclusively by Shaun Sutton and several of the plays on the bill were ones in which Nigel had performed in South Africa, placing him on familiar ground. The repertoire comprised the usual potboilers and perennial favourites, Emlyn Williams's *A Murder Has Been Arranged,* Arnold Ridley's *The Ghost Train,* and the inevitable *Charley's Aunt,* to name a few. These were the livelihood of weekly repertory companies up and down the country but were not, by and large, designed to test the range or depth of players.

The routine of rep was punishing, mentally and physically. A new production would open on Monday evening with rehearsals for the next week's play beginning the following morning. An act a day was rehearsed. Time not occupied by rehearsals and performance was for learning lines. Most actors lived with the perpetual danger of drying (suffering a memory lapse) on stage as well as the hidden terrors of props that could only be counted on for their unreliability. Lengthy read-throughs, detailed scene-blocking, and anything beyond a cursory analysis of the *dramatis personae* were luxuries the average rep company could ill afford. It was a system with obvious limitations but an invaluable discipline for which today there is no equivalent, a remote world recaptured (often hilariously) by Kate Dunn in her affectionate history *Exit Through the Fireplace.*[32] At Buxton amateurish transgressions such as corpsing (a particular problem for Nigel in those early days) were severely frowned upon and young actors had rapidly to cure themselves of these tendencies or face the sack. Sunday was the company's one day of rest but for Nigel, as part of the stage management, it was fraught with activity and tension as one set needed to be dismantled and another 'got in', the ephemeral nature of theatrical production nowhere more apparent than in weekly rep.

Towards the close of the season Anthony Hawtrey asked Nigel to be a member of his permanent company at the Embassy Theatre, beginning in October. Nigel was overjoyed at the prospect of a London season but was soon brought down to earth by the realisation that he was to continue in his capacity as assistant stage manager with no guarantee of regular acting parts. In the five months he spent at Swiss Cottage he appeared on stage only three times. His eagerly awaited London debut on 7 November 1951 was merely a walk-on part as a sailor in *Magnolia Street Story*, a new play by Emmanuel Litvinoff based on Louis Golding's best-selling novel of 1932. Nigel's second appearance at the Embassy was, bizarrely, in blackface; he played the (by today's standards politically incorrect) role of Donald, the happy-go-lucky boyfriend of the Sycamores' housekeeper in Moss Hart and George S. Kaufman's Pulitzer Prize-winning screwball comedy *You Can't Take It With You*. A month passed between this and his third and final acting assignment at Swiss Cottage as a waiter in a Christmas production of Thornton Wilder's *The Merchant of Yonkers,* a non-musical prototype of *Hello, Dolly!*

By February of the following year Nigel was utterly despondent, feeling that his career had ground to a halt. He confronted the Embassy's Manager, Oscar Lewenstein, about his concerns and, before he knew it, had unwittingly resigned. What followed was without question one of the bleakest periods of his life. He was now living the nightmarish scenario which, on leaving Cape Town, had filled him with dread but which he had hitherto narrowly avoided: in the middle of his first English winter he was unemployed and facing penury and starvation or, what for him was worse, an ignominious retreat to South Africa. Most days he trudged the length of Charing Cross Road and St Martin's Lane, knocking on the doors of the theatrical agents, great and small, and 'getting quite savagely rejected. I was like a Woody Allen character. People just looked through me.' At the same time, as if to underline the futility of his quest, the *Evening Standard* published an open letter from critic Kenneth Tynan dispensing to the stage-struck some sobering advice and statistics:

The desire to become an actor is today rather like pleading for admission to the Black Hole of Calcutta. Too many people have turned up at the party already. There is broken glass underfoot, and you are likely to be greeted with an elbow in the face.

These are the facts – and it will be helpful if you imagine that phrase in letters of fire; there are nearly 10,000 actors and actresses at present registered with Equity, the actors' trade union, of whom at least half are, at any given moment, unemployed. When the pantomime season ends, the proportion of actors in jobs falls to something like one in three.

You are, in short, redundant before you start.

The accession of the young Queen to the throne, upon the death of George VI on 6 February 1952, was portrayed by the media as the dawn of a new Elizabethan age. Britain regained a confidence and buoyancy it had lost in the dismal aftermath of war. But Nigel could not share in the national mood of optimism. Tynan's statistically grim warning and the constant rejection he suffered plunged him into a black depression. His goal of the Shakespeare Memorial Theatre seemed impossibly remote. He repeatedly failed to attract the attention of agents and producers or to be recalled for the second round of auditions. On one occasion he auditioned for Stratford before Glen Byam Shaw and Anthony Quayle, who talked throughout. 'Thank you,' they called out curtly. 'You weren't even listening,' Nigel snapped back in frustration.

A lot of people rise above it. I don't think I was ever able to quite. I always got sort of mortified and wounded and went into hiding because of it, and I suppose that was very much my nature.[33]

Nor was he any closer to finding personal happiness. In Britain in the early 1950s, especially in the wake of the defection of Burgess and Maclean, the notorious Montagu Affair and the prosecution of Rupert Croft-Cooke, political and public hostility towards homosexuality reached its height. The 1948 Kinsey Report had suggested that there was 'a huge domain of invisible perversion'[34] needing to be rooted out. A witch-hunt was vigorously implemented and suspected offenders, who had hitherto relied on the law turning a blind eye, were now baited by plain-clothes policemen and prosecuted. The theatre, widely regarded as a beacon and safe haven for men guilty of 'the West End vice',[35] provided easy quarry as John Gielgud's humiliating arrest in October 1953 for 'persistently importuning' confirmed. Until decriminalisation in 1967, homosexuals were driven into a clandestine underworld which operated on mostly discreet coded signals. Nigel, because of his natural reserve and propriety, and his acute sense of guilt, was repelled by this shadowy world and, as a consequence, lived in a protracted state of solitariness and displacement.

For years in England I lived a sort of double life and never felt in any way at ease with being gay as we call it now, never liking the world very much, finding the more extreme, more extrovert gay people offensive and alien to me. And so I was sort of somewhere in the middle of all that and not able to find somebody that I could share my life with because I found going into the bars and the clubs where you met those companions didn't suit me, although I used to do it but in a very half-hearted and embarrassed way, feeling that I was going to be recognised and reported to the police.

The temptation to return home to South Africa was almost overwhelming.

I got to the point where I wanted to give up and I just couldn't understand why I was doing it, but I knew that I really needed to justify to my father, and my mother too, my choice of career because they had been very against it. I think my mother had been softer about it than Dad. When occasionally he did write to me – and I suppose in the first six years I was away I had two letters maybe – they were always scribbled on the back of one of my mother's letters and ended up 'Best love, Dad.' And there were things like, 'If things aren't going well you can always come home', and I suppose those are the sort of things that are like a red rag to a bull to me, and I'd say, 'No, I'm not coming back.'

Nigel's close friend, South African-born actress Joyce Grant has traced back his persistence to something in his colonial background: 'South Africans have a kind of resilience, a kind of courage. They are not easily intimidated and not easily conned.'

A chance encounter with Oscar Lewenstein one evening led to Nigel's brief reinstatement at the Embassy as a call-boy at five pounds a performance. The indignity of having to accept a much-reduced rank and of waiting at the stage door for gratuities from the leading actors left a considerable dent in his pride. Soon after he was offered the job of understudying the dual role of the twin brothers Hugo and Frederic in a touring production of *Ring Round the Moon* by Manchester's Library Theatre. It was a far from ideal situation; the tour lasted three months and Nigel never once went on stage. But he was glad to be earning a weekly salary of eight pounds and to be granted a reprieve from the wretchedness of his London routine. Finally, at the end of June, after six long months of inactivity, his acting skills were put back to work. A quarter of the way through the new summer season at Buxton Anthony Hawtrey engaged him to 'play as cast' with, to Nigel's untold delight, no stage management. His second Buxton season, however, was not as happy as the first: Hawtrey was in poor health, and, although the first three plays in which Nigel performed were directed by his friend Shaun Sutton, the rest were directed by the Canadian character actor Raymond Lovell of whose capabilities Nigel and many others entertained no high opinion.

When the Buxton season ended Nigel returned to London and spent three weeks 'resting'. The Employment Exchange in Marylebone Road supplied him with a card to enable him to sort letters at Christmas time, but in the last week of October he was dispatched to Southampton by the minor theatrical agent Miriam Warner to perform in two twice-nightly rep pieces at the Grand

Theatre, and then to Walthamstow to appear with The Savoy Players in Patrick Hamilton's *Rope*. He had been recommended to Miriam Warner by his friend Helen Haye, the elderly but very regal doyenne of the English stage and star of the *Ring Round the Moon* tour. Warner's timely bookings came after months of silence from her office. She was not the sort of agent who could expedite a young actor's rise to the dizzying heights of the profession; out-of-the-way tours and twice-nightly rep were where the limits of her influence and acumen lay. The longest engagement she helped secure Nigel was also the most soul-destroying episode of his career, understudying in a West End hit for nineteen months without ever going on. Nigel recorded the beginning of this frustrating saga in his diary, in which, for the first time, one can perceive a tone of despair and glimpse his impecunious circumstances:

> *M. Warner phones me up late one wet December afternoon, telling me to go to Half Moon Street, for an interview with George and Alfred Black. The job is to understudy the lead (Leslie Phillips) and two others (Anthony Sharp and Ken Ruddington) in a new comedy. My interview was with Harold Boyes, and I remember my feet being soaking wet, as my shoes had a great hole in each. The audition was held by John Counsell the following day, and I got the job. Each day, for a week, I rehearsed at the Comedy – or rather watched the others rehearse – and then made my way to Walthamstow to play in Rope. We opened in Blackpool on December 8th, and then our first night – December 17th. It appears we are a success! Although how long I shall be able to bear sitting night after night in a dressing-room, I can't say.*

The comedy was Arthur Watkyn's *For Better, For Worse* and ran 607 performances. Playing opposite Leslie Phillips was twenty-year-old Geraldine McEwan who thirty years later made an outstanding Mrs Proudie, the nemesis of Nigel's equally outstanding Archdeacon Grantly in the BBC serialisation of Anthony Trollope's *The Warden* and *Barchester Towers*. Phillips remained in rude good health throughout the run but one night got Nigel's hopes up by fainting on stage in the middle of a performance. With the curtain still raised Nigel gathered up Phillips in his arms, carried him off, and deposited him on the bed in Phillips's dressing room. He then dashed off to his own dressing room to make-up in order to go on at Phillips's next entrance and rushed back to the wings only to be greeted by an apologetic Phillips in costume and fully recovered.

During the run of *For Better, For Worse* Nigel understudied in eight productions for The Repertory Players, a London Sunday theatre society, and walked on in just three of the plays. When, a few months later, he joined Northampton Rep, the local paper, to whom he told his tale of woe, speculated whether he had, in fact, created a record by understudying ten different productions without once being called on to give a performance.

His ordeal ended in July 1954 and within a fortnight he had landed a permanent acting job at Northampton's Royal Theatre, a beautiful Italianate style building, opened in 1884 and designed by the renowned Victorian theatre architect C. J. Phipps who was also responsible for the Theatre Royal Bath and The Lyceum in Edinburgh. The Northampton Repertory Players were one of the oldest repertory companies in England and counted among their past members the dashingly dissipated Errol Flynn (whose old digs Nigel now occupied), Nigel Patrick, Sonia Dresdel and Freda Jackson. Synonymous with the Royal was the theatre's resident scenic designer since 1928, Tom Osborne Robinson, whom Nigel, in a foreword to Richard Foulkes's history of the Company, described as 'a great character – flamboyant but very gentle. I can see him now striding round the town like some nobleman of the Italian Renaissance, big-bellied, big-nosed and bearded, glancing up at his favourite pieces of architecture as though he had fashioned them all himself and would guard them with his life.'[36]

On the first morning of rehearsals for Ian Hay's *The Sport of Kings* Robinson's assistant in the scenic department, Bruce Palmer, introduced himself to Nigel. A few years Nigel's senior, Palmer was an outgoing and seemingly carefree personality. Nigel welcomed his friendship and the two decided to rent a flat together, but within a short space of time Nigel became the object of Palmer's unrequited and possessive love, a situation that continued for twenty-seven years. For Nigel it was a demanding and claustrophobic relationship but in his lonely state he could not help but find some measure of solace in Palmer's companionship.

Apart from these emotional complications Nigel's fortunes had improved. At Northampton he played mostly leading roles with no stage management and was paid twelve pounds a week. He remained with the Company for eighteen months. In an instance of delayed justice one of his most critically acclaimed performances was as Tony (the role played by Leslie Phillips in London) in *For Better, For Worse*:

Among the players, Nigel Hawthorne is outstanding. This type of comedy seems to be his forte. He invests it with a calculated touch of farce, while never overstepping the borderline and brings to the part an individual style which is bound to be compared with that of Ralph Lynn.[37]

Jim Brent in *Quiet Weekend*, Northampton 1954. *(Courtesy of Trevor Bentham)*

His other long spell of understudying similarly paid off when he played 'with fine versatility'[38] Hugo and Frederic in *Ring Round the Moon:*

> *In a vast, grotesque winter garden, like a private Crystal Palace, and at the centre of a collection of wonderfully mad people we find Hugo, a violet-gloved blue-blooded young man about town (Nigel Hawthorne), who by means of a carefully staged party, is planning a complicated intrigue involving his sad soulful brother (a very different Hawthorne), a millionaire's daughter [...] and the millionaire's strident mistress.*[39]

On 30 October 1955 Nigel represented Northampton Rep in an audacious theatrical debate at the local Drama Club, an account of which was given in the *Chronicle and Echo:*

> *Mr Nigel Hawthorne and Mr John Bennett clashed in debate last night at Northampton Drama Club.*
>
> *Mr Hawthorne, well-known member of Northampton Repertory Company, moved 'That the average amateur actor is a menace.' Mr Bennett, who defended, is an amateur actor himself, though whether average was not stated.*

But what added piquancy to the situation was the fact that Mr Bennett, beside being an amateur actor, average or otherwise, is a director of Northampton Repertory Theatre.

So, virtually, Mr Hawthorne was clashing with one of his employers! With antipathy between amateurs and professionals as strong as it often is, here was a rich situation indeed.

Mr Hawthorne may be considered a bold man, not only on this score, but on the fact that he was singeing the beard of amateur drama right in the home port. He acknowledged his boldness – he began with a reference to 'a bodyguard of four Repertory permanent seatholders waiting outside.'

The bodyguard was fictitious but its absence did not deter Mr Hawthorne from some forthright remarks. Just a week before, in the Little Theatre which was the scene of last night's debate, he had seen the Drama Club's Dark of the Moon. Twenty-two people played in it. And of them, Mr Hawthorne indicated, there were only six whom he would retain in the club. [...]

I should add that everything was said in the spirit of debate.[40]

Having performed in a total of sixty-one plays at the Royal, Nigel returned to his well-rehearsed role of an out-of-work actor in London doing the rounds of the theatrical agents and producers. He was eventually interviewed by the director of the Bromley Repertory Company and, on the basis of an alleged resemblance to Frankie Howerd, was hired as the comic's look-alike in the farce *Tons of Money* which also starred Sheila Hancock. He followed this with parts in Bromley's Christmas pantomime *Cinderella* and the play *Night of the Fourth*.

After more than six years in England it was clear to him that he was no further advanced in his career than in 1951. He had managed to keep going, which in itself was no mean achievement, but he was caught in a Sisyphean cycle of weekly rep, futile auditions and unemployment. There was, however, an escape route to hand. Leonard Schach was currently in London in search of new productions to take home to South Africa. He contacted Nigel and offered him a place in his now fully professional company, the Cockpit Players, housed at the Hofmeyr Theatre. Nigel hesitated only momentarily. After a long winter of discontent he looked forward to the African summer and the possibility of a new beginning.

Notes to Chapter 1

1　*BBC Omnibus:* 'Yes, Sir Nigel', 1999.
2　*ibid.*
3　*ibid.*
4　*ibid.*
5　Interview with Andrew Duncan, 'If I'd had more courage, my life would have been totally different', *Radio Times,* 7-13 May 1994.
6　Schach (1996) 46.
7　*BBC Omnibus:* 'Yes, Sir Nigel', 1999.
8　Schach (1996) 11.
9　*Cape Argus,* 11 November 1947.
10　Schach (1996) 43.
11　Little Theatre programme.
12　Schach (1996) 43.
13　*Cape Argus,* 23 August 1948.
14　*Cape Times,* 11 July 1949, 3.
15　*Varsity* (University of Cape Town), Vol.8, no.8, 23 August 1949, 4.
16　*Cape Times,* 4 May 1949.
17　*ibid.*
18　*Cape Times,* 5 April 1950, 16.
19　*BBC Omnibus:* 'Yes, Sir Nigel', 1999.
20　*Cape Times,* 6 July 1950, 14.
21　*Rhodesia Herald,* 15 August 1950.
22　*Cape Argus,* 29 November 1950.
23　*Cape Times* 13 December 1950, 13.
24　*Cape Times,* 31 January 1951, 14.
25　Interview with Hugh Herbert, 'Yes … and no', *Guardian,* 9 January 1982.
26　*The Friend* (South Africa), 27 March 1981.
27　Interview with Alan Franks, *The Times Magazine,* 26 April 2003, 18.
28　Interview with Luaine Lee for *Scripps Howard News Service,* 'Nigel Hawthorne is More Than he Seems', 5 May 1999.
29　Quoted by Irene Worth in Harwood, ed., (1984) 96.
30　*BBC Omnibus:* 'Yes, Sir Nigel', 1999.
31　*Buxton Advertiser and Herald,* 15 June 1951, 3.
32　See Dunn (1998).
33　*BBC Omnibus:* 'Yes, Sir Nigel', 1999.
34　Rebellato (1999), 157.
35　On the association of the theatre with homosexuality in the 1950s, see Rebellato (1999), 160-3.
36　In Foulkes (1992) Foreword.
37　*Northampton Independent,* 3 September 1954.
38　*Northampton Independent,* 27 January 1956.
39　*Chronicle & Echo* (Northampton), 24 January 1956.
40　*Chronicle & Echo* (Northampton), 31 October 1955.

Chapter 2

African Summer

The Cockpit Players

For the first twenty years you are still growing
Bodily that is, as a poet, of course,
You are not born yet. It's the next ten
You cut your teeth on to emerge smirking
For your brash courtship of the muse.

(R. S. Thomas, 'To a Young Poet', ll. 1-5)

The premiere of John Osborne's first play *Look Back in Anger* in the English Stage Company's inaugural season at London's Royal Court ensured that 1956 has been ubiquitously acknowledged as a watershed in post-war British theatre. That same year a quieter 'revolution' was initiated half a world away when Leonard Schach's Cockpit Players, who, in common with the English Stage Company under the artistic direction of George Devine, were committed to the promotion of new writing and the pursuit of an artistic and progressive ideal, established a permanent home at the Hofmeyr Theatre in Cape Town.

From September 1956 until August 1962 Schach presided over an exciting, if short-lived, renaissance in South African theatre during which his unsubsidised resident company of actors and designers, drawn primarily from local talent, staged important plays freshly imported from overseas as well as the first modern tragedy indigenous to Cape Town. The Cockpit Players' repertoire of over thirty plays in six years represents a period when South African theatre was at its least insular and most responsive to the latest voices and movements in world drama, before domestic legislation and mounting international disapproval of the apartheid system combined to enforce South Africa's cultural exile, which was to last three decades. The new dynamism in the country's professional theatre structure also facilitated a critical phase in Nigel's development as an actor. When he returned to Cape Town in 1957, after six and a half frustrating years in which his career seemed to stagnate in the humblest ranks of English repertory, he was given, for the first time, the opportunity to be more than a jobbing actor and to have creative involvement in work far removed from the diet of light comedy, farce and melodrama that was the stock-in-trade of weekly rep.

Over the next five years, before his permanent relocation to England, he honed his skills as a thoughtful young character actor in plays by writers such as Osborne, O'Neill, Cocteau and Pinter, and in two works seminal to the maturing cultural identity of Australia and South Africa, Ray Lawler's *Summer of the Seventeenth Doll* and Basil Warner's *Try for White*. He also played an active part in the early translation of the inventive discourse of satiric comedy and iconoclasm pioneered by *Beyond the Fringe*. Commenting on the value of his time with the Cockpit Players, Nigel stated:

> *The main thing about it was it gave me a chance of playing huge leading parts of quality, with enough rehearsal time to really examine them and to be serious about my work. Instead of just doing a commercial job like a play a week or a bit on television, and just scraping a living by being an actor, I was actually able to be involved in a production and be excited by it, which is what I had always wanted.*

Leonard Schach was born in Cape Town in 1918. As his biographer Donald Inskip points out, 'His interest in theatre was in a sense a by-product of experiences none of which steered him purposefully towards the life in which he found fame and fulfillment.'[1] He graduated from the University of Cape Town with degrees in Arts and Law. As a student he began acting with the University Dramatic Society, becoming a competent interpreter of middle-aged character roles, and eventually made his less than auspicious directorial debut when co-opted to produce a stage reading of the ill-chosen Merton Hodge adaptation of Olive Schreiner's *African Farm*. He was admitted to the Cape Bar at the end of 1941 but was never to practise as a lawyer. War postponed the necessity for an immediate career decision and in 1942 he joined the South African Naval Forces in which, after a period of basic training, he was assigned to legal and administrative duties. At the conclusion of his service in 1946 Schach returned as a casual student to UCT's Speech and Drama Department, then headed by Rosalie van der Gucht, and over the next decade he directed several productions at the Dramatic Society's home, the Little Theatre, beginning with a sensitive staging of John Balderston's *Berkeley Square*.

From March 1947 he visited twelve countries in eighteen months in order to survey at first hand their organisation of national theatres and in June 1948 he represented South Africa at the first conference of the International Theatre Institute in Prague. The contact with leading foreign theatre practitioners, which this tour afforded him, and his exposure to audiences, particularly on the Continent, who cared deeply about the theatre, greatly influenced his ambition to be part of a similarly vital community – one that believed in the potential of theatre to change people's lives by endeavouring to inform, challenge and edify, as well as to entertain.

Not long after his return to Cape Town Schach was appointed Acting Controller of the Little Theatre for 1949, an opportunity which gave him a valuable introduction to the responsibilities of theatre management, through effectively a twelve-month apprenticeship, within a relatively secure environment, in day-to-day administration, policy making, and the leadership of an integrated creative team. It was at this time that Schach first demonstrated, what was undoubtedly his distinguishing asset as a director-manager, an uncanny success in obtaining the performance rights to new plays by top international playwrights. He had become close friends with Tennessee Williams's agent, Audrey Wood, who, in return for Schach's help in a personal matter concerning Williams, gave him the first foreign rights to *The Glass Menagerie* which he produced at the Little Theatre in December 1948 and toured nationally the following year. Much of his later success in importing new drama was also fortuitous, but Schach's good fortune was allied to an astute appreciation of the quality and currency of the writing and catholic personal tastes. According to Donald Inskip, 'Procuring performing rights for South Africa of many distinguished new plays ahead of other countries and managements was an often-realised ambition with Leonard, and he played an important part in keeping us in step with world theatre before this became increasingly difficult and impossible.'[2]

In the years before he established his own permanent company in Cape Town Leonard Schach built a reputation as an energetic and much-in-demand freelance director, producing plays for the Little Theatre Players, the repertory companies in Cape Town and Johannesburg, the National Theatre Organisation and two plays for the Brian Brooke Company.

In 1956 Brian Brooke, whose repertory company had staged 150 productions at the Hofmeyr Theatre since its inception in 1946, transferred his activities to Johannesburg where he started his own Brooke Theatre in De Villiers Street. The Hofmeyr was not dark for long. Brooke retained his lease of the theatre, while Schach became his sub-tenant and on 8 September launched the first season of his Cockpit Players. The opening performances under Schach's management, however, were given by the harmonica virtuoso Larry Adler and, along with the company's first full-scale production, Willard Stoker's *Spring Quartet,* which opened on 17 September, offered Cape Town's theatre-going public little in the way of a programmatic statement of the new regime. Audiences could better have gauged the Hofmeyr's future direction from the last production Schach presented there prior to the changeover, Samuel Beckett's *Waiting For Godot,* which had transferred from a packed season at the Little Theatre. Cape Town had been only the second English-speaking city after London to see the play in its entirety.

Nigel's association with Schach extended back to his student days when he had been a stage manager for *The Glass Menagerie.* Schach first directed him in 1949 in Bridget Boland's *Cockpit,* from which his company took its name and, as a result, had directed Nigel's final performance as an amateur in Arthur Laurents's *Home of the Brave,* which opened on the eve of the actor's twenty-first birthday. Even in those early days Schach had discerned something substantial about Nigel's talents and the makings of a fine character actor. He urged the young man to await patiently the recognition with which maturity would reward his peculiar gifts. When Nigel reunited with Schach at the start of the Cockpit Players' second season, both he and Cape Town theatre had reached an important liminal point.

With the change in management at the Hofmeyr came a transition in ethos and approach which did much to rescue Cape Town from the sort of parochialism and apathy that had partly prompted Brian Brooke's move to Johannesburg. Whereas Brooke was an actor-manager in the British theatrical tradition, Schach represented a new phenomenon in South African theatre, that of the director-manager. In the selection of plays to be produced Brooke followed an essentially, although not exclusively, commercial principle, while Schach's main criterion was that the work should be provocative and representative of the best modern writing without being esoteric. In his published reminiscences, *The Flag is Flying,* Schach outlined his agenda: 'I moved into the Hofmeyr determined to present plays that could bring cultured entertainment to the audience and would be a personal and intellectual challenge for me.'[3] A further difference in the modus operandi of these two men was their policy of recruitment. The Brian Brooke Company relied quite heavily on British imports of varying ages and experience. The Cockpit Players, on the other hand, did occasionally feature guest artists from abroad, most notably Dame Flora Robson and Beryl Reid, but their resident performers and technical staff were almost entirely local products.

The new management's philosophy was one with which Nigel found much sympathy and which greatly aided his growth as an actor, by enabling him to graduate from minor roles in rather lightweight commercial work to strong supporting and leading roles in some of the most significant drama of the twentieth century.

The important thing was that they were good plays and I was able to build up my confidence in playing leading roles and holding a play and leading a company and things like that, which I hadn't really done before, and I found that I was good at it and had a taste for it.

Evaluating Schach's strengths and weaknesses as a director-manager, Nigel recalled:

He was never a good director. His gift really was in being able to spot the sort of plays that would work. He used to come over here [to England] and somehow he managed to get these plays that nobody else got and they were all shunted across to South Africa and Leonard would come in and direct them. He would generally get to see the plays as often as he could in London or New York or wherever it was, and have a fair idea of the sort of set it was and what worked best. He was a very intelligent man, but he was not very good at communicating with actors. And so most of the time you let him surround you in the most expensively constructed set, always totally modelled on the original production, and the lighting was always immaculately done. He was very good at organising the lighting. And the thing he was least good at was really digging under the skin of a character and saying, like all good directors can do, 'Go for that', 'I wouldn't play that side of him; go for that side.' But his gift really was in choice and he was very successful.

The renewal of Nigel's association with Schach in 1957 coincided with the Cockpit Players' most noteworthy acquisition to date, the performing rights to *Look Back in Anger,* John Osborne's claustrophobic study of the desperate melancholy permeating a Sunday afternoon in a bleak suburban bed-sitter. The received reading of Osborne's shattering impact on a moribund British theatre has been most recently and impressively challenged, and its real complexity exposed, by Dan Rebellato in his book *1956 And All That,*[4] yet the mythology which surrounds *Look Back in Anger* has proved almost impossible to dismantle. As Richard Eyre and Nicholas Wright indicate, 'The British theatre still sets its clock by the revolution of 1956, accepts the theologies and pieties associated with that historical moment and talks about before and after *Look Back in Anger* as if it were before and after Darwin.'[5] The 'revolution', which popularised the ideologically loaded terms 'angry young man' and 'kitchen sink', and enshrined them in the theatrical lexicon, was, in fact, orchestrated by the Royal Court Press Officer and BBC Television, and given impetus and *gravitas* by the most influential drama critic of the time, Kenneth Tynan. When *Look Back in Anger* opened at the Royal Court on

Tuesday 8 May it received mixed, but generally lukewarm, reviews in the daily papers, but its critical fate was decided by Tynan's review which appeared the following Sunday in the *Observer* and, although not an unqualified rave, concluded with the famously flamboyant verdict: 'I doubt if I could love anyone who did not wish to see *Look Back in Anger*. It is the best young play of its decade.' Nigel had seen the original production during one of his 'resting' periods in London and certainly subscribed to this view.

In terms of its construction the play broke no boundaries. Its formal three-act structure and melodramatic climaxes had their archetype in the sort of 'drawing-room' dramas deemed typical of Terence Rattigan and the original 'angry young man' Noël Coward.[6] What was revolutionary and obviously arresting about *Look Back in Anger* was the way in which it rendered articulate the fiercely felt impotence and aimlessness of a new generation. Born in 1929, the same year as Nigel, John Osborne was, as Tynan claimed, the first spokesman of the classless and leaderless among this generation. In his excoriating rhetoric against his wife and the world at large, and his soliloquies alternately of self-love and self-loathing, the character of Jimmy Porter expressed the frustration and neuroses of post-war youth as well as its borrowed and troubled nostalgia for an Edwardian world of moral certainties and demarcations to which it never belonged.

Look Back in Anger, with Felicity Bosman, Leon Gluckman and Elspeth Bryce. *(Anne Fischer/ Courtesy of the National English Literary Museum, Grahamstown)*

Cliff Lewis in *Look Back in Anger* (1957), with Leon Gluckman. *(Anne Fischer/ Courtesy of the National English Literary Museum, Grahamstown)*

Leonard Schach's production of *Look Back in Anger* opened at the Hofmeyr Theatre on 20 November 1957 with Leon Gluckman as Jimmy Porter, Felicity Bosman as his wife Alison, Elspeth Bryce as her actress friend Helen, and Nigel in the role, created in London by Alan Bates, of Cliff Lewis, a self-characterised 'no-man's land' between Alison and Jimmy. Cliff was the first of many young character roles Nigel performed for Leonard Schach. Probably based on Osborne's friend Anthony Creighton, the character represents most of the things Jimmy is not: uneducated, burly, laconic, passive, and patient. Occasionally his sensitive and tolerant perspective of the marital war of attrition which, periodically, he referees, and his undramatic expression of this sensitivity and tolerance, contrast powerfully with Jimmy's vituperative eloquence:

> *Sometimes, it's been still and peaceful, no incidents, and we've all been reasonably happy. But most of the time, it's simply a very narrow strip of plain hell. But where I come from, we're used to brawling and excitement. Perhaps I even enjoy being in the thick of it. I love these two people very much. And I pity all of us.*

Look Back in Anger was the first significant new play in which Nigel had been involved as a professional actor, and one with profound resonance for his own generation. As such it was an exciting departure from his most recent work within the predictable and innocuous repertoire of provincial English rep. What Nigel could not have failed to discern in contemplating his debut with the Cockpit Players was the irony that, having retreated to South Africa when he did, he was at less of a distance than he had been in Northampton and Bromley, or as an understudy in the West End, from the revolutionary activity in London's Sloane Square.

Before rehearsals for *Look Back in Anger* began Nigel set up home in a modern flat in the Clifton area of Cape Town. He shared this home with his companion Bruce Palmer who had travelled with him from England and whom Schach had promised a job as one of his resident scenic designers. Nigel's own artistic talents as a caricaturist were also usefully employed in the company's publicity. Over the next five years, in addition to being one of the Cockpit Players' leading performers, he produced several cast drawings and production posters, as well as the company's Christmas cards. There was a definite correlation between his facility for drawing caricatures and his approach to creating characters on stage, which he himself analysed:

> *Like a caricaturist, an actor portraying a real-life character must find the essence of the man. In drawing caricatures you have to dig quite deep. You have to find what it is about that person that makes him identifiable, and it's usually nothing to do with the features at all. It's the inside of the person. Similarly, on stage, you find the drive, the energy of the man, the compassion of the man, the honesty of the man – those sorts of things I go for rather than the physical details.*

This process of internalisation, as applied to his acting, was something Nigel developed over many years and to which he finally found the key in a production of Christopher Hampton's *The Philanthropist* in 1973.

As soon as *Look Back in Anger* closed Nigel headed to Johannesburg to rehearse a supporting part in Ray Lawler's *Summer of the Seventeenth Doll*, which Schach directed for the National Theatre Organisation.[7] The play had first been performed in Melbourne in November 1955 and, like *Look Back in Anger* in Britain, it was a timely and original response to the need for some kind of national self-definition in the face of the social phenomena peculiar to the post-war period. The 1950s in Australia witnessed a boom in building and immigration and were typified by a suburban affluence and political and social conservatism. With regard to its national identity Australia had not yet

A Christmas card from the Cockpit Players drawn by Nigel.

reached full maturity and was still constrained by an indelible proneness to 'cultural cringe'.[8] Before *Summer of the Seventeenth Doll*, the country's unique psychology and evolving notion of self had not been adequately or accurately represented on stage. Lawler injected into a conventionally crafted dramatic framework recognisably indigenous content and colour. His unselfconscious and unsentimentalised characters spoke with authentic Australian accents and used the vernacular of the working class.

Summer of the Seventeenth Doll is the concluding part of a story which begins before the Second World War and concerns two Queensland canecutters, Barney and Roo, who every year spend the lay-off season, 'five months of heaven', in Melbourne with their girlfriends Olive and Nancy. When the curtain rises Nancy has married and moved away and been replaced by the prim barmaid Pearl who has difficulty reconciling her pretensions to respectable widowhood with her curiosity about the lifestyle of the lay-offs. The four characters are now approaching middle age and the play concentrates on their strained and altering relationships with each other, engendered by their reluctance to grow up and their fear of growing old. Despite its robust humour, it is possibly the first domestic and urban Australian tragedy. In it Lawler explores themes native to the bush – man's struggle against nature, mateship, and cheerful resilience – in the context of a tarnished suburban gentility. Although unmistakably Australian, *Summer of the Seventeenth Doll* was successfully transplanted to London in April 1957, where it was co-produced by Laurence Olivier at the New Theatre and contributed to the working-class revolution already underway in British drama.

Leonard Schach stole a considerable march on the play's New York premiere when his production opened twelve months earlier at the Alexander Theatre in Johannesburg on New Year's Eve 1957. His original cast included Joan Blake as Pearl, Marjorie Gordon as Olive, Bill Brewer as Roo and Michael Turner as Barney. Nigel played Johnnie Dowd, Roo's twenty-five-year-old rival in the cane fields, to whom, for the first time in his life, Roo had lost a fight. The play was greeted warmly by its South African audience who identified with Lawler's naturalistically drawn characters and appreciated Frank Graves's evocative recreation of a semi-squalid, faintly exotic Victorian cottage in Carlton. On 13 February 1958 *Summer of the Seventeenth Doll* transferred to Cape Town where it enjoyed a five-week run prior to a lengthy tour of Southern Africa and the Rhodesias. It was voted the best production of 1958 and inspired in Schach a determination to discover its South African equivalent. He had less than a year to wait until Basil Warner presented him with his first play *Try for White,* an authentic and contemporary Cape Town creation.

In the meantime the Cockpit Players' 1957-8 season concluded in March with *The Waltz of the Toreadors,* one of Jean Anouilh's *pièces grinçantes,* or harsh comedies, which was first performed in Paris in 1952 and staged at London's Arts Theatre Club by Peter Hall in 1956. In his review for the *Cape Times* Ivor Jones criticised the leading actor Gerald James's casual and one-key performance as General St Pé, before expressing the opinion, 'The Doctor Bonfant of Nigel Hawthorne is the best interpretation of the evening, and personally I feel that, given the chance, he would have made great guns of the General.'[9]

Immediately after *The Waltz of the Toreadors* Nigel and Bruce Palmer formed a company called The Eagle Players. The company enjoyed only a brief life but gave Nigel the opportunity to make his professional directorial debut with a production of *Doctor in the House,* presented at the Hofmeyr on 22 April 1958. The play was a rather broadly drawn and farcical adaptation of Richard Gordon's story of which there had already been a popular film version. Palmer designed the sets, while Nigel starred as Tony Grimsdyke, a perennial medical student, and recruited as his fellow students David Beattie and John Cundill. The production was reasonably well received and the players praised for their enthusiasm and hard work on an inadequate script. Ivor Jones of the *Cape Times* said of Nigel's direction, 'he […] leads them cheerfully, without any sign of the strain one might expect to beset an actor-producer in these days of box-office uncertainty.'[10]

Nigel's next excursion from the Cockpit Players was a second and very extensive tour for the National Theatre in Leon Gluckman's polished production of Sheridan's *The School for Scandal.* Among an experienced cast, which included Margaret Inglis, Siegfried Mynhardt, Frank Wise, Zoe Randall, David Beattie and Joyce Grant (in a beautiful performance as Mrs Candour), Nigel undertook, at his own suggestion, the exhausting but satisfying task of doubling the roles of Crabtree and Charles Surface. It was an eventful few months. The company travelled in a Kombi van from Johannesburg to Cape Town, playing many one-night *dorps* (small towns) along the way. In one of these *dorps,* an Afrikaans-speaking town in ostrich country, the audience threw stink bombs, rice and flour at the actors in their elaborate Restoration costumes. One morning along the route the wigs failed to arrive with the rest of the wardrobe and the actors had to improvise as best they could. The leading lady Margaret Inglis used white shoe polish to powder her hair, while the ever-resourceful Nigel went around to all the local barber shops, collecting crêpe which he fashioned into an elegant wig. Joyce Grant, who had become firm friends with Nigel, said 'he was so intelligent and inventive, and everything he did he did beautifully. He was a difficult person; he expected the best from you all the time.'

He returned to the Cockpit Players in October 1958 as Joe Ferguson, the hearty all-American football hero, and brawny third of a comic love triangle, in *The Male Animal,* which James Thurber wrote with Elliot Nugent. The company being short on tall men, Nigel's eligibility for the part of the hail-fellow-well-met quarter-back was decided solely on his height of six feet and his sturdy, albeit slim, build, and, although it was an otherwise improbable piece of casting, he 'walked off with the play'.[11] While it contained a serious sub-plot in the controversial issue of academic freedom, *The Male Animal* was an essentially orthodox domestic comedy, and for Cape Town audiences, who were becoming increasingly astute about new dramatic writing and were cultivating a taste for weighty and challenging scripts over merely diverting entertainment, it held limited appeal.

This taste for serious drama was well catered for by the company's next production, Eugene O'Neill's autobiographical *Long Day's Journey into Night*, in which Nigel made his second appearance of the new season. Schach had once again capitalised on his knack for acquiring performance rights so often withheld from larger and more established managements overseas. The actor Frederic March had introduced him to O'Neill's widow Carlotta who was notoriously mistrustful towards the more commercially motivated Broadway impresarios. Reassured, as Donald Inskip phrases it, by Schach's 'youthfulness and "non-establishment" approach to the play', she happily made the rights available to him. O'Neill wrote *Long Day's Journey into Night* in 1941 and had

Edmund Tyrone in *Long Day's Journey into Night* (1958), with Leon Gluckman. *(Anne Fischer/ Courtesy of the National English Literary Museum, Grahamstown)*

stipulated that it was not to be published until twenty-five years after his death and never to be performed. Fortunately his widow did not comply with these wishes and the play was first presented in Stockholm on 2 February 1956 and in New York the following November, earning O'Neill a posthumous Pulitzer Prize.

The action of the play occurs over a single day and night in 1912 within the Tyrone household. The father is a miserly Irish actor, his wife a morphine addict, their elder son Jamie a cynical alcoholic, and their younger son Edmund (based on the youthful O'Neill himself) a morbid consumptive with ambitions to be a poet. All four seem to be propelled on a course of self-destruction. On the day in question Edmund learns that he has tuberculosis, while his mother Mary renews her drug dependence and drifts in and out of madness. Around these incidents the family members participate in a series of scarifying exchanges of resentment and hatred, and competing crescendos of cruel reproach.

Schach staged the play in its entirety, which meant a running time of close to four and a half hours. John McKelvey was cast as James Tyrone, Joan Blake as Mary, Leon Gluckman as Jamie, and Nigel as Edmund. Paddy Canavan played the family maid. The South African premiere of *Long Day's Journey* at the Hofmeyr on 30 October 1958 coincided with the play's London run, which starred Nigel's boyhood heroine and, much later intimate friend, Gwen Ffrangcon-Davies. Opening night played to a half-empty auditorium, a fact lamented by Ivor Jones in his review the following day:

This apparent lack of support was deplorable, for the piece was memorably done, producer and cast obviously finding inspiration in a masterpiece of stage writing rarely seen in the theatre nowadays. [...] The casual theatregoer will find scant chance for laughter [...] though for the connoisseur there is masterly characterization and dialogue, to both of which Mr Schach's actors respond in full emotional flood. This talented quartet last night kept the audience hushed through every soul-searching scene, and, though slow, Mr Schach's decreed pace built constantly up to climaxes that are abundantly present in each of the four acts.

The production was a critical and (from its second night) popular triumph. The consistently high standard of the performances surpassed most people's expectations, including the critic for *Die Burger* who declared, 'I did not in my wildest dreams imagine that Leonard Schach and the Cockpit Players could produce and perform a play in this way.' Under the theatre listings in the *Cape Times* of 31 October the Cockpit Players posted the following notice:

> *May we*
> *thank*
> *the people of Cape Town*
> *for listening with such*
> *rapt attention and*
> *absorption last night to*
> *one of the*
> *truly great plays*
> *of all time.*
> *And we were sincerely moved by the audience's*
> *reception of the performances*
> *of*
> *Joan Blake*
> *John McKelvey*
> *Leon Gluckman*
> *Nigel Hawthorne*
> *Paddy Canavan*

Long Day's Journey was very much an ensemble piece with no exceptional star turn. In the role of Edmund the twenty-nine-year-old Nigel excelled, providing ample testimony of a new depth, virtuosity and maturity in his acting. The South African-born critic Clive Hirschhorn, who began his career with the Johannesburg *Sunday Times* and *Rand Daily Mail,* and was latterly theatre critic for London's *Sunday Express,* saw the production when he was an eighteen-year-old student: 'I had just come back from my first New York visit in 1957 where I saw the original *Long Day's Journey,* and remember thinking, on seeing Nigel in the part, how well he compared with Bradford Dillman.' When the play commenced a three-week run at the Intimate Theatre in Johannesburg on 9 February 1959, Oliver Walker of the *Star* remarked, 'Nigel Hawthorne's Edmund was […] painfully alive in the way he ranged between revulsion and rapture.'[12]

Between the end of the Cape Town run of *Long Day's Journey* and its Johannesburg opening Nigel appeared at the Hofmeyr in Terence Rattigan's *Separate Tables* as Charles Stratton, the young medical student who speaks in defence of the spurious Major. That same year the film version starring David Niven was released. A week before Christmas 1958 Nigel performed the role of Cornelius Hackl in Thornton Wilder's *The Matchmaker,* which, five years later, Michael Stewart and Jerry Herman remodelled as the Broadway musical *Hello Dolly!* In his third London appearance in 1951 Nigel had taken part in an even earlier incarnation of *Hello, Dolly!, The Merchant of Yonkers,* written by Wilder in 1938 and adapted from a nineteenth-century Viennese farce. Michael McGovern, who was also in the cast of *The Matchmaker* and became a good friend of Nigel, remembered, 'Nigel played Cornelius beautifully. The softness, gentleness and honesty of the character so suited Nigel's own personality.'

The first production of the new year was the Cockpit Players' most important contribution to indigenous theatre. Since forming his own company three years earlier Leonard Schach had introduced Cape Town, and much of the rest of the country, to some of the best examples of modern world drama, which in itself was a historic achievement, but what he still longed to uncover was a local play commensurable, in the potency and immediacy of its communication with the nation's soul, to the dramas of Tennessee Williams and Lawler's *Summer of the Seventeenth Doll*. Such a play he found in *Try for White*. Its author Basil Warner was a thirty-five-year-old advertising executive. Married to the actress Minna Millsten, and himself an amateur actor and occasional set designer, he was well known in theatre, radio and journalistic circles. *Try for White* was his first excursion as a dramatist. He had originally intended to send the manuscript to a London play agent, but at the eleventh hour offered it to Schach on the night before the final dress rehearsal of *Long Day's Journey*.

The three-act play, which deals with the human tragedy inherent in the country's race classification laws, is set inside and outside a house in the city's Malay Quarter on the eastern slopes of Signal Hill under the shadow of Table Mountain. At the centre of the plot is a coloured dressmaker Jane Matthews who, for many years, has successfully tried to pass for white. Her dark-skinned mother has lived in the house as the cook Mrs Adams. Robert, her son by a white father, is unaware of his mixed blood and has been educated as a white boy at a farming college in the Transvaal. Now twenty-one, he arrives home one New Year's Eve to learn of his mother's ten-year liaison with Hockey Jagger, an oafish and bigoted white bus conductor. He accepts the relationship and soon falls in love with a coloured girl, Lisa Samuels, who lives in the neighbourhood, but of whom his mother disapproves. Meanwhile Jane's friend Muriel Jordan, out of jealousy, betrays the secret of Jane's background to Jagger, who in turn dramatically denounces his lover in front of her son and abandons her to lonely despair. Confronted with the truth about his own situation, Robert is forced to choose on what side of the colour line to live. Against his mother's pleas, and despite his integration into the white community, he scorns the idea of continuing to try for white and assumes his identity as a coloured person.

Robert Matthews (far right) in *Try for White* (1959), with Heather Lloyd-Jones, Raymond Williams and Walter Glennie. *(Anne Fischer/ Courtesy of Percy Tucker)*

In his personal history of South African theatre Schach said of *Try for White*, 'Here at last was what every management in the country was waiting for: a play about South Africa by a local playwright, sociologically challenging, eminently stage-worthy, authoritatively accurate and dealing with the ills of racial segregation.'[13] It was not the first play to scrutinise the theme of 'trying for white'. Just four months before its opening, Cecil Williams staged *The Kimberley Train* at the Library Theatre in Johannesburg, a story about a young coloured girl's attempts to cross the colour divide, which took its title from a tune used by an underground group that protected coloured people who were able to pass for white. The author Lewis Sowdon was the theatre critic for the *Rand Daily Mail* and kept his identity out of the media until after the play had opened.

The impressive cast assembled for the world premiere in Cape Town of *Try for White* on 27 January 1959 included Marjorie Gordon as Jane Matthews, Michael Turner as Hockey Jagger, Nigel as Robert, Heather Lloyd Jones as his girlfriend, and Jane Fenn as his grandmother. The opening was well publicised as was the playwright's anonymity, the reasons for which Schach later explained:

These were early days in our theatre. Any reference to things local got a nervous titter as a response in the theatre. A recent murder play had degenerated into farce with the repeated mention of hotels, places and streets known familiarly to the audience. In addition, Basil had something of a reputation for flippancy. The public would not easily accept a theatre piece of his authorship. The cast readily agreed to this and were sworn to secrecy.[14]

The day after the opening the front page of the *Cape Times* bore the headline 'Mystery of Playwright Revealed', along with a photograph of Basil Warner, and proclaimed, 'Cape Town's biggest theatrical "tease" for years is over.' Inside appeared a rapturous review:

Basil Warner's Try for White, *which Leonard Schach produced last night at the Hofmeyr to a capacity audience giddy with expectation at the start, and clamorous with approval at the end, is unquestionably the finest drama with an essentially South African theme – the tragedy of Coloured people trying to pass for White – that I have yet seen in the theatre.*

This is no gaudy creation surrendering to showmanship, no smouldering slag heap of passionate complaint against racial discrimination, but a sincere and intelligent study of colour-bar problems confronting a Cape Town family during a critical period of reunion. [...]

This is Mr Warner's first essay as a dramatist, and as yet he is no Tennessee Williams, but to my mind their manner of creating characters is remarkably akin. Both evoke tense moods and create living people through a form of fluent dialogue that sketches allusively the outlines of an off-stage world, even while we take in the immediate matter behind the footlights. [...]

The situations reach out and touch sensitive chords of experience that must have twanged – personally or otherwise – in the hearts of many a Capetonian before to-day. We take a profound personal interest in Mr Warner's sharply drawn characters because we see them not as isolated specimens, but as people working out their destinies in relation to other people. [...]

In bringing these problems to us in the theatre the players could well have fallen into the booby-trap of exaggeration, but with Mr Schach's cunning hand to guide them nobody makes a mock of mockery in interpreting types too often caricatured on the stage. Performances are superb throughout. [...]

Here, indeed, is a more than adequate South African answer to Summer of the Seventeenth Doll, *and I sincerely hope that Mr Warner's throbbing document will, like the Australian play, go abroad some day to gather the acclaim it so richly deserves.*[15]

With *Try for White* English-language theatre in South Africa had truly come of age. The play epitomised a new maturity and vibrancy in the country's artistic consciousness and overcame the traditional sense South Africans had of being culturally backward and cut off from Europe. While cinema was still called the bioscope and television was not officially introduced to South Africa until 1976, in the 50s and 60s theatre was the leading cultural forum and was making people think about themselves and their environment. For Nigel the success of *Try for White* was extremely personally satisfying. It was the first time in his career that he had been responsible for creating an important role and he approached his character, which Warner had written from contemporary and local real life, with assurance and sensitivity. He represented the coloured boy's dilemma with understated anguish and a moving dignity.

Apart from the authenticity with which the characters were portrayed, what enabled Cape Town audiences instantly to connect with the story was the production's incredible evocation of the familiar sights, sounds and even smells of their city – the achievement of Bruce Palmer. Since his arrival in South Africa Palmer had designed the sets for *Look Back in Anger, The Waltz of the Toreadors, Inherit the Wind, Long Day's Journey into Night, Separate Tables* and *The Matchmaker,* which, despite the practical restrictions of the Hofmeyr's tiny stage, were faithful and detailed recreations of the London and New York originals. His set designs for *Try for White* accurately brought to life the descriptions and stage directions in Warner's atmospheric script. This precision astonished Schach, especially as Palmer had lived in Cape Town for less than two years. He had spent several days studying first hand the colourful Malay Quarter and the architecture and ambience of District Six, then a vibrant and multicultural ghetto area, but since the mass relocation of its residents to the Cape Flats between 1966 and 1982 a desolate strip of forgotten suburbia.

Before commencing a national tour, *Try for White* transferred to the Opera House in Pretoria and then to Johannesburg's Intimate Theatre. The first-night audience in Johannesburg on 2 March gave the cast fourteen curtain calls, but Oliver Walker, the theatre critic for the *Star,* was unimpressed by the play, maintaining that it had fallen short in daring and tragic substance:

> *This is strictly kitchen-sink or sewing-machine drama without enough elevation of speech or situation to wring our withers. Mrs Matthews' dilemma and her ultimate hard decision to stop playing white is only the small change of the colour question.*

> *Mr Warner has, one might suggest, been too busy laying on the local colour, to get to the core of the Colour crisis. The quaint, often comic 'accents' are all there, and the sordidness. But we miss that dyed-in-the-bone cynicism about Colour anomalies inherent in the South African outlook, and the hot summer climate ought to have been more fertile in dramatic invention to spread the situation more skilfully across three acts.*[16]

The play, nevertheless, repeated its Cape Town success in other parts of the country, crossing also into the Rhodesias, and Schach's dream of taking the production abroad seemed about to be realised. He had secured the backing of a London theatrical management for an English tour and London season. At the same time Georges Balay, the French ambassador to South Africa and an enthusiastic patron of the Cockpit Players, expressed interest in having *Try for White* as part of the 1961 International Theatre Festival in Paris. The Cockpit Players thus became the first professional theatre company in South Africa to be invited to stage a production at an international festival. The Paris visit would be linked to, and immediately precede, the play's British premiere. However, these plans were thwarted by political events outside the company's control. When South Africa quit the Commonwealth the London backers withdrew their financial support on the basis that a South African production might not be sympathetically received in view of the severance of formal ties, making the Cockpit Players' participation in the Paris Festival equally impossible. This was the beginning of the end of South Africa's theatrical renaissance.

In Johannesburg in early 1959 Nigel had reprised his roles in *Long Day's Journey into Night, Try for White,* and *The Matchmaker* within the space of six weeks. He and Bruce Palmer decided, at that time, to relocate temporarily to Johannesburg where Palmer found employment at the Alexander Theatre. Nigel briefly renewed his earlier South African theatrical associations, appearing at the Brooke Theatre in Petrina Fry's production of Hugh and Margaret Williams's comedy *The Grass is Greener,* in which he played the part of the dry and somewhat lugubrious butler Sellars. Also in the cast, as the madcap character Hattie (played with huge success in the West End by Joan Greenwood), was Shirley Firth, who recalls her personal experience of Nigel's quiet generosity towards his fellow actors:

> *I was way too young and inexperienced to touch the part, and the leading lady commented thereupon at the first read-through with 'Oh darling, you're not going to play that delicious part, are you?' Brookie, the management, heard this and came to my rescue by commenting that it was he who invited*

me to play the part, and he thought I'd be fine. My confidence was, however, dealt a blow, and my interpretation painfully tentative. Nigel must have registered this exchange, empathised, and observed me closely thereafter. Before the final dress rehearsal he took me aside and in his gentle way said it was all there but what I needed to do was to 'camp it up.' This was the cue or clue I needed. I rushed off and got myself some outrageous props – great floppy hat, outsize sunglasses, foot-long cigarette holder, backscratcher, and, as if that were not enough, cajoled a designer friend, who owed me a favour, to whip up a strapless black crepe dress that said it all. Needless to say I walked away with the notices. That really got me going and I owe it all to Nigel. Also, he knew I was undergoing domestic stress, and to enliven the little after-show Sunday night supper I was hosting for the cast in a very modest little downtown trattoria, he produced witty caricatures of the cast, which he tacked round the room, thereby enlivening the proceedings and got the evening off to a great start.

Over the next twelve months Nigel performed leading parts in Johannnesburg productions of *Under Milk Wood*, *Sabrina Fair* (as playboy David Larrabee, the role played by William Holden on screen), and Cocteau's daring comedy *Intimate Relations*. He was named Actor of the Year for his performance as the punch-drunk pugilist, Duke, in a National Theatre tour of William Saroyan's *The Cave Dwellers*, a strange tale about a group of decrepit performers living in an abandoned theatre. He also demonstrated his versatility as a director with productions of *Hansel and Gretel* for the Children's Theatre and the musical revue *Three's a Crowd* by Howard Dietz and Arthur Schwartz. On top of all these accomplishments, during this period he worked as a satirical cartoonist for the Johannesburg *Star*, producing disconcertingly accurate likenesses of well-known personalities like Flora Robson.

The end of 1960 saw Nigel's return to Cape Town and involvement in another landmark in South African theatre, the first production in English anywhere outside Britain of Harold Pinter's *The Caretaker*. Two years previously, in one of many instances throughout his life of being in the right place at the right time, Leonard Schach had met Harold Pinter in a kitchen at a first-night party of a local repertory company in Bristol. At that time Pinter was a struggling twenty-eight-year-old actor, trying to make it as a playwright. He had recently completed his second play *The Birthday Party* and gave the manuscript to Schach who passed it onto his London agent Jimmy Wax for something to read on a train journey. Wax eventually became Pinter's agent and almost exactly seven months after *The Caretaker* premiered at

London's Arts Theatre Club, Schach presented it at the Hofmeyr to tremendous critical acclaim.

The play is elliptical, cryptic, essentially plotless and relies greatly on mood, but is nevertheless arresting and revelatory. Its language seems simultaneously foreign and familiar. There is a single setting of a cluttered attic room in a west London house within which an intensive study is made, over three acts, of its mysterious characters who converse largely through silence or partially articulated sentences. Schach adopted a Brechtian approach to the play, experimenting with startling scenic and lighting devices. The South African three-man cast comprised Siegfried Mynhardt as the vagrant Davies, Nigel as

Aston in *The Caretaker* (1960), with Siegfried Mynhardt. *(Anne Fischer/ Courtesy of Trevor Bentham)*

the elder brother Aston, who has recently undergone electroconvulsive therapy in a mental institution, and Michael McGovern as the pugnacious and streetwise younger brother Mick. Geoffrey Tansley's review in the *Cape Times* reflected the general audience reaction:

> *Last night at the Hofmeyr I was fascinated at seeing and hearing an apparently meaningless script take on life. Words, which were disjointed and jumbled in print, painted a series of moods in which kindness, cruelty, laughter and pathos alternated, and gave structure to three totally different characters, all of whom reacted in his own way to the moods of the play. [...]*
>
> *Often the play seems incredibly funny; more often it is emotional; always it is compelling. Always too, it is delightfully unintelligible.*
>
> *Mr Mynhardt has capable support from Nigel Hawthorne as the fundamentally kind, slightly unbalanced, moody elder brother, and from Michael McGovern as the dominant, robust younger brother with a crudely sadistic sense of humour and an underlying kindness. Both these young men have got deeply into the subtleties of their parts.*[17]

Nigel's caricature of the *Caretaker* cast.

In the new year *The Caretaker* began a long tour which included Durban, Johannesburg, Port Elizabeth, Bloemfontein, Salisbury, Bulawayo, Umtali, Kitwe, Ndola, Chingola, Mufulira, Livingstone, Victoria Falls, Broken Hill, and went as far as the Copper Belt in northern Rhodesia. For the first time in South African theatre history an English-language play ran for over a year.

While preparations were being made for this tour Nigel made yet another foray into stage direction when he co-produced, with the company manager Aubrey Louw, Ben Travers's popular and perennial Aldwych farce *Rookery Nook* (written in 1926). This play, in which Nigel also starred as the newly married Gerald Popkiss, had been put on at the Hofmeyr for the duration of the Christmas season as suitable family entertainment.

The following April the Cockpit Players staged Agatha Christie's murder mystery *The Unexpected Guest* in which Nigel played the title role and Leonard Schach made a brief appearance as the corpse. The play was not a success and was regarded by Geoffrey Tansley of the *Cape Times* as an aberrant and unworthy choice of text on the part of a management who had recently presented *The Caretaker:* 'On the whole I feel that Mr Schach should stick to the kind of play in which he excels. The present production is the kind in which amateurs revel, and which they generally do quite well. Professional theatre should aim higher.' He described Nigel's performance as 'over confident'.[18]

During a rainy break in the rehearsals of *The Unexpected Guest* Michael McGovern accompanied Nigel to an early screening at the Labia Cinema of an old English comedy starring Alastair Sim:

During a particularly funny sequence, when the rest of the fairly small audience and I were laughing helplessly, I was suddenly aware that Nigel was totally still and silent. I looked at him, and by the light of the flickering screen I could see tears running down his cheeks. I asked him what was wrong and, still glued to the screen and smiling, he simply said, 'Isn't he wonderful?' I learned something about Nigel that day. He was quite unique.

Nigel later said that he admired Alastair Sim and his other hero Ralph Richardson 'precisely because they were *lost,* there was an absurdity to them in their given situations.'[19]

Nigel's penultimate performance for the Cockpit Players was as the young rabbi in Paddy Chayefsky's tragi-comedy *The Tenth Man,* who is confronted with the problem of keeping together a displaced European orthodox congregation in secular American society. The play was first presented on Broadway in 1959 under Tyrone Guthrie's direction and had been adapted from Ansky's 1914 drama *The Dybbuk* which dealt with demoniac possession. In *The Tenth Man* a *dybbuk,* or wandering spirit, has possessed a young woman and, in order to try to save her, a *minyan* (prayer group) consisting of ten Jewish men must be formed.

The last production in which Nigel appeared for the Cockpit Players was arguably Schach's greatest coup and the company's most challenging undertaking. This was the revue *Beyond the Fringe,* written and originally performed by Alan Bennett, Peter Cook, Jonathan Miller and Dudley Moore. Having seen the show in London, Schach had, true to form, promptly and successfully sought the first foreign performance rights to it. His production, which, along with Nigel, featured Siegfried Mynhardt, David Beattie and Leon Eagles, and eventually toured most of Southern Africa, opened at the Hofmeyr Theatre on Thursday 11 October 1961, exactly six months after the show's London premiere and a year before its transfer to Broadway. Thus, for several months the South African version of *Beyond the Fringe* ran concurrently with the London production in which the original cast was still performing.

Beyond the Fringe had its genesis in a plan, formulated by the Director of the Edinburgh Festival, Robert Ponsonby, and co-ordinated by his young assistant John Bassett, to stage a late-night revue, as part of the official Festival, which would rival the type of entertainment frequently presented on the Fringe by Oxbridge undergraduates. To devise such a revue Bassett recruited the precocious talents of four recent graduates, Dudley Moore and Alan Bennett from Oxford and Jonathan Miller and Peter Cook from Cambridge. Cook, the youngest member of the quartet, was the only one with experience in writing for the professional theatre. Each of the cast wrote and performed their own monologues or solos, many of which they had developed from their existing repertoire of skits or particular college 'party pieces'. The four also collaborated on a number of ensemble sketches. The result was a fresh, highly eclectic and extremely funny whole, groundbreaking in its sheer inventiveness and in the way it dissolved the distinction between private and public humour. The title was conceived by Ponsonby and was intended to suggest that the content of this revue surpassed the standard of the Edinburgh Fringe.

Beyond the Fringe opened at the Lyceum Theatre in Edinburgh on 22 August 1960. An expanded version of the show with material revised and added under the supervision of a professional director, Eleanor Fazan (who was later one of the choreographers for *Privates on Parade*), was produced by William Donaldson and Donald Albery at London's Fortune Theatre, opening on 10 May 1961 and collecting an *Evening Standard* Award for that year. This new version comprised twenty-three sketches. Among the most famous of these were 'Aftermyth of War' which lampooned the mawkish mythologising of Britain's war years, and especially the concept of 'The Few', by 1950s films like *Reach for the Sky;* a Shakespearean parody 'So That's the Way You Like It'; a lecture on civil defence and the H-bomb; Alan Bennett's sermon ('My brother Esau is an hairy man') composed entirely of meaningless phrases and hilarious *non sequiturs;* and Peter Cook's capriciously improvised monologue 'Sitting on the Bench' in which he played a dim coalminer who could have been a judge if he had only had the Latin.

One of the most enthusiastic reviews the show received was from Bernard Levin writing in the *Daily Express*:

> *The theatre came of age last night. Four young men [...] gave it the key of the door, and showed how the lock works. On the tiny stage of the tiny Fortune erupted a revue so brilliant, adult, hard-boiled, accurate, merciless, witty, unexpected, alive, exhilarating, cleansing, right, true and good [...] The satire [...] is real, barbed, deeply planted and aimed at things and people that need it.*[20]

Kenneth Tynan in the *Observer* provided a detailed description of the first sketch 'Steppes in the Right Direction,' designating it 'the moment when English comedy took its first decisive step into the second half of the twentieth century.'[21]

The label of satire so often applied to *Beyond the Fringe* is problematic and was not favoured by its creators, who disclaimed any specific satiric or didactic agenda. But, although its humour drew on several disparate traditions, many of which had nothing to do with satire, there was in the show an original and overarching attitude of mocking dissent directed at the complacency, hypocrisy and parochialism plaguing England in the Cold War era. As Humphrey Carpenter argues, 'Though *Beyond the Fringe* had not set out to be satirical, it had gradually developed into a devastating survey of the state of Britain in 1960.'[22]

In mounting their own production of *Beyond the Fringe*, the Cockpit Players were confronted by two obstacles. The first of these was very real and possibly unparalleled in theatre history – the non-existence of a definitive script. A published text of the London version of twenty-three sketches did not appear until 1963 and a second edition was produced to include additional material written for the 1964 production. The main difficulty the authors had in supplying a final script was the amount of improvisation that occurred nightly, making each performance a unique creation. The revised format of *Beyond the Fringe* had itself undergone substantial alteration during the course of the pre-London run in Cambridge and Brighton, and the London programme contained the warning 'This running order is liable to change.'

Schach thought he could solve this problem by obtaining permission to install a tape-recorder in the wings of the Fortune Theatre and having a transcription made from the recording. Nigel was one of the two hapless transcribers enlisted:

I remember the day very well. Leonard invited me over to his flat with the stage manager, a girl called Paddy Canavan, and Paddy and I listened to this thing and he said, 'I want you to write it all down' and he gave us a typewriter and left us alone. I can't remember how many days we spent on it, but it was very, very difficult to do as very often the laughter obscured some of the words because it was during a performance. And so there would be a wave of music or a huge burst of laughter and you could hear people talking in the background. We used to play it over and over and over and over and over again and then put down what we thought it was. And it wasn't until I saw the show in 1962, when I came back to England, that I realised to my horror, sitting there, that half the stuff we said was wrong.

Schach, who was the only one with first-hand knowledge of the show, was absolutely no help at all to them in this difficult task:

We had to sort of fill in the gaps and we would say to Leonard, 'What happened here?' and he said, 'Well, they were sort of wearing sweaters and they put them over their heads' and that was all. You just didn't know. I suppose he had seen it a few times, two or three times, but his memory of it wasn't all that accurate and sometimes it didn't fit.

Through this unorthodox as well as extremely laborious and fallible process a working script was finally produced which provided plenty of scope for the actors' resourcefulness and imagination.

The second obstacle facing the company was the question of whether the show's very Anglo-centric humour and the topicality of its references to Macmillan's England would translate to its new audience, particularly as no attempt was made to adapt the script to a South African context. Kenneth Tynan's sole criticism of *Beyond the Fringe* had been that it was too narrowly focussed on middle-class England: 'It can be justly urged against the show that it is too parochial, too much obsessed with BBC voices and BBC attitudes, too exclusively concerned with taunting the accents and values of John Betjeman's suburbia.'[23] The show's devisers and many of Schach's South African colleagues had also thought the humour of *Beyond the Fringe* too circumscribed to survive a major relocation. As it happened, however, the South African tour of *Beyond the Fringe* enjoyed phenomenal success, beginning in Cape Town and progressing through Johannesburg, Pretoria, the Rhodesias, East London and Bloemfontein. Ivor Jones in the *Cape Times* of 12 October reported:

The Hofmeyr has not often been the scene of such sustained hilarity and generous applause as was given there last night when Leonard Schach presented four of his Cockpit Players in Beyond the Fringe, *the satirical revue which has taken London by storm and will certainly do the same to Cape Town. [...] When brought to the Fortune Theatre in London five months ago it shattered all the established expectations of conventional revues by being an immediate and sensational success. Critics hailed it for going further and cutting deeper than anything of its kind had ever done in the British theatre, while applauding it for offering plenty of food for thought for those who wish it – or just sheer laughter for others. I whole-heartedly agree.*

The fervour of this reception and the fact that the show's Hofmeyr season had to be extended were not surprising given the Cape's doggedly English sensibilities and sympathies. The real surprise came in Bloemfontein, the heart of Afrikaans-language South Africa, where, as Donald Inskip relates, the audience 'showed a quick and appreciative grasp of even the finer points of this most quintessentially British satirical gallop. If indeed, as one has often heard, London is the spiritual home of all good Afrikaners, this season at the newly-built Bloemfontein Civic Theatre provided a pretty convincing demonstration.'[24] Nigel confirmed the universally warm response the production encountered:

We did a long tour and played two and three thousand-seater theatres and the original cast was at the Fortune in London which is tiny, so we must have made them a lot of money and yet we were, of course, without being aware of it, not playing the same show. It was a huge success. There was, I remember, an Observer *article which said that the reason it was liked in South Africa was because a lot of the humour was anti-British. It was nothing to do with that. It was just that the Englishness in a lot of South Africans embraced it. It was quite the reverse of what this man was saying.*

Of the original South African cast, David Beattie assumed the role of Peter Cook, Siegfried Mynhardt that of Alan Bennett, and Leon Eagles, newly arrived from Britain, that of Dudley Moore. Nigel played Jonathan Miller's part and thus performed such solos as the fantastical 'The Heat Death of the Universe' in which Miller had speculated on how there came to be four-hundred pairs of bright blue corduroy trousers in the London Passenger Transport Board Lost Property, concluding, 'it's obviously part of a London Passenger Transport Board plot – a rather complex economic scheme along Galbraithian or Keynesian lines – something rather baroque to expand the economy.' Exploring this theory to its most surreal extreme, he paints an image of four-hundred white, trouserless figures running through nocturnal London and, in an allusion to Kipling's 'Smuggler's Song' from *Puck of Pook's Hill*, of parents soothing their children to sleep with the words 'Turn your face to the wall, my darling, while the gentlemen trot by.' Ivor Jones, in his review, made special mention of Nigel in the sketch 'Porn Shopping' as a medical student scouting round the less salubrious bookshops along Charing Cross Road. Like the London cast, the South African quartet was dressed uniformly in dark grey lounge suits or sweaters, giving them the appearance of overgrown schoolboys. Pamela Lewis designed a striking set which reproduced the minimalism of the original and framed the stage in the monochrome of enlarged newspaper headlines.

Nigel's caricature of the *Beyond the Fringe* cast.

When Nigel returned to England the following year and saw the London production of *Beyond the Fringe* for himself, he was taken backstage to meet the cast. Neither he nor Alan Bennett could have had any inkling, during that first fleeting encounter, of their hugely successful collaboration thirty years later in *The Madness of George III*. Not too long after, a rumour was circulating town that a replacement cast was being sought for the show, prior to its Broadway transfer. Forty years later Nigel recalled, with scarcely muted horror, his personal interest in this news, which led to a case of paralysing stage fright:

> *This is quite a sad story [...] I got to know the management, or wrote to them – I can't remember how I did it – and got invited to an audition. And I thought it would be quite a novel idea to prepare – as I knew it so well – a couple of bits from the show itself, because I thought nobody else would have been able to do that as there wasn't a script and nobody, apart from the Cape Town production, had done the show. But, imagine my horror when*

I walked onto the stage and all four [of the original cast] were sitting out in the auditorium and they said, 'What are you going to do for us?' and I said, 'I can't. I can't do it.' They said, 'What do you want to do?' and I said, 'Well, I was going to do a couple of Jonathan Miller's pieces' and they said, 'Go ahead.' I said, 'I'd no idea you were going to be here, nobody had said you'd be here.' So they said, 'Well, it doesn't matter' and I said, 'It does. I'm terrified. It may not matter to you, but it matters terribly to me.' And the more I stood there, the more they tried to persuade me to begin and the further I got from wanting to do it. But eventually I took a deep breath and did both speeches rather badly and they gave the part to Joe Melia.

During Nigel's final two years with the Cockpit Players, South Africa underwent some of the most fateful political developments in its history, which marked the beginning of the country's repudiation by the international community. On 3 February 1960 the British Prime Minister Harold Macmillan delivered to the South African Parliament in Cape Town his 'Wind of Change' speech, in which he urged South Africa to face the fact of a growing national consciousness throughout the continent, and to move toward racial equality. Six weeks later, on 21 March, a massacre occurred in

Beyond the Fringe, 1961. Nigel (far left) with David Beattie, Leon Eagles and Siegfried Mynhardt. *(Anne Fischer/ Courtesy of Percy Tucker)*

the black township of Sharpeville in the Transvaal. Police killed fifty-six unarmed Africans who had been taking part in a campaign of civil disobedience against the pass laws, which required blacks always to carry identity cards. Soon afterwards, the government outlawed public meetings in certain areas and banned the ANC along with other political organisations it believed undermined national stability. On 31 May 1961, chiefly in response to the fierce denunciation of Dr Hendrik Verwoerd's apartheid policies by a group of Afro-Asian nations, South Africa withdrew from the Commonwealth and became a republic.

A fortnight before the Cape Town opening of *Beyond the Fringe* Schach had apparently told a reporter from the *Rand Daily Mail* of his intention to quit South African theatre within the coming year. In August 1962 his final production for the Cockpit Players, Tennessee Williams' *The Night of the Iguana,* was presented at the Hofmeyr. Two years later Schach directed Arthur Miller's *After the Fall,* which was his last South African production prior to settling permanently in Israel. His decision to disband the Cockpit Players and to go abroad was precipitated by the devastating cumulative effect on the performing arts, and especially independent theatre, of certain internal and external political actions.

From 1960 a series of acts, intended to separate the races, was promulgated, culminating in the Group Areas and Separate Amenities Act of 1965, under which theatres were effectively banned from presenting plays to racially mixed audiences or with racially mixed casts on stage. Theatre managers like Schach, in order 'not to condone but rather to circumvent the unhappy discrimination of the system',[25] arranged, when and where practicable, special performances of plays for non-white audiences. It is clear, however, from a sub-leader in the *Cape Times* of 2 March 1961, entitled 'Actors and Apartheid', and from subsequent letters to the editor, that many African theatregoers resented this practice, deeming it an inadequate and patronising expedient. This attitude, in turn, evoked a mixture of sympathy and frustration from some of the more enlightened members of the white population:

> *We can understand and sympathize with the cultural non-White whose aversion to apartheid is so strong that he cannot bring himself to attend a segregated performance. He must follow the dictates of his conscience, and should be respected for doing so. But there is a broader view which compels even greater respect – the view that the liberating power of culture can exert itself even in a segregated audience, and that the sense of human brotherhood can be communicated even in a building which denies it. [...] In terms of basic human significance art transcends politics.*[26]

The first reaction to these apartheid measures from the theatre community overseas came in the form of a resolution passed by Equity, the British actors' union, in June 1962, which forbade its members to perform before segregated audiences when visiting South Africa. This proscription, which only gradually came into full effect, made little impact on the Cockpit Players, since the company had always relied almost exclusively on local actors. For Leonard Schach the truly lethal blow was delivered a year later when, at South African playwright Athol Fugard's behest, nearly all British and American playwrights of consequence, together with some authors on the Continent, imposed a ban on the performance of their work to segregated audiences. This move struck at the core of Schach's artistic mission which had always been to enable South Africans to sample the best new international writing. These external boycotts were sealed within South Africa by Proclamation 26, which removed from the managements of all performance venues the discretion to admit non-European patrons.

The playwrights' boycott was undeniably the most injurious of the sanctions in the cultural sphere. 'Eventually,' Percy Tucker maintains, 'a positive corollary was seen in the growth of our own indigenous theatre, markedly linked to political protest.'[27] In 1963, for instance, Athol Fugard and his wife, the actress Sheila Meiring, formed an amateur drama group called the Serpent Players with non-white actors in the township of New Brighton, Port Elizabeth. Such initiatives, however, were slow in compensating for the country's lack of exposure to the foreign theatre scene. Schach went so far as to label the 1960s and 1970s the 'blackout' years of South African theatre:

The theatre in South Africa was seriously threatened. Local actors could, and they did, hold the fort. But new playwrights could not be developed overnight in South Africa. Furthermore, this boycott meant that the thinking South African public was being deprived of experiencing plays that serious-minded playwrights were writing (or should have been writing), attacking injustice wherever and in whatever form it was to be found. And, what is worse, when they did write plays of moral indignation, this ill-considered ban now prevented them from bringing consolation to those who suffered from these injustices. More important even, these writers were being prevented from making their criticisms of and opposition to apartheid known to the very people responsible for the injustice, for imposing these restrictions. In short, their opposition to apartheid was rendered voiceless. [...] Cultural boycott and sanction only encouraged injustice. Conditions were not ameliorated. Government, it could be argued, must actually have welcomed cultural boycott and sanction.[28]

At the same time as the boycotts came into effect, South Africa's National Theatre Organisation was dissolved and, in its place, heavily subsidised Performing Arts Councils (PACs) were introduced to foster the arts in each of the four provinces, a process which placed in further grave doubt the long-term feasibility of private companies like the Cockpit Players.

It was at the start of this process of nationalisation of the arts, and of South Africa's ostracism by the rest of the theatre world, that Nigel made his second and, as it transpired, permanent return to England. Although never a militant protester, or an especially political being, he felt, like many of his friends and colleagues, disaffected and disgusted by the multiplying injustices and the deeply unwholesome social structure engineered by the apartheid system. He also feared becoming desensitised to the evil around him. When he arrived back in South Africa in 1957 he was appalled at 'the terrible ease' with which he learnt to readjust to the system and accept it as normal: 'In no time at all I found I was no longer angry. I went on living in what I hoped was a liberal way – but blinkered.'

Strong and sincere as these feelings were, at the heart of Nigel's decision to leave the country early in 1962 was a profound need to confront his own demons:

> *I took a deep breath. It was very difficult to do because I was doing well over there and making a bit of money, not a lot but a bit. But I knew I had been untrue to myself by running away in '57 and thought that it would be better if I faced up to it and came back again, because I'd really burnt my boats in '57. So I saved up a thousand pounds this time, rather than twelve pounds, which is what I had originally, and came back again, not knowing anybody. Those people that I did know had moved on.*

He would not work again in South Africa until 1996 when he starred in *Inside,* Arthur Penn's film about political imprisonment. This was set almost entirely in a Johannesburg prison and switched between the 1980s and the present. In the film he played a sadistic Afrikaner colonel named Kruger whose interrogation methods provoke the suicide of a young white university professor. Ten years later the colonel is called to account by the Truth and Reconciliation Commission and the situations of inquisitor and prisoner are reversed.

The famous 'Round Africa' service provided by the Union-Castle mail ships was coming to an end and this time Nigel flew back to England. Unlike his arrival in 1951, he had no job awaiting him on this occasion and no friendly South African associate to take him under their wing. But he soon secured employment in provincial rep, signing on for two productions with the Connaught Theatre in Worthing. The first of these, on 30 April 1962, was Shaw's *Saint Joan* with Sarah Miles in the title role and Nigel as Gilles de Rais. This was followed a week later by Leslie Sands's thriller *Something To Hide* in which Nigel played the detective. Between 1945 and 1966 the Connaught was Britain's most important weekly repertory theatre and many of today's leading actors, writers, directors and designers began their careers there.[29] During its heyday in the 1950s it attracted the attention of London managements and critics who were keen to spot emerging talent and recognised in Melville Gillam, the company's head, the 'ability to see in a young actor that spark that takes him to the top of his profession.'[30] A Connaught season typically combined the canonical with the contemporary and experimental, making clear that it was no ordinary repertory bill. The year Nigel arrived the programme featured plays by Shakespeare, Coward and Delaney.

The one disappointing aspect of his sojourn in Worthing was that, after acquiring both status and self-esteem as a leading company player in South Africa, he had regressed to playing minor roles. However, his prospects seemed to improve when, a few months later, he landed his first substantial West End role. His previous on-stage experience in the West End consisted of a handful of 'spear-carrying' parts for the Repertory Players in the early 1950s. He had now been chosen for a double bill of one-act plays, under the blanket title *Talking to You*, by the American novelist and playwright William Saroyan.

After a short regional tour, *Talking to You* opened in London at the Duke of York's on 4 October 1962. Another member of the cast was a young actress by the name of Thelma Holt who would feature enormously in Nigel's private and working lives. Three years apart in age, the two quickly discovered a strong rapport and established a close friendship that endured until Nigel's death forty years later. A contemporary of Joe Orton's at RADA, Thelma Holt was an engaging and avant-garde performer, but rarely a leading lady. She eventually abandoned her acting career to become a producer. In 1968 she and Charles Marowitz founded the Open Space and from 1977 to 1983 she was the artistic director of the Round House. During Peter Hall's tenure at the National Theatre she was entrusted with special responsibility for bringing leading foreign companies to the South Bank. Since 1990 she has headed Thelma Holt Ltd and is one of London's leading impresarios and British theatre's most influential forces, renowned for her daring and uncompromising philosophy of theatre and her dedication to her actors. She produced Nigel's final two stage appearances, *The Clandestine Marriage* and *King Lear*.

At the time of *Talking to You,* she remembers:

Nige was larky, he was fun. He was very playful as a young man. Of course you hear about Nigel being very sensitive. I don't think he's easily depressed, but he has days when there's a black dog sitting on his shoulder. But as a young man that also had to be tempered with the fact that he was naturally extremely courteous and so he would always make an effort. So my early memories are of fun, of parties. He brought with him a lot of things that I soon realised were very South African: he liked to picnic, he liked to braaivleis.*[31] So the influence of growing up in the Cape was a very obvious one.*

Two years after *Talking To You,* and through Nigel's influence, Thelma Holt went out to work in South Africa. He had introduced her to the redoubtable director Taubie Kushlick and recommended her for Peter Shaffer's *The Private Ear and the Public Eye,* which played at the Intimate Theatre in Johannesburg. It was during her stay in South Africa that she met Nigel's family and got to know them well. In the process she gained a sympathetic impression of the normally difficult and overbearing Hawthorne patriarch. Nigel had always had a strained relationship with his father, although in later years he came increasingly to resemble him in some ways and would draw on characteristics of his father in the development of several roles:

I thought I was similar to my mother, but my older sister says I'm like him, which is a shock. He was very stubborn – and I suppose I am. Although I was at odds with him, I adored him and observed carefully. A lot of things I do are much influenced by what I remember of him.[32]

'Dad was, I suppose, quite eccentric and I use him all the time', he confessed in the 1999 *Omnibus* profile of his life. 'Very often now, quite unconsciously, I just remember things, the way he would do things, the way he spoke to people. I don't think he was ever as angry as he pretended to be. He always seemed to get quite a bit of amusement out of speaking to people in an angry way and I don't think that he really meant it.'[33] Charles Hawthorne equated acting with undergraduate frivolity and, what was worse, effeminacy, and his stern Victorian outlook and at times vociferous homophobia prevented him from finding much sympathy with his elder son's personal make-up or respect for his professional achievements. Nigel claimed that his father 'tried to like me, but didn't and felt disappointed in me. He wanted to be proud and I think he knew that he wasn't going to be.'[34]

Thelma Holt, however, saw a very different side to the authoritarian doctor, describing him as 'a great ladies' man. He was a great charmer, very laid back and easy with other people – within the family situation different and, like lots of doctors, tough. But with other people, particularly girls, a real sweetheart.'

According to a review in the *Times,* the Saroyan plays, *Talking to You* and *Across the Board on Tomorrow Morning,* were 'to all intents and purposes a rewriting of the Book of Job followed by a new Apocalypse. Mr Saroyan's Job, however, has no Voice from the Whirlwind, and his Apocalypse no new heaven but only the same old earth unaltered by a momentary transfiguration.'[35] The first play, *Talking to You,* featured Terence de Marney as 'The Tiger', a blind man ruling over a tiny paradise in the form of a basement room. The other inhabitants of this paradise included a Mexican guitarist (Andreas Markos), a black boxer known as Blackstone Boulevard (Johnny Sekka), and a young deaf boy (Graham Payne). Nigel's character Fancy Dan represented the intrusion of evil in the blind ruler's absence. *Across the Board on Tomorrow Morning* was set in Callaghan's Restaurant on East 52nd Street, New York. Its similarly eclectic group of characters symbolised the faces of contemporary anarchy.

The double bill, which was first produced on Broadway twenty years earlier, was not at all enthusiastically received by the London critics, who generally found the strong vein of allegory and fantasy in the plays, as well as Saroyan's insistently optimistic survey of human nature, pretentious and irritating. *The Times* reported, 'Mr Saroyan is a poet of profound simplicities who tends to inflate the simplicity and leave the profundity to look after itself', while Bernard Levin, writing in the *Daily Mail,* remarked biliously, 'He loves us all so much, and is so glad to be alive, and so glad that everybody else is alive that the effect can be a remarkably convincing feeling that one is developing a duodenal ulcer at a speed unprecedented in medical history.'[36] Thelma Holt believes the Saroyan plays presented an emotionalism which was somewhat discomforting and alien to British dramaturgical sensibility: 'I realise, with a bit more maturity, that that kind of sentiment, which works very well in America, – did work then and indeed works now – has never been well favoured in this island.' Nigel could at least take some comfort from his personal notices. John Percival in *Plays and Players,* for instance, wrote: 'Some of the acting in *Talking to You* was excellent, notably from Johnny Sekka, nervously eager as the pugilist, and Nigel Hawthorne as the edgy, ambiguous crook.'[37]

Despite the fact that, as Nigel commented, 'it was not even remotely successful,' *Talking to You* was a positive experience for the actor in terms of the access it allowed him to a stimulating vision of theatre and an approach to the craft that he found congenial to his abilities and personality. In the first place there was the personal contact with Saroyan, who was a leading experimental dramatist and, in Joan Littlewood's opinion, 'a master of improvisation'.[38] Thelma Holt asserts:

> *I think Nigel and I both agree that the most important thing about it was that Saroyan actually came and we got to meet Saroyan. He was quite an old man then[39] and was very charming. I remember that on the tour, before we met him – because we met him in London, we didn't meet him prior to that – we were excited – I can see now how young we were – that we were actually going to meet this great writer.*

Secondly, the plays were Nigel's initiation into the Method. The director was Arthur Storch, an actor and acclaimed Broadway director who subscribed to the tenets of the Method as adopted by New York's Actors' Studio, and who discovered in Nigel a receptive pupil:

> *I really found that I liked working with Storch enormously. It was a most peculiar transition for an actor who was, to all accounts, quite conventional, quite traditional, quite straightforward, and also a very shy person and a very self-conscious person, to suddenly come into the world of improvisation and an attitude to theatre which was really totally foreign to me and embrace it.*

This brief connection to the exciting and liberating possibilities of improvisation was the preliminary step towards his next big adventure in the theatre. He was soon to meet the woman who would become the major influence on his acting career.

> *I think that was the precursor really of my relationship with Joan Littlewood and why I found so much sympathy with her. And it's really helped me much more in the film world than it has in the theatre, because in the theatre there's an expectation of bravura, which is different from film and different from what I was trying to do.*

Joan Littlewood was an extraordinary maverick in the history of twentieth-century British theatre, a tormentor and challenger of the middle-class monopoly of theatre, who was ambitious to emancipate drama from impassivity and respectability by inventing an accessible theatrical language. In Nigel's eyes she was guru, mentor and a tyrannical monster. 'I think everyone meets someone who changes their whole life,' he once said, 'and she was the one who changed mine.'[40]

Notes to Chapter 2

1 Inskip (1977) 9.
2 Ibid 49.
3 Schach (1996) 82.
4 See Rebellato (1999).
5 Eyre & Wright (2000) 243.
6 The term 'angry young man' was first used of Noël Coward at the time of his scandalous play *The Vortex* in 1924.
7 Directed by P. P. B. Breytenbach, the NTO was a bilingual (Afrikaans and English) organisation, intended to provide employment for local performers and an outlet for local writers. During the fourteen years of its existence it undertook many national tours and presented over a hundred plays, both classical and modern.
8 'The Cultural Cringe' was the title of an essay by critic A. A. Phillips in a 1950 issue of the Melbourne arts journal *Meanjin*. Phillips defined the concept as 'an assumption that the domestic cultural product will be worse than the imported article.' Although in the context of this essay the term was applied specifically to Australian literature, 'cultural cringe' has subsequently been used of a general Australian tendency towards cultural self-depreciation and subservience to European culture.
9 *Cape Times,* 26 March 1958.
10 *Cape Times,* 23 April 1958.
11 *Cape Times,* 9 October 1958.
12 *Star* (Johannesburg), 10 February 1959.
13 Schach (1996) 88.
14 Ibid 89.
15 Ivor Jones, *Cape Times,* 28 January 1959.
16 *Star* (Johannesburg), 3 March 1959.
17 *Cape Times,* 1 December 1960.
18 *Cape Times,* 10 March 1961.
19 Interview with Kevin Kelly, 'Nigel Hawthorne retakes the colonies', *Boston Sunday Globe,* 24 October 1993.
20 *Daily Express,* 11 May 1961.
21 *Observer,* 14 May 1961.
22 Carpenter (2000) 121.
23 *Observer,* 14 May 1961.
24 Inskip (1977) 80.
25 Schach (1996) 108.
26 *Cape Times,* 2 March 1961, p.10.
27 Tucker (1997) 200.
28 Schach (1996) 109.
29 The impressive roll call of top theatre practitioners who worked at the Connaught includes Harold Pinter, Alan Ayckbourn, William Douglas Home, Ray Cooney, Michael Bryant, Maragaret Tyzack, Ian Holm, Elizabeth Spriggs, Daniel Massey, John Standing, John le Mesurier, Patricia Routledge, Dinsdale Landen, Andrew Sachs and Clive Francis.
30 Willmer (1999) 62.
31 An Afrikaans word meaning 'barbeque'. Often abbreviated to 'braai'.

32 Interview with Andrew Duncan, 'If I'd had more courage, my life would have been totally different', *Radio Times,* 7-13 May 1994.

33 *BBC Omnibus:* 'Yes, Sir Nigel', 1999.

34 *Ibid.*

35 *Times,* 5 October 1962.

36 *Daily Mail,* 5 October 1962.

37 *Plays and Players,* December 1962, 62-63.

38 Littlewood (1994) 552.

39 Saroyan was, in fact, only fifty-four years old at the time.

40 Interview with Paul Allen, 'A South African speaks out', *Morning Telegraph* (Sheffield), 30 November 1970.

Chapter 3

The Holy Terror of Stratford East

JOAN LITTLEWOOD AND THEATRE WORKSHOP

The Street-actors – as clowns, 'Billy Barlows,' 'Jim Crows,' and others.
(Henry Mayhew, *London Labour and the London Poor*)

When Nigel auditioned for Theatre Workshop in the summer of 1964, during a particularly lean and demoralising phase of his career, the company and its brilliant, implacable matriarch, Joan Littlewood, had already achieved legendary status. Workshop, as an ideal and as a permanent working unit, was past its heyday. Since 1960 its occupancy of its East End home, the Theatre Royal in Stratford E15, and its creative output had been episodic, the result of enervating West End success. *Oh, What a Lovely War!* in 1963 marked the return of Littlewood to Stratford East after an absence of two years as well as the regeneration of Workshop's practical philosophy and a restatement of its artistic strengths. In the four years that followed this triumphant regrouping Nigel appeared in three Theatre Workshop productions: the English and European tours of *Oh, What a Lovely War!, The Marie Lloyd Story* and *Mrs Wilson's Diary*. To characterise this period in Theatre Workshop's history as an Indian summer would imply a tranquillity the company never enjoyed. Rather, the years in which Nigel donned the mantle of a Littlewood 'scholar clown' represented a long last hurrah on the part of Workshop in defiance of intensifying financial pressures and a splintering membership.

Nigel's involvement with Joan Littlewood and Theatre Workshop was the most pivotal and enduring experience of his acting life and, with hindsight, is entirely consistent with the idiosyncratic nature of his professional development. At the time, however, his enlistment in the theatre militant of Stratford-atte-Bowe seemed to him an extremely aberrant career move and one symptomatic of his failure in the 1950s to attract attention at the annual mass auditions in London for Stratford-upon-Avon. It is worth speculating that had Nigel succeeded in his early bid to become a classical player in one of the leading companies like the Shakespeare Memorial Theatre or the Old Vic, in which actors conformed to a rigid *cursus honorum* dividing spear-carrier from star, his aptitude for risk-taking, improvisation and invention might never have fully declared itself. As it was, he acquired in Joan Littlewood his first real teacher, and under her austere but emboldening tutelage he learnt the lessons that ultimately defined him as a stage and film actor and transformed him into a highly professional, highly disciplined theatrical free spirit and free thinker:

> *She was somebody that saw in me something nobody else had seen. I became the blue-eyed boy for a while. She could be very heartless, very cruel, very demanding. But she taught me there was a diving board which was way up there and there was no point in stepping off the edge, you had to go up; climb the steps, go up the high diving board and dive off. There was no point in doing it if you couldn't.*[1]

Portrait of Joan Littlewood
(Peter Snow/National Portrait Gallery, London)

While Leonard Schach claimed to have been the first director to recognise the substance of Nigel's potential, Littlewood was the first to try to develop it. Richard Eyre and Nicholas Wright interpret Littlewood's capacity for spotting and nurturing untried talent as the essence of her political radicalism, her assertively left-wing conception of theatre: 'Her socialism lay less in believing in abstractions about redistribution of income than in realising the latent potential of every individual.'[2] John Wells, who collaborated with Littlewood many times, beginning with *Mrs Wilson's Diary*, perceived that, despite her notoriously difficult and combative temperament, 'her greatest gift is and always has been for extraordinary sensitivity, for unlocking inhibitions: people who had never spoken before told stories, offered suggestions and identified hidden conflicts – often in themselves.'[3] Littlewood's ambition, which she pursued with a missionary zeal, was to give a dramatic voice to the sort of people whom the British theatre establishment normally ignored, and she made a virtue out of strangeness. Her company was a motley band of 'nuts, clowns and villains', actors who were misfits under the West End reign of Hugh 'Binkie' Beaumont's H.M. Tennant Ltd, the ultimate purveyor of urbane, middle-brow theatrical fare – mainly boulevard drama and drawing-room comedy – and who were, perhaps, equally estranged from their fellow recusants against the commercialist orthodoxy, the angry young men (and women) of the Royal Court, many of them Oxbridge graduates, whose credo was the sanctity of the text.

Nigel, middle-class, politically undemonstrative and still an aspirant to the classical repertoire, with a solid grounding in traditional repertory, was not an obvious Workshop recruit, but he was, in many ways, that most prized of Littlewood discoveries, an outsider, a distinction made by Sheridan Morley:

> *He is not a natural Stratford East player, except that Joan was very good about outsiders, she recognised outsiders and Nigel was obviously, in London in the 50s and 60s, an outsider. He was also young, he wasn't getting much work, he even thought of giving it up for a period. Then Joan takes him up and suddenly he finds at Stratford East a kind of freedom, because she was a very funny, special woman and she didn't run theatres like other people. She took Barbara Windsor in and people who struck her as being not likely to end up at Stratford-upon-Avon. She liked people who, like Nigel at that time, seemed to be outsiders and weren't about to go and play Hamlet at the Old Vic. She recognised, I think, in Nigel something odd which was to do with Africa. I don't even know if she knew he came from there, but I can see how you would look at Nigel and think, this one is an odd one. He doesn't really fit the Old Vic or the Stratford of the 50s, he's not a classical player and that clearly appealed to Joan.*

In the two years since his second return to England Nigel had experienced no greater degree of success than he had a decade earlier in being noticed and having his talents properly utilised by the mainstream London managements. His first West End appearance of consequence had been in the ill-fated *Talking to You.* The critical battering and curtailed run of the Saroyan plays undercut any expectation he had of further West End exposure in the foreseeable future. Faced, at the end of his first year back in London, with an alarming dearth of job offers, he joined Thelma Holt on a decidedly unglamorous fit-up tour of south-west England with Theatre West, a short-lived company formed by James Roose-Evans under the aegis of Hampstead Theatre Club. The two plays they performed were Ibsen's *A Doll's House,* in which, Thelma Holt confidently affirms, 'Nigel and I bored for Oslo,' and a translation of Valentin Kataev's marital comedy, *Squaring the Circle,* dubiously dubbed the Russian *Private Lives*. Following this dispiriting tour, Nigel undertook odd jobs on television and performed occasionally in weekly rep at Bromley and in pantomime at Hornchurch (this last was for him the nadir of his acting career). In between these increasingly sporadic acting assignments he was employed as a domestic cleaner by a relatively up-market London agency, Your Servant, and among those for whom he cleaned was Cicely Berry, the voice coach at the Shakespeare Memorial Theatre, whose husband, Harry Moore, co-wrote *The Marie Lloyd Story*. Nigel was beginning to feel profoundly his isolation and sense of failure. His frail confidence in himself had all but disintegrated and when, eventually, he appeared before Gerry Raffles, Littlewood's General Manager and right-hand man, for an audition, he knew he had very little professionally to lose. What he gained by the end of his time at Stratford East was not security but his emancipation. In the beginning, however, he found himself in a totally unfamiliar environment, confronted with a theatre methodology which alienated him and undermined all his instincts and practices.

The composition, manifesto and overall aesthetic of Theatre Workshop had their genesis in the Red Megaphones, a small group of Salford teenagers formed by Jimmy Miller (later known as the folk-singer Ewan MacColl) in 1931, who enacted anti-capitalist sketches to dole queues outside the Labour Exchanges. The group was one of several operating under the standard of the Workers' Theatre Movement, a revolutionary confederacy closely identified with Communist policy and contributing to the daily class struggle through the performance of open-air sketches in a style known as 'agit-prop' (agitation and propaganda). In 1934, having begun to address the group's obvious need for training and technical knowledge by studying and applying in crude form the theories on stage lighting of the Swiss scenic designer Adolphe Appia,[4] the Red Megaphones changed their name to Theatre of Action and matured into a better organised and more skilled theatre collective, committed to experiment.

That same year they were joined by Joan Littlewood, a twenty-year-old drama student who had abandoned her course at RADA and arrived in Manchester disenchanted with the staleness and middle-class conservatism she deemed typical of West End theatre. She and MacColl, like-minded in their evolving vision of a political theatre relevant and accessible to working people, embarked on an intensive and, certainly in Littlewood's case, lifelong programme of self-education in the great theatres of the past and present. According to Howard Goorney, a founding member of Workshop and chronicler of its history:

Joan and Ewan's thirst for knowledge extended beyond their study of particular theatres and how they functioned, and their combined understanding of world dramaturgy was possibly unique in this country. It was not acquired in an academic sense, for its own sake, but in order to be able to relate it directly to their own work in the theatre.[5]

The development of training methods that would facilitate the group's driving philosophy was paramount; problems were solved as they arose and techniques invented as required, always through experimental processes. One area of training to which they were particularly committed was movement, and in this they were enormously influenced by Rudolf Laban whose revolutionary theories on free movement in modern dance they adapted to acting, continuing this work well into the years of Theatre Workshop.

In 1936 MacColl and Littlewood consolidated and redefined their ideas by founding Theatre Union, Workshop's immediate predecessor. This self-proclaimed 'Theatre of the People' played to audiences throughout England's industrial North-East before the outbreak of war and the dispersal of its members into the armed forces. Although by 1942 the company had ceased producing plays, its education continued for the duration of the war owing to the theatre studies undertaken by a core group of members, each of whom specialised in a particular subject such as Attic tragedy, *commedia dell'arte* or Chinese theatre. Books were exchanged and the fruits of their research shared through correspondence. When the war ended, those loyal to the cause of Theatre Union who had survived, reunited and, by pooling their army gratuities, launched Theatre Workshop – ironically from the top floor of the Conservative Party headquarters in Kendal. The ubiquity of theatre workshops today, and their usefulness to practitioners of all political and philosophical leanings, belies the fact that in 1945 this choice of name was not only a reflection of the company's utilitarian, hands-on approach to theatrical theory, but also a statement of its overtly socialist agenda. Theatre Workshop's manifesto was as follows:

The great theatres of all times have been popular theatres which reflected the dreams and struggles of the people. The theatre of Aeschylus and Sophocles, of Shakespeare and Ben Jonson, of the Commedia dell'Arte *and Molière derived their inspiration, their language, their art from the people.*

We want a theatre with a living language, a theatre which is not afraid of the sound of its own voice and which will comment as fearlessly on Society as did Ben Jonson and Aristophanes.

Theatre Workshop is an organisation of artists, technicians and actors who are experimenting in stage-craft. Its purpose is to create a flexible theatre-art, as swift moving and plastic as the cinema, by applying the recent technical advances in light and sound, and introducing music and the 'dance theatre' style of production.

Joan Littlewood became the company's director and producer, and Ewan MacColl its dramatist, with responsibility for in-service training. Also in Workshop's front ranks, and soon to prove himself an invaluable manager, was the youthful Gerry Raffles.

Over the next eight years the company's members lived the lives of strolling players, performing new works and revitalised classics in unconventional theatre venues and travelling abroad to Czechoslovakia, Sweden, Zurich and Moscow. A distinct Workshop style soon emerged which combined socialist documentary with the spirited entertainment of music hall, ribaldry with unforced lyricism, and which owed much to the influence of Elizabethan drama. In 1953 lack of subsidy forced the company to establish a permanent base and a decision was made to take over the lease of the Theatre Royal, a dilapidated Victorian building on the corner of Angel Lane, Stratford, in London's East End. No longer leading an itinerant troupe of social and theatrical reformers into traditionally non-theatre-going communities, Littlewood hoped that Workshop's new fixed location would attract a staunch working-class constituency, thereby preserving its central mission, a hope that was never more than partially fulfilled. In fact, as the years passed, Workshop attained considerable fashionableness, luring West End faithfuls eastwards, and even a measure of respectability through the approbation of critics like Harold Hobson. But in the early Stratford days, a time prior to the proliferation and popularity of experimental and fringe theatre, the company existed in a kind of limbo between metropolitan and regional theatre activity. This situation altered in May 1955 when Theatre Workshop became the first British company to win an award at the Théâtre des Nations Festival in Paris for its productions of *Arden of Faversham* and *Volpone*. The company's critical fortunes reached their height in the next three years as it staged the first works of Brendan Behan *(The Quare Fellow and The Hostage)* and Shelagh Delaney *(A Taste of Honey)*.

Increased fame and productivity exacted from Workshop a heavy price, one that endangered the very integrity and originality that were finally being recognised inside Britain. Between 1959 and 1961 five Workshop shows were successfully transferred to the West End, but these transfers were, in effect, a series of Pyrrhic victories. The conversion of a Stratford original into a mainstream hit eroded the company's constitution as a permanent repertory ensemble as casts settled into long runs on the other side of town. Its non-commercial, egalitarian ethos was compromised through contact and compliance with values Workshop had always eschewed and which bolstered the prevailing West End system and all that it implied (star billing, higher ticket prices and formulaic plots). These problems were compounded by the lamentably low financial support Theatre Workshop received from the Arts Council.[6] Thus, in 1961 Joan Littlewood left Theatre Workshop and England to work in Nigeria. Before her departure she told a *Daily Mail* reporter:

> *I'm leaving because I'm being hamstrung by the money-grubbing commercialism of the West End. […] It's slowly killing me. I build up a cast and I'm forced to export it to the West End. […]*
>
> *I just can't work for the money motive. And I hate to see shows which were successful here at Stratford becoming bad productions by the mere move to the staleness of the West End. […]*
>
> *So now I'm bequeathing whatever I've done to the enemy – the theatre owners, managements, the leaders who control the means of production.*[7]

During Littlewood's absence, and after her return in 1963, the Theatre Royal was leased to various companies around Workshop's increasingly sparse production schedule. It was with one of these visiting companies that Nigel made his inauspicious debut at Stratford East on 4 November 1963. *Oh, What a Lovely War!*, which had premiered at Stratford East in March of that year, was four and a half months into its West End run at Wyndham's Theatre when Howard Koch presented at the Theatre Royal his stage biography of Charles and Mary Lamb, *The Albatross,* in which Nigel played the part of the opium-addicted poet Samuel Taylor Coleridge. Koch had been the author of *Invasion from Mars,* the radio dramatisation of H.G. Wells's novel *The War of the Worlds,* which Orson Welles broadcast on CBS on Halloween 1938, sparking off mass panic in the streets of New York.

The Albatross was a ludicrous reconstruction, by turns bloodthirsty and mawkish, of the fifteen years or so from Mary Lamb's violent murder of her mother, and brief committal to a lunatic asylum, to Charles Lamb's retirement from his clerk's job at the East India Company. Koch set the relationship between brother and sister in a cursorily drawn literary context, leaving the actors to contend manfully with lines of embarrassing ineptitude such as 'Sorry I'm late; Hazlitt's in town' and 'Tell me, how are the Wordsworths?' Early on in the first act the cast became conscious of a simmering hysteria in the auditorium. The play's fate as a risible flop was sealed in the second act by Nigel's delivery, in an opium-induced haze, of a single word: when Mary, shocked at the alteration in Coleridge's appearance, asked, 'Samuel, where have you been?', he serenely replied, 'Everywhere ... !' and immediately plunged the audience into helpless gales of laughter. In the *Times* review the next morning Koch was summarily brought to justice for his latest 'stunt' and few among the wretched cast escaped unscathed. Nigel received a rare mention, but for all the wrong reasons: 'Nigel Hawthorne's Coleridge, a spruce ladies' man periodically rushing into the wings clutching his laudanum bottle, is a filmland absurdity.'[8] As compensation, to some extent, for the mortification he felt at such notices were the intimacy and geniality of the Theatre Royal, the scene of his nightly misery and of much more rewarding, if emotionally volatile, times to come.

Oh, What a Lovely War! was mounted in the context of the company's incipient decline, yet it is often thought to epitomise the best of what Workshop achieved as well as the paradoxes central to its achievements: the promotion, under a dominating director and personality, of ensemble playing and rehearsals built upon collaborative exploration; the communication of serious social messages through clowning; and the creation within a non-naturalistic setting of emotional realism. The show was jointly conceived and constructed by Charles Chilton, Joan Littlewood, Gerry Raffles and the members of the cast, although, as Kenneth Tynan discerned, the final version 'was essentially a one-woman show. The big, purposeful heart that beat throughout the evening belonged only to Joan. You felt that her actors had a common attitude toward something larger than acting, a shared vision that extended to life in general.'[9] From the established Workshop routine of research and improvisation issued an innovative documentary of the First World War in which the story was propelled by the songs of the period and sketches modelled on variety and seaside entertainments. It was Littlewood's inspired idea to present the war as a show-within-a-show by means of an Edwardian Pierrot troupe called The Merry Roosters, who performed 'the ever-popular War Game', complete with 'songs ... , a few battles and some jokes.' The other masterstroke was the use of a Brechtian device, a moving electronic newspanel which ran across the top of the proscenium arch and flashed messages such as 'OCT 12 ... PASSCHENDALE ... BRITISH LOSS 13,000 MEN IN 3 HOURS ... GAIN 100 YARDS.' The result of this imaginative staging was the continual juxtaposition of the end-of-the-pier gaiety and patriotic romanticism of the songs with the grim statistics of the carnage on the Western Front.

The West End production, with a cast that included Victor Spinetti, Brian Murphy and Avis Bunnage, ended its run in June 1964. A Broadway transfer was planned for October. In the interim an English and European tour was to be organised with an all-new cast of Pierrots, for which Nigel, urged on by his agent Barry Krost, warily agreed to try out. An audition was arranged for mid-morning at the Theatre Royal. Overcome with nerves at the prospect of having to improvise before the formidable Littlewood, and feeling acutely self-conscious, he first visited the nearby pub right on opening time, persuading himself that he could only survive the impending interview if he were drunk. He managed to arrive punctually at the stage door, fortified by six swiftly imbibed bottles of Guinness, and was relieved to learn that Littlewood was currently in America and it was Gerry Raffles and the on-site director Kevin Palmer for whom he would be auditioning. He included in his audition an impersonation of his agent, who was known to Raffles, and, to his delighted surprise, was hired on the spot.

At thirty-five years of age and as a veteran of weekly rep, Nigel was an anomalous example of Workshop's usual recruiting practice. Littlewood believed that established actors relied on their well-honed skills as a safety net, which in turn functioned as a barrier to experiment, risk-taking and the free exchange of ideas between groups of players. In general Workshop novices were young people newly graduated from drama school who had little or no professional experience and were, therefore, likely to be receptive to the training and ensemble methods prescribed at Stratford East. If older and more seasoned actors were to make the transition into Littlewood's dangerous world of improvisation, they had to prove themselves willing and able to retrench their steadily accumulated stock of techniques and thespian tricks and to relearn the rudiments of their craft.

In his initial attitude to the Workshop approach, Nigel demonstrated scant readiness to conform and was loath to jettison whatever in the way of a safety net he had already procured. Having had minimal formal training in his youth, he learned about acting and technique in the grind of weekly rep in Cape Town, Buxton and Northampton, acquiring excellent memory skills and a useful amount of theatrical nous and adaptability. The rigorous schedule of rep, however, and the necessity for actors to keep two and sometimes three plays in their heads at the same time, precluded opportunities for lengthy rehearsals or rehearsals of an experimental nature. Nor, for the most part, did managements and directors, or the standard of plays that were churned out, encourage collaborative invention and input from actors; competency and diligence (encapsulated in the old adage of remembering one's lines and not bumping into the furniture) were what guaranteed tenure within the average repertory company.

The company with whom Nigel had had the longest and most recent association, before joining Theatre Workshop, was the Cockpit Players in

South Africa. Here the calibre of plays in which he performed was exceptionally high and the parts he was offered, as a rule, genuine character roles of substance. Yet this was by no means an ideal preparation for Theatre Workshop. As discussed in the previous chapter, the Cockpit Players provided Hawthorne with vicarious exposure to the type of work, and something of the ethos, of George Devine's English Stage Company based at the Royal Court. For this reason the experience was also a partial introduction to an environment and a set of dramaturgical principles in conflict with those of Theatre Workshop. The English Stage Company and Theatre Workshop were opposite flanks of the same assault on the status quo of British theatre; they had ideals in common, but were geographically and methodologically divided. At one time Littlewood had tried to initiate a healthy 'war of the theatres' between Stratford East and the Royal Court, but she failed to draw any reaction from her less belligerent (or possibly more self-absorbed) rivals in Sloane Square.[10] The English Stage Company was founded specifically as a writers' theatre, whereas Theatre Workshop was a theatre of workers and pragmatists. A suitable analogy can be found in sixteenth-century Italy in the distinction between the scholarly *commedia erudita,* written drama performed to educated audiences, and the popular *commedia dell'arte* which was based on the collaboration and improvisation of a highly trained group of professional players. Littlewood was a discoverer and loyal supporter of individual writers, but she denounced absolutely the notion within theatre of the inviolability of the written word and the restraints upon actors that this imposed. She also dismissed the arbitrary differentiation between playwrights as creators and actors as interpreters; Theatre Workshop was a coalescence of equal creative elements.

In an address to the International Drama Conference at the 1963 Edinburgh Festival, Littlewood proclaimed:

> *I say to hell with geniuses in the theatre. Let's have the authors by all means, the Lorcas and the Brendan Behans, but let's get them together with their equals, the actors, with all their wit and stupidity and insight. And this clash, this collaboration, this* anti-collaboration *will create an explosion more important than any bomb.*

The execution of this philosophy made Littlewood a pioneer in Britain of collective creation, a process whereby the ideas of the entire company are considered at every stage of a play's development, including research and writing. Instead of the playwright working on a script in isolation and presenting it to the company as a *fait accompli,* the director and actors collaborate with the playwright from the outset. It was a process that embraced, and indeed necessitated, improvisation. A type of collective creation was practised by the *commedia dell'arte* troupes and by actor-playwrights like Shakespeare and Molière, but as a modern movement it grew out of a reaction, spearheaded by Dada and Surrealism, against the stringency of the set text and in favour of spontaneity in art, and had its formal beginning at New York's Living Theatre, established in 1947. In the mid to late 1960s collective creation became the basis on which much of British alternative theatre was founded,[11] yet Littlewood and Theatre Workshop anticipated this trend by more than two decades. In an *Observer* profile in 1959 Littlewood was quoted as saying, 'I really do believe in the community, I really do believe in the genius in every person: I have lived on this belief.'[12] John Wells remarked that by the time a Workshop production opened, 'everything was illuminated from within by a shared intelligence and insight.'[13]

With a theatre background apparently more conducive to the Royal Court's text-centred ideology, and with limited understanding of improvisation as a legitimate means of examining character and situation, Nigel had formed a preconception, reinforced by hearsay, of the Workshop methodology as anarchic and nihilistic, and therefore inimical to his need for order and some sense of certainty about what was expected of him. Having, over many years, witnessed at first hand his behaviour in rehearsals as an actor and a director, Thelma Holt identified the thing that distinguished Nigel's approach to each undertaking, and influenced his interaction with the other actors in a company, as 'an almost Presbyterian work ethic.' He himself said, 'I've always felt very conscientious and been very responsible in my attitude towards acting. I've never believed that there was much point in being an actor if you didn't take it seriously.' Guided by this attitude from the start of his career, he now feared, on entering the unknown theatrical territory of Stratford East, a chaotic free-for-all style of rehearsal in which actors, goaded by the director, would ride roughshod over the writer's script, using it as a mere springboard for furious ad libbing. The reality of what confronted him, however, was very different. On the first day of rehearsals for *Oh, What a Lovely War!* he quickly discovered that the Workshop style was, as the late Richard Wherrett, Founding Director of the Sydney Theatre Company, splendidly summarised it, 'knockabout, rough, improvisatory yet rigorously disciplined.'[14] Nigel and his fellow Pierrots were carefully drilled in the techniques evolved by Workshop and were expected to adhere to a structured and gruelling programme of study and practical exercises. Before any revision of the text was attempted, extensive background reading of primary and secondary source material on the First World War was required of every actor.

The aggressive nihilists he had anticipated were, in fact, a harmonious and committed body of hard-working and serious-minded individuals.

Yet, while many of Nigel's fears proved groundless, this did not mean that he was immediately reconciled to all of the company's working methods. He still dreaded the moment when he would be called upon to improvise. His only previous experience of improvisation had been under the direction of Arthur Storch during the brief life of *Talking to You*. He had found Storch's use of improvisation, in applying the Method, both comfortable and liberating, but he knew that Joan Littlewood's improvisatory techniques and her interpretation of Stanislavsky diverged significantly from those practised by the American schools, and were certainly not designed to put the actor at ease. In the days before Littlewood reappeared on the scene he became increasingly apprehensive and disconsolate. Not particularly gregarious at the best of times in those days, he now retreated further into himself, sensing Kevin Palmer's disfavour, and watched in silent dismay as his part was gradually pared away to insignificance.

By the time Littlewood returned to oversee the new company's progress, Nigel felt scarcely involved in the show and was, like the camels in Eliot's 'Journey of the Magi', 'galled, sore-footed, refractory.'[15] After a disarming introduction, Littlewood began by asking the actors for an improvisation exercise. A mixture of terror and disdain prompted Nigel to walk out at that point, and there might his association with Workshop have ended, but for some inner demon that, halfway to the tube station, compelled him to retrace his steps, re-enter the auditorium with an imperious flourish, and, ignoring the clever banter around him, hurl himself violently into the task of improvisation, demanding and, without question, getting full attention. That evening he received a phone call from Littlewood, who greatly augmented his role not only by restoring what Palmer had taken away, but also by taking parts from other actors and entrusting them to him. As a consequence, he went from being relegated to the company's periphery to occupying the position of *primus inter pares* and shouldering the lion's share of the show. More importantly, he had finally found a mentor and someone who took a real interest in helping him to realise his potential.

With Littlewood in charge of rehearsals, Nigel began to appreciate that Theatre Workshop was essentially a university founded on audaciously empirical principles. As well as being extremely well-read in theatrical theory and history, Littlewood was very aware of current and emergent movements in the work of theatre companies around the world, particularly on the Continent, and her knowledge was always applied to precise, practical ends. The rehearsals she conducted were, in a sense, tutorials, involving the actors in discussion, analysis and the mechanics of problem-solving. Her actors were encouraged to think intelligently about social and political issues and to consider how theatre in the modern world could address and illuminate those issues. They were to be, in her words, 'scholar clowns' or 'thinking clowns'.

Prefatory to his discussion of Theatre Workshop's production of Behan's *The Hostage* in 1958, Kenneth Tynan stated, 'From a critic's point of view, the history of twentieth-century drama is the history of a collapsing vocabulary.'[16] The hybrid quality of contemporary drama, he argued, confounded traditional generic description and the prolixity of Polonius: 'a modern play can, if it wishes, be tragical-comical-historical-pastoral-farcical-satirical-operatical-musical-music-hall, in any combination or all at the same time.' More than any other twentieth-century British director, Joan Littlewood was responsible for demolishing standard distinctions and merging disparate categories into an exciting and coherent whole. The heterogeneous style of *The Hostage* inspired Tynan to label it 'a *commedia dell'arte* production' and, therefore, 'a perfect embodiment of Miss Littlewood's methods.'[18]

The reason why a Workshop production usually defied straightforward critical classification was that Littlewood's well-established methodology was itself a synthesis of performance cultures, of ideas that were centuries old and others that were cutting-edge, and all of them, to a greater or lesser extent, modified or reinvented. Littlewood insisted that her vision of the theatre was nothing new, but rather the continuation of a long tradition stretching from Chinese theatre and the *commedia dell'arte* to music hall and Charlie Chaplin. She also drew a close comparison between her actors and the nineteenth-century London street performers described in vivid detail by Henry Mayhew in *London Labour and the London Poor* – the Punch and Judy showmen, acrobats, posturers, conjurers, stilt-vaulters, Guy Fawkes, knife-swallowers, Penny-Gaff clowns, Billy Barlows, mummers, hurdy-gurdy players and Jim Crows.[19]

Significantly Tynan listed Littlewood's Theatre Workshop alongside Stanislavsky's Moscow Art Theatre and Brecht's Berliner Ensemble as a prime example of the first of two main types of good repertory theatres, that is, one 'founded by a great director or playwright with a novel and often revolutionary approach to dramatic art. He creates a style for his own special purpose.'[20] Littlewood's approach to acting derived in great measure from Stanislavsky, her stagecraft from the alienation effects (*Verfremdungseffekte*) of Brecht's epic theatre. She thus amalgamated two seemingly irreconcilable methodologies – one aimed at producing the illusion of reality, the other at the destruction of theatrical illusion. Like Stanislavsky, Littlewood recognised the importance of inner realism in a performance and that this could be achieved through improvisation. The use of improvisation in rehearsal helped the actor to assemble a character's background and motivation, which in turn yielded a richer characterisation. Nigel was able to work quite contentedly within a Stanislavskian framework whilst managing to avoid its excesses and the hazards of insularity and self-absorption:

> *Exploration of character is fascinating, of course it is. It's wonderful to find out every aspect, every breath. But then, it's quite good to throw all that aside, and start working with your fellow actors, and evolve something. That can be a million times more exciting than anything else.*[21]

This was Stanislavsky as revised by Littlewood and integrated into the system of ensemble playing.

Littlewood's revision of Stanislavsky also incorporated theories opposed to naturalism in the theatre. As well as Brechtian alienation effects, these included the controversial theory of bio-mechanics developed by the avant-garde Russian director Vsevolod Emilievich Meyerhold. Bio-mechanics, which owed its origins in part to the stylised techniques of *commedia dell'arte* and *kabuki,* and even to Pavlov's theory of conditioning, involved subjugating the actor's mind and body to the will of the director, and stripping away all inessentials of production and stage design. In *Oh, What a Lovely War!* the use of slide projection, songs, costumes, placards and minimalist props and sets attested to the influence of Brecht. Part of the purpose of these distancing techniques was to provoke from the audience a critical response to what was happening on stage. Eyre and Wright contend that, in her training and deployment of actors as agents of alienation, Littlewood took this idea further than Brecht himself had:

> *She believed in the 'chemistry in the actual event', which included encouraging the audience to interrupt and the actors to reply – an active form of the kind of alienation that Brecht argued for but never practised.*[22]

As rehearsals for *Oh, What a Lovely War!* continued under Littlewood's supervision, Nigel was able to participate in, and observe closely, various exercises in improvisation and began to realise that, although improvisation was not necessarily the definitive solution to a problem, it could, when allied to research and other training methods, be an extremely useful point of entry into a character or situation, and was intended always to elicit truthfulness and behavioural authenticity from a performance. From his personal experience, John Wells outlined how a typical Workshop improvisation exercise worked:

> *Actors had to abandon the script and find 'parallels'. It seemed like a game. […] The players made it up, made each other laugh, frightened or surprised each other, sometimes themselves. Then they played the original scene, and it was almost always deeper and more secure.*[23]

It was an indelible Workshop conviction that clowning and humorous extemporisation could, in a way similar to Aristophanic comedy, promote serious inquiry and unearth fundamental human truths, and that the application of a broad brush need not obscure the fine detail of dramatic art. For Littlewood improvisation was also about freeing the actor physically, mentally and emotionally, giving him a literal and metaphorical space in which to determine the limits of his imagination. This process of self-discovery was very often punishing, nerve-rending and confidence-sapping, as the actor had to submerge totally his inhibitions and his instincts for caution and restraint, and to exploit his most deep-seated fears; this was the high diving board of which Nigel spoke in later years.

During these early weeks at Stratford East, Nigel's approach to improvisation was one of slow and grudging accommodation, as he was forced to concede its value. This was the first phase of his metamorphosis into a faithful disciple of Littlewood's and an exponent of improvisation without equal. Before too long, as his partner Trevor Bentham explained, Nigel made improvisation, and the freedom it afforded him, a crucial part of who and what he was as an actor:

> *She [Littlewood] changed his life. There's no question at all about that. Up until that time he had really been centred in repertory theatres, learning the part, learning the lines, knowing what he had to do, and he was used to running on very set rails. I think for the first time somebody came along, saw something in him that nobody else had seen, and picked him up, shook him out, and changed him totally for life. From that moment on nobody could improvise quite like Nigel; Nigel was one of the great movers and shakers on stage. He hated things being set in concrete, he hated things being stable, and that was entirely her doing.*[24]

Working with Littlewood he learnt that being in the same play night after night did not entail repeating the same performance. He came to abhor the idea that any aspect of his performance should be immutable. As Sheridan Morley noted:

You never quite know with Nigel what you've got till he does it, and he's always in that sense a wonderful actor to watch because he's unexpected, he comes at you from odd parts of the stage or the screen. [...] He is genuinely surprising.

In Nigel's view a lengthy stage run, such as he enjoyed with *Shadowlands* and *The Madness of George III,* was a journey towards truth rather than technical perfection. Jonathan Lynn, co-author of *Yes, Minister,* observed:

His acting is very fresh, it's never exactly the same. If you see him in a long run there's something different every night. He won't fix it. I worked with another great actor called Leonard Rossiter and Leonard was a machine. Once Leonard had discovered where the laugh was or how to play a moment, it never changed. Nigel's the opposite: as soon as Nigel has worked out how to do it one way perfectly, he then starts thinking about what other ways he can do it. That way, I think, he can keep it fresh over a long period of time. One of the problems in acting is, once you set something, you can start imitating yourself and so it loses its freshness and then it loses its truth. Nigel's very aware of this so he never does something this way because this is the way he did it yesterday. He just goes with the truth of the moment and how he feels about it at the moment that he plays the line.

This awareness was formulated in the ensemble spirit of Theatre Workshop. No actor, who is part of a company, can operate in a vacuum and this was especially true for Littlewood's actors who were the factory-floor workers under a radical theatrical communism. Interdependence was vital: nightly improvisation and alterations to an individual performance succeeded or failed according to the adaptability of other cast members in their timing and responses. Outside Theatre Workshop Nigel's eagerness to keep a performance fresh and not to confine experiment merely to rehearsals sometimes disconcerted and exasperated those of his fellow actors who preferred to live less dangerously on stage and who struggled to meet the demands his versatility made upon them continually to rethink their own performances. The changes Nigel would make to his performance each night were not necessarily major or drastic; according to Lynn they could be 'very subtle, just not exactly the same. It makes the other actors have to react freshly too because they see a slightly different look in his eye or whatever.'

In 1997 Nigel told Carole Zucker:

To go down the same journey, night after night, for a year or eighteen months, I find increasingly difficult to do. It's such an unnatural way of behaving, to go in every night, and to say exactly the same words, maybe in slightly different order, or with different emotions attached to them. And, also, the people you work with, must necessarily, because they're different from you, work in different ways. Sooner or later, you're going to come into conflict with somebody who works in a different way from you, and what you're doing is upsetting them.

I'm not really that technically adept, you know. I just go for it, and I know exactly what I'm going for. I have a very good instinct, and I'm very lucky about that. It sometimes lets me down, like everybody's does. But generally speaking, I know what's right, and I have a certain amount of taste: 'No, that feels wrong, I don't think I'll do that,' and then I'll start to change things. In the course of a play I'll totally change my performance, every night, totally. Moves, everything, which always angers a number of my colleagues. I had a terrible row with this English actress. She said 'I think you change things just for the sake of changing them,' and I said 'Yes, of course I do.' She said the art of acting is to be able to come into the theatre very night and give exactly the same performance that you gave the previous night, and I said 'I don't agree with that, it's boring. Surely the important thing is to keep it fresh, I would have thought'. Once you've left the rehearsal, it's out of the director's hands, it's in your hands as a group, to maintain the thrill, the danger, the spontaneity of it. You make it a happening every night. [25]

This insight into his general attitude to the craft of stage acting reveals how thoroughly Nigel had assimilated the lessons Littlewood taught him and which, according to the American-born director Charles Marowitz, set Theatre Workshop actors apart from their peers. Writing at the end of 1965, Marowitz maintained that the unique training Workshop players received gave them the means to create for themselves and their audiences a revivifying and almost primal experience of theatre:

Joan Littlewood [...] is the only Continental producer in England. By which I mean, the only one who consistently used – and to an extent still uses – an acting-company as a creative tool. With both the Royal Shakespeare and the National Theatre, one never feels the same sense of company identity. One talks of 'a Littlewood actor' as a very special sort of creature; Royal Shakespeare and National Theatre actors are largely interchangeable. (And this is curious as officially, Littlewood's company no longer exists. What does exist is about 35 actors with unshakable loyalty prepared to follow Joan wherever she cares to pitch her tent.)

> *What confers the somewhat dubious distinction of being 'a Littlewood actor' is an appetite for hazard, the improvisation and experiment, for risk-taking which can so easily be construed as idiocy; qualities which most West End actors both lack and abhor. Like Planchon, like the early Vilar, like the Becks of the Living Theatre, Littlewood operates a benevolent monarchy – or rather matriarchy. Despite rigid supervision from above, there is a group product, collectively arrived at, and not the execution of a premeditated plan. When these concert-parties work (and they don't always), the theatre, returning to some pre-Hellenic root, once more becomes fun-and-games which, broadly speaking, is what every play should be no matter how serious its intent.[26]*

The English tour of *Oh, What a Lovely War!* began in Golders Green on 31 August 1964 and continued throughout the autumn and winter with engagements in the south as far as Brighton and up into the Midlands as far as Nottingham. This was immediately followed by a European tour encompassing Antwerp, Brussels, Rotterdam, Zurich and West Germany. Throughout Germany the show made a powerful impact:

> *The basis of the evening remains kitsch worn smooth with use, weak operetta sweetness, crammed second-rate night-club entertainment for provincials. Here families can make merry. This is the stuff of British sea resorts, at least of Osborne's* Entertainer *and comparable entertainment – in this country too we certainly have shows like this that are familiar to us all. Admittedly, in our country, all of this has become less set in traditional forms: here we content ourselves with St Pauli, Blauer Bock and traditional jigs: and unfortunately nothing of it seems to be very suitable to use as polish for our art, in the way the English do it here in their 'Pierrot Show' within their entertainment tradition.*
>
> *Puns and cheap jokes and a mask of schmaltz, clown costumes and girls' legs, a show parade performed with routine swing, and sentimentality sold with tired charm – this is the basis of the most wicked and serious satire conceivable on stage. Merriness as the fruit of bitterness and happy leg-swinging – just to kick us in the stomach. [...]*
>
> *The world of the operetta, the music halls, is turned upside down and placed at the service of amusing insights that come in a flash: kitsch is wedded to bloody madness, the clown jokes are mixed in with the unfeeling roar of machine guns and the ridiculous planning games of the superior officers, and the ring-a-ring o' roses of the decorated armed soldiers is juxtaposed with the brutalities of the front. [...]* Commedia dell'arte *serves*

here not to scale down the subject matter in question, nor to render it harmless; rather, classification as a discovered game pattern strengthens it here. [...]

Incidentally, Kalus Budzinski, taking up motifs from Littlewood, has written a German version of Lovely War: *his libretto is called* Hurra, wir sterben [Hurray, we are dying]. *It directs its attacks more clearly at its own, the German side, it uses couplet text and melodies from the pre-war and war years, extracts from German armed forces' reports and flag-waving patriotic literature and – typically – a potpourri from Karl Kraus. We wait in eager anticipation to find out which German director will take up the subject and create a comparison with Joan Littlewood. It is certain that the success of the guest tour will provide encouragement in this regard.*[27]

The extraordinary critical reception and capacity houses enjoyed by Theatre Workshop in West Germany inspired Littlewood to take the production in late 1965 to East Germany. This second tour, launched four years after the construction of the Berlin Wall and at the height of Cold War tensions, encompassed Leipzig, Dresden, KarlMarxstadt and an extended booking in East Berlin. The show also transferred to West Berlin, making Theatre Workshop the first British company to perform on consecutive nights in the Russian and American sectors of Berlin. The fact that audiences in the Eastern sector had been the first to see *Oh, What a Lovely War!* was noted with suspicion and resentment by the West Berlin press. As far as Nigel was concerned the bleak and dimly lit urban landscape of East Berlin held far more fascination than its colourful and decadent Western neighbour. He and a number of others in the company billeted themselves at an Eastern sector hotel and, having been issued with special visas, passed each evening through Checkpoint Charlie on Friedrichstrasse. While in East Berlin Theatre Workshop was treated to a production of Brecht's *Koriolan* (an adaptation of Shakespeare's *Coriolanus*) and dined as guests of the Berliner Ensemble where the actor Wolf Kaiser made a speech in which he deferred to Workshop's supremacy. A decade later Joan Littlewood became one of the very few English personalities to be included in Meyer's Lexikon, the new East German encyclopaedia.

In between the two European tours of *Oh, What a Lovely War!* Nigel had made a brief return to the Connaught Theatre in Worthing, taking part in two productions – Sheridan's *The Rivals* and an English version of Jean-Louis Roncoroni's *Summer's Ending* – before reuniting with his South African friends Leon Gluckman and Joyce Grant for a West End revue on race relations called *Nymphs and Satires*. The latter opened at the Apollo Theatre on Shaftesbury Avenue on 25 May 1965 and was directed and co-written by Gluckman as a sequel to his first highly successful London revue *Wait a Minim*. The show featured an international and multi-racial cast and relied heavily on the artifice of mixing up or interchanging black and white stereotypes and testing the reaction of the two groups to the same situation. Nigel appeared in several sketches including the solo, 'Zebra Crossing', presented as a parliamentary address on zebra pigmentation as the next stage in human evolution, and was at his best as an Afrikaans sergeant teaching a group of schoolgirls to shoot pistols. Unfortunately, for all the good intentions and proven talent of those involved, in attempting to carve a provocative morality tale on racial tolerance from what was essentially fluid but standardised West End entertainment, *Nymphs and Satires* failed dismally. Joyce Grant remembers the production as 'a total disaster' and that, despite Gluckman's liberalism, 'it was somehow totally misconceived; the material was not up to it.' The critic for *The Times* attributed the show's inefficacy to its oversimplified design and the sheltered idealism of its expatriate creators:

> *Where* Wait a Minim *seemed to have sprung from its South African background, the new show seems to have been composed at a safe distance from the scene. Its picturesque work, songs and figures in gaudy blankets facing a setting sun are directed at the tourist; and devices such as framing the show between an opening chorus of race hatred and a closing chorus of racial harmony are directed at the armchair liberal.*[28]

After the adventure of touring *Oh, What a Lovely War!* across Cold War Germany and being fêted by the famous Berliner Ensemble, Nigel resumed his more prosaic pre-Workshop stage work, beginning with a Sunday-night performance at Hampstead Theatre Club of David Wilson's uninspired social parable *Are You Normal Mr Norman?* Six months later, at a considerable loose end, he revisited his old stamping ground, the Royal Theatre in Northampton, where he appeared with the Repertory Players in six productions directed by Willard Stoker, for a weekly salary of twenty-five pounds. Among the leading roles he performed were Charles Condomine in Noël Coward's *Blithe Spirit,* Arthur Winslow in Rattigan's *The Winslow Boy,* a part he memorably repeated on film for David Mamet thirty-three years later, and Edward Kimberley in Pauline Macauley's *The Creeper.* The following spring he returned to London and added to his depressing list of West End failures by playing the Angry Neighbour of Jean Kent and Terence Alexander in Ray Cooney's production of Duncan Greenwood and Robert King's *In At the Death* at the Phoenix Theatre, which the critic for *The Times* damned as a 'hopelessly outdated, wordy and cliché-ridden comedy-thriller. [...] Landed with some of the most deadeningly tedious lines imaginable, the cast can do little except go down fighting.'[29]

Without question the only significant and stimulating plays in which Nigel was involved in the mid-sixties were those produced by Joan Littlewood. He was invited back into the company in 1967 to undertake various supporting roles in a musical biography of Marie Lloyd written by Daniel Farson and Harry Moore from their book *Thanks for Nothing,* with original music composed by Norman Kay. *The Marie Lloyd Story,* which was only the sixth Workshop production mounted in four years, opened at Stratford East on 25 November and starred Avis Bunnage as the idol of the British music halls who won enormous popularity with her risqué presentation of numbers like 'A Little of What You Fancy Does You Good', and whose private life was marred by domestic violence and by scandals on both sides of the Atlantic. The show focused on the turbulent decline of the middle-aged artist. Act One concluded with Marie playing to a packed house at the Pavilion, 'by Command of the British Public', on the same evening in July 1912 that the first Royal Command Variety Performance, from which she had been excluded, was staged at the Palace. Act Two opened with her detention on New York's Ellis Island on a charge of moral turpitude and closed with her fatal collapse in the wings of the Edmonton Empire after singing 'I'm one of the Ruins that Cromwell knocked abaht a bit.'

The show's opening, originally scheduled for Wednesday 22 November, had to be postponed until Saturday after Avis Bunnage was struck on the head by a heavy piece of wood when the stage cloth fell during the penultimate rehearsal of her death scene. A fortnight earlier a looming lawsuit had made an indefinite postponement seem likely. Marie Aylin, the daughter of Marie Lloyd and Percy Courtenay, threatened to seek an injunction in the High Court to stop the show, claiming that she had already signed an agreement with Binkie Beaumont for a musical based on her mother's life. Fortunately, as Gerry Raffles told the *Daily Telegraph* on 6 November, 'Our solicitors advised us that our version does not infringe copyright,' and the show went ahead legally and unimpeded.

On 22 September the *Times* 'Diary' announced the emergence of another potential rival to the show, a musical on Marie Lloyd by Ned Sherrin and Caryl Brahms which was due to open in the West End early the following year. Sherrin claimed that the two productions 'will be so different there will not be any comparison between them.'[30] As it turned out, his show, *Sing a Rude Song,* was not presented until February 1970.[31] Intriguingly, it starred the Theatre Workshop darling Barbara Windsor, Denis Quilley, and Bee Gee Maurice Gibb, and included additional material by Alan Bennett.

As the subject of a stage musical, the earthy Marie Lloyd, with a heart as big as Waterloo Station,[32] was more obviously within Littlewood's domain than either Beaumont's or that of the Sherrin-Brahms partnership. One of Lloyd's most ardent devotees, T. S. Eliot, who saw in her 'the expressive figure of the lower classes', wrote:

> *Whereas other comedians amuse their audiences as much and sometimes more than Marie Lloyd, no other comedian succeeded so well in giving expression to the life of that audience, in raising it to a kind of art. It was, I think, this capacity for expressing the soul of the people that made Marie Lloyd unique and that made her audiences, even when they joined in the chorus, not so much hilarious as happy. [...] The working man who went to the music-hall and saw Marie Lloyd and joined in the chorus was himself performing part of the act; he was engaged in that collaboration of the audience with the artist which is necessary in all art and most obviously in dramatic art.*[33]

It was this singular type of theatrical experience, which was consonant with the style and objectives of Theatre Workshop, that fascinated Joan Littlewood.

In spite of Littlewood's indisputable credentials as a student and masterly documenter of music hall entertainment, *The Marie Lloyd Story* did not amount to the roaring success that all its ingredients presaged. Far more attention was paid to recreating atmosphere than to dramatic structure, to refining the details rather than the whole. Philip Hope-Wallace reasoned:

> *The result is perhaps bound to be sketchy, since Miss Littlewood arranges to tell the story in a series of back-stage vignettes, in a style which is that of a music hall sketch. No doubt, the laconic and rather unfocussed style of playing these real life episodes was deliberately planned to set off the brassy on-stage acts which are bounced straight over to the audience with gusto. But one feels that more might have been extracted from the history of this incautious star and her loves.*[34]

J. C. Trewin's was perhaps the most astute assessment of the 'capriciously chaotic' production's virtues and shortcomings:

> *I suppose we can say that Joan Littlewood's production has something of the restlessness of Marie herself; and that such a figure as this is served better by hit-or-miss impression than by the solemnities of a full-scale musical. Even so, the piece does want more shape, more rigorous selection. [...]*

With all its imperfections on its head, the piece does linger. It was strange to come up that murky street from the station, and to move into a lost world. The world is much too easy to sentimentalize; but, on the whole, this is not a Littlewood fault.[35]

Among the several roles Nigel played was that of Sir Oswald Stoll, a loyal friend of Marie Lloyd's, although he never invited her to appear at the Coliseum during his management of it. His portrayal of Stoll drew an incensed reaction from Felix Barker who reviled it as one of a number of 'gross caricatures': As Sir Oswald Stoll's biographer I can only let out a howl of outrage at the way he is presented.'[36] The majority of critics, however, were full of praise for Nigel's excellent supporting contributions and versatility. Alan Brien was particularly admiring of Workshop's latest acquisition: 'The company is strengthened by two newcomers: Nigel Hawthorne who slips in and out of half-a-dozen disguises with the slippery ingenuity of a young Guinness, and Valerie Walsh […].'[37] Irving Wardle reported: 'The company's extensive doubling is of no help to the plot-line but in the course of changing their hats Griffith Davies, Gaye Brown and Nigel Hawthorne flood the house with warmth.'[38]

A proposed West End transfer for *The Marie Lloyd Story* did not eventuate and the show ended its run on 23 December 1967. Meanwhile, *Mrs Wilson's Diary,* 'an affectionate lampoon' interspersed with songs, had opened on 21 September, breaking all box-office records at the Theatre Royal, Stratford East. A month later it transferred to London's Criterion where it ran for 255 performances. Based on a current *Private Eye* serial of the same title, the show was the successful result of an improbable alliance between Theatre Workshop and the public school and Oxbridge alumni who were leading the satire boom of the Swinging Sixties. For Nigel, who joined the cast in January, it was the first time he acted in a West End hit.

As a fortnightly column, the Diary was the whimsical invention of Peter Cook and co-author Richard Ingrams. It first appeared in the *Eye* on 30 October 1964, the issue immediately following the British General Election on 15 October, which saw Labour narrowly returned to power under the premiership of Harold Wilson, after thirteen years in opposition. This initial entry recorded the move to Number 10 Downing Street of the new Prime Minister and his wife Mary (whom the writers impishly renamed Gladys), a Pooterish, Ovaltine-drinking couple of lower-middle-class sensibilities. The political manoeuvring as well as the various domestic and international crises that followed Wilson's election were fashioned into the stuff of suburban soap opera, the homespun narrative of an ordinary housewife. John Wells eventually replaced Cook as Ingrams's collaborator, while Willie Rushton (whose caricatures were reproduced in the programme for the stage version) illustrated the spurious diary entries.

Early in 1967 Joan Littlewood discussed with Ingrams and Wells the feasibility of translating the Diary to the stage. A working script was prepared along with short but spirited musical numbers created by Wells and Jeremy Taylor including 'Who are the Bastards Now?', The Terrible Mr Brown' and 'Harold's Last Waltz'. The basic plot revolved around the farcical machinations of Wilson and his public relations guru Gerald 'Hoffman' (a thinly disguised Gerald Kaufman) in their obsessive endeavour to improve Wilson's rating in the opinion polls. In the course of one hectic day of fawning to the press, securing a guest spot on the *David Frost Programme* and hatching a scheme to parachute the Foreign Secretary, George Brown, into North Vietnam, Wilson and his advisers manage to overlook the threat of an American nuclear attack on London until it is too late. Theatre Workshop was compelled to submit to three months' consultation over the finished script with the Lord Chamberlain who, despite the fact that his days as the arbiter of theatrical good taste were numbered, insisted upon savage cuts. The end product was an exuberant but satirically rather tame offering with only occasional infusions of scurrility such as the depiction of George Brown, for whom *Private Eye* coined the euphemism 'tired and emotional', as 'a puffed-up old soak'.[39]

The cast of *Mrs Wilson's Diary* featured Myvanwy Jenn in the title role and the jowly, heavy-lidded Bill Wallis as Harold Wilson. Critical reaction to the production was predominantly very positive, although there was little consensus about the level and impact of its putative satirical content. Harold Hobson, writing in the *Sunday Times,* gave the show a rave review:

> Mrs Wilson's Diary *[…] is immensely enjoyable, keenly satirical both of personal mannerisms and political policy, acted with joyous finesse, extremely funny, and it makes one happy to be alive. […]*
>
> *The play has been made by people who are in love with living, and this joy is infectious. Miss Littlewood has never directed better entertainment.*[40]

In *The Times* Irving Wardle declared:

> *It is not a major Littlewood production, but it is a very lively show and it establishes an important precedent in British censorship which has at last allowed the stage to handle our politicians with the same freedom that television and newspapers take for granted.*

> *The style is that of undergraduate revue, and it marries quite well with Miss Littlewood's music hall low comedy. The effect is not one of political satire but of a good-natured party.*[41]

Not everyone was seduced by this species of benign satire. The critic for the monthly magazine *The Queen* felt Theatre Workshop had sold out to the unchallenging and self-satisfied humour characteristic of old-fashioned West End revue:

> *It is a gentle, mildly funny, fairly snobbish evening with the bite of a soft-centred chocolate. I think there's a place for this kind of theatre, usually written by Hugh and Margaret Williams, usually at a theatre convenient for the Savoy Grill. But that Joan Littlewood has moved into this market seems a sad, bad thing.*[42]

Benedict Nightingale viewed the lack of edge and pungency in *Mrs Wilson's Diary*, the leniency of its gibes, as symptomatic of an ingrained national apathy:

> *The mockery never goes very far beyond what a moderately permissive headmaster would accept from the Founder's Day revue. […] It is extraordinary that British satire is content to remain as good-tempered as it invariably is. Is no-one politically angry? It seems not: we go on happily snorting, nudging each other in the ribs and generally indulging our national vanity (so vastly over-rated abroad) of 'laughing at ourselves.'*[43]

One notable personage who was dismissive of the show's humour was Mrs Wilson herself. In March 1975, a year after her husband's return to Number 10, Mary Wilson recalled, 'I didn't go to see the play, but I read the script. I didn't care for that very much; because […] it was too much of the banana skin technique, and I don't like putting banana skins under people.'[44] The following year she confessed to *Woman's Own* that should she ever meet John Wells she would like to bite him.

Throughout its long run *Mrs Wilson's Diary* kept pace with the changing political scene. The actors were expected to know on a daily basis what their real-life counterparts in Westminster were up to. Cabinet reshuffles were replayed, and occasionally anticipated, on stage, entailing regular cast changes. On 29 November 1967, the day following the premiere of *The Marie Lloyd Story,* James Callaghan became Home Secretary and Roy Jenkins Chancellor of the Exchequer in a direct exchange of senior ministerial posts. Callaghan had resigned as Chancellor after the Cabinet accepted his recommendation to devalue the pound, cancelling the pledges he had given to a number of overseas countries about the value of their sterling holdings. His successor Jenkins was the son of a Welsh miners' MP, liberal, passionately pro-European, a mix of Anglo-Saxon sang-froid and Celtic flair, and widely regarded as an able economist as well as a civilised and imaginative social reformer.[45] As Home Secretary he had championed radical legislation on divorce, abortion and homosexuality, earning himself the title 'the architect of the permissive society'. One of his last actions in this capacity had been to countenance the decision of George Strauss, the Labour MP for Vauxhall, to introduce a Private Members' Bill to abolish the Lord Chamberlain's power to censor plays, an issue in which Nigel was shortly to become directly and dramatically involved.

In the new year Ingrams and Wells added the character of Roy Jenkins to the *dramatis personae* of *Mrs Wilson's Diary* and as soon as the part had been typed Littlewood offered it to Nigel. After a costume fitting and a quick read-through of his scenes, he was informed that he would be going on stage that night and given barely an hour to learn his lines. It was the most intimidating challenge he had yet faced in the theatre. He had no opportunity to familiarise himself with the rest of the script, to mug up on current political events and parliamentary concerns, or to study Jenkins's mannerisms. What he did have, however, was the unique benefit of his experience as a satirical performer in *Beyond the Fringe* and two years' instruction under Littlewood in how to take danger and the unexpected in his stride.

Although Nigel was slimmer and nine years younger than the owl-like Chancellor, Littlewood and the writers saw a resemblance between the two, which Nigel enlarged upon by flattening his hair with pomade, wearing thick spectacles and lisping his 'R's. He made his character instantly recognisable and was cheered by the audience on his entrance. The real Roy Jenkins, who was later made Lord Jenkins of Hillhead and Chancellor of Oxford University, saw *Mrs Wilson's Diary* earlier in its run, but neither he nor his wife[46] were curious enough to make a second visit to watch their namesakes performing at the Criterion.

Having survived this baptism of fire, and enjoying the unaccustomed security and prestige of an extended West End run, Nigel slipped more and more comfortably into his role and the show, too comfortably for Littlewood's liking. It was at this point that Littlewood began a ruthless war of attrition with Nigel, ignoring him in the weekly rehearsals and only communicating with him through her disparaging and publicly displayed director's notes. Nigel's fall from favour occurred rapidly and without warning. In Littlewood's opinion he had allowed his performance to become flat and predictable and her curious form of reproval was justified; he needed jolting out of his comfort and complacency. Ignorant of what offence he had given, Nigel endured Littlewood's draconian treatment for six weeks before finally exploding in anger in the middle of a rehearsal. Possibly this was the reaction Littlewood was hoping to provoke. In any case she ended her silence, explained to him over dinner the cause of her displeasure and a fragile accord ensued.

One member of Theatre Workshop, Julia Jones, claimed, 'Two years was about the longest anyone with real acting talent could stay with Joan and not be destroyed. She had a very destructive element – she had to break people down and destroy their confidence.'[47] Nigel had become keenly aware of this destructive element and suspected that underlying Littlewood's extreme behaviour towards him during *Mrs Wilson's Diary* was a resentment of his burgeoning independence. He never recovered his position as Littlewood's blue-eyed boy and never worked with her again. In later years, whenever he spoke about his mentor, he revealed an intense ambivalence. In two separate radio interviews in the late 1980s he expressed his respect and affection for her, but said that she could be a monster, a remark Littlewood refused to look at in context or to forgive. His repeated efforts to explain and to repair the breach between them only fuelled her hostility at what she chose to paint as his ingratitude and betrayal. Peace came at the eleventh hour when Nigel's illness forced her to relent. Littlewood died nine months after Nigel on 20 September 2002.

If one were seeking a succinct description of Nigel as an actor, Joan Littlewood's phrase 'scholar clown' would serve particularly well. Of Nigel's millennial interpretation of King Lear, John Stokes wrote in the *Times Literary Supplement*:

Hawthorne gives his movements the precision, the allusive subtlety, that is paradoxically available only to actors steeped in comic technique. When he essays a dance, he shows us not so much the thing itself as the thought of it – a juddering of the ankle.[48]

It was this ability to combine intellect with physicality, literally to make the word flesh, to embody an idea, either tragic or comic, in all its subtlety and complexity (an ability which likened him to, and in which he surpassed, his great hero Alastair Sim) that made Nigel the consummate scholar clown.

Notes to Chapter 3

1 Interview with Luaine Lee for *Scripps Howard News Service,* 'Nigel Hawthorne is More Than He Seems', 5 May 1999.
2 Eyre & Wright (2000) 259.
3 *The Independent Magazine,* 29 February 1992.
4 On Theatre Workshop's discovery and application of Appia's theories and his belief in 'a synthesis of all the arts', see Goorney (1981) 5.
5 Goorney (1981) 165.
6 On the history of the relationship between Theatre Workshop and the Arts Council, see Holdsworth (1999) 3-16.
7 *Daily Mail,* 11 July 1961.
8 *Times,* 5 November 1963, 14.
9 Tynan (1989) 184.
10 See Littlewood (1994) 538.
11 Companies based on collective creation included the People Show (founded 1966), Pip Simmons Theatre Group (1968) and Welfare State International (1968).
12 *Observer,* 15 March 1959.
13 *The Independent Magazine,* 29 February 1992.
14 Wherrett (2000) 36.
15 T. S. Eliot, 'Journey of the Magi', line 6.
16 Tynan (1975) 226.
17 Ibid 227.
18 Ibid 257.
19 See Mayhew (1861) Vol.3.
20 Tynan (1975) 362.
21 Recorded in Zucker (1999) 75.
22 Eyre & Wright (2000) 264.
23 *The Independent Magazine,* 29 February 1992.
24 In conversation with Sheridan Morley on *The Arts Programme,* BBC Radio 2, 21 June 2002.
25 Recorded in Zucker (1999) 73.
26 *Plays and Players,* December 1965, 7.
27 Ernst Wendt, *Theater heute,* March 1965, 29-31.
28 *Times,* 26 May 1965, 16.
29 *Times,* 22 April 1967, 7.
30 *Times,* 22 September 1967, 8.
31 The show opened at the Greenwich Theatre on 18 February 1970 and transferred to the Garrick Theatre on 26 May of the same year.
32 This description was reported by the *Sunday Times* critic James Agate (1945) 210: 'Returning from Kempton a party of bookmakers fell to speaking of the dead artist. One said with tears in his eyes, "She had a heart, had Marie!" "The size of Waterloo Station," another rejoined.'
33 Eliot (1951) 457-58.
34 *Guardian,* 27 November 1967.
35 *Illustrated London News,* 9 December 1967.
36 *Evening News,* 27 November 1967. Barker was the author of *The House that Stoll Built: The Story of the Coliseum Theatre,* published in 1957.

37 *Daily Telegraph,* 3 December 1967.
38 *Times,* 27 November 1967.
39 Benedict Nightingale, *Plays and Players,* November 1967, 15.
40 *Sunday Times,* 24 September 1967.
41 *Times,* 22 September 1967.
42 *The Queen,* 11 October 1967.
43 *Plays and Players,* November 1967, 14-15.
44 *Sunday Times,* 30 March 1975.
45 See Ian Trethowan's profile of Roy Jenkins in *The Times,* 30 November 1967, 11.
46 The character of Mrs Jenkins was introduced to the show in May 1968.
47 In Goorney (1981) 176.
48 *Times Literary Supplement,* 5 November 1999.

Chapter 4

In Anger's Wake

THE ENGLISH STAGE COMPANY AT THE ROYAL COURT

If you've no world of your own, it's rather pleasant
to regret the passing of someone else's.

(John Osborne, *West of Suez*)

'There aren't any good brave causes left,' declaimed Osborne's anti-hero Jimmy Porter in 1956. 'If the big bang does come and we all get killed off, it won't be in aid of the old-fashioned, grand design. It'll just be for the Brave New nothing-very-much-thank-you.' Articulated in this famous outburst is the British post-war equivalent of what in *fin-de-siècle* Vienna the playwright Hugo von Hofmannsthal diagnosed as a pervasive sense of 'das Gleitende'[1] (sliding or slipping away), the belief of the young that the institutions taken for granted by previous generations, and all the old convictions, had for them neither substance nor permanence. For the individual, denied purpose and made incapable of faith, this meant a loss of identity and self-worth.

When Nigel was invited into the English Stage Company, twelve years after Kenneth Haigh, in the character of Jimmy Porter, first made his despairing plea for 'a little ordinary human enthusiasm', the Royal Court Theatre was continuing to produce plays that examined humanity's moral inertia or disenfranchisement, while, at the same time, it had adopted its own good brave cause in its urgent and ultimately successful crusade against the pre-censorship of theatre. Nigel arrived at the Court three years into the second definable phase of the English Stage Company's history – post-Devine, post-*Anger*.

In September 1965 William Gaskill replaced George Devine as the Company's Artistic Director. Devine had retired owing to ill health and died prematurely the following year, canonised a secular saint by his theatrical votaries. In his judgement of the succeeding regime, the *Times* critic Irving Wardle unjustly pronounced that the Court had outlived its heroic phase. On Devine's retirement, Eric Shorter extolled the Court's admirably old-fashioned bohemianism and socialism – 'corduroyed radicalism, bearded irreverence, artiness but above all youth' – but expressed concern that its pioneering fervour was fading: 'Much of that early creative, leftish gusto has disappeared in recent years; the old salt has lost its savour.'[2] The English Stage Company's initial decade and its dominant figures – Devine, Tony Richardson, Osborne and Arnold Wesker – had unquestionably become the stuff of legend, but, significant though its achievements were, this group represented only the first wave of an ongoing campaign to which the reinforcements, mustered under Gaskill's command, brought their own creativity, commitment and combative energy. Perhaps, by the mid-sixties, the shock of the new, so palpable in 1956, had abated, but the Court's celebrated anger had not. Rather, it had become less rhetorical and more real, and was vented both on stage and in off-stage skirmishes as the Company felt itself increasingly under siege from external forces such as the Lord Chamberlain and the critics, and occasionally, when artistic and administrative interests clashed, on the verge of implosion. At a conference in celebration of the English Stage Company's twenty-fifth anniversary, Gaskill recollected the period of his tenure as one of intensive conflict mitigated by artistic solidarity:

> We were an embattled theatre. And that united us strongly in a way that the theatre had also been united in the past by its group of writers. All my memories of that period are of fights really, fights with the Lord Chamberlain, with the Arts Council, with the British Council, with members of Parliament. It was draining because it was really external, outside the work itself.[3]

The particular challenges confronting the Royal Court at the end of the 1960s required a pragmatic as well as an ideological heroism. Theatre generally was undergoing one of its periodic crises and its practitioners and advocates were being compelled to defend its relevance in a rapidly changing society, and to determine its future direction.

In 1968 the Court's old order had by no means disappeared, nor had the precepts established by Devine been discarded. Gaskill and his associates Lindsay Anderson and Anthony Page had all done apprenticeships under the Devine-Richardson alliance and were resolved to carry on the work commenced during those years. They were now joined by younger directors like Robert Kidd, Jane Howell and Peter Gill. Among the Court writers John Osborne was still a presence and about to embark on an unmellowed middle age, with his 'characteristic rancid eloquence'[4] and gift for elegiac hatred largely undiminished. Yet his anger, described by Richard Eyre and Nicholas Wright as 'an existential force',[5] had acquired an ignoble dimension; his manner of retrospection was sometimes less demonstrative of sincere passion and regret than of choleric prejudice for the past.

As Osborne settled into the role of grand old man of anger, the Royal Court discovered a new and much misunderstood *enfant terrible* in Edward Bond and its first resident dramatist in Christopher Hampton, fresh from his finals at Oxford. The Court playwrights of the late 1960s and 1970s had, as David Hare perceives, a somewhat different agenda from their predecessors:

> *Whatever agony may have marked our private lives, we did not see it as part of our mission to put our souls on stage. The job description was different. Whereas the generation before ours was involved in a passionate defence of the individual, in which self-exposure, self-excoriation and even self-annihilation were regular ingredients, we, in our beginnings, were much more concerned to tell stories which might offer some equally passionate defence of the collective.*[6]

A further generational distinction was that Hare and his contemporaries, who included Howard Brenton, Howard Barker, Caryl Churchill and Trevor Griffiths, had the benefit of alternative platforms for their writing. When the English Stage Company was formed in 1956, Sloane Square and Stratford East were really the only major venues for contemporary or experimental plays in Britain, but in the next decade opportunities for writers improved with the creation of the Royal Shakespeare Company in 1962, the foundation of the National Theatre at the Old Vic a year later, and the growth of fringe theatre after the opening of the Traverse Theatre Club in Edinburgh in January 1963.

The English Stage Company of 1968, faced with fresh ordeals and competition, retained fundamentally the same ethos it had espoused twelve years earlier. Like Theatre Workshop, the Company functioned on paradoxes, a peculiar blend of philosophy and circumstance which had distinguished its work since its inception. For Devine and his successors theatre was a serious pursuit and, in a co-ordinated effort to dissociate themselves from the froth and high camp they considered to be the worst excesses of the West End, they evolved a dramaturgical style that was virile, unmannered and of eloquent simplicity. Lindsay Anderson compared the Royal Court aesthetic with the Periclean ideal: 'We pursue beauty without extravagance, knowledge without effeminacy.'[7] In other words, Dan Rebellato infers, 'The theatre was a serious place, not to be compromised by homosexual frippery.'[8] This aversion to 'theatricality' in its most pejorative sense of artificiality and inconsequential campery was never about persecuting homosexuals within the theatre or purging plays of the love that dare not speak its name; it was principally a reaction against the coded, Rattiganesque treatment of 'queerness', which the current generation of writers and directors (hastily and with little clemency) branded emotional dishonesty. Paradoxically, the Court's programmatic heterosexual stance was earnestly taken up by directors who were themselves homosexual, as William Gaskill commented in his memoirs: 'Although George Devine would have been horrified if he'd realized it, most of his directors were homosexual, ranging from closet queen and bisexual to the fairly blatant [John] Dexter and myself.'[9]

Another paradox characteristic of the English Stage Company was the idealisation of the 'redbrick actor' under directors who hailed predominantly from Oxford. With the democratisation of the stage and the relocation of dramatic action from the drawing-room to the kitchen sink and ironing board, a genus of non-heroic actor emerged, equipped with regional accent, whose prototype was Wilfred Rawson, the idol of Albert Finney and Peter O'Toole. The Court's apparent preference for northern, working-class actors drew from disgruntled members of the newly displaced theatre breed, such as Noël Coward,[10] accusations of inverted class snobbery. In truth the Company was not as exclusively proletarian as its kitchen-sink image suggested, and even, from time to time, accommodated the drama's patrician elders, its classical heavyweights Olivier, Gielgud and Richardson. But, if the Royal Court was tolerant of diversity, it demonstrated a lack of imagination in utilising some of the talent at its disposal.

Nigel, who, partly because of his South African background, defied regional classification, was no more a typical Royal Court actor than he had been a typical Theatre Workshop actor. Thanks to Littlewood's gift for nurturing outsiders, Workshop proved in the end an energising and liberating education for him. Littlewood created the conditions necessary to the actor's self-discovery and maturation. Conversely, the Royal Court's priorities lay in creating the conditions necessary to the writer's development; its attitude to actors was always rather a grey area. With one or two notable exceptions, throughout the period in which he worked at the Court Nigel was assigned a series of fairly uninspiring parts, ranging from authoritarian or Blimpish characters to ones that, on the page, simply faded into the background. What he made of these roles is a different matter and, indeed, the consistently good notices he received belied his lack of encouragement and opportunity. Although at the time he could not help feeling cheated of the responsibility his experience and perseverance merited, with hindsight, and a certain generosity of spirit, he could rationalise his non-selection for meatier and more arresting parts as a backhanded compliment to his ability to fashion, sometimes from next to nothing, a three-dimensional and credible character.

At the end of 1967 William Gaskill, trawling for fresh talent, went to see *The Marie Lloyd Story* at Stratford East and offered Nigel the part of Prince Albert in Edward Bond's latest play *Early Morning,* which was originally scheduled for a three-week season in the Court's main bill, opening on 23 January 1968. After the script was refused a licence, Gaskill resolved to stage *Early Morning* as a club performance on two consecutive Sunday nights, as a means of circumventing the Lord Chamberlain's authority. These planned Sunday night productions (the second of which was, at the eleventh hour, aborted and redesignated a 'critics' dress rehearsal') eventually took place on 31 March and 7 April, by which time Nigel was appearing at the Criterion as Roy Jenkins in Theatre Workshop's *Mrs Wilson's Diary.* Gaskill's invitation thus placed him temporarily in the unique position of having a foot in both camps of the theatre revolution.

Nigel's rudimentary introduction to Royal Court work in the Cockpit Players did not reduce the culture shock he suffered on entering the English Stage Company proper. The reason for this was the intervening influence of Joan Littlewood. While she was never the easiest person to work with, Littlewood managed to inspire Nigel as nobody in the theatre had before or since, and his conversion to her methodology and way of thinking, albeit slow, was lasting and complete. She taught him that freedom of imagination, not the inviolability of the text, was the *sine qua non* of powerful theatre, a lesson which, he believed, left him temperamentally unsuited to the Court system. After the regulated anarchy of Theatre Workshop, he found the directorial approach of the Royal Court stiflingly pedagogic and puritan.

The dynamic in the two companies was very different. Workshop had a dominant and charismatic leader in Littlewood, but it was essentially an egalitarian working unit in which actors were co-authors in the development of a new play. Its success depended on its inclusive, outward-looking philosophy. In marked contrast, the Court was tenaciously hierarchical and, sadly, its high principles often translated into exclusivity and insularity. Irving Wardle, whose bias against the post-Devine Royal Court has already been noted, charged Gaskill in 1970 with running 'the place more as a professional studio for a chosen circle of colleagues, pursuing some extremely fruitful lines of development, but at the expense of surrendering the theatre's former openness to the world outside, and its established flair for brilliant ad hoc casting.'[11] At the end of the next decade Benedict Nightingale characterised the Company's aggressive idealism as a two-edged sword: 'its fault was a tendency to become austere, self-righteous and insular, and its virtues were cheek, a crusading spirit, and an eagerness to utter contentiously on matters of moment.'[12] In Nigel's view this '"us" and "them"' trait was nowhere more perceptible than in the tacit segregation of actors from directors and playwrights. As one of Littlewood's scholar clowns, he had been entrusted with an equal share in the creative process. Now he felt that his creativity was being constricted and his commission as an actor was merely to preserve, under the director's stern control, the integrity and primacy of the writers' words. Moreover, the Workshop idea of deriving profound truth from intelligent clowning was admired without being emulated at the Court, where piety and stringency tended to prevail.

One of the most pithy and incisive descriptions of the actor's plight in this artistic hierarchy was Nigel's congratulatory message to the Royal Court on the occasion of the theatre's one-hundredth anniversary in 1988:

> *May one who has been directionally Gaskilled, Paged, Howelled, Dunloped, Hansoned, Andersoned and on more than one occasion Kidded, humbly wish them and all those deemed higher in the pecking order than mere actors, an exceedingly theatrical centenary.*[13]

In this witty and seemingly good-natured jibe at the loftiness of the Court's directors, he has converted their surnames into violent-sounding transitive verbs. These verbs are in the passive voice with Nigel, the humble and mightily abused actor, their hapless subject. His use of the adjective 'theatrical', with its camp associations, cleverly undercuts the cultivated solemnity of the Court. The sentence is a small masterpiece of sly and charming invective.

Nigel had very much an actor's perspective (with its accompanying prejudices and just grievances) of this proudly christened writers' theatre. The term 'writers' theatre', it has latterly been argued, is something of a misnomer, for, in reality, the Royal Court could be unhesitatingly and brutally dismissive of individual writers just as surely as it was loyal and protective towards them. Nigel's centenary message is an indictment of the English Stage Company as primarily the jealously guarded province of schoolmasterly directors but, without doubt, the text, if not always the author, was the focus of the directors' collective attention.

From the start the Company conspicuously centred its mission in the written word, believing like Yeats that 'Words alone are certain good'[14] and thereby declaring its non-allegiance to the cult of personality holding sway over West End theatre, with its Olympian impresarios and ennobled actors: 'Ours is not to be a producer's theatre or an actors' theatre; it is a writer's theatre.'[15] This bold statement of purpose was reiterated and amplified in a pamphlet entitled *Royal Court Theatre Box:* 'The policy of this Company is reminiscent of the Vedrenne-Barker management – to revive the drama by placing emphasis on the play and the writer rather than the actor or the producer, and to relate the stage to contemporary life and problems.' In an interview with *Plays and Players* in March 1969, the twenty-five-year-old Robert Kidd defined this policy as 'a kind of purism. Plays done without distortion of direction, acting or production',[16] a remark endorsed by William Gaskill, who maintained that the Company's real aim was 'to present new writing in a form of staging centred in the play and without any extraneous decoration from the director or the designer.'[17] Such purism had a negative side, as Eyre and Wright reveal: 'At its best the work had a limpid beauty, at its worst asceticism looked like poverty of imagination and purity became sanctimoniousness.'[18]

Nigel had great respect and, in many cases, personal liking for writers, but he saw no virtue in affecting an unyieldingly reverential attitude to their work. No text intended for performance, he reasoned, whether it be Shakespeare or a new play, should be regarded as entire of itself:

> *I don't feel that any text is sacrosanct, and I know that Harold Pinter would probably reach out and strangle me if he was near enough, and so would Edward Bond, and say that I was wrong. But I think that when a writer writes something, it's really only the beginning, and then people take it over, and start forming the characters, and you gradually find, very, very often that some lines are unnecessary.*[19]

As far as the Royal Court was concerned, this Littlewood-inspired conviction was nothing short of heresy. Nigel had two indelible memories of Court rehearsals which he often recalled as telling instances of the Company's purism in action: on one occasion he was roundly chastised for failing to observe the correct, i.e. typed, punctuation in a sentence – specifically, playing a comma instead of a semi-colon – and on another, someone brazenly (or naïvely) suggested cutting one of John Osborne's lines, whereupon the playwright stormed out of the theatre and stayed away for three weeks in a sulk worthy of Achilles.

At the Royal Court actors were unapologetically placed in a servile relationship to the text. Jack Shepherd, who appeared with Nigel in the Bond plays *Early Morning* and *Narrow Road to the Deep North*, recognised the advantages of this situation as well as its inherent problems:

> *During the period when I worked intensively at the Court a defined way of rehearsing the actors (of getting there) was in the process of being evolved.*

The actors were encouraged to regard themselves as servants of the play. The text had to be spoken in such a way that the audience would be drawn to the narrative of the play – not the charismatic (or otherwise) nature of the performance. A good actor was someone who could draw attention to the thing that was said, as opposed to the way it was being spoken. Naturalness, not naturalism. Altruism, not egotism. And above all, in rehearsal, there was no substitute for doing. *As Bill Gaskill repeatedly said: 'Don't talk about it – do it.' And much more.*

What made it difficult was that a lot of the theory tended to run right across the grain of an actor's instinct. It was very hard to find a synthesis.[20]

Whether there was ever a style of acting that could confidently be identified as typical of the Royal Court is problematic. However, as Jack Shepherd indicates, there was some consensus of opinion on the question of what qualities constituted a good Court actor. In the programme for his production of John Antrobus's *Crete and Sergeant Pepper,*[21] Peter Gill wrote that good acting 'is more an informing value than a style. It can be described perhaps as a feeling for observed reality and a belief that while the actor is uniquely himself, he must still meet all the demands of a particular writer.' William Gaskill gradually embraced the Aristotelian thesis that the actor was first and foremost a promoter of action, an illuminator of plot rather than character:

I began to understand that in the theatre it is the action itself that counts, that character is a secondary consideration. Theatre is about what happens, not what people are. But the actor will always pull back towards characterization and the writer move the action forward. The director has to moderate between them.[22]

As Gaskill himself conceded, this notion ran contrary to the actor's instincts, but it certainly found favour among his fellow directors. Jane Howell, for example, subscribed to it in directing *Narrow Road to the Deep North:* 'I didn't work on character at all in this play, which is very unusual for me. I always told the actors to play the action. I didn't want emotional involvement.'[23]

The absence of emotional involvement seemed to Nigel to be a feature of the improvisation exercises which were a daily component of rehearsals. Improvisation at the Court was a mental discipline that involved putting the actors through a form of basic drill, and was far removed from the imaginative brainstorming sessions Nigel was accustomed to in Theatre Workshop, where actors were expected to experiment freely and fully inhabit their roles. The conclusion he drew from the Court's more conservative use of improvisation was that actors were to be discouraged from thinking too much for themselves; experimentation was the prerogative of writers.

In spite of the constraints Nigel endured as a member of the English Stage Company, the Royal Court was, for several reasons, a positive experience. It provided him with reasonably steady employment for a number of years and the chance to work with some of the leading playwrights of the day. Between 1968 and 1974 he performed with the English Stage Company in three 'Sunday night productions without décor', seven main-bill productions, one Theatre Upstairs production, two West End transfers, and one European tour. All but two of these were new plays. One of the Court's most successful and long-running productions, Christopher Hampton's *The Philanthropist*, afforded Nigel what was arguably the seminal role of his acting career. For his very first Royal Court assignment he had landed a part in an exciting moment of British theatre history – the final battle against the Lord Chamberlain.

Early Morning was the last play to be banned *in toto* by the Lord Chamberlain's office. When the script arrived on his desk early in 1967, Gaskill 'was completely unprepared for the fantasy unleashed.'[24] Originally entitled *Recent Morning Died Queen Victoria,* the play is written in the form of a dream sequence in which the Queen and Florence Nightingale are depicted as lesbian lovers, Prince Albert and Disraeli as co-conspirators in a failed *coup,* Princes Arthur and George as Siamese twins (the latter becoming a decaying corpse still attached to his brother), and everyone is reunited in Heaven at a cannibalistic feast. Bond set the story in Victorian England but introduced deliberate anachronisms, such as cinema queues and airports, which became an important feature of his dramatic style. He later explained to Gaskill, in relation to his *Lear:*

> *The anachronisms are for the horrible moments in a dream when you know it's a dream but can't help being afraid. The anachronisms must increase and not lessen the seriousness. They are like a debt that has to be paid.*[25]

In the printed text of *Early Morning* Bond prefaces the nightmarish fantasy with the assertion, 'The events of this play are true', by which, Hay and Roberts contend:

> *He means that the events of the play present in surreal form the significance of the actions taken by Victorian and modern society. If people do not literally eat each other in reality, they effectively do so by destroying the humanity of*

themselves and each other. What might be termed the 'sub-text' in another work becomes here the main text.[26]

Quite apart from the practical problems of staging a work that, with its special effects and abrupt scene shifts, was very similar to a film script, Gaskill foresaw formidable opposition from both the censor and his own Council. But, despite any personal reservations he may have had, his championship of Bond's 'freedom play' never faltered; he committed himself, at some physical and emotional cost, to making certain that *Early Morning* was performed, if only to an audience of English Stage Society members. 'In fighting for *Early Morning,*' Roberts states, '[Gaskill] was defending everything the Court stood for.'[27] His policy of 'no surrender' with regard to the play placed the Royal Court on the front line of the censorship battle. It is perhaps difficult in the present climate, in which anything goes, and with a surfeit of violence constantly available, to conceive of the Lord Chamberlain's absolute jurisdiction or what this meant for writers trying accurately to portray contemporary life, but, as Gaskill points out, 'to us at the time it was a tremendous battle with a real enemy.'[28]

A disturbing scene in Bond's previous play *Saved,* involving a baby being stoned to death in its pram, had sensationally put the whole issue of censorship under the spotlight and led to the successful prosecution of Gaskill and the Royal Court's licensee, Alfred Esdaile, for contravening the Theatres Act of 1843. Under Section 12 of this Act new plays and additions to existing ones had to be submitted to the Lord Chamberlain's office for scrutiny by the Examiner of Plays. A licence could be withheld or withdrawn from a play on such grounds as sacrilege, profanity, indecency, sedition or for the offensive representation of personalities. There was no appeal against the Lord Chamberlain's decision, which was made on the advice of his readers, and he was not legally bound to provide reasons for his decision. By the late 1960s these powers had become an absurd anomaly in an otherwise permissive society, especially as television and radio were not subject to pre-censorship.

In practice a play was seldom banned in its entirety, as happened with *Early Morning,* and the Lord Chamberlain's office was usually more than willing to suggest cuts or alterations in the text that would enable a licence to be issued. The last Lord Chamberlain, Lord Cobbold, was, like his immediate predecessor Lord Scarborough, a reluctant censor, and generally considered scrupulously fair and unfailingly polite in his dealings with theatre managements.[29] Nevertheless, his unqualified right to interfere was a constant source of frustration and resentment for theatre practitioners. What particularly rankled was that the Lord Chamberlain was an officer of the Royal Household.[30] In an interview with J. W. Lambert in 1965, Lord Cobbold protested his complete impartiality:

> *My personal objective is to try to assess the norm of educated, adult opinion and if possible to keep just a touch ahead of it. I find I have to make a positive effort to keep my own personal tastes, likes and dislikes right out of the picture. They are obviously irrelevant for censorship purposes.*[31]

It seemed clear to those in the theatre, however, that the Lord Chamberlain's supreme duty was to safeguard the *dignitas* of the Crown, a belief confirmed by his intransigent stance on *Early Morning*.

In October 1967 the English Stage Company submitted Bond's script to the Lord Chamberlain. On 8 November the play was returned with the sole comment, 'His Lordship would not allow it.' When, in the new year, Gaskill requested elaboration, John Johnston, Comptroller of the Lord Chamberlain's office, replied:

> *The play* Early Morning *comprises mainly historical characters, who are subjected throughout to highly offensive and untrue accusations of gross indecency. They are selected for insult apparently as being nationally respected figures with long records of devoted service to their country and fellow citizens … If allegory is required then the characters should be allegorical.*[32]

Edward Bond's position was equally uncompromising and a repetition of the stand he took over *Saved*:

> *I would do almost anything to prevent my play being banned except alter one comma at the request of the Lord Chamberlain.*
>
> *If the director asked me to change a word or alter a scene, I would do so, because he would be trying to improve the clarity, or truth, or theatrical force of the play. But the Lord Chamberlain is not helping, he is interfering. His aim is extra-theatrical. […]*
>
> *You <u>cannot</u> have the present censorship, and a culturally virile theatre. The censorship is an aesthetic obstacle.*[33]

Concurrent with Gaskill's personal mission to have *Early Morning* produced were the introduction, reading and drafting of George Strauss's Private Members' Bill for the abolition of theatre censorship.[34] Paying no heed to the parliamentary timetable or to pressure from the Chairman of the English Stage Company Council, Neville Blond, and the Arts Council, who were anxious that the Bill's progress not be jeopardised by the theatre inviting prosecution, Gaskill scheduled *Early Morning* for two 'Sunday night productions without décor'.

Besides Nigel the cast included Malcolm Tierney, Peter Eyre, Tom Chadbon, Roger Booth, Norman Eshley, Dennis Waterman, Jane Howell, Hugh Armstrong, Harry Meacher, Gavin Reed, Jack Shepherd and Bruce Robinson. Gaskill had wanted somebody like Maggie Smith to play Florence Nightingale, but the part went to Mick Jagger's then girlfriend Marianne Faithfull, adding to the media hype that surrounded the play's off-stage fortunes. Several months earlier the role of Queen Victoria had been offered to John Bird, who had played the monarch in the BBC1 satirical film *My Father Knew Lloyd George*. After some deliberation Bird declined the offer and the part was given to Moira Redmond.

The deputy stage manager for *Early Morning* was twenty-four-year-old Trevor Bentham, a handsome and good-humoured young man, who would become the most important person in Nigel's life. Trevor was from a family of lawyers and had himself been expected to join the Bar, but his burning ambition was to become an actor. He trained at London's prestigious Central School of Speech and Drama in the same year as Julie Christie and, like Nigel, he did his acting apprenticeship in provincial rep. After a while he moved into stage management and one of his first jobs was with the Phoenix Theatre Company in Leicester where the star attraction was a young, hell-raising Welsh actor by the name of Anthony Hopkins.

Rehearsal time for *Early Morning* was limited and the actors struggled with fatigue and a script that was more than usually demanding. Nigel informed the *Evening Standard* that the cast was 'fascinated by the play, if exhausted at the end.'[35] The first Sunday night production was presented on 31 March and celebrated the twelfth anniversary of the English Stage Company. The programme cover bore the announcement:

> Early Morning *was commissioned by the English Stage Company and was scheduled to be presented in the main bill. It has been refused a licence by the Lord Chamberlain and is therefore being presented by the English Stage Society to society members for two Sunday evenings only.*
>
> *If the Bill for the abolition of Theatre censorship, at present before parliament, becomes law, the English Stage Company intend to present the play at the earliest opportunity in the main bill.*

The play's running time of three hours elapsed without incident, but after the performance two police officers – one of them a Detective Chief Inspector – interviewed Gaskill and cautioned that the Company risked prosecution for obscenity if a second performance went ahead. They argued that, because a Vice Squad Inspector had been admitted to the theatre without having to produce his club membership card, the performance could not legitimately be called private. On this advice Alfred Esdaile overruled the Management Committee's wishes and cancelled the performance scheduled for 7 April. Gaskill was furious but could not count on support from even his staunchest allies like Kenneth Tynan, who had little enough time for the play. In his *Observer* column of 7 April, Tynan wrote:

> *If only it had been better done, we would have realised how bad a play it was. William Gaskill's desultory production left room for doubt: that mumbled line might hide some pivotal clue, that inexplicable pause might be the key to some grand satiric design. What the evening lacked was a quality I have long relished and would now like to designate as High Definition Performance.*[36]

Notwithstanding Esdaile's ban, a matinée performance of *Early Morning* was given on 7 April, thanks to a clever expedient thought up by Greville Poke, Secretary of the English Stage Council. Poke's idea was to redesignate the performance a 'critics' dress rehearsal' and admit the audience free of charge through a side entrance. The cloak-and-dagger aspect of these proceedings appealed strongly to Nigel who was warned that, because he spoke the first words of the play, he might, in the event of a police raid, be a prime target for arrest. A police presence was maintained outside the theatre but the 'rehearsal' was not interrupted. In place of the scheduled evening performance Gaskill, Bond, Tynan and the publisher John Calder[37] conducted a 'teach-in' on censorship.

The critics could not understand all the fuss being made about the play and deplored the fact that the momentous censorship debate had become focused on a work unworthy of such attention. Peter Lewis of the *Daily Telegraph* ridiculed the play's martyrdom:

> *For the Lord Chamberlain, so near the end of his censorship functions, to ban it as the offensive representation of historic and royal persons is solemn to the point of idiocy.*
>
> *But it would be equally idiotic to make a great issue of principle and liberty out of the play, which seemed to me obscure, inconsistent,*

pointless, boring, and greatly inferior to Mr Bond's previously banned play, Saved.[38]

His sentiments were echoed by Irving Wardle in *The Times:*

What I regret is that the Royal Court's just and necessary fight for theatrical free speech should be conducted on behalf of a piece as muddled and untalented as this. […]

THE ENGLISH STAGE SOCIETY

ROYAL COURT THEATRE, SLOANE SQUARE
LONDON, S.W.1.

Telephone: SLOane 2273

The Council of the English Stage Society
request the pleasure of your representative's company
at the

ROYAL COURT THEATRE

on

SUNDAY, APRIL 7th

at 8 p.m.

when they will present

EARLY MORNING

by Edward Bond

Directed by William Gaskill

Designed by Deirdre Clancy

Two tickets are enclosed. If you are unable
to use either or both, please return to the
Box Office Manager, Royal Court Theatre, Sloane
Square, S.W.1.

Press Representative: Frank Rainbow, 45 Clarges Street, W.1.
HYD 4620

15 Springcroft Ave
N.2.
April 8th, 1968

Here's Riches for you.

Tickets for the Show
THAT WAS NEVER PLAYED !

Regards,

Charles.
(Charles Landstone).

ROYAL COURT THEATRE
SLOANE SQUARE, S.W.1 SLOane 1745

2nd Perf. 8 pm — SECOND PERFORMANCE 8 pm
Sun 7/4/68 — Sunday APR 7
STALLS 12/6 — STALLS 12/6
H 18 — H 18
TO BE RETAINED — TO BE GIVEN UP

Invitation and tickets to *Early Morning* (1968), the last play to be banned by the Lord Chamberlain.
(Courtesy of The Raymond Mander & Joe Mitchenson Theatre Collection)

What on earth is being proved by taking a group of well-known historical figures and inventing an action fantastically at variance with their lives? It would not be necessary to ask this question if Early Morning *were simply a joke at the expense of not-so-sacred British cows. [...]*

But on the whole Early Morning *is not, and is not intended to be funny. [...]*

The message is clear enough. What remains unclear is the relationship of this monstrous image to the facts of existence; or any sign of the theatrical imagination that might give it self-sufficient authority. As in 'Saved', we are confronted by savage events and numb inert language. And the performance of an excellent cast, playing in a cold throwaway style and constantly breaking the line of performance by dropping out of the action, reflects not on these characters but on the author's lack of technique. Given a chance, there was good comedy from Moira Redmond as the Queen and Nigel Hawthorne, Malcolm Tierney and Jack Shepherd as the frock-coated hatchet men.[39]

Two days later the playwright John Arden responded to these fulminations in a letter to the Editor of *The Times*:

Sir, – Your Drama Critic, Mr Wardle, is of course entitled to his opinion that Early Morning *is a 'muddled and untalented' play (April 8). I do not agree with him, but even if I did I would still find his review unfortunately expressed. The whole point of Sunday evening performances at the Royal Court is that works which may well be untalented or muddled, should nevertheless be given an inexpensive and experimental production in the only way that matters to a dramatist – on a stage, before an audience. [...]*

It is therefore all the more horrifying that the work of an obviously talented writer should be snuffed out in its very beginnings by a sinister confederation of the Lord Chamberlain (and his bravoes, the police) and the licensee of the Royal Court – a gentleman whose interests in the bricks-and-mortar of the building should weigh in the scales alongside those of the artists concerned, not against them.

It seems a pity that Mr Wardle could not have added to his legitimate criticisms of Early Morning *a note of joy that he was enabled to see the play at all. [...] Our censorship difficulties are almost entirely due to rank cowardice in theatre offices and boardrooms, and an occasion upon which this attitude has been overcome, however briefly, should not go unnoticed by the critics.*[40]

One problem was that the production was under-rehearsed and had foundered under the weight of so many conflicting outside pressures. A more significant problem was Bond's complexity as a writer. Nigel always thought *Early Morning* had been much maligned and that the critics had failed to get beyond the surface difficulties and confronting subject matter to appreciate the play's intrinsic humour and morality.

Strauss's Bill became law on 28 September and six months later *Early Morning* opened in the Court's main bill with a new and slightly larger cast. Of the original cast only Nigel, Moira Redmond, Jack Shepherd and Tom Chadbon remained. As a consequence of the Theatres Act, 1968 theatre managements were now subject to common law and there was the danger that the production could provoke a string of prosecutions by members of the public. The public, however, showed that they were quite sensible and sophisticated, and not a single prosecution ensued. This time around the critical reception was considerably warmer and a genuine effort made to understand, in Martin Esslin's words, 'this strange, significant and important play'.[41]

In between the not so clandestine critics' dress rehearsal of *Early Morning* and its premiere in the main bill, Nigel made his official English Stage Company debut in *Total Eclipse.* This was Christopher Hampton's second play and his first as the Company's resident dramatist. It dealt with the tempestuous relationship between the nineteenth-century poets Paul Verlaine and Arthur Rimbaud, a story with elements of Oscar Wilde's affair with Bosie, and of the violent jealousy that destroyed Joe Orton and Kenneth Halliwell. Jeremy Kingston, reviewing the play for *Punch,* styled the liaison 'a monster from Dostoievsky meets an hysteric out of Chekhov.'[42] The two principals delivered impressive performances: the older and weaker Verlaine was played by John Grillo, and the banefully attractive boy genius Rimbaud by the notoriously obstreperous and intemperate Court prodigy Victor Henry, whom Jack Shepherd described as 'the only truly ungovernable person I have ever known.'[43]

'The rest of the cast,' reported Martin Esslin, 'do extremely well, notably Nigel Hawthorne, in a succession of character vignettes: each quite different and equally memorable.'[44] These character vignettes included Verlaine's father-in-law M. Mauté de Fleurville, the caricaturist and photographer Étienne Carjat, and Judge Théodore T'Serstevens, the magistrate in Verlaine's trial. In what became the pattern of his Royal Court years, Nigel earned considerable critical approval for his small, finely crafted performances. Alan Bennett, who saw a number of these performances, said, 'You were always pleased to see him because you knew you'd get something not out of stock, you'd get something peculiar. He always surprised you.'

The play itself received mixed reviews but, much to the director Robert Kidd's chagrin, the critics devoted more space to treatises on the lives and love of Rimbaud and Verlaine than to a discussion of the production's qualities. Appreciative attention was paid to the striking decadence of Patrick Procktor's red and green sets. In the opening scene a Moorish lamp turned in front of the stage, 'casting hypnotic shadows of drugged intensity on deep red walls.'[45] Kidd incorporated the scene-shifting into the play. The climax of most scenes was frozen into a tableau, preceded and followed by a black-out, and the scenery was changed in full view of the audience. Martin Esslin admired this fashionable technique as 'a most effective device of epic theatre',[46] but the majority of critics found it a tiresome distraction.

Total Eclipse opened on 11 September 1968 and, although the Theatres Bill was well on the way to becoming law, it did not escape the touch of the Lord Chamberlain's blue pencil. Towards the end of its nineteen performances, however, censorship was formally abolished and the offending lines reinstated, adding a couple of minutes to the play's running time.

In October Nigel appeared as Count Wermuth in the Court's Sunday night production of a translation of Brecht's adaptation of *The Tutor,* a class satire by Jakob Lenz. The play takes place in Prussia in the 1770s after the Seven Years War and concerns a private tutor who seduces his employer's daughter and afterwards castrates himself. It was one of a number of adaptations Brecht made of classical texts during his final years at the Berliner Ensemble and through which he could more safely voice his political views.

To celebrate the Court's hard-won freedom from the Lord Chamberlain's authority, William Gaskill decided to start off 1969 with an Edward Bond season, comprising revivals of the previously banned *Saved* and *Early Morning* as well as his newest offering *Narrow Road to the Deep North.* This last play, which Bond wrote in two and a half days, had premiered at the Belgrade Theatre in Coventry on 24 June 1968 as part of an international conference on People and Cities. The work was commissioned by the conference Chairman, Stephen Verney, Canon of Coventry Cathedral, who 'wanted a play that dealt powerfully with the problems of people living in big cities, with the violence that breaks out in them, and with the crushing weight of authority, colonial, national, civic, and religious.'[47]

In a departure from the social realism of *Saved* and the surrealist fantasy of *Early Morning,* Bond presents *Narrow Road* as a parable about government, which he sets in feudal Japan, and employs a semi-stylised, poetic idiom. The story is told mainly from the point of view of the seventeenth-century haiku poet Basho and features a bloody and despotic warlord Shogo in his struggle against the Western barbarians, the British, for possession of his city. Jane

Howell's spare and rhythmic production made good use of some of the formal conventions of Noh theatre as well as alienation techniques. In defining the overall style achieved, John Barber coined the term 'the Brechtian Oriental'.[48]

Nigel played the British Commodore, epitome of colonial and missionary fatuity. Although his performance was commended by the critics, he afterwards suspected that he had made the Commodore too much a caricature of bewildered English pomposity. This lapse may be attributable to Jane Howell's direction and, as mentioned previously, her studied rejection in rehearsals of character and emotional involvement.

On the whole the play was well received, even though, as typically with Bond's work, it was the object of both praise and perplexity. In the autumn of 1969 the English Stage Company took *Saved* and *Narrow Road* to Europe for a tour sponsored by the British Council. The tour started at the Belgrade International Theatre Festival in Prague, where *Saved* collected joint first prize, and ended in Warsaw, stopping at Venice and Lublin on the way.

Lindsay Anderson once observed of Gaskill that he directed classics like new plays and new plays like classics.[49] For better or worse this was true of his production of Congreve's *The Double Dealer,* which Rosemary Say dubbed 'a modern naturalistic interpretation of what was intended to be an aesthetic romp.'[50] The play was performed in period costume, but the mannered style of Restoration comedy had been radically rethought. In John Barber's estimation:

> *Clearly an attempt has been made to seek a modern style of playing the comedy. But without superlative speaking, and without the gloss of elegant manners, some of the amusement must be lost. Further, when real passions break through the artificial manners, they cannot shock if the manners have simply been absent.*[51]

The Royal Court insistence on textual lucidity and unembellished acting, in this instance, detracted from the play's workability:

> *Extremely respectful towards the text, the cast acquire individual clarity at the expense of general coherence. They play at a deliberate measured pace, using the minimum detail, and usually coming to a stop when they have nothing to say. The impression, which may change during the run, is over-careful and dislocated: and you take away a memory of sharply isolated moments rather than a purposeful flow of dramatic energy.*[52]

In *The Double Dealer* Nigel played the cuckolded husband Lord Touchwood and demonstrated one of his most outstanding gifts as an actor, his practice of taking an audience unawares by discovering in even a stock character of comedy moments of exquisite pathos. One reviewer presciently compared him in this role to Molière's Orgon, a character he later played to perfection for the Royal Shakespeare Company: 'As the husband who admits an irreligious Tartuffe to his wife's bosom, Nigel Hawthorne is dismayingly moving.'

The previews and opening of the production had the ill fortune to coincide with both the televised excitement of the Apollo 11 space mission and a fierce heatwave. First night on 22 July was a humid 27° C. Robert Cushman began his review by declaring:

> *I am now the survivor of a semi-cathartic experience. For one could only feel pity, unalloyed with terror, for any bunch of actors called on to disport themselves in Restoration wigs and costumes on one of the most stifling nights of the July heatwave.*[53]

The oppressive conditions resulted in a discouraging 37 per cent return at the Box Office.

At the end of the run Nigel made a cameo appearance in an episode of the popular television sitcom *Dad's Army*. He is seen in the final minutes of 'The Armoured Might of Lance-Corporal Jones' as the Angry Man whose bicycle is commandeered by the Walmington-on-Sea platoon. The part was offered to him by the show's creator Jimmy Perry, with whom he had shared a dressing room when they were performing together at Stratford East in *The Marie Lloyd Story* (Perry played the part of music hall singer Alec Hurley, Marie's second husband). In the unenviable position of having just two lines to deliver in the midst of a chaotic scene, Nigel understandably failed to impress. His fleeting performance was slightly stilted and almost wrecked by nerves and the pressing sense of being a fish out of water. He would have to wait another decade before his television career really took off.

Nigel's final Court performance for 1969 was as the Governor, Pemberton, in Frank Norman's prison play *Insideout,* adapted, on Peggy Ashcroft's suggestion, from the playwright's book *Bang to Rights*. Norman, who had served four prison sentences prior to his writing career, came to prominence with the enormously successful Theatre Workshop production of his *Fings Ain't Wot They Used T'be*, a musical on which he collaborated with Lionel Bart. *Insideout* was initially commissioned by Peter Hall at the Royal Shakespeare Company, before being forsaken, passed to Kenneth Tynan (then Literary

Manager at the National Theatre), and finally ending up at the Royal Court, a full three years after Norman completed work on it. Nor did its tribulations end there; the play became the innocent victim in an acrimonious dispute between the Court and the London critics.

The Court's traditional hostility towards the critics culminated in October 1969 with the withdrawal of facilities from Hilary Spurling, the theatre critic of the *Spectator,* because of her 'unilluminating attitude to our work'. Spurling was struck from the free-ticket list and effectively barred from Court productions, a petulant move that the critical fraternity was quick to denounce as a blow against the freedom of the press. By the time *Insideout* opened on 24 November, a number of critics had undertaken to boycott Court productions in protest. However, several of them attended the opening in an unofficial capacity. The few critics who published reviews held wildly differing opinions of the tone of Norman's work. Irving Wardle called *Insideout* 'much the mildest prison play I have ever seen. You would not expect Mr. Norman to write as an outraged liberal outsider; what is surprising is the tone almost of affection which he bestows on the system. It is like someone casting his memory back to schooldays, with all the pain and anger erased by time.'[54] John Barber, on the other hand, saw in the play 'a blistering angry account of life in gaol', and 'a vivid and hideously convincing realisation of prison life, its duties and petty routines laid on the line with the thoroughness and explicitness of a Zola.'[55]

Nigel spent the following year as a leading light of Sheffield Repertory Company (see Chapter Five), returning briefly to the Royal Court in a Sunday night club performance of Sheffield's latest and most divisive play, *Strip Jack Naked.* The guest performance was arranged by the Court's assistant director, Roger Williams, after he saw the world premiere at Sheffield Playhouse. It was the first time in over twenty years that a Sheffield production had been invited to go to London, and in the words of Playhouse Director, Colin George, who commissioned the play, 'it put Sheffield in the first division.'[56]

His last performances downstairs at the Royal Court were in two new plays by John Osborne. The first of these, *West of Suez,* was an obvious star vehicle of the sort normally disdained by the Court. It provided Sir Ralph Richardson with a plum role as a raffish, spoilt and dissemblingly eccentric old writer. Ninety-seven percent of seats were sold (well above the Court average) and each night Richardson was respectfully applauded on his late entrance. Two months after it opened, *West of Suez* transferred to the Cambridge Theatre in the West End.

It was not just the audience who was under Sir Ralph's spell. Nigel idolised Richardson, and when given his choice of parts in the play selected the one he judged would ensure his constant close proximity to the great man on stage. What captivated him was not Richardson's histrionic talents but his charisma as a man. Nigel had a sneaking regard for Sir Ralph's repertoire of tricks, but always saw straight through them, and he harboured no longing to be more like him as an actor: 'I didn't think he was a wonderful actor. As a personality he was extraordinary.' He recognised in Richardson a flamboyant character, wonderfully off-centre and larger than life in his virtues and foibles, and that, as Alec Guinness said, 'Of all the actors of repute in our time he was, I think, the most interesting as a man: original, shrewd, knowledgeable, commonsensical and yet visionary.'[57]

In later years Nigel was several times compared to Ralph Richardson, particularly for his portrayal of C. S. Lewis in *Shadowlands* in London and New York. As an older man he bore some physical resemblance to Richardson and, if one studies carefully his facial expressions on film, especially during sad, contemplative or wistful moments, it is possible to catch traces of Richardson. But in most respects the two actors were not alike. Sheridan Morley, who identified in Nigel's acting a 'sense of another world, a spirituality, a secretness', dismisses any notion of him as a latter-day Richardson:

> *Ralph Richardson was so much more up-front and mad. Ralph is Michael Gambon now – Michael Gambon is doing Ralph all over the place. Ralph was barking mad but he wasn't secretive. When he came on you bloody watched and he had that extraordinary voice. He was never invisible. [...] What you saw is what you got. With Nigel Hawthorne what you see is never what you get and what you get is never what you see, and that's why it's clever.*

West of Suez is set in a villa 'on a sub-tropical island, neither Africa nor Europe, but some of both, also less than both', and 'perched between one civilization and the next'. Here the English writer Wyatt Gillman is holidaying with his four daughters and their husbands. In exploring the imperfect relationships between the various characters, Osborne builds up a picture 'of a whole society – very English, self-centred, self-lacerating, civilised in its way, and pathetically aware of its own limitations.'[58] The play ends suddenly with Wyatt being shot to death by local revolutionaries.

There are echoes of Jimmy Porter in *West of Suez* (notably in the line 'If you've no world of your own, it's rather pleasant to regret the passing of someone else's') and a powerful sense of displacement. But fifteen years on anger has been supplanted by a bleak chord of scornful elegy.

Mary Holland, writing in *Plays and Players,* regretted the passing of Osborne's 'wilful, lacerating streak':

> *One remembers the early Osborne, the passionate pain for what he saw happening to a country he loved, which he articulated in the classical tradition of English rhetoric, and one's inclination is to keep silence. I cannot find it in myself to castigate his increasingly maudlin chauvinism, his petty resentment against the young, the un-British, journalists, the un-hip.*[59]

Sheridan Morley read Osborne's latest offering as a depressing but richly layered essay on the new abyss:

> *The frames of reference within which it has been constructed are a curious amalgam of Chekovian nostalgia, present despair and future terror. […]Osborne's purpose […] is to build a play for our uneasy time on the ground plans of earlier theatrical writers; not only Chekov and Shaw but even Coward (in his* South Sea Bubble *mood) are invoked here like dramatic ghosts at a banquet, and the result is a densely packed, multi-levelled celebration of the void … a sardonic, almost bitchy realisation that, as none of Osborne's predecessors had to accept or even to realise, the emptiness is all.*[60]

Lindsay Anderson allowed Nigel to nominate which character he would like to play and Nigel had chosen Christopher, Wyatt's secretary-cum-nursemaid and protector. The role entailed comparatively few lines and seemed to Anderson an odd and excessively unassuming choice, but on reading the script Nigel had perceived Christopher as Wyatt's shadow and envisaged himself at Sir Ralph's side throughout the play. Unfortunately, Anthony Page, who directed the production, tried to turn Christopher into a cipher and to stifle Nigel's best efforts to give the character a presence. In one beautifully played scene towards the end, however, Nigel brought Christopher compellingly to life. At the beginning of Act 2, scene 2 he shared an exchange with Osborne's wife, Jill Bennett, into which he compressed his character's tragic past and present suffering, his failed marriage, his forlorn love for Bennett's character Frederica, his devotion to Wyatt, and his haunting memory of the young unarmed prisoner he killed in the war. In Jill Bennett, Nigel discovered a stage partner totally responsive to his method of changing a performance without altering the text, of keeping the performance fresh and unanchored. To their surprise they managed to dodge directorial strictures and regularly changed the way they played this understated and very revealing scene. It was one of the most personally satisfying experiences Nigel had during his involvement with the Royal Court.

A Sense of Detachment, which opened on 4 December 1972, was the twelfth and most controversial of John Osborne's plays to be presented at the Court. The controversy raged mainly around the work's absence of recognisable form and its excess of hatred and contumely. The curtain rose on 'a virtually empty stage except for a projection screen at the back, a barrel organ downstage and an upright piano.' The principal cast members, identified only as Chairman, Chap, Girl, Older Lady, Father and Grandfather, walked on carrying bentwood chairs and proceeded to insult first the audience, then each other, and to deconstruct every proffered theatrical device as an absurd cliché. Every so often actors, planted in the auditorium, shouted opprobrious slogans to which the actors on stage responded in kind. There was nothing resembling a plot in the conventional sense and, as Sheridan Morley observed, 'Osborne's sustained search for the ultimate hatred leads him further and further away from an actual play'.[61] The language was deliberately offensive and the evening's most shocking episode involved explicit excerpts from a pornographic film catalogue being gravely intoned by the genteel Older Lady (Rachel Kempson). Osborne stated that *A Sense of Detachment* was about the horror of living in the twentieth century. His utter damnation of everything the century symbolised, its adulteration of all goodness ('We are not language. We are lingua. We do not love, eat, or cherish. We exchange.'), refuted the clamorous imputation in the press that the Osborne anger was a spent force.

Not surprisingly critical opinion was deeply divided. Felix Barker (who had been so outraged at Nigel's portrayal of Oswald Stoll in *The Marie Lloyd Story*) attacked the play as a 'meandering, intemperate charade', and pitied Rachel Kempson for having 'to speak filth of a kind never before heard on a London stage.' J. C. Trewin loftily questioned the soundness of the Court's literary judgement: 'Surely the Council of the English Stage Company should have had courage enough to refuse *A Sense of Detachment?* Such an affair as this does credit to neither the theatre nor the author'. But *A Sense of Detachment* attracted its share of apologists and even ardent admirers.

Rachel Kemspson voiced the cast's frustration when she told the *Evening Standard:* 'I understand why a lot of people don't get the play. Only highly intelligent people seem to really understand and then they have to come back a second time to get it all. It's like an enormous canvas in a very short space.'[62] Michael Billington of the *Guardian* did not believe that the play's erratic constitution reduced its forcefulness as a piece of theatre, or that its ostensible flippancy obscured the sensitivity and seriousness at its core:

How to describe John Osborne's A Sense of Detachment? *A thinking-man's
'Hellzapopin'? A spiky, satirical, inconsequential collage? An attack on our
own heartless, loveless, profiteering society in which language is corrupted
daily? A moving threnody for a dying civilisation? The paradox of this (to
me) provocative, innovatory and exciting work is that it manages to be all
of these things, moving outwards from purely theatrical satire to an eloquent
examination of the world at large. [...]*

*Snooks are deftly cocked at elliptical, poignant chat in front of an empty
cyclorama; at inconsequential Littlewoodian bursts into song-and-dance; at
audience participation; at pseudo-documentary; and at first person singular
theatrical autobiography.*

*But what at first seems like a kaleidoscopic cabaret gradually turns into
something sharper and sourer. [...]*

*Bravos and boos greeted this strange hypnotic pot-pourri at the end but I
would defend it on several grounds. It is, at the very least, sustainedly
entertaining. It uses an apparently inconsequential form to defend timeless
human values. [...] And it goads, provokes and agitates its audience as only
a truly vital theatrical work can.*[63]

The drama critic for the *Sunday Times* lamented the 'universal failure to
perceive that *A Sense of Detachment* is a play which will be one of the treasures
of the British theatre.' The cast, he said, 'sustained by no obvious line of story,
but inspired by Mr Osborne's superlative vision of loveliness despised and
grandeur of soul destroyed, give performances which, in passion, emotional
tension, and almost miraculous orchestration make *A Sense of Detachment* the
one play in London which only clodhoppers would willingly miss.'[64] Oscar
Lewenstein, who in July 1972 had taken over from Gaskill as Artistic Director
of the Court, claimed his 'wife was moved to tears by this play, which
expressed all Osborne's heartfelt concern for England.'[65]

In his stage directions Osborne wrote: 'If there are any genuine
interruptions from members of the audience at any time, and it would be a
pity if there were not, the actors must naturally be prepared to deal with such
a situation, preferably the CHAIRMAN, the CHAP or the GIRL. These
can be obvious, inventive or spontaneous.' For this reason, the cast of
A Sense of Detachment was specially selected from actors who had worked very
closely to, and interacted with, an audience, and could, therefore,
adeptly field any unscripted interjections. Nigel's invaluable Theatre
Workshop training made him an obvious choice and he was entrusted
with the role of the Chairman. In the week before previews began, the
director Frank Dunlop outlined to Ronald Hastings of the *Daily Telegraph*

what was required of both the actors and the audience in Osborne's unorthodox scenario:

> *If the audience is interested and wants to take an active part the performance will change, so that performances may differ from one night to the next. There are two or three actors who will take the lead over any changes in plan as a result of the audience's reaction. [...] All we want them [the audience] to do is to react truly and sincerely to what they see on the stage. We don't want them to make exhibitions of themselves for that would be only another theatrical cliché.*[66]

This worked well in the abstract, but the highly confrontational nature of the piece placed the actors dangerously in the audience's firing-line. Each night abuse and convenient missiles were hurled at them by otherwise respectable patrons, who felt they had been disgracefully short-changed, and by pockets of loutish hecklers willingly egged on. As Alan Bennett once remarked, 'Knighthoods nothing: Actors should be decorated for gallantry.'[67] The fractious behaviour the play incited took its toll on the company's nerves, prompting a reporter from the *Sunday Times* to ask, 'If audiences are going to continue to play speaking roles, would it not be only fair if Equity insisted the author too should sit on stage and field their loose balls?'[68] On the fourth night, in reply to an exceptionally audible barracker, Denise Coffey, playing the Girl, exclaimed, 'Who'd have thought old Sam Beckett was in tonight and nobody knew!' Back came the riposte, 'A very funny line and not in the script,' at which Coffey snapped irritably, 'Yes it is, and so are you.'

Things got much further out of control several weeks into the run, when two boorish young men in the third row of the stalls continually interrupted and repeated the actors' words. At the curtain call Rachel Kempson leapt over the footlights and, to the rest of the cast's horror, started pummelling the men. She was afterwards quoted as saying: 'I saw red. [...] We were all pretty tired by this time and I jumped off the stage and hit both of them. I think the cast cried out for me to stop because they were afraid the men would hit back.' Far from retaliating, the men beat a hasty retreat up the aisle. They were then apprehended outside the theatre by irritated members of the audience who decided to pick up where Kempson had left off. Middle-class theatregoers metamorphosed into an enraged lynch-mob: one of the men had two teeth knocked out and both received black eyes. It was all a long way from the decorous deportment expected of audiences in Binkie Beaumont's West End. In reporting the incident the newspapers made pointed and, in a few cases, snide reference to Rachel Kempson's age (sixty-two) and married name (Lady Redgrave).

Most critics saw past the ugliness on and off stage to the fine performances, which extracted from the play what beauty and nuances of meaning it held:

The Chairman of the conversation is Nigel Hawthorne; Mr Hawthorne is suave, anxious to please, and pacificatory. And it is one of Mr Osborne's celebrated coups de théâtre *to make him, in the last thirty seconds of the evening, suddenly exchange his kindness and geniality for a merciless and vindictive display of scorn and hatred that leaves the audience shocked and disorientated. […]*

Miss Kempson, Miss Coffey, Mr Michael, Mr Standing, and Mr Hawthorne himself reach in [the play] a pathos and a translucent beauty of the most memorable kind. […] Mr Hawthorne delivers its terrible conclusion with a miraculous amazement, recoiling from a vision of evil that makes his face unforgettably appalled.[69]

1973 signalled a turning point in Nigel's career, one that forced him to assess exactly who he was as an actor, and to which he ascribed his later success. In March of that year he took over from George Cole the lead in Christopher Hampton's *The Philanthropist,* his first starring role in the West End. The play had premiered at the Royal Court in August 1970, directed by Robert Kidd and with Alec McCowen as the philanthropic Philip, an amiable and uncritical philologist who is incorrigibly indecisive ('My trouble is, I'm a man of no convictions. *(Longish pause.)* At least, I think I am.') A month later the production transferred to the Mayfair Theatre where it ran for three highly profitable years, a financial boon that allowed the Court a period of risk-taking on less financially viable projects.

As well as finally knowing the singular contentment of being the star of a critical and commercial West End hit, Nigel experienced with *The Philanthropist* his road to Damascus, a moment of illumination which had a profound impact on his personal and professional development. This revelatory moment occurred as a result of his extraordinary empathy with the character of Philip, Hampton's skilful inversion of Alceste, the protagonist of Molière's *Le Misanthrope,* and who, as Irving Wardle noticed, 'approximates so closely to the wryly defeated character that comes through the poems of Philip Larkin.'[70]

I didn't get going really till Privates on Parade. *That was when the wheels really sort of cranked into place. Before that I was going from job to job. Maybe I wasn't ready as a young actor, and I'm sure I wasn't. I hadn't settled into myself and I hadn't found out who I was or what I was, what I did best, and what I looked like and sounded like. But when I did, it was an instantaneous recognition and I think it was* The Philanthropist *that did it. Christopher Hampton always said that I was the nearest to the part of Philip of anybody who had played it. And, in fact, when I went to see Alec McCowen playing it at the Royal Court, I started to get almost panicky, almost shaking with nerves because the character was so like me. I totally identified with him, his indecisions, his general attitudes, his apprehensions and vulnerabilities. And it was really after that that I started to be successful because I knew that admitting my own vulnerabilities was the best way through. And it wasn't to do what Olivier did, which was to plaster everything on top; it was to find out really what was going on underneath.*

Nigel was forty-three when he came to this realisation, and had been a professional actor for over two decades. It was the beginning of the end of his long struggle, not merely towards recognition, but, more importantly, towards a determination of what for him was the essence of acting. He learnt that the more he revealed of himself, the more interesting and truthful was his performance. His point of entry into a character was not a walk or a voice, costume or make-up, but an examination of his inner self.

In February 1969 the Court's upstairs space and late-night drinking club, which for many years had functioned as a *de facto* second house, opened as the Theatre Upstairs. Here in 1974 Nigel gave a superb final Court performance as the police chief, Colonel Krou, in *Bird Child*, written by David Lan, a twenty-one-year-old White South African (now Artistic Director of the Young Vic), and directed by Nicholas Wright. The play, set in apartheid South Africa, was a slightly cumbersome creation with a laborious, expository first act, but it had sincerity and quiet humour, and Lan's characters were fresh, deftly drawn and well served by the standard of acting.

In many ways the decade of the 1960s had been for Nigel a delayed education as well as the toughest, most exciting and unpredictable phase of his development as an actor. He began the decade as a South African stage star, then returned once and for all to England where he retraced his path through the dismal routine of weekly rep, unemployment, failed auditions and West End misses, before he was adopted and transformed by the visionary Joan Littlewood. From Theatre Workshop the Royal Court was not a logical progression, but Nigel's trials as part of the English Stage Company, at the very least, established the resilience of his faith in Littlewood's teachings. But the Royal Court offered him more than just a negative comparison with the invigorating irreverence and creative freedom of Theatre Workshop; it gave him exposure to the cutting-edge of dramatic writing at a critical point in British theatre history, and was a vital step towards the maturity of his talent.

Notes to Chapter 4

1 Hofmannsthal (1874-1929) introduced the concept of 'das Gleitende' in his most famous essay *Ein Brief,* written in 1902. In this fictional letter from Lord Chandos to Francis Bacon, Chandos confesses a crisis of language ('Sprachkrise'), which Hofmannsthal represents as symptomatic of 'das Gleitende', the impermanence of existing cultural and social institutions.

2 'Devine and After', *Plays and Players,* November 1965, 21.

3 See Doty & Harbin, eds, (1990) 58. The conference, entitled 'The English Stage Company at the Royal Court Theatre: Production Practices and Legacies, 1956-1981', was held at Louisiana State University, 7-10 October 1981. Gaskill's remarks here were made in the second session of the conference, 'Artistic Directors Talk: The Court After George Devine, 1965-1981'.

4 The phrase is used by Michael Billington in his review of Osborne's *A Sense of Detachment, Guardian,* 5 December 1972.

5 Eyre & Wright (2000) 242.

6 Hare, 'Theatre's great malcontent', John Osborne Memorial Lecture, delivered at the *Guardian* Hay Festival 2002 and reprinted (in abridged form) in *Guardian,* 8 June 2002.

7 In Findlater, ed., (1981) 148.

8 Rebellato (1999) 215. On the Court's 'freedom from camp' policy, see Rebellato 213-23.

9 Gaskill (1988) 24.

10 In 1961 Coward penned a series of dismissive articles on the kitchen-sink school of drama for the *Sunday Times.*

11 Wardle, 'Vintage Year at the Court', in *The Times,* 'Saturday Review', 5 September 1970.

12 Nightingale, 'How the Court makes a drama out of a crisis', *Daily Telegraph,* 20 September 1988.

13 Printed with other anniversary messages inside the Royal Court Theatre Centenary programme. One omission from the list of directors is Ken Campbell who directed Hawthorne in *Insideout* in 1969.

14 Yeats, 'The Song of the Happy Shepherd' (1885), v.10.

15 *New Statesman,* 24 March 1956.

16 Kidd in conversation with Robert Waterhouse, *Plays and Players,* March 1969, 56.

17 In Findlater, ed., (1981) 61.

18 Eyre & Wright (2000) 251.

19 Recorded in Zucker (1999) 75.

20 In Findlater, ed., (1981) 109.

21 This production premiered at the Royal Court on 24 May 1972.

22 Gaskill (1988) 51. Cf. Aristotle, *Poetics* 1450a: 'Tragedy is not a representation of men but of a piece of action, of life, of happiness and unhappiness, which come under the head of action, and the end aimed at is the representation not of qualities of character but of some action; and while character makes men what they are, it is their actions and experiences that make them happy or the opposite. They do not therefore act to represent character, but character-study is included for the sake of the action. It follows that the incidents and the plot are the end at which tragedy aims, and in everything the end aimed at is of prime importance. Moreover, you could not have a tragedy without action, but you can have one without character-study.'

23 Howell in an interview with Peter Ansorge, *Plays and Players,* October 1968, 71.

24 Gaskill (1988) 95.

25 In a letter of 18 May 1971.

26 Hay & Roberts (1980) 66.

27 Roberts (1999) 124.

28 Gaskill (1988) 68.

29 See Johnston (1990) 243-44.

30 Originally stage censorship was the responsibility of the Master of the Revels, who was subordinate to the Lord Chamberlain and first appointed in the reign of Henry VII to supervise Court entertainments. From 1660 the Lord Chamberlain himself began to intervene directly in censorship and the regulation of theatres. The Licensing Act of 1737 conferred on him the statutory right to issue theatre licences and his powers were modified by the Theatres Act of 1843.

31 Printed in *Sunday Times,* 11 April 1965.

32 This reply was made on 18 January 1968 and reprinted in Johnston (1990) 107.

33 Bond recorded these comments on the Lord Chamberlain in his notebook on 1 August 1965. See Stuart, ed., (2000) Vol 1, 87-8.

34 The Theatres Bill was formally introduced and read for the first time on 29 November 1967. The first draft appeared on 26 January 1968.

35 'Dazed Reception', *Evening Standard,* 1 April 1968.

36 'Shouts and Murmurs', *Observer,* 7 April 1968, 26.

37 Calder and his partner Marion Boyars had been prosecuted under the Obscene Publications Act of 1959 for the publication of Hubert Selby's novel *Last Exit to Brooklyn.* John Mortimer led a successful appeal.

38 'Don't ban this play, just let it fade away', *Daily Telegraph,* 8 April 1968.

39 'Muddled fantasy on brutalization', *Times,* 8 April 19868.

40 'A Dramatist's Choice', *Times,* 10 April 1968.

41 *Plays and Players,* May 1969, 25.

42 *Punch,* 18 September 1968.

43 In Findlater, ed., (1981) 107.

44 *Plays and Players,* November 1968, 19.

45 *The Queen,* 25 September 1968.

46 *Plays and Players,* November 1968, 19.

47 Robert Waterhouse, *Guardian,* 20 February 1969.

48 *Daily Telegraph,* 20 February 1969.

49 See Gaskill (1988) 84.

50 *The Queen,* 20 August 1969.

51 *Daily Telegraph,* 23 July 1969.

52 Irving Wardle, *Times,* 23 July 1969.

53 *Plays and Players,* September 1969, 28.

54 'Smiling view of prison', *Times,* 2 December 1969.

55 'Blistering drama of life in prison', *Daily Telegraph,* 2 December 1969.

56 'New play will go to Royal Court', *Morning Telegraph* (Sheffield), 2 May 1970.

57 Guinness (1996) 192.

58 John Barber, 'Osborne's tingling look at life', *Daily Telegraph,* 18 August 1971.

59 *Plays and Players,* October 1971, 38.

60 *The Tatler,* October 1971.

61 *The Tatler,* February 1973.
62 *Evening Standard,* 8 December 1972.
63 *Guardian,* 5 December 1972.
64 *Sunday Times,* 28 January 1973.
65 In Findlater, ed., (1981) 166-67.
66 *Daily Telegraph,* 25 November 1972.
67 Bennett (1994) 293.
68 *Sunday Times,* 10 December 1972.
69 Ibid.
70 *Times,* 4 August 1970.

Chapter 5

A Strolling Player

A troupe of strolling players are we,
Not stars like L. B. Mayer's are we,
But just a simple band
Who roams about the land
Dispensing fol-de-rol frivolity.
Mere folk who give distraction are we,
No Theater Guild attraction are we,
But just a crazy group
That never ceases to troop.

(Cole Porter, *Kiss Me Kate*)

In a welcome and liberating interlude between Royal Court appearances, Nigel spent most of 1970 in the north of England as a principal member of Sheffield Playhouse's permanent ensemble. It was the last year of the company's occupancy of the Playhouse, a converted British Legion hall, which was to be replaced by the new Crucible Theatre with its thrust stage, minimalist design and doubled capacity. Herbert Prentice started Sheffield Repertory Company in 1923 when he transformed his amateur troupe into a professional one. By the 1960s the company had gained an outstanding reputation for its high standards and productivity, being recognised by the Arts Council of Great Britain as a major repertory group. During the nine months of his tenure at the Playhouse, Nigel was given a wide variety of testing lead roles and the chance to make his British directorial debut (see Chapter 6). In the process he proved himself an intrepid and innovative interpreter of Shakespearean classics and controversial modern plays alike.

What originally drew Nigel to Sheffield was a surprising offer from the Texan-born theatre director Michael Rudman. Rudman was mounting a production of *Henry IV, Part I* at the Playhouse and was determined to have Nigel as his Falstaff. Nigel was considerably more startled than flattered by this proposal, thinking the idea risible. He gently declined the offer, reasoning that he lacked the ample proportions and personality, and the vocal authority necessary to play Shakespeare's corpulent, roistering knight. Rudman persisted and Nigel finally yielded to a fourth entreaty, but his acceptance of the role did not silence his qualms; he still believed that, at forty years of age and weighing twelve and a half stone, he was an ill-equipped and unlikely Jack Falstaff. Yet, he was not normally one to resist an unusual challenge, and, as it turned out, Falstaff was for many years his favourite part and certainly one of his proudest achievements.

Rudman's most significant alteration to the text was his interpolation of the Bishop of Carlisle's curse from Act IV, scene one of *Richard II*, delivered shortly before Bolingbroke's coronation as Henry IV:

> *I speak to subjects, and a subject speaks,*
> *Stirr'd up by God, thus boldly for his king.*
> *My Lord of Hereford here, whom you call king,*
> *Is a foul traitor to proud Hereford's king;*
> *And if you crown him, let me prophesy, –*
> *The blood of English shall manure the ground,*
> *And future ages groan for this foul act;*
> *Peace shall go sleep with Turk and infidels,*
> *And in this seat of peace tumultuous wars*
> *Shall kin with kin and kind with kind confound;*
> *Disorder, horror, fear, and mutiny,*
> *Shall here inhabit, and this land be call'd*
> *The field of Golgotha and dead men's skulls.*

The production began with this prophecy, amplified by echo machine, ringing in King Henry's ears as he lay in bed gripped by nightmare. The device underlined the guilt that dominates Henry's thoughts and actions, and the crime that propagates rebellion and 'civil butchery'. At the close of the production the curse was heard again – with the words spoken by the dead of Shrewsbury battlefield – and thereby encapsulated the play in a dramatic as well as intellectual frame.

The young actor who played Prince Hal was Michael Gwilym, an alumnus of OUDS (Oxford University Dramatic Society) and a future star of the Royal Shakespeare Company. His was an understated and contemplative Hal; as Paul Allen of Sheffield's *Morning Telegraph* put it, he was 'a basically serious-minded undergraduate sorting himself out in London's fleshpots.'[1] He was the perfect foil to his dissolute mentor, Falstaff. Nigel, in fact, acknowledged Gwilym's energising performance as the source of the courage he found in himself to make of Falstaff what he did. He also responded to the younger man's humour and gentleness which reminded him of another precocious acting talent, his school chum Jobie Stewart. The father-son relationship that Nigel and Gwilym developed so well on stage became the basis of their joint adaptation of *Henry IV, Parts I* and *II, Stand For My Father,* written in the run-up to that year's Edinburgh Festival.

Falstaff in *Henry IV, Part I* (1970), with Mike Gwilym (2nd left). *(Courtesy of Sheffield Theatres Trust Ltd)*

Nigel's Falstaff, generously padded and bearded, was the highlight of the production. It was an uncommonly sensitive portrayal which, as Paul Allen discerned, pointed up how flawed and unsatisfactory are the values by which great men live in the public domain, and the hollowness of 'honour' as a worldly abstraction:

> The [...] outstanding feature of the production is a Falstaff from Nigel Hawthorne which enacts with great conviction the theory that the fat knight is Shakespeare's tool for parody and rejection of conventional honour and virtue.
>
> The scene in which he takes time off from marching to war to enjoy a picnic hamper – tiny camper's stool and all – and then gives a dissertation on honour full of Muggeridgian irony (and more than a hint of Muggeridge's voice) is a gem.[2]

One critic proclaimed this Falstaff 'the best I have seen':

He was a marvellous combination of yer Alf Garnett, Terry Scott and Robin Day all rolled in one bucolic ball.

This performance was outstanding in what must be one of the finest productions at Sheffield Playhouse.[3]

In the audience one evening was Kenneth McReddie who had recently set himself up as a London agent. The performance he witnessed filled him with awe:

I was bowled over by this actor of whom I had never heard. I thought, this is absolutely a great actor. This is the real article. He was doing something special. There was a vitality, a sense of depth, a terrific wit in his performance and it was very real. You believed him. He mesmerised you.[4]

McReddie sent a congratulatory note to Nigel and secured the actor as a loyal client for the next thirty-one years.

In late March and April *Henry IV, Part I* ran in repertoire with Peter Nichols's semi-autobiographical first stage play, *A Day in the Death of Joe Egg.* Nigel, the star of both productions, alternated his Falstaff with a very different but equally impressive performance as the demoralised father of a severely handicapped child. *Joe Egg* is the prime example of what Eyre and Wright classify as Nichols's 'comedy of discomfort',[5] and remains his greatest commercial hit in spite of its distressing subject matter and blacker than black humour. First produced at the Glasgow Citizens' Theatre in 1967, under Michael Blakemore's direction, it subsequently ran for several months in London with Joe Melia and Zena Walker heading the cast.

The play analyses the actions and innermost thoughts of Bri and Sheila in caring for their daughter Josephine, a ten-year-old vegetable they have nicknamed 'Joe Egg' after Bri's childhood bogeyman. After a decade of tormented parenthood their marriage is at breaking point. Sheila cannot bear to part with her daughter and clings vainly to the hope that something can yet be done to improve the child's quality of life. Bri, on the other hand, can no longer bear to nurture the irreparably brain-damaged and totally dependent girl. The sick jokes and protective flippancy he has used to cope with the situation give way to attempted euthanasia. His and Sheila's own self-engineered palliative therapy involves re-enacting, as a series of vaudevillian routines, the cycle of Joe Egg's sub-life, and satirising their fruitless encounters with doctors and do-gooders of varying persuasions.

Bri was a demanding role which Nigel played with compassion and without facile pathos. He did not try to soften the character's sense of

Bri in *A Day in the Death of Joe Egg* (1970), with Anne Kristen and Wendy Wax. *(Courtesy of Sheffield Theatres Trust Ltd)*

suffering, outrage or murderous despair. It was an accomplished and finely judged tragi-comic reading of the part.

> *Nichols cheats a bit: he introduces the tragedy only when he has you firmly in his hand with the jokes, and from the beginning it is a mighty manipulation of cast and audience by the author through the character of Bri, the husband whose brittle and explosive (and very funny) charades are a last desperate device to help him deal with a situation which is slipping inevitably away.*
>
> *The play depends on the actor who plays him, and Nigel Hawthorne gives a performance which if anything enhances the good work he is currently doing as Falstaff.*
>
> *From the opening scene he plays off his audience and his fellows in a way which suggests he is really enjoying himself and has not been equalled by anyone else I have seen at the Playhouse in the last two years.*
>
> *With rapid changes of pace and mood, allied to an impressive stage presence, he strings us along on a tide of fantasy and comedy until he can jerk the string and tug us all back to the tragic heart of the matter.*[6]

Robin Thornber of the *Guardian* attributed the production's more than usual honesty and power to the commanding humanity of the central performances:

As it is played at Sheffield Playhouse under the direction of Paul Hellyer, the play seems less of a tract and more of a simple human drama, an honest and revealing account of the strains imposed on the relationship between the parents.

Perhaps it is because in this performance these two actors dominate the stage even more than is usual in this play. Anne Kristen is Sheila, in every weary movement, every knowing grin, every familiar cry of 'Bri'. And Nigel Hawthorne achieves the right balance of sympathy and alienation as Brian the husband, bravely quipping his way out of facing the truth about his subhuman daughter and his equally smothering mother.[7]

Nigel's next Sheffield appearance was in Christopher Wilkinson's confronting first full-length play, *Strip Jack Naked,* which also ran concurrently with the hugely popular *Henry IV.* Wilkinson had worked with Sheffield Repertory for six years as an actor before being awarded an Arts Council Bursary to assist with his fledgling writing career. Director Colin George promptly commissioned a script from him with a view to producing it at the Playhouse. The ensuing work, *Strip Jack Naked,* was a macabre and complicated piece, consisting of a staccato sequence of disturbing scenes that amounted to a surrealist, Kafkaesque persecution pantomime about the brutal infringement of individual liberty. As far as it could be followed, the story dealt with the interrogation and ritualistic degradation of a, possibly schizophrenic, young man by the agents of an unspecified authority, for an unnamed offence.

Nigel received good notices for his performance as Wyngate, the group's chief assailant, but the play scandalised the regional critics. The *Yorkshire Post* set the general tone:

The play is a tale of torment, a perverted view of the savage baiting of the human spirit, relentless and horrible to watch. It is unnecessary and tasteless theatrical nightmare. It is crude in its language and in its thought, for the thought of the spirit of man in torment should have dignity which this play singularly lacks. [...]

The play is stated to be unsuitable for children and I would think distasteful to any intelligent adult other than those who laughed at what they did not comprehend.[8]

The critic for the *Sheffield Star* reported:

If sex, violence, sadism and murder are the makings of a new and exciting play then this one is certain for success. Whether or not Mr Wilkinson absorbed all these factors into one long nightmare for a purpose or for sheer cheap sensationalism is obviously a matter for each member of the audience to decide.[9]

Certainly audiences did decide for themselves the validity of these factors. The play's relentless profanity and nastiness alienated a substantial portion of the Playhouse's faithful supporters and generated a steady stream of correspondence and editorial comment in the local press. Every one of its nine performances was punctuated by patrons' disgusted departures.

At the conclusion of its Sheffield run the production was given a far more suitable venue and presentation when it was staged as a Sunday night club performance at London's Royal Court. With his typical pinpoint accuracy and scrupulous even-handedness, Michael Billington delivered his ruling on the play's problems and merits:

A surrealist nightmare is perhaps the hardest thing for even the most experienced dramatist to try to reproduce in the theatre: for a beginner the task is almost impossible. Watching Christopher Wilkinson's play, brought to town for one night by the Sheffield Playhouse Company, I kept wishing that his evident gift for writing jazzy, nerve-pricking dialogue had been tethered to a theme dramatically within his reach.

In racing parlance, the piece would seem to be by Kafka out of Pinter. [...]

[Wilkinson] mistakenly seems to assume that the nightmarish framework gives him a licence to introduce any amount of wildly sensational material: he forgets that nightmares are often frightening precisely because of their impeccable logic and that in theatrical terms even surrealist material needs to be employed with iron control. Unlike Kafka, he fails to root his fantasy of persecution in explicit prosaic detail: unlike Pinter, he weakens the power of his symbolic intruders by tying them too closely to specific professions.

If he can rid himself of the notion that nothing succeeds like excess, I am sure he will go on to write good plays: the talent for dialogue is already there. Here he is also extremely well served by Colin George's production [...] and by the performances of Nigel Hawthorne as the persecutor-in-chief and Barrie Smith as the anguished recluse.[10]

Over the summer Nigel was stationed at Edinburgh's Traverse Theatre, which American expatriate Jim Haynes had created as a centre of experimental activity outside the intensive three weeks of the city's world-famous Festival. There, in addition to presenting *Stand For My Father*, his first piece of writing for the professional stage (discussed in Chapter Six), Nigel played the sadistic, and eventually emasculated, husband in Tom Mallin's dark sex-war drama, *Curtains*. Directed by Michael Rudman, the production was later remounted at London's Open Space. This was a small adaptable playhouse in Tottenham Court Road, built by Haynes's fellow American Charles Marowitz and Thelma Holt as London's answer to the Traverse. Holt remembers Nigel's first, unpromising association with the avant-garde basement theatre:

> *When I built the Open Space he was part of the Charles Marowitz workshops. He used to tell a wonderful story about Charles taking one look at him during a workshop, when we used to do all these crazy Antonin Artaud things – 'I am a daffodil, I am a daffodil' – and, finding that Nigel wasn't very good at it, telling him not to come back anymore. So Nigel got sent away, which was fun.*

Before returning to Sheffield in the autumn, Nigel appeared at the Traverse in the title role of *Ubu and Ubu are Dead*, a musical biography of the anarchic French playwright Alfred Jarry, who was an important forefather of French Surrealism and Theatre of the Absurd.

In November, while Nigel was playing a fascist Macbeth to great acclaim in Colin George's strikingly imaginative Playhouse production, a feature article in Sheffield's *Morning Telegraph* considered his intelligent and contemporary approach to the classics:

> *As actors go his head is more important than his heart: he prefers to make sense of a play (hence his Falstaff last spring and now Macbeth) than an emotional blockbuster or a slab of dramatic rhetoric.*
>
> *Perhaps because of this he believes that he hasn't the weight for the great classical parts and certainly he has little experience of them, but if you believe, as I do, that the great parts and the great plays need to be reinterpreted by each generation in the manner to which its taste and needs are suited, he is probably as capable as anyone of finding the less towering, more tortured moods demanded by the seventies.*[11]

This appreciation of Nigel's subtle gifts foreshadowed his unconventional reading of King Lear nearly thirty years later. For Nigel the head was not more important than the heart, but making sense of a character's behaviour, and thus making believable his journey, was central to his methods. He was expert at reasoning madness; he could precisely prefigure the elements of irrationality by distilling the sane man's obsessions. His madmen were literate, self-aware characters.

Clad in black leather, and with a sleek scalp, Nigel's Macbeth was a menacing and mesmerising figure of Faustian ambition and weakness. The critics unanimously applauded the articulacy and audacious understatement of the interpretation:

> *At the centre of the whole thing is the Macbeth of Nigel Hawthorne. You will watch in vain for conventional heroics and thunderous speech-making but this is an articulate hero who makes sense of his appointment with doom and whose gradual decline into blood and something like madness is more believable and finally sympathetic than any I have seen.*
> (Morning Telegraph)[12]

> *Not for this ambitious knight the expected orations and over-colourful beating of his brow – but a subtle and cunning approach which lifted the already marvellous production into the masterpiece class.* (Star)[13]

> *Nigel Hawthorne's Macbeth might at first be a highly articulate and sensitive Tamburlaine, and his degradation is finely exploited.*
> (Doncaster Gazette)[14]

The production itself was praised as 'a most unusual interpretation which is stark, barbaric and timeless,'[15] and 'a most telling, consuming, vibrant-with-life-and-meaning presentation.'[16] 'What is so distinguishing about this production', declared the *Star's* drama critic, 'is that it defies all conventional concepts of Shakespeare – and yet is sensationally successful in the bargain.'[17] The costumes and settings were the work of Polish designer Josef Szajna who received a programme credit equal to that of the director Colin George. With the sparest means he created an ambience of monstrous fantasy but, at the same time, naturalistic nightmare. His witches were unearthly creatures, giant white slugs with horribly inflated skulls for heads. Banquo had the appearance of a comic-strip spaceman, and the forest in which his assassination was carried out was illuminated by a hideously glowing moon. Both the staging and Nigel's performance were among the most exciting and cutting-edge in the history of Sheffield Repertory.

Nigel's final performance at Sheffield was as the 14th Earl of Gurney, a paranoid schizophrenic peer who believes he is God, in Peter Barnes's irreverent comedy *The Ruling Class.* The play, originally staged at Nottingham Playhouse and later in the West End, contained a scathing send-up of the extant feudal practice of primogeniture. Its alleged blasphemy and a fleeting striptease ensured that it became an instant *cause célèbre* at Sheffield and reopened the censorship debate two years after the abolition of the Lord Chamberlain's authority to pre-censor plays. Much was made in the press of the fact that Frank Hatherley's production was the first at the Playhouse to feature, however hurriedly, a partially naked actress (Patricia Franklin).

A week after the play opened, a local Conservative councillor, Charles Macdonald, walked out in the middle of a performance, leading other audience members in noisy protest. The walk-out brought a temporary halt to the production as the small band of protestors stood in the Playhouse foyer and shouted their disapproval. Macdonald did not let the matter rest there. He tried to pressure Sheffield City Council, which had a £350,000 stake in the new Crucible Theatre, into exercising some formal control over the material performed there. His comments to the Council concerning *The Ruling Class* were duly reported in the *Star*:

> *The play was blasphemous and portrayed perversion. I don't feel that is suitable for young teenagers and for many mature people.*
> *Some people may be quite happy to grovel in the gutter, but when it gets down to sewer level I believe it is time to make a protest.*[18]

The Council resisted Macdonald's call for state interference in the Crucible's choice of plays, but a fierce war of words raged around the whole issue of theatre censorship and was fought by local politicians and their constituents with equal conviction. Paul Allen, the drama critic for the *Morning Telegraph*, responded to the controversy with a lengthy article, headed 'How to Treat Shock', in which he cautioned against the re-introduction of pre-censorship:

> *If Sheffield City Council had taken up Coun. Charles Macdonald's wish for 'a certain amount of control' over what goes on in the Crucible it would have been the beginning of the end.*
> *Shock is at the root of all the great moments of theatre from the Old Vic to the village hall and from farce to tragedy. Once you set out to guard against some arbitrarily established mark being overstepped you lay a dead hand on the theatre which has crippled it enough times in the past already.*[19]

The controversy did not diminish the enthusiasm which greeted Nigel's performance, possibly his toughest Playhouse assignment. Sporting shoulder-length hair and a white T-shirt emblazoned with the slogan 'God is love', he had to move convincingly from a condition of benign lunacy to the role of 'a vengeful and bloodthirsty Jehova-cum-Jack the Ripper'.[20]

The Barnsley Chronicle announced that Nigel had triumphed absolutely in 'a leading part that would be any actor's dream':

> *It is like a gigantic fireworks display, with brilliant, and often startling, coruscations bursting out in rapid succession at all points of the compass, flashing, crackling and shooting in every direction, a continuous challenge to the ear and the eye, and to the mind which directs and interprets for them.*
>
> *Nigel Hawthorne's 14th Earl is the finest individual performance of the season (and perhaps for some seasons past). The taxing range of the role is encompassed with an apparent facility which can only have stemmed from uncommon ability and total dedication; he deserves a clutch of 'Oscars'.*

In 1972 Nigel broadened his Shakespearean experience when he joined the company of the Young Vic in London's Waterloo. The first Young Vic Theatre opened in 1945 under George Devine's directorship, as part of the Old Vic Drama School, but was disbanded in 1951 owing to financial problems. Its successor was founded by Frank Dunlop under the auspices of the National Theatre. This new theatre opened in 1970 in a converted butcher's shop in The Cut and in the shadow of the venerable Old Vic. Like its post-war precursor, Dunlop's company was committed to presenting, at reasonable prices, professional adult performers in plays suitable for young audiences. Constructed from breezeblock and steel, the building's unprepossessing, functional design reflected the company's democratic, no-nonsense philosophy. The auditorium was a large square space enclosed by tiered wooden benches and penetrated by a long thrust stage. The emphasis of the theatre's productions was on the text and acting rather than elaborate staging, and the aim was to create an informal atmosphere which encouraged audience participation. All this, Nigel quickly discovered, required of the performers enormous energy and concentration. Dunlop, who had formerly been in charge of the Nottingham Playhouse and joined the National Theatre Company in 1967, had about him, as Nigel noted, 'a touch of the Joan Littlewoods'. He favoured a flexible, egalitarian approach to theatre and was an admirer of Theatre Workshop's modernised *commedia dell'arte* techniques.

Nigel's first Young Vic part was Baptista in *The Taming of the Shrew*, which Dunlop directed as a none too subtle but enjoyable and festive farce. The production had opened at the previous year's Madrid Festival and now had an almost entirely fresh cast that included Denise Coffey as Bianca, Trevor Peacock as Petruchio, and Nicky Henson as Grumio. This was closely followed by Dunlop's experimental, and occasionally baffling, concoction entitled *An Alchemist*, mounted in celebration of the quatercentenary of Ben

Jonson's birth. The use of the indefinite article in the title was qualified by the description, 'an entertainment mainly by Ben Jonson.'

A decade earlier at the Old Vic, Tyrone Guthrie had staged a modern-dress version of *The Alchemist* in which he substituted current idioms for Jacobean slang. Dunlop's production, however, was a much more vigorous and wholesale modernisation. The pace was frenzied and the text abounded in anachronisms. Trendy Seventies Chelsea replaced Blackfriars as the play's setting. The programme carried a rationale for the updated allusions and references:

> *Because we would like to achieve something of the outrageousness that the play must have had on its first performance, we have set the play in today and taken some liberties with parts of the play which are in Elizabethan slang and refer to the Billy Grahams, Georgie Bests and Lord Goodmans of Jonson's London. We have tried to find as near as possible exact equivalents for persons and phrases that had an immediate and probably very shocking impact on the original audience.*

The overall effect was boisterous and uneven. It was a highly diverting if unholy alliance between the contemporary insertions and Jonsonian verse. The *Sunday Times* observed that the Young Vic was 'camping uneasily on the no-man's land between classical and modern', and suggested the solution to this stylistic ambivalence might be 'less Jonson and more Dunlop. This is just what happens in the second half, and the show blossoms out into uninhibited (if sometimes overacted) lunacy.'[21]

Nigel appeared as the brazen butler Face, a role played by Ralph Richardson at the Old Vic in 1947. He would have been more cleverly cast in the small part of Face's innocent gull, Abel Drugger, once played by David Garrick and made memorable by Alec Guinness in the 1947 Vic production. But he served his allotted character well, giving him a calm insolence and a military air. J. C. Trewin singled out in his review Nigel's 'zestfully protean'[22] performance, while Eric Shorter said, 'Mr Hawthorne's subaltern-type Face is a general joy.'[23] In July the company took both *The Taming of the Shrew* and *An Alchemist* to Ottawa as part of Festival Canada. It was Nigel's first visit to North America.

Back at the Young Vic the following month he played Brutus, opposite Richard Beale's Caesar and Hywel Bennett's Mark Anthony, in *Julius Caesar* which director Peter James set in a Fascist dictatorship of the 1930s. The setting, designed by John Napier, was an elevated rostrum resembling the Victor Emmanuel monument, fronted by a battery of microphones and backed by imperial standards bearing the state insignia of two jagged streaks of crimson lightning. The conspiratorial senators were represented as 'thin-lipped gauleiters in high jackboots'.[24] Fascist renderings of Shakespeare's tragedies about totalitarian regimes had not quite become the theatrical cliché they are now considered, but critics already treated them with some weariness and circumspection. In the case of James's version the transposition worked well up to a point but, as Nicholas de Jongh of the *Guardian* argued, the parallels between first-century BC Rome and the Axis powers of the 30s were sometimes 'confused' and 'strangely perfunctory'.[25]

Interestingly, in view of Nigel's earlier performance in Theatre Workshop's *Mrs Wilson's Diary*, his Brutus was described by the reviewer for the *Sunday Times* as 'a worried little figure peering up through gold-rimmed spectacles, [who] kept reminding me of Mr Roy Jenkins.'[26] In *Punch* Jeremy Kingston wrote:

> *Nigel Hawthorne's good performance as the brooding Brutus, a civil servant ordering everything by the book, almost persuades one that the character is as noble as everyone says — and his own lines contradict. The 'Portia is dead' description emerges as an encouragement to stoicism not an act of hypocrisy.*[27]

Alan Riddle of the *Daily Telegraph,* however, believed Nigel's Brutus to be more good than noble, but he demonstrated that the actor's more muted interpretation of the great Shakespearean roles did not lack power or resonance: 'he spoke the line "Look in the calendar and bring me word" with a resonant quietude that sent a chill up my spine.'[28]

After its triumphant showing at the 1971 Edinburgh Festival, Frank Dunlop's whimsical production of *The Comedy of Errors* was invited back for the 1972 Festival. With a new Young Vic cast that included Nigel as the bewildered Duke, the revival was staged inside a circus tent within the Haymarket Ice Rink. Taking more liberties with the text than any production since Komisarjevsky's in 1938 at the Shakespeare Memorial Theatre, Dunlop's *Comedy of Errors* was credited to 'William Shakespeare and others'. The action was translated from Ephesus to Edinburgh with accents to match. The play was presented more in the fashion of a revue and began with community singing of the songs of Scotland, led by Ian Charleson. After repeating its success from the year before, the production was given a short season of three and a half weeks at the company's London home. This was Nigel's last appearance as a permanent member of the Young Vic. He returned briefly to the company ten years later in the rather tired vehicle *John Mortimer's Casebook.*

Late in 1973 Nigel reunited with Michael Rudman, who was now Artistic Director of Hampstead Theatre Club, for the British premiere of Austrian playwright Peter Handke's *Der Ritt über den Bodensee (The Ride Across Lake Constance)*. The play was first staged in Berlin in 1971 and a year later in New York. It is one of several provocatively anti-theatrical investigations by Handke into the problems of language and communication. Subtitled 'Are You Dreaming or Are You Speaking', it shows how people can become imprisoned by language. Four women and three men, who are identified only by the actors' given names, express themselves, and interact with each other, purely by means of fascinating but inconsequential word patterns or through stereotyped phrases and gestures. But lurking beneath the strange, and often witty, dialogue are a nameless anxiety and lethal terror. The play is the dramatic translation of an old German legend about a horseman who sets out on a winter's day to cross Lake Constance and, as darkness falls, loses his way. He reaches a village and, upon asking some of the inhabitants how he can traverse the lake, is told that he has already managed to cross the lake's thin surface of ice. The horseman then realises the danger he has unwittingly escaped and drops dead from fright. W. Stephen Gilbert, writing in *Plays and Players,* emphasised the 'foreignness' of the play's preoccupations and structure, and the subliminal depths of the author's loaded word games:

Handke is a writer who does away with surface altogether. He writes, as it were, from the nine-tenths of speech and behaviour that go unsaid and undone, rather than the one tenth that passes right through the system and actually communicates itself to others. In Lake Constance *we see not so much an edgy encounter between several persons, in what is presumably the neutral ground of an hotel, as a subterranean account of unexpressed desires, fears, fantasies, nightmares and manoeuvres in a game of dominance and submission.*[29]

The Ride Across Lake Constance provoked and perturbed many of the critics. J. C. Trewin admitted the task of explication was beyond him: 'It seems to me to be an anti-play; further than that I cannot go',[30] while Milton Shulman remarked dryly that the play's obscurity, by comparison, made 'Harold Pinter as crystal clear as Beatrix Potter'.[31] Michael Billington prefaced his brave attempt at interpretative paraphrase by confessing:

I sometimes wish that instead of dramatic criticism I had chosen one of life's simpler, less demanding jobs like that of senior mathematician,

Arctic explorer, or Foreign Secretary. I would not then be expected to produce instant elucidation of plays like The Ride Across Lake Constance.[32]

By contrast, Harold Hobson of the *Sunday Times* seemed singularly and proudly unflummoxed:

When I saw it the first time The Ride Across Lake Constance *seemed to be, theatrically speaking, a very simple play; and this impression was strengthened at a second visit, when I was more than ever struck by the sheer dazzling brilliance of the performance and production. Nevertheless, I cannot deny that many people whose acuity of mind and theatrical judgement and experience are not to be questioned consider it to be almost incomprehensible.*[33]

The play's enigmatic quality did little to inhibit its success, and on 12 December, exactly one month after its opening, it transferred to the Mayfair Theatre.

To tackle this extraordinary, and extraordinarily difficult, piece Rudman had assembled an enviable cast of strong personalities. Together with Nigel were Nicky Henson, Alan Howard, and the glamorous female quartet of Jenny Agutter, Faith Brook, Gayle Hunnicutt and Nicola Pagett. Hobson declared the company to be 'the finest example of ensemble acting to be seen in London.'[34] Irving Wardle of *The Times* likened the perils that the actors faced to the legendary horseman's plight:

There are on stage a group of actors who, no matter how well they have rehearsed, are always liable to go through the ice. By a typical Handke paradox, their task is to convey the terrors of stage fright by never putting a foot wrong.

They certainly achieve this in Michael Rudman's superbly cast production. Mr Rudman has rightly looked beyond the film stereotypes of the script and chosen actors of powerfully individual presence.[35]

Stephen Gilbert was not altogether impressed with the production but named Nigel, with his verbal dexterity and strain of controlled anarchy, as its most redeeming feature:

Only Nigel Hawthorne is at home, convincing that those lines actually are coming blithely off the top of his head. His stream-of-consciousness soliloquy is a gem of comic timing, balance of effect and nuance. It's a truly Milliganesque performance that lifts the play.[36]

The following year Clifford Williams invited Nigel to play Touchstone in a revival of his famous all-male production of *As You Like It*. It was seven years since the production had first been staged at the National Theatre, and now, by arrangement with the National, it was to tour North America, beginning at the Geary Theatre in San Francisco and finishing up at the Mark Hellinger Theatre on Broadway. In spite of the fact that he deemed the role incorrigibly unfunny, Nigel was keen to go to America and to make his Broadway debut. He accepted Williams's offer but was then confronted with the seemingly impossible job of giving his character a convincing comic dynamism. In the original production Derek Jacobi had played Touchstone as a Frankie Howerd figure. Nigel conceived the idea of crafting his portrayal as an impersonation of W. C. Fields. He carefully studied recordings and old footage of the American vaudevillian and film star, and delivered his closely observed impersonation at the read-through of the play. When no mention was made of the originality of his reading, Nigel lost heart and by the first rehearsal had abandoned the idea of the impersonation. He reverted to a straighter and, as he felt, flatter interpretation.

The tour lasted six months with little or no time between engagements. The venues in which the company played were disconcertingly vast and the actors were forced, for the sake of audibility and visibility, to scale their performances accordingly. Subtlety had swiftly to be dispensed with. But if the cross-country tour had its discouraging elements, the Broadway run of just five performances was disastrous. The New York critics dismissed the production as a pale imitation of its resoundingly successful original. Clive Barnes listed among its faults a loss of sweetness; an over-emphasis on the transvestite aspect; and an outdated sense of Carnaby Street pop and swinging Shakespeare. He also believed that the play was undercast; only one member of the company had actually appeared with the National Theatre proper. His passing and faintly approving comment on Nigel's performance was that he had 'some nicely broad moments.'[37] Notwithstanding its multifarious disappointments, Nigel always regarded the tour as an exciting and valuable experience.

Up until this point Nigel had been attached to various theatre companies. In the second half of his career he emerged as very much an individual artist. Even when he worked with the illustrious Royal Shakespeare Company and National Theatre, he was his own man and a star in his own right.

Notes to Chapter 5

1   Paul Allen, 'Not a school book Shakespeare', *Morning Telegraph* (Sheffield), 5 March 1970.
2   Ibid.
3   'An outstanding Falstaff', *Star* (Sheffield), 5 March 1970.
4   Interview with Stephen Pile, 'The Fortunes of Nigel', *Telegraph Magazine*, 19 April 1992.
5   Eyre & Wright (2000) 331.
6   Paul Allen, 'Humour and Tragedy of Joe Egg', *Morning Telegraph* (Sheffield), 26 March 1970.
7   *Guardian*, 26 March 1970.
8   Desmond Pratt, 'A nasty way to empty theatres', *Yorkshire Post*, 1 May 1970.
9   'Mesmerised into a very unpleasant stupor', *Star* (Sheffield), 30 April 1970.
10 'Nightmare enough', *Sunday Times*, 10 May 1970.
11 Paul Allen, 'A South African speaks out', *Morning Telegraph* (Sheffield), 30 November 1970.
12 Paul Allen, 'Macabre Macbeth is a hit', *Morning Telegraph* (Sheffield), 22 October 1970.
13 'A triumph for the Playhouse', *Star* (Sheffield), 22 October 1970.
14 *Doncaster Gazette*, 30 October 1970.
15 Ibid.
16 Paul Allen, 'Macabre Macbeth is a hit', *Morning Telegraph* (Sheffield), 22 October 1970.
17 'A triumph for the Playhouse', *Star* (Sheffield), 22 October 1970.
18 'Councillor accuses Playhouse of sinking to "sewer level"', *Star* (Sheffield), 3 December 1970.
19 *Morning Telegraph*, 5 December 1970.
20 M. H. Stevenson, 'Penetrating questions on sanity', *Daily Telegraph*, 19 November 1970.
21 *Sunday Times*, 11 June 1972.
22 *Lady*, 29 June 1972.
23 'Glib Bawdry To Relieve Monotony', *Daily Telegraph*, 9 June 1972.
24 Jeremy Kingston, *Punch*, 6 September 1972.
25 *Guardian*, 23 August 1972.
26 *Sunday Times*, 27 August 1972.
27 *Punch*, 6 September 1972.
28 'Magic plus meaning in Caesar', *Daily Telegraph*, 23 August 1972.
29 *Plays and Players*, December 1973, 48.
30 *Lady*, 29 November 1973.
31 'Thrown in at the deep end …', *Evening Standard*, 13 November 1973.
32 *Guardian*, 13 November 1973.
33 'Horsemen, pass by', *Sunday Times*, 9 December 1973.
34 Ibid.
35 *Times*, 13 November 1973.
36 *Plays and Players*, December 1973, 49.
37 *New York Times*, 4 December 1974

INTERVAL

Chapter 6

Changing Direction

WRITING AND DIRECTING FOR THE STAGE

'The real voyage of discovery consists not in seeking new lands,
but in seeing with new eyes.
(Marcel Proust, *Remembrance of Things Past*)

In the theatre Nigel was happiest, and at his most commanding and assured, as an actor. Performance was certainly his most eloquent and expressive mode of communication, but his artistry and ambition were not confined to the performative sphere. Just as many established writers and directors can be frustrated performers at heart, conversely, actors, being natural storytellers, may often covet the autonomy and control apparently enjoyed by their creative arbitrators, the playwright and director.

Nigel was a highly intelligent and articulate actor with the rare advantages of directorial acumen and literary sensitivity. From early on he acquired a thorough understanding of the entire process involved in the making of theatre. He wrote in his spare time and relished the chance to direct. As his career progressed, lack of time and opportunity meant that his significant excursions into writing and directing for the stage were infrequent, even haphazard or digressive in nature. What is more, his talents in these fields were both overshadowed and subsumed by his prodigious acting talent.

Nigel's small body of work as a professional playwright and director was eclectic and quirky and, like his far more sizeable acting record, a testament to his versatility. It is also interesting for what it reveals about his *modus operandi* as a performer as well as his theatrical and broader outlook. In common with his acting counterpart, Nigel the director was an ideas man, inventive, adaptable and discriminating. Similarly his dramatic prose displayed something of the facility, clarity and elegance that distinguished his acting, and something of the same whimsy and observation. His auxiliary skills as writer and director made him a multi-faceted theatre practitioner, and they enriched, and gave added finesse to, his performance work. It is no coincidence that the person who exerted the greatest influence on him professionally was Joan Littlewood, a woman who, in defiance of the conventional theatrical hierarchy, famously bestowed on the writer, director and actor equal creative status and whose methodology incorporated the insights and practical experience she had gained in all three capacities. She understood how vital it was for actors to have not only the freedom to explore and experiment, but also an authorial right to make artistic decisions and alterations.

Every part Nigel undertook, particularly in his later years, was informed by the critical and analytical faculties of a director allied to an actor's good sense and intuitive notion of what would and would not work. Without being at all clinical in his approach, he was able to step back from his character and assess the degree of workability or suitability of the slightest detail in the context of the whole play. Instances of this directorial detachment occurred several times during rehearsals for *The Madness of George III* and were, paradoxically, a consequence of the degree to which he was involved with his character. 'Nick, I've got an idea!' became his catchphrase and a standing joke among the rest of the cast who trailed admiringly and exasperatedly in the wake of his powerful, watchful imagination. One of the endings Alan Bennett originally envisaged for the play had the King reappear amid his squabbling physicians and ministers and explain to them the future course of his illness and its eventual diagnosis as porphyria. Nigel managed to persuade Bennett that such an anachronistic expedient would undermine the emotional integrity and force of the play, that he could not so easily divest himself of his character and, if he did, the audience would feel cheated.[1] Writers and directors were not always as amenable as Bennett and Hytner to Nigel's back-seat direction and editing, but most were forced to concede that his instincts were usually flawless.

As an actor Nigel's relationships with directors were often characterised by a wariness on both sides. He responded most positively to directors who, like Hytner, were happy for him to find his own imaginative horizons:

> *The sort of directors that I work best with are those who don't try to pin me down; who don't say 'Yesterday you did it like that, and I like it that way', because that hems me in. Most directors will want to work towards an opening night, and that's the thing I want to work away from. I don't want an occasion, I want more of a happening. I think directors either steer clear of me, or they go along with it.*[2]

Thelma Holt, who first knew Nigel as a struggling fellow actor and years later produced his West End directorial debut, recalls that his director's shrewdness and resourcefulness were evident from the start:

[At the time of Talking to You*] I was aware that he was a good actor, but I was too young to appreciate how much a good actor. My first appreciation of Nigel and what he had to give to other members of the profession was when we did* A Doll's House *which was directed by Jimmy Roose-Evans, Hampstead Theatre Club. And on* A Doll's House, *like everybody who ever does that play, there were enormous problems, and Nigel had in him then, though he would deny it, the instincts of a director. Whereas most actors when things are difficult have … a survival instinct is very obvious in actors, you know how to survive, you've got your little box of tricks and you delve deeply into it in order to compensate for whatever is wrong with either your performance or the production. In Nigel's case – and I'm sure Jimmy Roose-Evans would not take this amiss – I don't remember the direction I got from the director (and Jimmy's a good director); what I do remember is the direction I got from Nigel Hawthorne, and I was in my twenties and he was great.*

In South Africa in the late 1950s and early 60s Nigel had directed four shows, all rather lightweight vehicles with little or no scope for injecting serious political and social comment despite the momentous nature of the times, but through which he proved himself a deft engineer of comedy and revue. Ironically, the first play he directed in England provided him with the means to make a bold statement about the political situation in South Africa and to expose in cathartic fashion the sorrow and impotent fury he felt towards the deeply divided and troubled society of which he had been part. This was Edward Bond's *Black Mass,* a short one-act play[3] in his *Sharpeville Sequence: A Scene, a Story and Three Poems,* written for the Anti-Apartheid Movement and first produced at London's Lyceum Theatre on 22 March 1970 for the Sharpeville Massacre Tenth Anniversary Commemoration Evening. In December of the same year Nigel, through his personal friendship with Bond, obtained the playwright's permission to stage his own lunchtime production of *Black Mass* at the Sheffield Playhouse where he was currently based. Characteristic of Bond's provocativeness, savage comedy and surrealism, the plot entails Christ's place on the cross being assumed by a succession of policemen after he poisons the South African Prime Minister with communion wine. In Nigel's production the character of Christ was played by Duncan Preston and the Prime Minister by Sam Kelly, while Colin George, who ran the Playhouse, took the part of the Priest. *Black Mass* was the only play Nigel directed in which he did not also act.

Four days before the performance Nigel gave an interview to Paul Allen of Sheffield's *Morning Telegraph* under the heading 'A South African speaks out'. In this he confessed his motivation in directing the play:

One of the things I want to stress is the terrible ease with which one can accept a high standard of living – a servant, a couple of cars, a sun that never stops shining, lots of fruit, cheap meat.

It can happen in a matter of weeks. Your servant comes in drunk one day and you suddenly realise how much ruder you are being to him than you would ever be to a white charwoman.[4]

Allen postulated that the ease with which Nigel's initial shock in 1957 at the way people behaved to each other wore off 'may indicate an element of expiation in Friday's production, an atonement.'[5] In 1968 Nigel had returned to South Africa to see his dying father and on this occasion the shock did not dissipate. He was appalled at the insularity of white South Africans (including his family), the poverty of the black population, and the ludicrousness and obscenity of official policy. During his visit, at a party held in his honour, a woman said to him dismissively, 'You know your trouble: you're a humanitarian.' The fact that she intended this as an insult, and that at the same time he felt himself rebuked for his passive brand of liberalism, remained with him. He told Allen:

I hope it [the production] will be of some significance. The point is there are thousands of people like me, English people who have gone out there. It is not all something to do with a foreign country 6000 miles away. I don't think people can say they are not involved. We all are.[6]

In order to underline their involvement and the danger of complicity through inaction and indifference, Nigel devised a daring plan to make the audience part of the drama and the system it attacked. He arranged for two types of tickets to be issued at the box office – white and coloured. A few minutes into the play the house lights suddenly went up and two actors in the guise of Afrikaner policemen walked on stage to announce that, as it was illegal for holders of coloured tickets to occupy seats other than in the last two rows, all tickets would be subject to inspection. Undergraduates from Sheffield University then entered the auditorium bearing torches and proceeded to inspect the audience's tickets. Patrons with coloured tickets were herded into a pen at the rear of the auditorium before the play was allowed to continue. Tickets were again scrutinised at the interval and the same law of segregation enforced. The bar was partitioned, with drinks served in glasses on the spacious and comfortably appointed white side and in paper cups on the cramped and primitively furnished coloured side. Even the use of the lavatories was controlled by strict observance of the colour divide.

The audience readily co-operated in their brief initiation into apartheid conditions. The play was well received and Nigel's comprehensive plan to include the audience in the action enhanced the message at its core. Information about the work of the Anti-Apartheid Movement together with its membership forms were made available at the Box Office counter where anti-apartheid posters could be purchased. Playhouse patrons were also able to sign forms of declaration for presentation to the Commonwealth Prime Ministers' Conference which was held in Singapore the following month.

If *Black Mass* showed Nigel at his most political and penitent, his next major project as a director, exactly twenty-four years later, showed him at his most mischievously and unashamedly camp, his most irresistibly droll. In December 1994 he directed and starred in Thelma Holt's revival at the Queen's Theatre in Shaftesbury Avenue of the Georgian comedy *The Clandestine Marriage* by David Garrick and George Colman the Elder. The play is a genial satire on the pragmatic matchmaking between the rich social-climbing merchant class and the impoverished aristocracy, in which noble actions save the day and young love triumphs. It had last been staged in London by Ian McKellen in 1975 at the Savoy Theatre with Alastair Sim as the delightfully decrepit Lord Ogleby, a part he had previously performed at Chichester in 1966. Sim's association with the role was no doubt partly what attracted Nigel to the play. *The Clandestine Marriage* was also one of the first productions he had seen on his arrival in London in 1951 when Donald Wolfit played Lord Ogleby at the Old Vic. But like so much of his career, Nigel's West End directorial debut owed more to chance than to premeditation.

Having recently completed both the stage and film versions of *The Madness of George III*, he was approached by Thelma Holt to appear in a play she had in mind to produce, which was not *The Clandestine Marriage*. She remembers how Nigel gently thwarted her plans:

> I asked him to do another play, I had another play in mind, and he came back immediately with, 'Can I ask a rhetorical question?' I said, 'What is it?' He said, 'I don't want to do this play, but I would like to do The Clandestine Marriage.' And I said, 'Well, I know The Clandestine Marriage *was done in the early 70s at the Savoy. I don't think I've read it, Nige. I don't think I've ever read the play* The Clandestine Marriage *and*

I certainly haven't seen it.' He sent me a copy. I got it that day, he had it biked over. I rang him up. It was clear that it was a cinch for him, it was great. I said, 'Come and have lunch,' and we had lunch just round the corner [from Holt's office in Aldwych] and we started to talk about who could play things in it, ideas about directors. It was a very lovely, casual lunch. And then he started talking about his costume and he said, 'I have this idea that I'd wear those beautiful little Louis heels and we'd all have these grey shoes, but my stacks would be painted red.' And I said, 'Only your stacks?' And he said, 'Mmm. Everybody else can just have the grey proper shoes but I want red stacks, and then this jacket will obviously be made by a very wonderful tailor and should be a sort of faded pink ...' And I stopped him and said, Nigel, I don't actually think you should do the costumes for the play but I think you should direct it.' And he went, 'Oooh! [squeal of surprised delight] I can't do that.' I said, 'Well, I don't know who we're going to get to direct you because you've obviously sunk into the play', which, of course, is Nigel's thing. He was already there. I can't think of a director who is going to want to direct a play when, weeks before you've even started, you've painted your heels, your stacks, red. He said he couldn't, he was sixty-five. I said, 'What do you mean you're sixty-five? You'd better do it quickly, dear, while you're still alive. Do it now!' And he was persuaded to do it across the luncheon table.

While the part of the rheumatic roué Lord Ogleby, a vain but ultimately magnanimous old popinjay, was clearly meat and drink to Nigel, as the director of a large West End show he had some unfamiliar and invidious responsibilities to shoulder. Holt and her managerial team quickly discovered that, when it came to casting decisions, Nigel did not have in him the streak of ruthlessness which is a necessary component of the director's job description:

It was absolutely wonderful, it was a joyous time. We got together the most marvellous cast. But there were actually sixteen people in it and the first ghastly we had was that we did all the auditions here in the big room at the end of the corridor and people were going out all grinning and smiling and waving, and everybody Nigel met thought they were in the play. I had about 150 actors to get rid of. He didn't know how to say, 'Go away, I don't want you,' so he was offering everybody work and if he wasn't actually offering it, he was implying an offer by his general demeanour of 'It's wonderful seeing you, I'm longing to see you again.' Actors interpret that as an offer, they go home and tell their agent they got a job, which, of course, they hadn't. So we dealt with that very well, but we could have cast the play twenty times by the time he'd finished.

The resolution Nigel lacked in the audition room he more than compensated for in the rehearsal room. He was a dedicated and wise leader of a company, a mix of amiable paterfamilias and stern taskmaster, and, as Thelma Holt observed, his preparation and investigation into the text were exhaustive:

God help anybody who goes to a first rehearsal not knowing what the play is – they don't have to know what it's about – and not having read it extremely carefully, because Nigel will have done enough homework to sink a ship. When we came to rehearsals for The Clandestine Marriage *they all got the usual shock you get with Nigel because the book is down before the end of the first week and it's very clear from day one that he's not looking at it. He does tremendous homework.*

He is the most patient … he's certainly one of the most sensitive men I've ever known. He's very sensitive to atmosphere, he knows if people aren't feeling happy without them saying anything, he's delicate. He is mortified if he feels that in any unintentional way he has ever given offence, but when he encounters somebody who is sloppy or has not given a piece of work the respect it merits, he can be very, very acidic and very unforgiving. He doesn't like it and that's the work ethic which results in this incredibly delicate attention to everything he does, incredibly delicate.

Illustrative of Nigel's delicate attention to detail were things like the red Louis heels he insisted on for Lord Ogleby and the eccentric stage props he invented such as a pedal-powered rowing boat and a shaggy lump of carpet masquerading as a dog. He also came up with the idea to stage one of the indoor scenes outdoors, deploying the actors as walking garden hedges, a clever and amusing piece of choreography. But Nigel felt that his attempts to emphasise what he regarded as the play's vital element of vulgarity were frustrated by Timothy O'Brien's too tasteful and restrained set designs.

After a successful tour of Newcastle, Malvern, Guildford and Bath, *The Clandestine Marriage* opened in London on 5 December, the same day on which the film *The Madness of King George* was seen by the American critics. There was generally high praise for Nigel's portrayal of Lord Ogleby: 'a ruthlessly observant but deeply generous performance […] a jewel of a performance, lovingly crafted and irresistibly appealing'[7] ruled the *Sunday Times,* while the *Sunday Telegraph* declared, 'As the arthritic old gallant Lord Ogleby, Nigel Hawthorne confirms – if confirmation is needed – that he is a comic actor of the first rank.'[8] Nicholas de Jongh wrote in the *Evening Standard:*

Lord Ogleby remains the satirical centrepiece: this rouged, tottering relic, an ancient Narcissus still trying to rise to romance's challenge, despite rheumatic joints, is deftly played with valiant, careful swagger by Hawthorne in lilac stockings and gaudy accessories.

And there's a beautiful interjection of comic pathos when the wig slips to reveal the bald truth. But Hawthorne misses Ogleby's preening affectation and gleeful insincerity. Perhaps he's too truthful an actor for this mendacious role.[9]

Charles Spencer of the *Daily Telegraph* believed Nigel had found his finest comic role since Sir Humphrey:

The actor's leery smiles of complacent delight when he believes his love is returned are a joy to behold, but he makes the character much more than a laughing stock. After the farcical capers of the final act, with the whole cast rushing about in their nightshirts, he belatedly realises what an ass he has made of himself and reveals a real generosity of spirit. It is a lovely moment and Hawthorne plays it to perfection.[10]

Many of the reviewers, however, reacted less enthusiastically and with some suspicion to Nigel's twin role as director, possibly viewing it as an actor's hubristic overstepping of the mark. Nigel had deliberately not tried to superimpose onto the text any political or social agenda of a personal or contemporary nature. He chose instead to direct the play as a jovial, warm-hearted romp, scattered with pathos, an approach some critics found old-fashioned and unsatisfying. Nicholas de Jongh, in particular, regretted the absence of 'real social cut and thrust beneath the surface fun' and felt that Nigel had missed 'the thoroughly English obsession with class' in order to exploit the 'comic ructions' of the secret marriage and multiple misunderstandings. By contrast, the critic for the *Observer* caught the mood Nigel was aiming for, describing his 'spartan, grotesque direction' as 'a joy'.[11] Michael Ward of the *Sunday Times* applauded the 'skill, pace and elegant invention' with which Nigel directed the play. In the *Financial Times* Alastair Macauley noted perceptively in relation to Susan Engel's interpretation of Mrs Heidelberg, a termagant with fashionably deformed vowels: 'That such a performance can flower here is credit to Hawthorne; so is the very acute playing in small roles.'[12]

In 1999 *The Clandestine Marriage* was translated to film in a splendidly crisp adaptation by Trevor Bentham, who had left stage management in the early 1980s to become a screenwriter. Nigel reprised his role as Lord Ogleby although the rest of the cast, headed by Joan Collins and Timothy Spall, was entirely new. Shot on location in Gloucestershire, the film was directed by Christopher Miles but the finished product was largely the result of Nigel's careful editing with Trevor as patient collaborator.

Nigel's passion for research, his gift for textual analysis and for collating historical and biographical facts, was something he nurtured outside his job as an actor and which frequently fed into his writing pursuits. For example, resting between work in the late 1960s he began studying the Russian Revolution, spending many hours in the British Library Reading Room. His focus was the brutal execution of Tsar Nicholas II and his family, and the events immediately preceding this, by which he was moved and fascinated. Out of his intensive research he produced a script, provisionally titled *Mind the Steppes* and giving what he styled 'the Marx Brothers'-eye view of the Revolution'.

One evening backstage at the Royal Court during the run of *Early Morning*, Nigel's agent introduced him to the twenty-year-old pop singer and songwriter Cat Stevens who confided to Nigel his thoughts of writing a stage musical. Without any hesitation Nigel offered to send him his Russian Revolution script and, to his astonishment, Stevens expressed instant enthusiasm. Over the next three years the two worked extremely happily together on *Revolussia*, composing somewhere in the region of fifteen songs. Unfortunately, after such a pleasant and fruitful partnership the project was never completed as Stevens eventually opted to concentrate his efforts on his concert work and Nigel's script remained unproduced.

However, another work on which he collaborated at about the same time did reach the stage. In the summer of 1970, following on from the huge success of *Henry IV, Part I* at the Sheffield Playhouse, Michael Rudman, then in charge of Edinburgh's Traverse Theatre, invited Nigel and Mike Gwilym to devise a show, as a prelude to the annual Festival, based on *Chimes at Midnight*, an amalgamation by Orson Welles of *Henry IV, Parts I* and *II*. Nigel and Gwilym accepted the challenge and, writing under the pen-names John Hudson and Francis Coleridge, they concocted *Stand For My Father*, an adaptation which pared away the plays' political concerns and consolidated the scenes involving Hal's real father (Henry IV) and his father figure (Falstaff). Gwilym played Hal, Nigel doubled as King Henry and Falstaff, and his old friend Jobie Stewart was cast in the roles of Justice Shallow and Mistress Quickly. *Stand For My Father* was enjoyable to perform, but it was treated by the critics as something of a curiosity piece, and its audiences were rather sparse.

Nigel's first major solo effort as a playwright was his double bill *Sitting Ducks* which premiered at the Soho Poly in Oxford Circus on 29 March 1976 under Andrew Carr's direction. The Soho Poly, a lunchtime theatre and one of London's first fringe venues, had showcased the early work of writers such as Timberlake Wertenbaker, Sue Townsend, David Edgar, Barrie Keefe, Sam Shepherd, Caryl Churchill and Pam Gems, providing several of them with their big break. *Sitting Ducks* comprised what were essentially two monologues: 'Prompt!', set in a seedy summer season repertory theatre with shades of Osborne's *The Entertainer*, and 'Mummy', set in an Edinburgh hospital ward.

The first of these was a tableau depicting 'the desperation of an ageing minor actor alone on stage without a prompter before an audience'.[13] Currently appearing at the Queen's Theatre in the long-running *Otherwise Engaged*, Nigel himself featured as the woebegone actor Harry Figdore, a prosecuting counsel in the last act of a tatty murder thriller, applying Leichner in his dressing room and oppressed by nightmarish fancies. The critic for the *Daily Telegraph*, Eric Shorter, judged the monologue Chekhovian in style and said, 'Mr Hawthorne brings to this particular plight a skilful and pathetic sense of comedy.'[14] Of Nigel's performance as Harry, Michael Coveney in the *Financial Times* wrote:

> *Mumbling what he can remember of the script, scowling at the absent stage-management, frothing at the absurdity of his physical plight – Mr Hawthorne presents a touching spectacle of sweat and confusion before being submerged in the National Anthem and jolted from discomfort by his half-hour call.*[15]

In 'Mummy', the second more-or-less monologue, Nigel's friend Joyce Grant played the part of a garrulous and overbearing mother, fussing at the bedside of her critically ill son, a probably homosexual film star. Although in the play the woman is Scottish, according to Joyce Grant Nigel 'based the character on the mother of a dear friend he had in South Africa who was a brilliant young actor and something of a tragic figure. The mother was disappointed in her son. She was typical of certain narrow-minded South African women, a very unsympathetic character.' Putting Eric Shorter in mind of 'a sketch by the late Tony Hancock',[16] 'Mummy' suffered from weak direction and was the less successful of the two pieces, but both plays were entertaining and showed a good sense of tragi-comedy.

Despite his desultory forays into other theatrical disciplines, Nigel was always and primarily an actor. The intelligence and sensitivity that informed and shaped his acting not surprisingly sought other means of expression. In those pursuits, however, he was experimenting and extending his gifts, and his main course, indeed, his life's journey, remained the same. The distinguishing factor common to all his creative work was a truthfulness, an imaginative precision.

Notes to Chapter 6

1 See Bennett (1992) xix.
2 In Zucker (1999) 72-3.
3 In a letter to Tony Coult on 16 September 1971, David Jones, the play's original director, called it 'very much an extended review [sic] sketch'. See Hay & Roberts (1980) 112.
4 Interview with Paul Allen, 'A South African speaks out', *Morning Telegraph* (Sheffield), 30 November 1970.
5 Paul Allen, 'A South African speaks out', *Morning Telegraph* (Sheffield), 30 November 1970.
6 Interview with Paul Allen, 'A South African speaks out', *Morning Telegraph* (Sheffield), 30 November 1970.
7 Michael Ward, *Sunday Times,* 11 December 1994.
8 John Gross, *Sunday Telegraph,* 11 December 1994.
9 *Evening Standard,* 6 December 1994.
10 *Daily Telegraph,* 7 December 1994.
11 *Observer,* 11 December 1994.
12 *Financial Times,* 6 December 1994.
13 Eric Shorter, 'Skilful sense of comedy', *Daily Telegraph,* 31 March 1976.
14 'Skilful sense of comedy', *Daily Telegraph,* 31 March 1976.
15 *Financial Times,* 31 March 19776.
16 Skilful sense of comedy', *Daily Telegraph,* 31 March 1976.

ACT TWO:

The Arrival

(1975-2001)

For I have learned
To look on nature, not as in the hour
Of thoughtless youth; but hearing oftentimes
The still, sad music of humanity.

(William Wordsworth, 'Lines composed a few
miles above Tintern Abbey', ll. 88-91)

Chapter 7

Joining the Establishment

PRIVATES ON PARADE AND SIR HUMPHREY

*The most perfect caricature is that which, on a small surface,
with the simplest means, most accurately exaggerates,
to the highest point, the peculiarities of a human being,
at his most characteristic moment in the most beautiful manner.*

(Sir Max Beerbohm, 'The Spirit of Caricature')

By 1975, the halfway point in his career, Nigel was nearing the end of his prolonged 'struggle for dignity and justification, to prove that I'd made the right decision to be an actor in the first place.'[1] Since his permanent relocation to England thirteen years earlier he had survived a rigorous apprenticeship with those famous and opposite bastions of Britain's theatrical avant-garde, Theatre Workshop and the English Stage Company, and in studying and adapting their discrete methodologies he learnt as much about himself and what he valued as an actor as he did about his craft. His role in *The Philanthropist* in 1973 had paved the way ahead for him, unlocking his most deep-rooted inhibitions and arming him with a new confidence, a confidence paradoxically grounded in his admission of fear and emotional assailability. The next twelve years witnessed a series of professional milestones for Nigel, including his overdue first appearances with the two pillars of the acting establishment, the Royal Shakespeare Company and the National Theatre, and the invention of *Yes, Minister* and *Yes, Prime Minister,* which made him an internationally celebrated star and a cherished national institution. It was a time of constant employment. He was much in demand in two media and able finally to pick and choose his assignments. During these years a major change occurred in the public consciousness and critical reception of Nigel's dramatic powers. He had long been recognised as an eminently watchable and clever character actor, an always surprising support act. Now he was beginning to be appreciated as a leading player of venerability and *gravitas;* as one journalist phrased it, he was the 'scene-stealer grown to master practitioner'.[2]

To this period between the mid-1970s and mid-1980s belong two of Nigel's best-known and most lauded characterisations, Major Giles Flack in

Privates on Parade and Sir Humphrey Appleby in *Yes, Minister,* which exemplify the essence of his genius, namely his magical transformation of caricature into something palpably real and richly textured. On paper both men are caricatures of quintessentially English species of authority and fanaticism: Flack, a patrician army officer in the Montgomery mould, is a fervent, wonderfully obtuse and dangerously misguided muscular Christian, while Sir Humphrey, a suave and supercilious mandarin and potent mixture of sophist and sophisticate, Mephistopheles and Machiavelli, is the supremely smug face of faceless officialdom. In Nigel's hands they became extraordinarily believable, sympathetic and appealing characters as he dared to expose their complexity and humanity.

Before these roles launched him into the upper echelons of his profession, Nigel enjoyed successful London runs in two new plays. The first was Simon Gray's *Otherwise Engaged,* which opened on 30 July 1975 and reunited Gray with the director and star, respectively, of his acclaimed *Butley* (1971), Harold Pinter and Alan Bates.

The basic plot of *Otherwise Engaged* concerns the frustrated attempts of the selfish and emotionally disengaged central character, publisher Simon Hench, to listen in peace to his new recording of Wagner's *Parsifal.* His carefully erected sanctum of calm is invaded by a steady stream of unannounced visitors – his objectionable, scrounging upstairs lodger; his pitiable and paranoiac schoolmaster brother; a drunken critic; a ruthless young author and temptress; a morbidly obsessed old schoolfellow; and lastly his unfaithful, exasperated wife – each one presenting a sub-plot of extreme anguish and personal disorder to contrast with Simon's cruel, impenetrable equanimity. Harold Hobson characterised Simon, 'in the witty urbanity of his detached mind,' as 'the West's fine flower after the lifeblood has departed from it,' and observed that structurally the play was 'the brilliant converse of Alan Ayckbourn's *Absent Friends.* Everyone comes to comfort Ayckbourn's hero, though he is in no need of comfort. Gray's hero, on the other hand, is in most desperate need, though he does not know it himself; all his visitors are themselves in search of comfort.'[13] The poet and critic Craig Raine offered this eloquent appreciation of a difficult and determinedly unsympathetic dramatic creation, a character that hardly changes from beginning to end:

> *Simon Hench, the hero of Simon Gray's excellent* Otherwise Engaged, *exists at the still point of the turning world. Lapped in contentment, he just doesn't want to know about the centrifugal stresses on the outer edges where normal people live. [...] Like a comic Mersault, he picks his way through normality with a dazed indifference, a detachment almost self-centred, and, as in*

L'Etranger, attracts the bitter hatred of the conventional who resent his straightforward hedonism and his rejection of the boring myths which corrode pleasure. Insulted by his philosophical attitude, knowing their delimited place in his consciousness, the normal megalomaniacs wage a dullard vendetta against his impregnable calm. No one likes to be tolerated – it dwarfs our self-importance. Simon is too clear a mirror, too exact a yardstick: facing him, the other characters know the precise dimensions and the intimate details of their failure to succeed and be happy.[4]

Interesting comparisons can be made between Simon and the title philanthropist of Christopher Hampton's long-running third play, another literary type prone to pedantry and whose equilibrium is endlessly threatened. Each is the passive centre within a small universe of intellectual and emotional flux, but whereas Philip's passivity is a condition arising from his defeatism and pliancy, Simon's similarly dogged passivity, his emotional stasis, functions as a carapace with which he lethally repels true feeling. It is fascinating, therefore, to consider what Nigel, perfect in the part of the put-upon Philip, might have made of the complacent, imperturbable Simon. But the role went to Alan Bates who proved ideal casting, and when he left the production the following February, owing to other commitments, he was replaced by the equally effective Michael Gambon.

Nigel played Simon's elder brother Stephen, a failed teacher at Amplesides, a very minor public school, desperately seeking the Assistant Headmastership by swallowing his fragile pride and the Headmaster's wife's herbal coffee, nut cutlets and pansy wine. As a playwright Simon Gray is very adroit at communicating with great economy the personal and psychological history of his characters, and he was well served in this respect by Nigel's performance. Nigel was consistently singled out by the critics for his moving realisation of this deeply unhappy, excitable and ridiculous schoolmaster. He achieved tragic depth as well as comic precision. In his published journal Gray recalled:

During the early rehearsals of Otherwise Engaged *Alan Bates and Nigel Hawthorne were physically incapable of getting past a moment when Nigel Hawthorne, playing a minor-public-school teacher, had to step forward and announce aggressively, 'I am the latent pederast.' Both Alan and Nigel doubled up with laughter again and again. Weeks later, when the same moment arrived before an audience, they were bewildered by its reacting exactly as they once had done. Within a few nights they'd not only come to expect the response, but had incorporated it smoothly into their performances, and might even, if they had been less puritanical performers, have found themselves milking it by prolonging it a little.*[5]

The rest of the production's blue-chip ensemble consisted of Julian Glover, Mary Miller, Benjamin Whitrow, Jaqueline Pearce and, in his first West End role, Ian Charleson, a gifted and charismatic young actor who had performed with Nigel in the Young Vic Company and who delivered an unforgettably powerful Hamlet at the National in 1989 while terminally ill with Aids. *Otherwise Engaged* received all the year's awards for Best Play, although its press night was slightly overshadowed by the off-stage drama attending director Harold Pinter's highly publicised impending divorce from his actress wife Vivien Merchant.

In the week before the play's pre-London premiere in Oxford, Alan Bates gave an interview to the *Evening Standard* in which he commented on Pinter's main strength as a director:

He is an actor and a writer and as a director he's there for the sake of the author and actor and at the end that's what the word director is about. He's there to present the play written by someone else, not to try and say he's the great wizard of all time. I learnt that from Lindsay Anderson.[6]

As a fellow writer and as a director Pinter had a special affinity with Simon Gray and the two collaborated on several projects. Having begun his career performing in weekly rep and never really abandoned acting, he could also empathise with, and minister to, the needs of his company of players. He understood, for instance, how important it was for actors to be free to explore and to make mistakes, and that a surfeit of input from the director early on in rehearsals only inhibited their progress. His approach was an editorial one. He was able to accommodate the actors' individual working methods, to allow them to undertake their own journey. Nigel, in particular, responded extremely well to this style of direction which afforded the actors considerable creative latitude.

Towards the end of the run Nigel appeared as Touchstone in a revival of Peter Gill's production of *As You Like It* which had first been staged by the Nottingham Playhouse for the previous year's Edinburgh Festival. The revival, with a cast that also included Zoe Wanamaker, Jane Lapotaire, John Norrington, John Price and Malcolm Ingram, was performed on the evening of Sunday 30 May 1976 as a part of the opening festival of the Riverside Studios, an arts centre housing a theatre and cinema as well as concert, dance and exhibition spaces. Situated on the banks of the Thames in Hammersmith, the venue was originally a foundry and converted into film studios between the wars. At one time, with the BBC as lessee, it became the largest television centre in Europe and the first to broadcast colour television. Gill's *As You Like It* was tailored especially to fit the informal scenery of the new Studios and featured alongside the professional actors local musicians and child acrobats. Audience involvement was encouraged and during the interval the spectators gathered around a Punch and Judy show.

In profiles of Michael Frayn's work, Tom Courtenay is usually credited as the original star of the writer's 1976 comedy *Clouds,* but, although he headed the play's transfer to the Duke of York's, it was Nigel who created the lead role of Owen. *Clouds* premiered in August at Hampstead Theatre where it broke box-office records. It was the fifth play, and the second at Hampstead, in which Nigel was directed by Michael Rudman.

This was six years before Frayn achieved instant commercial success and attracted worldwide attention for his brilliantly conceived farce-within-a-farce *Noises Off.* He made his theatrical debut in 1970 at London's Garrick Theatre with a collection of four short plays under the title *The Two of Us,* but he was already an established novelist and journalist, a former columnist on the *Guardian* and *Observer.* After he left the *Observer* in 1968 he continued to contribute features to the paper on foreign countries, including a substantial piece on Cuba[7] of which *Clouds* is clearly a by-product.

The play's setting, according to the programme, is 'Cuba. Or, at any rate, an empty blue sky', and its focus a journalistic junket. The main characters, Mara and Owen, are English writers sent to Cuba by rival colour supplements to report on life after the revolution. Their companions on the tour of the country are their Cuban guide Angel, their cigar-smoking driver Hilberto, and an idealistic American academic named Ed. Frayn had read Moral Sciences (i.e. Philosophy) at Cambridge in the 1950s and in his dramatic writing he regularly explores philosophical ideas through comedy and farce. Many of his plays reflect Wittgenstein's concerns with the relationship of reality and perception, as he readily points out:

What they are all about in one way or another, it seems to me, is the way in which we impose our ideas upon the world around us. [...] The world plainly exists independently of us – and yet it equally plainly only exists through our consciousness.

Clouds is an entertaining though not terribly profound meditation on this question of objective reality, its premise being that the characters' responses to an unfamiliar land are primarily determined by what they think and feel, and that what they think and feel is affected by what they see. Michael Billington of the *Guardian* said that Frayn 'says something useful about the visitor abroad seeing a country through the prism of his own particular emotional state. [...] Above all, the play questions the whole notion of documentary reporting.'[8] The play's anonymous *mise en scène* was a playful challenge to the audience's assumptions concerning material reality and progress; the action unfolded against a set comprising only a multi-levelled platform, a table and six continually rearranged chairs.

Owen in *Clouds* (1976), with Barbara Ferris and (front row, l. to r.) James Berwick, Paul Chapman and Olu Jacobs. *(John Haynes / The Raymond Mander & Joe Mitchenson Theatre Collection)*

The *Sunday Telegraph* greeted *Clouds* as 'far and away Michael Frayn's best play to date,'[9] while the majority of reviewers thought it engaging but, as a dramatic and philosophical construction, rather slight. J. C. Trewin in the *Birmingham Post* judged it 'not so much a play as a sequence of mood impressions, as fleeting as the clouds,'[10] and in the *Daily Telegraph* Eric Shorter wrote: 'the whole entertainment gives an impression of having been stretched beyond its theatrical reach – a lengthy feature article, satirical and well-turned but flourishing best in descriptive rather than dramatic passages.'[11] There was general praise for Frayn's acute wordplay and Rudman's fluid and assured direction, but the play really owed its box-office success to the acting of the principals.

The comic burden of the evening was carried by Nigel who, in Milton Shulman's alliterative phrase, played the neurotic and cynical Owen with 'dithering disdainful delight'[12]: 'A born worrier, combining anxiety and fanaticism unleavened by humour, Mr Hawthorne is not only totally convincing but also hilariously funny.'[13] Two particularly revealing observations were made of the performance. Michael Billington noted how physically expressive an actor Nigel was:

> The play [...] elicits a marvellous comic performance from Nigel Hawthorne as the waspish Fleet Street scribe. His body is constantly alive with ire, illness, depression or exhilaration, and he even manages to turn a tentative love-affair into a source of fret.[14]

Robert Cushman's analysis of the character of Owen perceptively identified in Nigel's interpretation a peculiar truthfulness, subtlety and ingenuity, and just as accurately describes what Nigel accomplished with his next stage character Major Flack:

> The gentleman, given an enchantingly bilious acidity by Nigel Hawthorne, is inclined to slight the achievements of the revolution, and even more inclined to slight those of his competitor. [...] He proceeds to exclaim 'Oh God!' three times. There is no great passion in the exclamations; they are rattled off in a vein almost of self-caricature. For a moment I suspected Mr Hawthorne of stylising his performance, then realised that in fact he was giving a wholly realistic performance of a man who stylises his own life.[15]

Among those who saw and admired *Clouds* was playwright Peter Nichols, a near contemporary of Frayn's and, being similarly lean and bespectacled, some say his doppelgänger. Nichols had recently finished his latest play, a tragi-comic scrapbook of memories from his unconventional National Service, which was initially working-titled *Malayan Moonshine* and later *Jungle Jamboree*.

Late in 1976, while visiting his old friend and co-writer Mike Gwilym in Stratford, Nigel faced a rare embarrassment of riches. Having been emphatically ignored by the Royal Shakespeare Company and the National Theatre for years, he suddenly found himself being resolutely courted by both companies simultaneously with two tempting new scripts. The National offered him Alan Ayckbourn's *Bedroom Farce,* and the Royal Shakespeare

Company Nichols's *Jungle Jamboree,* now definitively retitled *Privates on Parade.* No sooner had Nigel opted to do the former than he was approached by a small but distinguished deputation made up of Ian McKellen and Judi Dench, who were currently performing in Trevor Nunn's production of *Macbeth* at The Other Place, and persuaded to join the National's marginally older rival instead. It was typical of the way in which Nigel's career developed, however, that his debut with this illustrious classical institution, the cynosure of his youthful dreams, was not made in Stratford but at the RSC's London home, the Aldwych Theatre, where the accent was on new plays and non-Shakespearean classics. Moreover, this particular new play could with some legitimacy be classified a musical and, a decade earlier, would have kept the Lord Chamberlain and his infamous blue pencil busily employed.

Peter Nichols maintains that he can only write dialogue when he hears people's voices in his mind and that his writing comes from memory and imitation. Like so much of his work, *Privates on Parade* is strongly autobiographical. Following on from *Forget-Me-Not Lane* (1971), in which Nichols recalls his adolescence in the 1940s, it is based on his experiences in post-war Singapore and Malaya as a troupe member of CSE, Combined Services Entertainments (or Chaos Succeeds ENSA, according to Nichols), in company with John Schlesinger, Stanley Baxter, Kenneth Williams and a succession of hopeful tap-dancers, accordionists and impressionists. Nichols claimed that it was in CSE – against a backdrop of spirited, makeshift revue, guerrilla warfare, corruption and suicide – that his education began:

> *I read* The Ragged Trousered Philanthropists *and Bernard Shaw's* Political What's What *and became a lifelong leftie. Stanley Baxter explained Existentialism and the rest of us nodded intelligently, lounging in our Chinese kimonos, smoking through cigarette-holders. We even had a sub-culture – the world of queans [sic] with its own lingo and world-view.*[16]

It occurred to him some years after he resumed civilian life that this colourful sub-culture, and the crisis which had made such strange bedfellows of the army and show business, provided ample material for a potential stage play. 'My first shot at it,' he said, 'was made when Danny La Rue was unknown, glamorous drag confined to gay clubs and the 1940s still too close to be camp.'[17] He subsequently revised the idea of the show twenty times or more, but it was not until December 1974 that he applied himself in earnest to its construction, by which time Jimmy Perry and David Croft had stolen some of his thunder with their immensely popular BBC1 sitcom *It Ain't Half Hot Mum.* A much less subtle effort than their first classic creation *Dad's Army,* this focused on a Royal Artillery concert party in India at the end of the war, the comic predicament of 'a load of poofs' under the charge of a bawling, homophobic Welsh sergeant-major. Undeterred, Nichols began collecting facts and anecdotes for his play, enlisting the aid of 'the unofficial archivist of that brief outpost of showbiz',[18] the troupe's conjurer Rae Hammond, who had transferred to CSE from the Intelligence Corps. He eventually showed the script to another of his old CSE comrades, Kenneth Williams, who recorded his reactions in his diary:

> I read Peter Nichols' play Privates on Parade. He's done some clever and adroit things with it but the obscenity and blasphemy are unwarranted: the second half is not as good as the first and a proper dénouement is lacking. The character Terri (based on Barri Chat I should think) is a gift for somebody. He's got a capacity for creating an evil and corrupt atmosphere of astonishing nastiness, with amazing economy.[19]

Set in 1948 during the Malayan Emergency, *Privates on Parade* details the exploits on and off stage of the eclectic conscripts to SADUSEA (Song and Dance Unit South East Asia). Among the military mummers are a callow new recruit, a foul-mouthed Brummie corporal, a brutal and crooked sergeant-major and an outrageous queen, Acting Captain Terri Dennis, modelled, as Kenneth Williams correctly assumed, on the civilian dancer and drag artiste Barri Chat. Dennis, with a voice that is 'Shaftesbury Avenue pasted over Lancashire' cautions an NCO, 'You dare speak to an officer like that I'll scream the place down!' and uses an exclusively feminine nomenclature (hence Bernadette Shaw, Clementina Atlee, Georgina the Sixth and even Jessica Christ). His musical repertoire consists of full-blown impersonations of Marlene Dietrich, Vera Lynn, Carmen Miranda and Noël Coward.

The unit's commanding officer, Major Giles Flack, is 'a spare ascetic man, authoritative, quiet, with the air of an earnest scoutmaster'. He tries solemnly to inject military discipline upon the tide of camp and chaotic entertainments ('no perfume on guard duty, eh? No mufti either. Properly dressed, fixed bayonets.'), and remains oblivious to 'polari', the macaronic theatrical slang. He toasts with lemonade 'the defeat of Communism in South-East Asia Command Malaya and Singapore and the victory of Christian enlightenment' and treats a suicidal mission into the jungle against the Chinese communists as a *Boys' Own* adventure. Moreover, he routinely addresses his men in what he fondly imagines to be their accustomed vernacular:

Now some of you may be saying 'Yes, that's all very well, but law-luv-a-duck, we're only peace-time conscripts waiting for the boat back to dear old Blighty.' And others may say 'but cor-stone-the-crows, this is a non-combatant unit after all.' But, as we see from last night's episode, we are *a military target.*

Unlike many of the characters in the play, Flack bears no resemblance to his counterpart from Nichols's days in CSE. He was an imaginary fusion of Baden-Powell and Field Marshal Montgomery, with an onomatopoeic surname (i.e. flak = anti-aircraft fire). The invention of this character lent the show much of its intended satirical flavour, as Nichols outlined in his diary during his research:

I've been reading about the Malayan emergency for the new play, now retitled Jungle Jamboree, *which suggests a cheap show and carries undertones of Baden-Powell. The Chambers gives 'jamboree' as a great Scout rally' but lists the origin as unknown. Partridge traces it to US, 1872. I always thought it was out of Afrikaans by old* Be Prepared *himself. Anyway the Boy Scout tinges are right for my view of the Malayan 'war' as described in such accounts as* Jungle Green *by Arthur Campbell MC, an officer with the Suffolks who operated in the Kuala Lumpur region, which shows the viewpoint of the professional soldier. His tone of voice will fit my officer commanding, to set the decent and dutiful viewpoint against the hedonism of the old-queen dancer who becomes his second-in-command.*

Montgomery's books are also hilarious – Forward to Victory *and* The Path to Leadership, *exhortations to soldiers and when all of them had been demobbed, to youth leaders and Mothers' Unions. Sad, funny and frightening all at once.*[20]

A lot of the play's humour derives from the collision of cultures between the professional trouper Terri Dennis and the professional soldier Major Flack. The casting of Denis Quilley and Nigel in these polar parts was inspired. Nichols originally wanted Stanley Baxter to play Terri, or failing him Kenneth Williams, but the director Michael Blakemore wisely pointed out that the presence of either star comedian would overbalance the show. The playwright, however, had reservations about the suitability of Quilley, who was Blakemore's suggestion, an undoubtedly versatile performer but perhaps too masculine a personality: 'I'd seen him as *Candide* [in 1959] and in revue, so knew he could sing and dance as well as play straight. But wasn't he too straight? Certainly not the campest actor around.'[21] During rehearsals Quilley quickly dispelled any doubt that he could camp with the best of them, while Nigel, who actually was homosexual, slipped consummately into the role of the officer who is 'straighter than a Roman road'[22] and to whom the theatre is a closed book. Nichols remarked, 'You believed that Nigel was a soldier. He had the bearing of a soldier. He was strong and tall and looked dignified and robust.' But this authoritative portrayal very nearly never was.

Early on in the rehearsal period Nigel had serious thoughts of quitting the production, convinced of his own inadequacy. He experienced the same sense of displacement and isolation that had plagued him during rehearsals for *Oh, What a Lovely War!* What was happening to him was a reflection of his character's position in the show. Flack is a solitary and abstemious figure whose attempts at bonhomie are awkward and often embarrassing. At one point he confides to the young private whom he has taken a fatherly shine to that 'Command can be lonely.' Nigel the actor felt similarly cut off from the other members of the cast who all had musical numbers to perform, and he could see no means of bringing to life what appeared to be a humourless and unpopular caricature. Two weeks into rehearsals Peter Nichols returned from Minneapolis, where he was Visiting Playwright at the Guthrie Theatre, to find Nigel alone and unhappy:

> *He was walking around very depressed and I buttonholed him in one of the anterooms at Floral Street [the RSC's rehearsals rooms in Covent Garden]. He said he didn't know what he was doing with the part, he was going to let me down, and he couldn't see his way forward at all. Then he suddenly got it.*

Nigel discovered the key to his character quite by accident, as a result of two insignificant typographical errors in the script of the Major's long funeral oration, which he delivers in Act I, Scene 11 at the grave of the miscreant sergeant-major who has been murdered. The sermon, as Nichols wrote it, begins:

> *We mourn the loss of our comrade-in-arms. Both as a man and a Company Sergeant-Major, Mr Drummond deserved the admiration of us all. Not least in his attention to detail.*

In Nigel's copy of the text the first full stop was printed after 'Sergeant-Major', and the second had been replaced by a comma. When Nichols casually indicated these mistakes at a rehearsal, the subtle discrepancy in the punctuation triggered in Nigel a brainwave that was the breakthrough he needed. He decided that an odd alternation between enjambment and sudden, unaccountable pauses was idiosyncratic of the dotty Major's speech. What had simply been an erroneous reading of the text became a studied and consistent component of Nigel's performance, a distinctive and dislocated verbal rhythm out of which the whole character evolved.

Privates on Parade opened at the Aldwych Theatre on 22 February 1977. The Royal Shakespeare Company had not been Nichols's first choice as producer. The Bristol Old Vic turned the play down on the grounds that its patrons were 'not yet ready to hear Our Lord referred to as "Jessica Christ".'[23] Denis King composed the show's ten musical numbers, including the title anthem; an Astaire-Rogers pastiche 'Better Far than Sitting This Life Out'; and 'Could You Please Inform Us', the best song Noël Coward never wrote. The three-hour show had plenty of dark elements – Nichols originally conceived of a much more 'raw and Brechtian'[24] play about war – but it was also a tremendously enjoyable song-and-dance extravaganza infused with bitter-sweet nostalgia. In a review for *Plays and Players* Charles Marowitz traced the dominant tone of *Privates on Parade* to the uncomplicated, morally clear-cut and unmistakably British war films of the 40s:

> *Peter Nichols' newest play is full of solid, old-fashioned virtues. There is a maze of story-line; a lot of sympathetic, clearly delineated characters; an unmistakeable sense of location; tenderness, conventional morality, comedy, high-spirits and human reassurance. [...]*
>
> *The show strongly resembles the war-films from which so much of its nostalgia is derived. [...]*
>
> *These films were invariably filled with colourful characters who, despite their outward flippancy, were cast in the heroic mould. [...] They were as distinct as* Commedia dell'Arte *types. [...] It was a universe as ordered as Shakespeare's; as circumscribed by Christian values as the Elizabethans were by the chain-of-being. [...]*
>
> *Nichols' play is rooted in that kind of simplicity. [...] Mainly it is demonstrating a kind of playwriting which hasn't been around for a very long time, which indeed has fallen out of fashion. [...]*
>
> *As a piece of comic engineering, one must salute the ingenuity that could construct such a play in the 1970s. To be so profoundly tuned into the ambience of another time and to be able to work it to your advantage, is no mean feat. Although it is not uncritical of those halcyon years, it is palpably affectionate about them, and to encounter a play motivated by affection rather than social loathing or class prejudice is itself a rarity these days. [...]*
>
> Privates on Parade *is a displaced Ealing comedy; a delayed legacy from the Boulting Brothers. It is 'the play of the film' and if nostalgia, now waning,*

ever gets a second wind in England, it could be Lew Grade's next big cinematic blockbuster. In so being it will have found its most natural form.[25]

The play was lavished with honours, including three Society of West End Theatre (SWET) Awards (renamed the Laurence Olivier Awards in 1984), the *Evening Standard* Award for Best Comedy, and, to Peter Nichols's amazement, an Ivor Novello Award for Best Musical. Nigel's superlative Major was decorated with the SWET and Clarence Derwent Awards for Best Supporting Actor. The London critics were deeply impressed by the richness, delicacy and originality of the performance, and most made mention of the vocal peculiarities Nigel invented for Flack. Charles Marowitz summed up the character with admirable precision:

Nigel Hawthorne, playing the kind of deadly British officer whose historical prototype is Haig and whom Guinness played to perfection in Bridge on The River Kwai, *is the very embodiment of county values, militarily displaced. In a highly eccentric but entirely appropriate drawling rhythm, Hawthorne doodles little details around this Blimpish Major whisking him away from caricature just long enough to remind us the type is rooted, not in stage-history, but in the country manors of England. It is a beautifully-observed, precisely escalated characterisation.*[26]

Michael Billington, always an admirer of Nigel's imaginative range and physical inventiveness, wrote:

Nigel Hawthorne's Major, bristling with mad enthusiasms, swinging his legs like stilts, gives a major creative performance. In his vocal, physical and emotional observations Mr Hawthorne is faultless and extracts every nuance of humour.[27]

B. A. Young of the *Financial Times* was particularly entertained by Flack's readiness 'to go into an improving speech to his men about their duty to God and King, his gently rolling periods given sudden emphasis on the final words of each speech.'[28] In the *Daily Telegraph* Frank Marcus, commenting generally on how Nichols and the company had made the characters sympathetic and human, said:

The author's compassion ensures that we come to care for this absurd band of idiots, and the actors are so marvellous that they are capable of suggesting the truth behind the caricatures with a mere look or a gesture. [...]

Nigel Hawthorne's Major is a blinkered but zealous advocate of a somewhat simplistic kind of Christianity. He is a buffoon, but also suggests an innate decency. It is a subtle, as well as uproariously funny, performance.[29]

According to Peter Nichols, Nigel captured superbly the major's blind zeal, his rugged piety and devout belief in God as the ultimate Englishman:

Flack was marvellously obtuse as a character and Nigel got that beautifully. He characterised even Jesus as a sort of officer type, very much as Montgomery did. Montgomery used to go around for years after the war being muscular Christian to everybody and talking about the army as the world's finest youth club.

In the show Nigel had a limited amount of singing and dancing to do and with this he coped exceedingly well, remaining at all times true to his character. At the conclusion of his absurd eulogy he sang a short solo, 'The Prince of Peace', a mock hymn in the vein of 'Onward Christian Soldiers':

Behold the army of the Prince of Peace
Conquering that his kingdom may increase
Taking to some distant Asian shore
His cleansing and redemption evermore.

Major Giles Flack (centre) in *Privates on Parade* (1977), with (l. to r.) Ben Cross, Tim Wylton, Simon Jones, Emma Williams, Ian Gelder and Denis Quilley. *(Donald Cooper/Photostage)*

In Act II, Scene 4, in preparation for their doomed expedition up-country, Flack puts his men through a refresher course in basic training, during which they sing and countermarch to 'Privates on Parade'. In the middle of this number Nigel, reprimanding a flight-sergeant for blasphemy, sang, or rather said to music:

> *Wise soldiers generally refrain*
> *From taking Jesus' name in vain.*
> *One day you'll need to call him in the clamour of a war*
> *Then he would say 'Look here, you've often called on me before.*
> *I'm an extremely busy bloke.*
> *You shouldn't use my name in joke.'*

To the accompaniment of the next few bars of music, he then went into an eccentric dance which was so unexpected and so delightfully executed that every night it got a round. Nichols remembers that 'when the audience applauded Nigel used to motion them, in a self-effacing manner, to stop, as if to protest, "No, no, no, I'm not worth it." It was a lovely little thing he did.'

Nigel's performance was a funny, surprising and acutely observed portrait of a ridiculous and deluded paternalist. It was also at times a profoundly moving and unsentimental study of a lonely, well-meaning and decent man. At the end of Act II, Scene 2, after his interview with Steve, the lad for whom he displays a genuine affection and concern, Giles, alone on stage, composes aloud a letter to his wife:

> *Dear Margaret, there's a young soldier here I'd like to invite down to the mill-house when I get home. Decent, intelligent boy, very much the kind I'd have liked as a son, had God so willed. He's in a spot of bother at the moment but I mean to help him out of that. As I would my own.* (Moving off, putting on his cap) *How splendid your roses winning first prize again this year ...*

As Nigel spoke these words the stiffness and absurdity of his character disappeared to reveal a very human figure. He brought a simplicity and pathos to the scene which were, like so much of his interpretation, unpredictable and commanding.

In his autobiography *Indirect Journey*, published in 1978, the critic Harold Hobson, whom Eyre and Wright label 'a Christian uplift-chaser',[30] identified *Privates on Parade* as one of two plays[31] in which he had encountered, and been most deeply stirred by, 'a faith absolute and compelling'. This was quite an astounding admission as Hobson was, as a rule, no champion of Nichols's work. The playwright had been especially angered by what he regarded as Hobson's subjective, short-sighted and commercially damaging assessment of *A Day in the Death of Joe Egg*.[32] But it was Nigel's transcendent performance, rather than any reform or recantation on Nichols's part, to which the critic attributed the momentary miracle of theatre he witnessed in *Privates on Parade*, an experience he defined as nothing short of an epiphany:

> *It would be a very risky thing to attribute to Peter Nichols the beliefs held by this Major, who is on every possible occasion held up to the audience's derision. Flack is, in fact, a reactionary of extreme folly and incompetence. He is well-meaning, but preposterous. He has the ridiculous idea of talking to his men in their own language, of which his mastery, to say the least, is not unqualified. In Malaya he leads them just about as incompetently as it is possible to do. Nichols encourages the audience to jeer at him as a figure of fun who totally misunderstands everyone he meets and every situation he finds himself in. He reaches the summit of absurdity when at the funeral service held for a particularly foul-mouthed sergeant he thinks it appropriate to apply to him the tremendous words in which John Bunyan described the death of Mr Valiant-for-Truth (which he symbolizes in the crossing of a river): 'And so he passed over, and all the trumpets sounded for him on the other side.' It would be difficult to conceive of anything more ludicrous than this, and it is quite possible that Mr Nichols intended it ludicrously. But at that moment one of those miracles of the theatre happened when in an instant the whole mood of a play and of its audience becomes transformed. The change does not come gradually, like the bud of the spring, nor the dawning of the day. Suddenly where all was barren the harvest shines with gold; where was total darkness, there is the blaze of eternal light; where, in Major Flack, there had hitherto been nothing but folly, there came over him, as he spoke the magnificent and wildly incongruous words, something very like sublimity. Nigel Hawthorne, who played the Major, spoke them with such certainty and commitment that the spirit of jeering was silenced in our realization that, whatever might be the case with us, this ridiculous officer could actually hear the triumphant peal of the ringing trumpets which are in heaven. I have known people, a theatrical manager of long experience among them, who at this moment in the play, such being the grandeur of Nigel Hawthorne's performance, could not restrain their tears.*

One of the legion of admirers Nigel received backstage was the RSC's Artistic Director, Trevor Nunn, who embraced him exuberantly and pleaded,

'Please, please, please promise me that you'll join the company and come to Stratford.' Nigel muttered under his breath, 'I've been trying to get to bloody Stratford since I was twenty-one!'

At the Aldwych *Privates on Parade* ran for a limited season of fifty packed performances. Almost exactly a year later the show transferred to the Piccadilly Theatre, which was temporarily housing some of the RSC's productions prior to the opening of the company's new London base, the Barbican. When he was asked by the RSC whether he would be willing to continue in his role for the remounted production, Nigel vacillated. He had achieved his most outstanding success so far in *Privates on Parade* but under trying circumstances and after a good deal of angst, which he was not eager to revisit. While he was deliberating, he was contacted unexpectedly by Trevor Bentham who had been offered the job of company manager on the production and, being in a similar quandary, sought Nigel's advice.

Having first met at the Royal Court in 1968 Nigel and Trevor had seen little of one another over the next few years, but in 1975 they found themselves working on Shaftesbury Avenue at the same time. Nigel was performing in *Otherwise Engaged* at the Queen's and, three doors down at the Lyric, Trevor was stage and company manager for Lindsay Anderson's productions of Ben Travers's *The Bed Before Yesterday* and Chekhov's *The Seagull*. On matinée days Nigel and other members of the cast would go for tea at Cranks on Carnaby Street, Britain's first vegetarian restaurant. Most weeks they were joined by Trevor who recalls that during those relaxed afternoons he and Nigel 'just got on terribly well. We liked each other very much.' Unbeknown to them at the time, their mutual decision to sign on for the Piccadilly production of *Privates on Parade* was to change both their lives.

Both men were going through a troubled period in their personal lives and their despondency drew them closer together. Trevor's partner, an Australian actor named Kevin Lindsay, had died from a heart attack four years earlier, while Nigel was feeling increasingly trapped in his unsatisfactory relationship with Bruce Palmer with whom he was sharing a house in Islington. Trevor frequently drove Nigel home after the show and the friendship that developed between them was the beginning of a long and loving union which lasted until Nigel's death. They eventually set up home together on the outskirts of London and later in rural Hertfordshire where they became highly active in the local community, especially as fund-raisers for several charities.

As he approached fifty, Nigel had finally discovered his soul mate. In an interview two years before he died he said of his partnership with Trevor:

We are very like brothers. We think exactly the same way, we have the same tastes, the same sense of humour. There is a very good relationship between us. I couldn't have wished for a better one, really.[33]

Nigel and partner Trevor Bentham on holiday in Venice. (Courtesy of Trevor Bentham)

It is impossible to overestimate the importance of this extremely happy and solid relationship to Nigel's career and it is no coincidence that Nigel began to enjoy enormous success on stage and television at the same time as he began his life with Trevor. Out of his new personal and domestic contentment grew a greater professional confidence, as Trevor modestly explained:

He was quite inhibited generally. Certainly when I first met him he was a very shy man, he didn't come forward at all. In fact, one thing I noticed during rehearsals was he always used to sit in the background, looking somewhat aloof I have to say. He later confessed it was because he wished he wasn't there. That was very typical of Nigel. He was very insecure and that changed for him really, I suppose, at the time of Privates on Parade *when for the first time people began to notice him. Then, I suppose, because he found somebody who could kind of back him, talk him through it.*[34]

'Trevor,' Nigel said, 'has been wonderful for me. Not only is he an incredibly nice man but he's very gentle and totally unselfish.' He was the centre and mainstay of Nigel's life. Nigel discussed and shared everything with him, and the impact on Nigel's work, not only of Trevor's support but also his wisdom and insight, is immeasurable.

In 1982 *Privates on Parade* was translated to film. Peter Nichols wrote the screenplay, Michael Blakemore directed and Denis Quilley repeated his award-winning performance as Terri Dennis. Nigel, however, was not even offered the part of Major Flack and only learnt that the film was being made when he read about it in the newspapers. In his place was John Cleese, a comic genius but, in contrast with Nigel, not a character actor of great range or subtlety. Cleese had seen the show in London and believed Flack to be an ideal role for himself. Nigel had been on friendly terms with Nichols, Blakemore and Cleese, and, while he could force himself to rise above the insult of being passed over in favour of a more high-profile and bankable star, he found it difficult to forgive their collective discourtesy and pusillanimity in not explaining the situation to his face. Nichols regrets the way matters were handled:

> *Nigel took umbrage quite rightly at the fact that he didn't get the film but, as I explained to him later, the film was only made because John Cleese wanted to make it. I did wrong. I should have gone to him and said, 'I'm sorry, Nigel, but you're not going to do the film because John Cleese is going to do it.' He said, 'That's all I wanted you to do, to just explain what happened and why I wasn't going to do it.' And I said, 'Well, it's not the play they wanted to do, it's just that John Cleese liked the play and wanted to do that part.' I have to say that John in the reading that we did in the rehearsal room was very good, but I didn't feel that he brought it through to the film properly. I think he fell for doing his 'silly walks' routine. There are some scenes where he's terrific in it, but he was never as good as Nigel. He didn't have an original slant on it the way Nigel did.*

In 1974 Antony Jay was reading a speech by Labour minister Barbara Castle, the then Secretary of State for Social Services, when he realised that there was a difference between Ministry policy and the Minister's policy. This realisation provided the dichotomy that is the crucial comic dynamic of *Yes, Minister*, the brilliant and iconic television sitcom which Jay and co-author Jonathan Lynn set in the heart of Whitehall. As John Adams observed: 'Underpinning each episode is the opposition between the centrifugal force of change, of which Hacker is the agent, and the centripetal resistance represented by Sir Humphrey Appleby.'[35] The Right Hon. James Hacker MP, newly appointed Minister for Administrative Affairs, epitomised private idealism and conscience sabotaged by political expediency and hypocrisy. His Permanent Secretary Sir Humphrey Appleby KCB, the smooth and seasoned civil servant, was the incarnation of bureaucratic intrigue and self-interest. The relationship between them was, as Jonathan Lynn indicated in an interview with Maria Aitken (the sister of disgraced Tory MP Jonathan Aitken), one of the classic comic formulae, that of 'the servant who is more able than the master, which is the same as Jeeves and Bertie Wooster or *The Admirable Crichton.*'[36]

In the early 1960s Jay had been a writer on the satirical *That Was the Week That Was (TW3)* and a senior producer on *Tonight,* programmes which gave him valuable insights into the political mind and the workings of government. Lynn, who had studied law at Cambridge where he was also a member of Footlights, was an experienced actor, writer and director in theatre and television. He and Jay met in 1975 as fellow writers for John Cleese's Video Arts training films. Two years later they started work on *Yes, Minister,* a curiously well-timed collaboration, with a historic general election in the offing and the emergence of the ministerial diarist as a publishing phenomenon.

The accuracy of the writing as well as the up-to-the-minute and sometimes prescient quality of the storylines, for which the series was widely acclaimed, were the product of the creators' thorough research. The basis of this research was Richard Crossman's posthumously released *The Diaries of a Cabinet Minister* which first appeared in 1975. Crossman had kept a detailed journal since entering the House of Commons in 1945. He became a minister during Harold Wilson's premiership and his diaries were the first to reveal the inner machinations of government and what it was really like to be a member of the Cabinet. Jay and Lynn also cultivated a host of loquacious first-hand sources inside Whitehall and Westminster, whose anonymity they continue to preserve. 'The higher up you get,' Lynn asserts, 'the more indiscreet they become, until people very near the top, you give them a good lunch and a good bottle of wine and they'll tell you absolutely anything.'[37] Many of the incidents that occur in the show were written down as they had been reported to the authors by unguarded insiders. Antony Jay maintains, 'That's why it was so funny. We couldn't think up things as funny as the real things that happened.'[38] Lady Falkender, Harold Wilson's secretary, scrutinised the first season's scripts for political detail and could not fault them. The show's 'authenticity' led, strangely enough, to its exuberant endorsement by personages across the political spectrum. Among the parliamentarians keen to declare themselves *Yes, Minister* devotees were Roy Hattersley, Gerald Kaufman, Paul Channon and Margaret Thatcher herself. There was also avid speculation as to the possible real-life identities of the featured antagonists.

Jay and Lynn submitted a pilot script to the BBC with the parts of Hacker and Sir Humphrey already firmly cast in their minds. To their delight, says Jonathan Lynn, not only were their choices not questioned, they had been anticipated:

> *I thought Nigel gave a really brilliantly funny performance in* Otherwise Engaged. *I'd also seen him on TV in a few very good supporting parts and when we came to write the pilot of* Yes Minister *we had only two people in mind for the two main parts, who were Paul [Eddington] and Nigel. So we went to the BBC thinking we were going to have an argument with them about it. And, in fact, the Head of Comedy, who was called John Howard Davies, said 'I'd like to suggest a couple of people. For Jim Hacker I'd like to suggest Paul Eddington,' and we said, 'Good, we agree with that.' Then he said, 'Have you any thoughts about Sir Humphrey?' and we said, 'Nigel Hawthorne.' And he said, 'Oh, that's who I was going to suggest.' So there was never any disagreement about that.*

The problem, however, was winning round the actors, who, though enthusiastic about the pilot script, were reluctant to commit themselves to a series and kept delaying their decision. Their procrastination seems extraordinary in hindsight, but, as Lynn recounts, the writers expedited matters by issuing an ultimatum:

> *There were two problems. Both of them were very cautious about committing to a series on the basis of one pilot. They said they loved the pilot but could they read another script. Then they read another one and said, 'Well, that's very nice. What else happens in this series?' We wrote four scripts and they kept asking for more. Finally we said after four, 'Look, you've got four scripts, now you've got to make up your mind,' at which point they both committed. The other problem was that Paul wanted to play Sir Humphrey. It wasn't clear at that point that Sir Humphrey was the character that was going to catch the public's imagination more than Jim. We had no way of predicting that. We could have predicted it if we'd thought about it, because the public had seen politicians before but they had not seen civil servants. On the other hand, we didn't know if Sir Humphrey was going to seem rather abstruse and not so accessible a character, and we knew that the public would love seeing a politician behaving the way politicians do. So I told Paul*

that Jim Hacker was the main character, as it were, the Minister, which is how it seemed actually, and I said that anyway we just thought that he was the right man for the part. I don't think he really ever forgave me because the last thing he said to me, two months before he died, was, 'You know I always wanted to play Humphrey.' He did say it with a twinkle in his eye. Nigel played it perfectly. He was the perfect man for the part.

To Nigel and Eddington's dismay the director of the pilot, Stuart Allen, wanted to add jokes, fearful that the script was too wordy. Eddington said in his memoirs:

Both Nigel and I were [...] uneasy about the director. He had made a big hit with On the Buses, *a TV series designed to appeal to the most popular taste and which had had a long run. The sophistications of our show did not, I suspect, appeal to him very strongly and he was inclined to fall back on well-tried visual gags. One which particularly jarred was a scene in which Diana Hoddinott, absolutely right as the Minister's wife, was scrabbling on the floor for her tranquillisers. Large close-up of her behind. Wrong!*[39]

Fortunately, the actors and writers were united in their refusal to compromise the show's intelligent wit, and, throughout the entire series, *Yes, Minister* was spared the deplorably familiar process of 'dumbing down'. Its success rested largely on the fact that it never patronised its audience.

Filming should have commenced in 1979 but the May general election, which brought Mrs Thatcher to power, intervened. The BBC, anxious not to prejudice either side's campaign or lay itself open to the imputation of political bias, decided to shelve the series until after the election. As Jay explained:

They were a bit worried, not knowing what the series was going to be like at that stage, that there might be something that touched on a hot political issue bang in the middle of the election and might be heartily objected to by one or other of the parties.[40]

The first season of seven episodes, directed by Sydney Lotterby, was eventually transmitted between 25 February and 7 April 1980. The delay meant that many people wrongly assumed the series was about the Thatcher government. In the interim Nigel scored his first major television success as Mr Burgess ('The Vampire'), the sadistic and manic examiner of London's would-be cabbies in Jack Rosenthal's play *The Knowledge*. Although this went on the air in 1979, Nigel secured the role on the strength of his performance as Sir

Humphrey. Rosenthal, one of Jonathan Lynn's closest friends, had been present at the filming of the *Yes, Minister* pilot in order to lend moral support. Afterwards he and Lynn, who appeared in *The Knowledge* as one of the hapless examinees, agreed that Nigel would be ideal casting as 'The Vampire'.

Yes, Minister was always recorded before a studio audience, something to which Nigel and Eddington strenuously objected despite their having performed in front of theatre audiences all their lives. The writers, however, remained impervious to their objections, and, as Lynn has disclosed, for very sound reasons:

> *Nigel didn't like the hybrid situation of working with cameras and an audience. It took him a long time to get used to that. Both he and Paul repeatedly asked us to get rid of the audience. We always said no. For us it was like a deal breaker: if we didn't have the audience, we wouldn't do the show. The reason for that primarily was political insurance. The show would always have been subject to political pressure and, in fact, we did one episode ['The Challenge'] where we showed how the BBC was subject to political pressure. The one insurance against that is that the audience is laughing. So that you can't have a real-life Sir Humphrey saying to the chairman of the BBC, 'Look, you chaps think this all very funny and amusing but nobody else does,' because the chairman of the BBC can say, 'That actually isn't the case. We bring in 350 random people every week and they howl with laughter.' So as a protection for the show we regarded the audience as essential. Governments like to interfere much more than is acknowledged here, either by the government or by the BBC, in the way politics and government are shown on television.*
>
> *I also think that the actors play better with an audience than without, and that's where Paul and Nigel and we all disagreed. They would much have preferred to have no audience. They said they would have acted better. We said not in our opinion. Nigel, who is a perfectionist, hated the fact that he occasionally made a mistake in front of the TV audience due to the fact that there was only five half days of rehearsal and I think he also didn't like the business of having to talk to the audience between scenes and include them in the evening's events as it were. He did get very good at it in the end. Paul was very good at it from the start because Paul had done another situation comedy,* The Good Life. *At the beginning Nigel didn't even pretend that he liked having the audience there.*

Yes, Minister, which became *Yes, Prime Minister* at the start of its fourth season, set exceptionally high standards in the genre of situation comedy.

The series benefited from having the same two writers over eight years and five seasons. The scripts were consistently polished and clever creations, the issues satirised at once current and immutable, and the relationships between the characters sensitively developed. Sheridan Morley also ascribes the show's stature to the actors' substantial training and experience in the theatre:

> *Nigel and Paul Eddington were theatre animals and that showed. That's why the television series was so good; these were stage people. Rather like* The Good Life *where you had Felicity Kendal, Eddington again, Briers, Penny Keith – they were stage-trained and that's what made those shows much more exciting than the usual television sitcom where you have a telly actor who has never done the classics.*

As with his approach to theatre, Nigel was primarily concerned with the journey of his character. Lynn recalls that during rehearsals he and Antony Jay would often use Shakespearean analogies as a shorthand method of elucidating for the actor certain facets of Sir Humphrey's character or motivation:

> *Nigel was never very interested in politics or government. He was interested in Sir Humphrey's character. Sometimes when we were talking about the character or the episode with Nigel we would say 'This week it's Iago' or 'This week it's Malvolio', and I think those were the comments that he found most helpful from us. Whereas if we ever got into the nitty gritty of policy, that wasn't something that interested him at all. The issues don't interest him. The issues interested Paul; he was much more political, he was very political. Nigel was interested in the character and it's absolutely true, of course, that to play a part like Sir Humphrey you don't have to be interested in the issues. That's our job as writers. That was up to Tony and me. What Nigel had to do was play the man convincingly. It was a very complicated and difficult part to play actually, although he made it look extremely simple. Because Tony and I wrote the whole series, we always knew the characters as well as Nigel and Paul but no better really. In the end Nigel knew Humphrey completely and that's what he was interested in much more than the day-to-day political issues. Nigel's not completely apolitical. He has his own political views but I don't think he regards them as anything to do with his work in public.*

Nigel's theatre training and the memory skills he acquired early in his career served him well when learning and reciting Humphrey's long and convoluted speeches which Lynn and Jay composed as parodies of laboured bureaucratic language. In one episode of *Yes, Prime Minister*, 'The Ministerial Broadcast', Humphrey 'summarised' the response of the Cabinet Committee to the Prime Minister's radical new defence policy as follows:

After careful consideration, the considered view of the committee was that while they considered the proposal met with broad approval in principle, it was felt that some of the principles were sufficiently fundamental in principle, and some of the considerations so complex and finely balanced in practice that in principle it was proposed that the sensible and prudent practice would be to subject the proposal to more detailed consideration with and across the relevant departments with a view to preparing and proposing a more thorough and wide-ranging proposal, laying stress on the less controversial elements and giving consideration to the essential continuity of the new proposal with existing principles, to be presented for parliamentary consideration and public discussion on some more propitious occasion when the climate of opinion is deemed to be more amenable for consideration of the approach and the principle of the principal arguments which the proposal proposes and propounds for approval.[41]

In the preceding episode, 'The Grand Design', debating with the Prime Minister the effectiveness of the nuclear deterrent, Humphrey reached a frantic climax with the line:

But even though they probably *certainly know that you probably wouldn't, they don't* certainly *know that although you* probably *wouldn't, there is no* probability *that you certainly would.*[42]

Nigel discovered that the best way through such linguistic stunts was to observe the inherent logic of each sentence and deliver the whole with panache. He likened the technique involved to playing Restoration comedy. These verbose passages became familiar set pieces to which the audience looked forward each week. A large part of our enjoyment of them lies in witnessing the performance feat they entail. John Adams has analysed the metatheatrical dimension Nigel added to his performance of these set pieces:

There are significant shifts in imaginative focus between the two basic components of character – the persona *(the scripted entity) and the* player *(the actor embodying the part). For example, in a characteristic set-piece, the bounds of realist convention are perilously tested when Humphrey takes language into realms where it is detached from meaning; as we the audience become aware that he has embarked on a lengthy sentence of bureaucratic unintelligibility, the performance skills of the actor become part of the pleasure, taking us close to the point where the actor's linguistic dexterity is foregrounded. The oration over, Hawthorne 'freezes', and at that moment the frame of reference changes again; without dropping the mask of the persona, the player pauses for appreciation of his skills, creating one of those vital moments that suture the audience into the comic drama as* event *through a shared recognition of its fundamental artifice.*[43]

When the opening episode of *Yes, Minister* was first broadcast, Russell Davies noted how, in common with all of Nigel's recent characterisations, the character of Sir Humphrey was a many-layered construction: 'he is always giving us a performance within a performance, and sometimes several.'[44] Sir Humphrey was one of Nigel's most significant creative achievements, a character as complex and incisively drawn as any he played on stage. Both writers acknowledge that Nigel uncovered aspects of this arch-bureaucrat's behaviour and thinking which had not been obvious to them when they conceived the character. Lynn states:

What Nigel did was take scripts that could have been a little dry and flesh them out in various ways. The possibilities were all there but they weren't specified in the script, and Nigel found extremes of behaviour in a character that is fundamentally extremely buttoned up. So that, although it was almost always repressed, you could see the megalomania and the rage and all the other qualities.

Antony Jay was similarly impressed by Nigel's discovery and controlled communication of these extremes of behaviour:

He was enormously creative. It was he who pointed out that Sir Humphrey was more than the voice of good sense and stability. He realised that Humphrey was in fact very nearly mad.

Behind the veneer of control there was a streak of mania – and it was Nigel who made us see this. He brought a dimension of danger that added great richness to the role.[45]

Without in any way compromising the character or being ingratiating, Nigel also humanised Humphrey, a man who construes the epithet 'moral vacuum' as a gracious compliment, and who is, as Jonathan Lynn points out, unequivocally the show's villain:

There is nothing good about Sir Humphrey on paper. He's the bad guy, he's the devil. He manipulates everybody into doing what he wants. He has all kinds of good motives and rationalisations he can use to justify his behaviour: he believes that he's saving the country from the squalid politicians who are only interested in short-term electoral advantage. But Sir Humphrey is not really a good guy. Yet Nigel somehow made him appealing and you liked him no matter how bad he was.

Yes, Minister was sold to forty-six countries, pirated in Eastern Europe and South Africa, and by 1986 translated into Urdu and Chinese. The published scripts, *The Complete Yes, Minister* and *Yes, Prime Minister volumes I* and *II,* sold over one million copies in hardback. In the process Nigel became a household name. His performance as Sir Humphrey earned him a Broadcasting Press Guild Award and a total of four BAFTAs, and in the 1987 New Year's Honours List he was made a CBE. In the corridors of Whitehall and Westminster he was a revered icon; Mrs Thatcher invited him to lunch at Number 10, in Israel he was taken off to meet the Prime Minister, Yitzhak Shamir, and at the American embassy he attracted a long queue of diplomats and dignitaries eager to shake hands with Sir Humphrey. Greatly to Nigel's amusement, even the Queen appeared to believe that he was one of her faithful senior officials:

I used to meet the Queen and she kept saying, 'What are you doing here, in the theatre? I would say, 'Well I work here, ma'am.' And she'd say 'Do you?' She had obviously got locked into her mind that I was Sir Humphrey and so she couldn't quite see what I was doing in these strange buildings.

To his new mass audience, unfamiliar with his stage work, it seemed he had emerged from nowhere, an overnight success at the age of fifty. He was suddenly a ubiquitous face on the small screen. In the same week that *Yes, Minister* premiered, Nigel could be seen on Thames in the title role of *Jukes of Piccadilly,* a teatime detection series, and on BBC2 as Stephano in *The Tempest.* Russell Davies drolly drew attention to the current televisual feast of Nigel Hawthorne in his *Sunday Times* column:

> *Home-grown drama, fortunately, is coming at us in superabundance just now. For viewers bewildered rather than pleased by this, I have the following advice: try to think of it all as the Nigel Hawthorne Show. You'll find the star recurs often enough to lend a cheerful continuity to the most bizarre diversity of texts. Since last December, when he drew attention to himself by sticking an inhaler up each nostril in Jack Rosenthal's* The Knowledge, *Mr Hawthorne has more or less taken up residence in the TV rehearsal rooms.*

While enjoying his television success in the early 1980s, Nigel underwent an acute crisis of professional faith. After thirty years treading the boards he became temporarily disenchanted with the theatre, or at least with its elaborate artifice and pretence, the dressing up and the curtain calls. He told a *Times* reporter in 1983:

> *I keep asking what I am doing dressing up every night, and it all seems a bit silly. I enjoy working for the camera because you are not stuck with it night after night. You don't have to have constant loyalty to it. You can do it once and don't even have to watch it. I used to love my theatre days, the magic and make-up and pretending, but suddenly these things seem a little empty and you wonder what you are doing it for. It is like waking up after a nice dream and thinking, now it's daylight I can see through it.*[46]

Throughout the first three seasons of *Yes, Minister* he appeared infrequently on stage, always in leading parts but in material that was, on the whole, unexciting. In the spring of 1980 he played Dr Austin Sloper in a touring production of *The Heiress,* a somewhat dated adaptation of Henry James's 1880 novel *Washington Square.* This was the third time Nigel and Trevor worked together – Trevor was Production Co-ordinator. Unfortunately, the play failed for two reasons. Nigel's co-star Juliet Mills completely misread her character Catherine Sloper, giving her a fallacious beauty and a personality that was almost vivacious, convinced that the girl was merely shy rather than plain. Nigel, meanwhile, fell prey to an equally serious misconception. Fascinated with James's novel, he embarked on an inordinate amount of research for his role, based on the character in the book. As a consequence his performance, which may well have been true to the subtleties of the original text, was not consonant with the structure of the more melodramatic stage version as written by Ruth and Augustus Goetz in 1947. More happily a year later he toured with Jonathan Lynn's Cambridge Theatre Company in a new play by Jack Rosenthal titled *Smash!*

Nigel's next theatre venture promised a great deal from the names involved but, in the end, only contributed to his growing aversion to the stage. He starred with John Alderton in Denise Coffey's Young Vic production of *John Mortimer's Casebook,* a triptych of one-act plays wrapped up in the device of a prison concert party. The evening's centrepiece was Mortimer's enjoyable but rather antiquated 'The Dock Brief', first produced in 1957 and the precursor to his television masterpiece *Rumpole of the Bailey.* Framing this gentle burlesque aimed at the Bar, were the hastily contrived curtain-raiser 'Interlude' and the dubiously resurrected 'The Prince of Darkness', lampooning the medical profession and the Church respectively. According to Michael Billington, the overall effect combined 'a Shavian cynicism about the professions with a Dickensian love of the grotesque'.[47] The production received mixed reviews, although the consensus was that Nigel and Alderton's creditable efforts were ultimately defeated by the tired material.

In 'The Dock Brief' Nigel played the dilapidated barrister Morgenhall. His interpretation was a cognate of the character of the dilapidated repertory actor Harry Figdore in his own one-act play 'Prompt!' Francis King in the *Sunday Telegraph* remarked:

> *The dim and dusty barrister, fruitlessly waiting for a brief, is so much akin to some dim and dusty actor, fruitlessly waiting for a role, that the way Nigel Hawthorne plays him, with histrionic gestures, flowing locks and plummy voice, is wholly right.*[48]

In 'The Prince of Darkness' Nigel took the part of a demonic fundamentalist curate with intimations of another religious mountebank, Tartuffe, and in 'the medical pantomime 'Interlude' he played probably his least favourite role ever, that of a hospital matron dressed as Widow Twankey, complete with titian wig and frilly cap. It was the second time he had had to don full drag since his ignominious appearance as a chorus girl in *The Pirates of Penzance* at the Christian Brothers' College, Cape Town, and he made sure it was the last. This particular humiliation no doubt intensified his general disillusionment with the medium of theatre. In the week *John Mortimer's Casebook* opened he revealed his waning faith to Hugh Herbert of the *Guardian*:

> *Really, I feel I'd like to get out – direct, write, or make films. I've lost the appetite I used to have for the theatre. I sometimes think that it's a horrendous profession, it scares the daylights out of me. I have a dreadful reluctance … a defiance. I don't know why I should, which makes it rather like the Christians going out in front of the Romans.*[49]

Although he continued for the next few years to harbour such grave misgivings, Nigel never made the decisive break he often talked about, but instead kept returning to the stage. In the summer of 1983 he rejoined the Royal Shakespeare Company for two productions at The Pit, the Barbican's flexible studio theatre designed for small-scale transfers from Stratford. The first of these was David Rudkin's translation of Ibsen's mordant comic fantasy *Peer Gynt,* which opened on 9 June, directed by Ron Daniels and starring Derek Jacobi. This production, in which the story was relocated from rural Norway to Northern Ireland, had originally been staged at The Other Place the previous year. Nigel took over the parts initially played by Derek Godfrey – Solveig's father, von Eberkopf, the Strange Passenger and the Buttonmoulder. Each of these character vignettes was well thought through and well delineated, and his Buttonmoulder was an especially haunting presence in this 'metaphysical pantomime'.[50]

The following month Nigel gave a memorable performance as Orgon in Christopher Hampton's blank verse translation of Molière's *Tartuffe.* Directed by Bill Alexander, the production was the first London revival of the play since its presentation at the Old Vic in 1967. As part of the RSC's short French season it ran in repertoire with Bulgakov's *Molière.* On the eve of the play's press night Nigel explained to Clare Colvin of *The Times* the purpose of this new adaptation:

> *In the past, audiences have been very suspicious about French plays, and the translators truncated Molière's long and complicated speeches to make them acceptable to English ears. We were concerned that the production should be a genuine version, rather than taking the original idea and turning it into a funny play: it is not in rhyming couplets but blank verse, in order to keep it as near as possible to Molière's words.*
>
> *The basic of good comedy is truth, so the more real the situation is, the funnier. You don't need arbitrary business and jokes. Underneath there is an extraordinary emotional situation, in which Orgon, an ordinary middle-class family man, has invited into his house a religious nut, who is also a conman. The more he is warned, the more obstinate he becomes that the man should remain in their lives. When the moment of realization does arrive, it is almost too painful to watch.*[51]

The comic design of simplicity and emotional truth of which Nigel spoke was nearly undermined by the outrageous overacting and blatant scene-stealing tactics of Antony Sher's Rasputin-like Tartuffe, 'Richard III with a rosary',[52] who repeatedly gave vent to extravagant glee at his own malevolent duplicity. But the corrective factor in the production was Nigel's restrained and 'powerfully centred conception of Orgon'.[53] Most reviewers commented on the pronounced contradistinction in acting styles and effectiveness between the two principals, which Eric Shorter expressed as the difference between character and caricature.[54] Michael Billington recognised in Nigel's performance what Michael Rudman designates as the actor's gift for rich anger:

Because Mr Sher is so robustly malign, Nigel Hawthorne has no alternative but to play Orgon as a sublime dupe, which he does with great skill. He is particularly good at half-checked gestures of throttled rage and at smiling at relations (particularly his mother) through wittily gritted teeth. It is a fine comic performance full of rich detail, such as his look of thunderstruck disbelief when told by his wife to hide under the table. Yet I couldn't escape a nagging feeling that Mr Hawthorne's visible intelligence was slightly at odds with an interpretation that forced him into the role of gulled idiot.[55]

Ned Chaillet commended the calming dignity and delicacy of Nigel's interpretation, describing him as 'a drawn bow who vibrates every pang of devotion, and then the later remorse'.[56] Benedict Nightingale believed Nigel had humanised Orgon and made sympathetic and plausible his costly infatuation with the fraudulent holy man:

Mr Hawthorne, without exaggeration or embarrassment, presents us with a remarkably humane picture of a peppery, volatile man unself-knowingly in the grip of the love that dares not tell its name. He is besotted, disoriented, lost – and then suddenly, painfully found. If you want to see bravura acting, go and admire Sher; if you want to see feeling, intelligence and skill unobtrusively at work, go and enjoy that hardy perennial Hawthorne.[57]

A year later the production was filmed for television and Nigel reprised his role. He had distinguished himself in all three of his RSC performances, but he had yet to play Stratford and his first Shakespearean part as a member of the company. In the meantime he made his National Theatre debut in what proved to be a less than ideal vehicle for his talents. He appeared as Colonel Tadeusz Stjerbinsky opposite Geoffrey Hutching's Jacobowsky in the rather laboured comedy *Jacobowsky and the Colonel*, S. N. Behrman's Broadway treatment of Franz Werfel's last play *(Jacobowsky und der Oberst)* about the reluctant alliance between two very different refugees during the fall of France in June 1940. The production opened on

22 July 1986 in the National's largest auditorium, the Olivier, and was directed by Jonathan Lynn.

With the exceptions of Jack Tinker's rave review (a 'spectacular production' containing 'magnificent, mesmerising and utterly memorable performances [...] by Nigel Hawthorne and Geoffrey Hutchings')[58] and Robert Hewison's scathing harangue (*Jacobowsky and the Colonel* is the worst play I have seen at the National, in the worst production'),[59] critical reaction was either tolerant or tepid. Since its premiere in New York in 1944, and in London the following year (with Michael Redgrave as the Colonel), the play had been revived several times and in a variety of forms, including a Hollywood film in 1957 starring Danny Kaye and a stage musical in 1979 featuring Joel Grey. But notwithstanding its previous success, any claim the comedy had to being a minor modern classic worthy of lavish rehabilitation by Britain's subsidised National Theatre was doubtful.

The odd couple of the play's title are an astute and resourceful Jewish accountant and an aristocratic, anti-Semitic Polish cavalry officer with 'one of the finest minds of the fifteenth century'. The men are forced by the imminent occupation of Paris, and a shortage of available transport, to motor together across France, dodging the Gestapo. En route to their rendezvous at Hendaye with a night boat bound for England, they collect the Colonel's French fiancée Marianne, whose presence in the escape party makes romantic rivals of the mismatched travelling companions.

The character of the Colonel is a modern incarnation of Plautus's asinine *miles gloriosus* (swaggering soldier). Nigel lacked the necessary braggadocio and conceit for the part. He was extremely skilled at portraying characters prone to fanaticism and mania, but dullards and absurdly jealous lovers were not his strong suit. He was too intelligent an actor merely to play the buffoon. But, although Nigel could not, as Eric Shorter noted, 'swagger instinctively',[60] he did work his own brand of magic on this particular buffoon, making the Colonel, in the course of his adventures, change in himself and in his relationships with Jacobowsky and Marianne. Jonathan Lynn declares:

> *He brought dignity to the role. The Colonel was an extremely humourless character and Nigel made this rather stiff, unappealing, humourless man warm and attractive and, finally, someone that you really loved and cared about.*

In giving substance to a fairly hollow role and penetrating the truth behind the caricature, Nigel again demonstrated his manifold gifts as a 'thinking clown'. Francis King discerned, 'he adroitly brings out not merely what is comic but what is sad.'[61] Michael Billington indicated the physical eloquence and insight of the characterisation:

Hawthorne's colonel stiff backed, sleek haired and high-chinned, exists on some lofty, unearthly plane; other people are merely things in his dream and when he asks 'Where is style? Who has elegance?' he sweeps the air grandly like a man living purely on the Platonic level. Hawthorne gives us not only the man but a criticism of all he stands for.[62]

Nigel had, as Irving Wardle concluded, exploited and far exceeded the meagre possibilities of an improbable part:

Nigel Hawthorne, as the Colonel, makes up for romantic dash with a crazed patrician arrogance, excelling in passages of apoplectic defeat and holding on to the character long after it should legitimately have expired.[63]

Nigel's next role at the National, in September of that year, fitted him like the proverbial glove and showed him to be an inspired farceur of rare emotional subtlety and depth. As director Michael Rudman's choice, he undertook the title role in Arthur Wing Pinero's *The Magistrate,* the first of three Royal Court farces which established the playwright's popularity.[64] Not for the first, nor the last, time Nigel was following in the venerated footsteps of Alastair Sim, who had given a masterly performance as the Magistrate at the Chichester Festival and in London in 1969.

The production was staged in the Lyttelton, a traditional proscenium theatre, and the entire run was sold out. Under Rudman's direction the farce was played seriously and at a sensible pace which did not shroud Pinero's verbal wit. In his review Irving Wardle catalogued the virtues of this daring approach:

This is by far the funniest Pinero production I have seen, and its secret is to play the text as though it were not a farce at all. There are no super-energetic figures bouncing on to identify the stage as fun-corner. The pace throughout is measured and deliberate with no frantic accelerations. Characters are treated in deadly earnest and it is their pursuit of ruling obsessions that reduces the audience to ecstasies of helpless laughter. Such a style is always being laid down as the basic rule for farce; but it is very seldom that you see a production with the nerve to carry it out. [65]

It was an approach that completely accorded with Nigel's personal tenet that 'the basic of good comedy is truth', that humour derives from emotional accuracy rather than arbitrary jokes or contrived capering. The truthfulness of the performances and the production was a striking achievement since the action of the play evolves, in a foreseeable sequence of complications and coincidences, from a preposterous premise. Mr Posket, Magistrate of Mulberry Street Police Court, is the second husband of the widowed Agatha, who has lied about her age and consequently passed off her nineteen-year-old son Cis Farringdon, a sophisticated and likeable scapegrace, as a lad of fourteen. Alarmed at the boy's precociously raffish tastes, and with the object of gently reforming him, the blameless Posket tentatively accompanies his stepson one evening to a seedy Soho resort. When the hotel is raided by the police for infringing the licensing laws, he narrowly escapes exposure by falling from a balcony.

In more than one review Nigel's magisterial Magistrate, 'wondrous in his innocence, hilarious in his discomfiture and disarray,'[66] evoked gratifyingly positive comparisons with Sim:

The Magistrate, National Theatre 1986. *(John Haynes/ The Raymond Mander & Joe Mitchenson Theatre Collection)*

In Nigel Hawthorne's marvellous performance the part does take on a satiric edge which puts it even beyond the long shadow of Alastair Sim.

At home, Hawthorne's Posket is a blissful innocent, pitiable even with his servants, and absolute putty in the hands of his gambling, hell-raising stepson. But see him after the night out, crawling back into the Mulberry Street Court and gradually reassuming the majesty of the law; the mild beaming features contorted into self-righteous fury as he informs his arrested friend, Lukyn, that the events in court may oblige him to cancel his evening's dinner engagement. As Hawthorne rises to his climax he dons a pair of pince-nez and collapses in agony, as his adventures have left him with a scarred nose: a superb detail that precisely encapsulates the contradiction of private and public life.[67]

The *Daily Telegraph* hailed the performance a triumph of emotional comedy:

Mr Hawthorne's Posket lurches into the magistrates' room at Mulberry Street, looking like Banquo's ghost. Bruised, bedraggled and scarcely able to walk, he staggers across the room, eyed by his chief clerk; and as we learn what befell him in his flight from the raided hotel where his sophisticated stepson had led him such a dance, Mr Hawthorne's plight becomes so pitiable in its absurdity that you almost wish the actor would leave the stage and give you time to pull yourself together as well.

This is without question the funniest piece of comic acting on the London stage because it is utterly and agonisingly self-absorbed and because Mr Hawthorne as the good natured Posket who has just undergone a trek through the north London suburbs has made that off-stage nightmare so vivid.

If you never expected this player to rival memories of Blakelock, Hordern or Sim, visit the Lyttelton and have your prejudices happily dashed.[68]

Nigel's successful association during the late 1970s and 1980s with Britain's theatrical establishment and his superlative embodiment on television of the governing establishment were, ironically, confirmation of his maverick abilities. His acting defied expectation and generic pinpointing; he constantly redefined the boundaries of comedy and tragedy, often by means of a single facial expression or gesture. *The Magistrate* had not only restored Nigel's faith in the theatre, it had also made people more aware of the emotional power of which he was capable. His greatest stage performances were still to come and would surprise everyone, including Nigel himself, with their emotional magnitude and rawness.

Notes to Chapter 7

1 Interview with Sheridan Morley, 'Life's equation solved', *Times,* 7 March 1988.
2 'By George, Hollywood will be mad about him', *Sunday Times,* 15 January 1995.
3 *Sunday Times,* 3 August 1975.
4 *New Statesman,* 8 August 1974.
5 Gray (1985) 147.
6 *Evening Standard,* 4 July 1975.
7 Michael Frayn, 'In Cuba', *Observer Review,* 26 January 1969.
8 *Guardian,* 17 August 1976.
9 *Sunday Telegraph,* 22 August 1976.
10 *Birmingham Post,* 18 August 1976.
11 'Patronising humour misses the point', *Daily Telegraph,* 17 August 1976.
12 *Evening Standard,* 17 August 1976.
13 *Sunday Telegraph,* 22 August 1976.
14 *Guardian,* 17 August 1976.
15 'Clouds over Cuba', *Observer,* 22 August 1976.
16 'Tropical scandals', *Times,* 7 February 1978.
17 In programme for *Privates on Parade.*
18 Nichols (2000) 401 (diary entry for 10 February 1975).
19 Davies, ed., (1994) 512 (diary entry for 23 March 1976).
20 Nichols (2000) 409-10 (diary entry for 10 April 1975).
21 Nichols (2000) 426-7.
22 Jack Tinker, *Daily Mail,* 9 February 1978.
23 Nichols (2000) 426.
24 Nichols in interview with Jim Hiley, *Plays and Players,* March 1978, 15.
25 *Plays and Players,* April 1977, 22-3.
26 Ibid, 24.
27 *Guardian,* 9 February 1978.
28 *Financial Times,* 9 February 1978.
29 'Private Lives,', *Daily Telegraph,* 12 February 1978.
30 Eyre & Wright (2000) 130.
31 The other play was James Bridie's *Marriage is No Joke,* produced in February 1934, with Ralph Richardson as the Scots Calvinist John MacGregor.
32 In his published *Diaries* Nichols ((2000) 56-57) wrote: 'Penelope Gilliatt made the famous joke about the sound of a typical English Sunday morning being Hobson barking up the wrong tree. This was never more true than when he allowed his own experience to distort his view of *Joe Egg.* He was lame and walked with sticks, due to his parents having trusted Christian Science to cure his infantile polio. He allowed that I'd 'taken a limiting case', as though I'd gone shopping for it, but thought I had too easily scorned The Laying-On of Hands. 'Miracles do sometimes happen' he wrote, then went on to exemplify his own history (presumably) where a doctor had said he'd never be able to earn his living and that child 'went on subsequently to earn about £6,000 a year more than the doctor ever did. But I admit the author has *chosen* (my italics) an instance graver than this.' I kept quiet at the time, his review probably costing us the audience we might have had if he'd been more honest. He was, as we've seen, even more intolerant of my next play, though here his view was muddied by his family relations with Lord Chandos (né Lyttelton), Chairman of the Board and prime opponent of the play.'

33 Interview with Jan Moir, 'I proved them wrong … Eventually', *Daily Telegraph,* 3 September 1999.

34 In conversation with Sheridan Morley on *The Arts Programme,* BBC Radio 2, 21 June2002.

35 Adams (1993) 62-85, at 71.

36 Interview with Maria Aitken on BBC's *Friday Night … Saturday Morning,* 27 November 1981.

37 *A Short History of Yes, Minister,* BBC 1999.

38 *Ibid.*

39 Eddington (1995) 142.

40 *A Short History of Yes, Minister,* BBC 1999.

41 Lynn & Jay (1986) 112. Playwright Alan Bennett read out this particular speech at Nigel's memorial service held at the National Theatre on 6 June 2002.

42 Lynn & Jay (1986) 80.

43 Adams (1993) 62-85, at 75-6.

44 *Sunday Times,* 2 March 1980.

45 'By George, Hollywood will be mad about him', *Sunday Times,* 15 January 1995.

46 Interview with Clare Colvin, 'The reality of humour', *Times,* 27 July 1983.

47 *Guardian,* 7 January 1982.

48 'The asinine law', *Sunday Telegraph,* 10 January 1982.

49 Interview with Hugh Herbert, 'Yes … and no', *Guardian,* 9 January 1982.

50 John Barber, *Daily Telegraph,* 16 June 1982.

51 Interview with Clare Colvin, 'The reality of humour', *Times,* 27 July 1983.

52 Michael Billington, *Guardian,* 29 July 1983.

53 Ned Chaillet, *Plays and Players,* October 1983, 34.

54 See Eric Shorter, 'Tartuffe with the stops out', *Daily Telegraph,* 29 July 1983.

55 *Guardian,* 29 July 1983.

56 *Plays and Players,* October 1983, 34.

57 *New Statesman,* 5 August 1983.

58 'Badge of courage, and of excellence', *Daily Mail,* 24 July 1986.

59 'Telling tales from Hollywood', *Sunday Times,* 27 July 1986.

60 'Poles apart', *Daily Telegraph,* 24 July 1986.

61 'Poles apart, yet flung together', *Sunday Telegraph,* 27 July 1986.

62 *Guardian,* 24 July 1986.

63 *Times,* 23 July 1986.

64 *The Magistrate* premiered at the Royal Court in 1885. It was followed by Pinero's *The Schoolmistress* (1886) and *Dandy Dick* (1887).

65 'Measured farce with a serious side', *Times,* 25 September 1986.

66 Kenneth Hurren, *Plays and Players,* December 1986, 23.

67 'Measured farce with a serious side', *Times,* 25 September 1986.

68 'Laughter, but with feeling', *Daily Telegraph,* 26 September 1986.

Chapter 8

Leap of Faith

SHADOWLANDS AND OTHER PLAYS

*There can be no knowledge without emotion. We may be aware of a truth,
yet until we have felt its force, it is not ours. To the cognition of the brain
must be added the experience of the soul.*

(Arnold Bennett, *The Journals*, entry for 18 March 1897)

*But for them it was only the beginning of the real story. All their life in
this world and all their adventures in Narnia had only been the cover and
the title page: now at last they were beginning Chapter One of the
Great Story which no one on earth has read: which goes on forever: in
which every chapter is better than the one before.*

(C. S. Lewis, *The Last Battle*)

While appearing in *Shadowlands* on Broadway in 1990, Nigel explained, in
an interview with the Long Island newspaper *Newsday*, how he had acquired
with maturity greater authority and fresh awareness as an actor:

> *I became middle-aged and started to recognize my vulnerabilities and
> incorporate them into what I was doing. It was a bright thing [to do]
> because we're all a mass of faults, and English people spend their lives trying
> to cover them up. There's a sort of closetedness about people, and what I look
> and sound like seems to coincide with this characteristic. So I'm able to be
> hurt, to be pompous, to expose myself to danger, to go in where angels fear to
> tread and be smashed in the face.*[1]

The discovery he made in his middle years, and which he had obviously
carefully analysed, was the turning-point of what was as much a spiritual
odyssey as a professional one. Analogous to his personal journey was the
journey he undertook every night on stage in the role of C. S. (Jack) Lewis,
the Oxford don and popular theologian best known as the author of
The Chronicles of Narnia.

Shadowlands begins with Lewis addressing a public meeting on the subject of human suffering and God's apparent indifference to it; having unconsciously sequestered his adult self from the anguish of love and loss, he protests the value of pain as 'a mechanism that will penetrate our selfishness'. He returns to the theme of suffering three times in the course of the play, and his initial complacency is jolted first by fear born of love, then by grief, and finally by true wisdom founded upon a faith sorely tested. By the end his intellectual certainty has been subverted by an empirical understanding of suffering; his faith, and his relationship with God, made richer by his vulnerability and confusion. Nigel never enjoyed the sort of certainty characteristic of Lewis's earlier writings, but at a critical juncture in his life, and in relation to his own work, he did learn the importance of confronting and utilising his doubts, and, like Lewis, he chose suffering over safety.

With the success of *Privates on Parade* Nigel entered a new phase of his theatrical career as a leading London player able to alternate between dramatic and comedic roles. What came to light in his performances of the late 1970s and 80s was a hitherto unexplored epic quality. This had nothing to do with technique but, rather, the ever-increasing reserves of emotional power on which he drew. Guided by his principles of restraint and accuracy, he emerged as a tragedian unmistakably of the modern era.

More than a decade before his portrayal of C. S. Lewis, Nigel forcefully depicted the intense spiritual conflict of a fictional man of faith, Henri de Montherlant's tormented priest and pedagogue, Father de Pradts, in *The Fire That Consumes*. The play's original title, *La Ville dont le prince est un enfant,* is taken from Ecclesiastes 10.16: 'Woe to thee, O land, when thy king is a child'. The land in this instance is a Catholic boys' college in the Paris suburb of Auteuil between the wars. Also under scrutiny is the land of the soul in which is fought a fierce battle between sacramental, self-negating love and secular passion. The child is fourteen-year-old Serge Souplier, a wanton innocent, who is loved by both a senior pupil, André Servais, and his form master, de Pradts. When the boys swear eternal devotion to one another in the Games Pavilion, they are apprehended by de Pradts who has his rival expelled, out of jealousy and not from the pure motives he would claim for himself. The priest is then forced by the Father Superior of the college to examine his conscience and the limits of his faith.

Montherlant first conceived the idea of *La Ville* in 1913, after his expulsion from school, at the hands of an Abbé of not unimpeachable rectitude, on account of his 'sentimental friendship' *(amitié particulière)* with a younger boy. It was not until 1951, however, that he began to dramatise these events, and then only with the intention of publishing rather than staging the final work.

M. L' Abbé de Pradts in *The Fire That Consumes* (1977), with Adam Bareham. *(Donald Cooper / Photostage)*

Two years later the play received a private amateur performance in Geneva, but, being sensitive about the delicate and autobiographical subject matter, Montherlant continually refused permission for a professional production. He finally relented in 1967, authorising a performance under the direction of Jean Meyer at the Comédie Française where the play caused an immediate sensation. In 1971 Peter Daubney brought the French production to London as part of his annual World Theatre Season. *The Fire That Consumes,* adapted by Vivian Cox with Bernard Miles, was the first English translation of *La Ville* staged in England.

The venue for the production was the Mermaid Theatre at Puddle Dock, near Blackfriars Bridge. Founded by the comic actor turned impresario Bernard Miles and his wife Josephine Wilson, the Mermaid opened in 1959, financed entirely by public subscription and built within the walls of a bomb-damaged warehouse. The surrounding area abounded in Elizabethan theatre history. Nearby, in the converted buttery of a dissolved Dominican friary had stood James Burbage's Blackfriars Theatre (one of the first candle-lit indoor playhouses in London), for which Shakespeare wrote his later plays. The Mermaid Tavern in Bread Street, off neighbouring Cheapside, had been the meeting place of the Friday Street Club whose members included Sir Walter

Raleigh, Francis Beaumont, John Fletcher, Ben Jonson and Shakespeare. Moreover, the theatre was positioned directly opposite Bankside, the site of the great Elizabethan theatres, the Rose, the Swan and the Globe. The Mermaid had a steep single-tier auditorium and an open Elizabethan-style stage. Although its repertoire was extensive, it tended to specialise in reworkings of neglected minor classics as well as Jacobean and Elizabethan revivals.

The Fire That Consumes was directed by Bernard Miles and opened at the Mermaid on 13 October 1977. Nigel's principal fellow performers were Dai Bradley as Souplier, Adam Bareham as Servais and David William as the Father Superior. The anglicised style of the production was seen by the critics as its greatest shortcoming. The translation, which had the merits of clarity and performability, lacked the resonance of the French original. Michael Billington lamented the loss of an asceticism as well as aestheticism belonging to French classical tragedy:

> *Henry de Montherlant's* The Fire That Consumes *is a very fine play indeed and I am glad that the Mermaid has had the courage to stage it. But, compared to the Racine-like severity of Jean Meyer's production which played at the World Theatre Season six years ago, Bernard Miles's is unduly coarse and corporeal. It is, in fact, about as French as boiled beef and carrots.*[2]

The drama critic for the *Observer* surmised that the purposed Gallic severity of the *La Ville* was quite possibly untranslatable within the context of the English stage tradition:

> *When the older schoolboy of the play's twosome proclaims his passion to be higher than that of Racine's Andromache, he clues us in as to feeling and style. They may not be attainable by an English cast. [...] With its ice melted the play looks like a protracted and mealy-mouthed restatement of a theme once thought daring.*[3]

This was a view shared by Milton Shulman of the *Evening Standard*:

> *This story of the overwhelming passion of a priest for a French schoolboy could conceivably maintain its austere, spiritual authority in a Spanish, German or even Japanese version.*
>
> *But [...] these schoolboys by the very nature of the tongue they speak, become relentlessly English. [...]*
>
> *Only in the intellectual debate between the Father Superior and the priest*

does this play attain that mystical, almost symbolic, quality, that would make its cerebral, rather priggish, characters acceptable.[4]

But, if Miles's production missed the austerity and discipline of Meyer's staging of the original, it compensated for its deficiencies with a forceful and original emotional core, for which Nigel was largely responsible. Irving Wardle of *The Times* recommended the production 'as a work of manifest integrity with a superb central performance by Nigel Hawthorne as the Abbé (witness the impulsive slips of his authoritative mask) and a matching display of volatile danger from Dai Bradley as the boy friend.'[5] Billington wished the human vulnerability the play described had been placed against a believable background of Catholic rigour and repression, but allowed that 'Nigel Hawthorne's Abbé, who earlier misses entirely the priest's poker-backed cruelty, becomes very moving in his breakdown into an unmanned hysteria, his nails biting into the palms of his hands in desperation.'[6] A critique of the play in the *Theatre Newsletter* stated: 'Nigel Hawthorne's portrayal of the Abbé contains the pent-up passion, the anguish and the pain of one who is being consumed by a fire that, as the Father Superior points out, is not the one St Bernard was speaking of.'[7] The anguish Nigel released on stage was made more potent by the actor's truthfulness and avoidance of the snare of excess. As the *Sunday Times* pointed out, 'Nigel Hawthorne as the tormented priest gives a remarkably powerful portrait of suffering, also the more convincing for its restraint.'[8] The reviewer for the *Sunday Telegraph* responded to criticisms of the un-French character of the production with a sensitive appraisal of the unique qualities Nigel's reading of de Pradts had brought to the play:

> *Nigel Hawthorne's playing of the Abbé is a revelation. He endows the man – played in the French production as a tight-lipped, cruel disciplinarian – with his innate warmth and humanity. Not that he glosses over the priest's duplicity – indeed, he takes him daringly to the edge of comedy – but he never forfeits our sympathy. The more cerebral French may quarrel with his interpretation but he moved me deeply.*[9]

During the Christmas season of 1978 Nigel appeared at the stately Theatre Royal, Haymarket in only the second West End presentation of Bernard Shaw's *The Millionairess*.[10] Written in 1935, when Shaw was seventy-nine, and styled by its author 'a Jonsonian comedy in four acts', the play is a trifling piece cursorily concerned with serious themes such as economic inequity and capitalist ideology. It is devoid of both the political and dramatic verve of Shaw's earlier work, but the general tedium is alleviated by flashes of Shavian wit and perspicacity. The thin plot features an arrogant millionairess being challenged by an Egyptian doctor, whom she wishes to wed, to make her own living for six months, and subsequently turning an East End sweatshop into a thriving business and an old inn into a smart hotel.

Starring in Michael Lindsay-Hogg's handsome production, as the imperious plutocrat Epifania, was Penelope Keith, who was then riding the crest of her popularity after four series of *The Good Life* on television and her recent stage appearances in Ayckbourn's *The Norman Conquests* and Shaw's *The Apple Cart*. Nigel, sharing second billing with Charles Kay (who later created the role of Dr Willis in *The Madness of George III*), portrayed Epifania's suave and cynical solicitor, Julius Sagamore. In Anthony Asquith's 1961 film version of the play, this part had been played by Alastair Sim opposite Sophia Loren's Epifania. Nigel received uniformly good notices for his performance but it was an otherwise unhappy experience.

The pairing of Nigel and Penelope Keith was not the most professionally congenial owing to the polarity between their methodologies and temperaments as stage performers. Keith is a very polished comedienne with a natural authority. Variety and vulnerability, however, are not generally attributes which distinguish her acting. In contrast to the unpredictability, the danger and excitement of Nigel's approach, Keith's objective was to reproduce the same exquisitely chiselled, well-honed performance night after night. She accused Nigel of changing things just for the sake of changing them. As soon as he had perfected the playing of a line or scene, he introduced variations, experimenting with different readings and emotions. Keith strove for technical perfection, Nigel for freshness and constant reinvention.

Thirty years after his performance as Stepan Stepanovitch in Chekhov's 1889 one-act comedy *The Proposal* at the Muizenberg Pavilion, Nigel led an all-star cast in a specially commissioned new version of *Uncle Vanya* by Pam Gems at Hampstead Theatre.

Sheridan Morley remarked on the careful use of the term 'version' to describe Gems's treatment of the play:

Not a translation, you understand, nor strictly an adaptation, simply an arrangement of a masterpiece, one which manages ever so slightly to sharpen and highlight our knowledge of the play without ever being untrue to its original mood or intent.[11]

Gems, well known as the author of *Dusa, Fish, Stas and Vi, Queen Christina,* and *Piaf,* made it clear in an afterword to the text that she was 'not very interested in Chekhov's plays as literature, whatever that word means.'[12]

What fascinated her were 'the spaces between the lines,' of which Chekhov was master, and the playwright's trained musical ear that enabled him to compose wonderful rhythms for the stage. These things, she correctly argued, can be fully realised and appreciated only in live performance and through the unscripted, and potentially stimulating, communication between actors and audience which is integral to the creation of theatre:

> *Dramatic line proffers not information, not explication, but clue. Not only the emotion, but the cognition, too, is supplied, not by the actor supported by production for the benefit of the paying public, but by the public itself. The audience is a member of the cast, playing its role every night – and not always knowing its lines. The play on the page is a diagram, a blueprint; and a pretty odd blueprint at that, since most of it is not there at all but in the spaces between the lines. (Just about all of which, come to think of it, was invented by Anton Chekhov.)*[13]

Gems's version of *Uncle Vanya*, which J. C. Trewin pronounced 'both colloquial and theatrical',[14] was a fluid and idiomatic rendering with shortened speeches and only the occasional lapse of taste and authenticity.

The new version under Nancy Meckler's direction opened at Hampstead on 22 November 1979, appropriately twenty years after James Roose-Evans had founded the theatre with his own production of *The Seagull*. Meckler and her husband David Aukin, who was currently the Hampstead's Artistic Director, had met Nigel socially and, on hearing that he had never played Vanya, they undertook to mount a revival of the play. Nigel relished, and was grateful for, this opportunity, but he discovered that Meckler was not the kind of director with whom he worked best. In the first week of rehearsals she told him over the telephone to stop interfering. When he asked her what she meant, Meckler complained that he kept telling the actors things she did not want them to know for another three weeks. This was a not atypical example of how Nigel's method of participating fully and freely in the creative and decision-making process could be perceived as a threat to the director's authority. For his part, Nigel disliked the autocratic attempts of directors to restrict the actors' collaborative involvement in the production and to ration information according to directorial judgement or convenience.

While Nigel occupied the play's title role, the rest of the formidable cast included Maurice Denham as Professor Serebryakov, Jean Anderson as Vanya's mother Marya, Alison Steadman as Sonya, Susan Littler as Yelena and Ian Holm as Astrov. Morley observed how harmoniously this elite ensemble worked together:

Given a cast the NT or the RSC would have been proud (and must now be envious) of, this new production by Nancy Meckler is very much an actor's evening. [...] Indeed with the exception of the Olivier-Redgrave-Plowright production which launched Chichester in the early 1960s[15] it is hard to believe there can anywhere have been a better post-war Vanya. *[...]*

What makes it so infinitely impressive is the feeling that this company has been together, reacting to each other's reflexes, for a matter of months rather than weeks; they will, if there is any justice, be staying together for a matter of years.[16]

Ian Holm had been Nigel's tentative suggestion for the part of the doctor – tentative because three years earlier Holm withdrew completely from the theatre as the result of a sudden and debilitating attack of stage fright he suffered in the middle of the second preview performance of Eugene O'Neill's *The Iceman Cometh* at the Aldwych. Since then he had been busily occupied in television and had lately acted with Nigel in the BBC *Play for Today, The Misanthrope*. That he committed himself to *Uncle Vanya* against everyone's expectations was due entirely to his personal and professional regard for Nigel, as he revealed in an interview with the *Evening Standard* a week before the premiere of the production: ' I accepted this for one reason and one reason only and that's because Nigel Hawthorne's in it. We are a mutual admiration society.'[17] After *Uncle Vanya* Holm did not work on the stage again until 1993 when he starred in Pinter's *Moonlight* at the Almeida.

The Hampstead being an intimate performance space, the production was what Charles Spencer called 'a chamber Chekhov'.[18] In the writing, direction and acting the emphasis was on detail and nuance, on small, precise effects. Pam Gems said of Chekhov: 'More than any other playwright he saw that drama lies in the particular, and not in the general statement which belongs, if at all, elsewhere. Those small, piercing moments of truth …'.[19] It was the 'small, piercing moments of truth' at which Nigel excelled, as Arthur Schmidt noted in his review of *Uncle Vanya* for *Plays and Players*:

As he looks at Yelena and back upon twenty years of a life not so much mis- as unspent, he makes yearning as physical an act as walking. When he brings the autumn roses to apologise to Yelena and discovers her about to surrender to Astrov, his grip on the stems and the intake of breath are if anything understated, even on the Hampstead's small stage.[20]

According to Gems's reading, Vanya 'is the poetic truth of the play, he cries out what the others deny, or try to suffer.'[21] What Nigel succeeded in capturing wholly and accurately in his interpretation of this chronically disillusioned and unfulfilled character was Chekhov's lyricism of grief. In Act Three Vanya rails resentfully at the Professor, whom he once worshipped and who, he now feels, has made a drudge and a dupe of him:

Uncle Vanya, with Jean Anderson, Hampstead 1979. *(John Haynes/ The Raymond Mander & Joe Mitchenson Theatre Collection)*

You've ruined my life! I was talented … I had courage, intelligence – given a chance I might have been a Schopenhauer, a Dostoevsky … oh I'm talking rubbish! I'm going mad … Mother I'm in agony!

Nigel's delivery of this outburst was heartfelt and full of poignancy, while the humour and absurdity of his literary comparisons were significantly muted. James Fenton in the *Sunday Times* commented, 'I admired and was moved by Nigel Hawthorne's Vanya. His weeping was manly. There was no self-indulgence.'[22] Especially moving were Nigel's stillness, his silent tears and visibly broken heart in the final scene in which Vanya and Sonya return to their joyless existence and Sonya tries desperately to comfort her uncle with the assurance 'We shall find peace'. The truthfulness and tenderness of Nigel's performance were aided by his strong identification with the character's suffering:

Vanya is obsessed with the fact that he's wasted his life. He's put all his energies and talents into supporting this professor whom he suddenly finds to be bogus and without any talent.

   As an actor I did not get going at all until I was forty, which is a lot younger than Vanya, but even at forty when nothing was happening to me in the profession I had chosen I had a tremendous feeling that I had wasted my time.[23]

In 1986, after an absence of nearly two and a half years from the stage, Nigel was lured back, at Glenda Jackson's request, to be her co-star in Charles Wood's new comedy *Across from the Garden of Allah*. Following a short pre-London tour in Guildford and Bath, the play, directed by RSC Associate Director Ron Daniels, opened at the Comedy Theatre on 27 February. Thirty-three years earlier that particular theatre had been the scene of Nigel's fleeting, but highly dramatic, first West End appearance when, as Leslie Phillips's understudy in *For Better, For Worse,* he had rushed behind the footlights to carry off the show's temporarily insensible star.

Between 1927 and 1959 The Garden of Allah, a Spanish-style hotel on the corner of Sunset Boulevard and Crescent Heights and within walking distance of Ciro's, the Players Club and Schwab's Drugstore, was a prominent Hollywood landmark, an oasis for the cinema aristocracy, and the setting for fights, suicide and murder. Wood's play, a three-hander composed in semi-blank verse, is a savage indictment of the professed Dream Factory in all its nauseating, neon-lit decadence. Through the contrasting reactions of his two protagonists, a middle-aged English couple, the playwright paints a garish, unsettling landscape suggestive of the worlds of Kafka and Hieronymus Bosch. Nigel's character was Douglas, a fifty-year-old unproduced screenwriter from Banbury, summoned to Hollywood to rewrite his adaptation of Evelyn Waugh's *Vile Bodies*. Douglas is a frequent, and therefore battle-hardened, visitor to Hollywood, able to let the bizarre mores of this weirdly closed community wash over him. His wife Barbara, on the other hand, a former actress and 'faded English rose with thorns'[24] played by Jackson (with whom Nigel had recently appeared in the film *Turtle Diary* in a cameo role as her publisher), is a first-time visitor appalled at the sleazy, synthetic and exploitative reality of the movie capital and its denizens. Both outsiders display a voyeuristic fascination with the ugly beauty of their alien surroundings and, specifically, the naked poolside posturing of their fellow hotel guests. The play's only other window onto Hollywood is a Mexican bellhop who is also an occasional masseur and film extra.

In an introduction to a collection of Charles Wood's plays, Richard Eyre made the general observation:

> *The work is not easy to perform. It's hard for actors to find naturalness within dialogue that is so highly distilled and so insistently singular, and it takes time, imagination and confidence to allow his scenes to realise their full potential.*[25]

Nigel and Jackson received high praise for their expert handling of these inherent difficulties. Nigel's timing and control were particularly impressive. But for the critics and sparse audiences, the play as a whole remained steadfastly unpalatable and unengaging, as John Barber's summation indicated:

> *Although it finally packs a Puritanical punch, this little morality – Mr Wood's third and sourest play about movie people – develops insufficient interest in its three characters, and is too scant of incident, to make enthralling theatre.*[26]

One reviewer, however, was undaunted by the problems and pungency of the script. Giles Gordon in *Plays and Players* credited the comedy with a broader and more incisive agenda than was commonly appreciated:

> *The text, which has a dazzling array of funny lines, is taken by Ms Jackson and Mr Hawthorne at a terrific lick: they serve this most adult, and sophisticated and allusive of texts with commendable lack of ego.*

I believe the play has been seriously underrated, yet had it been put on in the subsidised sector rather than the West End it might have been overpraised. Mr Wood's skill is that his clever dialogue is, on the face of it, casual and superficial but, if you listen to what is going on below, the aspirations and disappointments of the twentieth century – private relationships, public gloss – are there. It is a subversive piece of drama, akin to many contemporary American novels, of singular power, perfectly realised by all concerned.[27]

The production remained at the Comedy for many weeks, which would normally have been a cause for celebration, but, in view of the mostly poor notices and waning attendance, the length of the run cast a pall of gloom over the proceedings and became a test of the actors' fortitude. However, this dismal episode had at least one positive outcome as far as Nigel was concerned: it got him to the National after Michael Rudman saw the play and decided he wanted Nigel to star in his production of *The Magistrate*.

Nigel's next West End excursion was in Tom Stoppard's cerebral spy thriller *Hapgood,* which opened at the Aldwych on 8 March 1988, directed by Peter Wood and starring Stoppard's muse Felicity Kendal as Mother of a British intelligence unit. He played Kendal's classically educated section chief, Paul Blair, a Sir Humphrey of counter intelligence ('I gave a chap a job with us once because he said he'd read physics and I thought he meant the book by Aristotle.'). Robert Gore-Langton in *Plays and Players* declared that Nigel performed 'faultlessly his accustomed role of urbane civil servant with First Class arts degree'. It was around this time that critics began to compare Nigel to Ralph Richardson. Now in his late fifties, Nigel did bear a passing resemblance to Richardson, especially round the mouth, and he showed, without the same flamboyance, something of the unconventionality of this intriguing actor. In his review of *Hapgood* in the *Daily Telegraph,* Charles Osborne wrote: 'Nigel Hawthorne engagingly invests the head of MI6 […] with some of the quirkier mannerisms of the late Ralph Richardson.'[28]

In complexity of plot *Hapgood* outstripped the spycatcher novels of John le Carré, drawing parallels, in dense explicatory passages, between espionage, quantum mechanics and particle physics. Stoppard's complicated hypothesis was 'that the dual nature of light works for people as well as things'. He applied Heisenberg's Uncertainty Principle to the field of human perception. In Act One, scene 2 the defected Russian physicist Kerner tells an irritated and slightly mystified Blair:

Every time we don't look, we get wave pattern. Every time we look to see how we get wave pattern we get particle pattern. The art of observing determines what's what. [...] Somehow light is continuous and also discontinuous. The experimenter makes the choice. You get what you interrogate for. And you want to know if I'm a wave or a particle.

Not surprisingly, this sort of discourse, and the constant semantic interplay between the boffins and spooks, also provoked considerable irritation and mystification among West End audiences and their arbiters of taste, the critics. As a consequence, *Hapgood* was Stoppard's only major play not to win a London award. The review sub-headings alone are a measure of the general bemusement at the dualities the play explored: 'Molecules match up with moles' *(Observer)*[29]; 'Tricks of the light' *(Guardian)*[30]; 'Going nowhere fast' *(The Times)*[31]; 'Now you see it' *(Times Literary Supplement)*[32]; 'Tom Stoppard gets physical' *(Daily Telegraph)*[33]; 'Indefinite particles' *(Independent)*.[34] One piqued critic quipped, 'It would need a seeing-eye dog with A-level physics to guide most of us through what was going on.' Robert Gore-Langton was ultimately more forgiving in his evaluation:

What we are finally left with is a cumbersome dramatic contrivance, an irritatingly impossible poser, and a spy buff's dream come true. But if Hapgood *inflicts a pointless puzzlement, it's a mighty impressive card trick nonetheless.*[35]

Audiences, meanwhile, voted with their feet. When the play received its first performances, prior to the West End, at the Wimbledon Theatre several patrons left at the interval. This trend repeated itself at the Aldwych much to the delight of the maître d' of the Covent Garden restaurant Orso, one of the main beneficiaries of the *Hapgood* exodus.

The frustrations of the average spectator, however, paled beside those experienced by the cast. Ira Nadel, in his recent biography of Stoppard, gives a vivid indication of how the actors had not only to assimilate convoluted abstractions of double and triple meaning and application, but also to contend with a complex choreography:

Hapgood *depicts the unpredictability of individuals, doubled by the language itself as words themselves become puns, double agents in the play. The work explores the randomness behind our perceived realities as the spy story becomes a metaphor for theoretical physics. Agents cross and recross London and meet or miss each other at municipal bars, in a curious choreography whereby randomness attains a rhythm akin to ballet. Peter Wood added a whistled tune and occasional drumbeats to accentuate the dance, as the actors' movements become blurred and we lose track of the simultaneous exchange of briefcases between two Russians and what we later learn are two Ridleys.*

As the house lights went down in its original production, a street map was projected on to three hexagonal panels above the empty stage, allowing the audience to follow the route of a Russian agent driving across London (his route plotted by red lights on the map).[36]

In an interview with Sheridan Morley on the eve of the play's London premiere, Nigel likened the degree of difficulty involved in performing such a cryptic piece to 'playing chess without a board':

There's a plot of hugely elaborate labyrinthine complexity, set within the framework of physics. On the pre-London tour in Wimbledon we had a little trouble with an overcrowded grid, so we had to open without a full dress rehearsal and on the first night there I stood on stage, frequently without the faintest idea of what was supposed to be happening next.

But I stayed very calm and pretended it was all a dream: luckily Felicity went ploughing on, and although one or two people left in some bewilderment, it seemed to work out in the end.[37]

This was a diplomatic account of the problems the text was causing the company and about which Nigel felt very strongly. During the Wimbledon run of *Hapgood* Stoppard, dissatisfied with the scene between Blair and Kerner in Act One, scene 2, put his concerns in a note to Nigel and Roger Rees in which he maintained that the scene was 'too much about reactions'. Nigel's written reply to the note has been condensed and annotated by Nadel and is extremely revealing of the actor's razor-sharp analytical skills as well as his fundamental approach to, and ethos concerning, dramatic explication:

The note elicited a four-page critical response from Nigel Hawthorne, beginning with a comment on the complexity of the opening scene at the zoo and how odd it seemed that Stoppard wanted Hawthorne and Lewis [sic][38] *to 'reduce the degree of humanity and by doing so, your contention is that the scene will be easier to follow'. The opposite should be the case. Hawthorne then astutely analyses the relationship between Kerner and Blair and questions further why Felicity Kendal is told to make Hapgood colder and less approachable. 'Any thought of the four of us working as a "team" went out of the window weeks ago ... You seem to be advocating the sacrifice of relationships to theories by telling us that the characters are getting in the way of the physics.'*

The result of this emphasis made the play harder to perform night after night; any energy had to be artificially injected, Hawthorne explains, because there are 'no emotional areas'. He also disliked the idea that he had to play his character, Blair, with more ruthlessness. He indicts Stoppard and Peter Wood for dominating rehearsals by 'playing games with the cast to see how much of the play they understood'. Feeling patronized, Hawthorne resisted the direction of Wood and Stoppard and resented the way 'the invention [was] thrown on the responsibility of the actors at the last moment', while the director's heart 'never really seemed in the production'. The final paragraph summed up Stoppard's weaknesses and strengths with this trenchant sentence: 'I love you as a man and puzzle that the warmth you give out so constantly and effortlessly is excluded from your plays. You have written a brilliant but élitist play ...'[39]

The problem that Nigel isolated was the play's absence of emotional weight and cohesion, the forfeiture of subtleties of character to intricacies of plot. Although a lover of words and ideas, Nigel believed that a playwright should not try to dazzle an audience with science, that linguistic and conceptual cleverness should not obscure the journey taken by the characters in a drama. The following year he found the perfect antidote to the strategic and emotionally static *Hapgood* in William Nicholson's heart-rending *Shadowlands*, as he told Blake Green in New York:

The role [in Hapgood*] had no heart, so I was wrong to do it. The part [in* Shadowlands*] is absolutely wonderful because it takes you on that journey: you see a man who appears to be one thing, and you see him become someone else.[40]*

Shadowlands was Nicholson's first work for the stage, adapted from his own award-winning BBC television film of 1985, which featured Joss Ackland and Claire Bloom as C. S. Lewis and the American poet Joy Davidman-Gresham. The earlier version was essentially a love story about unlikely soulmates, whereas the stage play focuses on the spiritual journey at the centre of the love story and is the dramatisation of a theological conundrum – 'if God loves us, why does He allow us to suffer so much?' The title of the play, and much of its meaning, is taken from 'Farewell to Shadowlands', the final chapter of the seventh and final book in the *Narnia* series, *The Last Battle*, which Lewis wrote in 1956, the year of his marriage to Joy. In this chapter the children have left the old and shadowy Narnia and gone 'further up and further in' the new, sunlit and real Narnia. There, leaping towards them 'like a living cataract of power and beauty' is the Lion and Christ-like figure of Aslan, their awesome yet tender protector:

> Lucy said, 'We're so afraid of being sent away, Aslan. And you have sent us back into our own world so often.'
>
> 'No fear of that,' said Aslan. 'Have you not guessed?'
>
> Their hearts leaped and a wild hope rose within them.
>
> 'There was a real railway accident,' said Aslan softly. 'Your father and mother and all of you are – as you used to call it in the Shadowlands – dead. The term is over: the holidays have begun. The dream is ended: this is the morning.'
>
> And as He spoke He no longer looked to them like a lion; but the things that began to happen after that were so great and beautiful that I cannot write them. And for us this is the end of all the stories, and we can most truly say that they all lived happily ever after.[41]

Lewis's conception of the Shadowlands had two main sources. The first of these was Plato's allegory of the Cave from the beginning of Book VII of the *Republic* where Plato represents knowledge as a kind of conversion of the soul from darkness to light. Socrates, the narrator, asks Glaucon to imagine a group of prisoners, chained in an underground cave since their formative years, whose physical constraint and limited sphere of vision cause them to mistake shadows for reality. He then develops this image, employing it as a simile to describe human nature in its education and want of education. Lewis acknowledges his debt to this Platonic parable in the penultimate chapter of *The Last Battle* where Lord Diggory tells Peter and Lucy:

> 'When Aslan said you could never go back to Narnia, he meant the Narnia you were thinking of. But that was not the real Narnia. That had a beginning and an end. It was only a shadow or a copy of the real Narnia which has always been here and always will be here: just as our world, England and all, is only a shadow or a copy of something in Aslan's real world. [...] All of the old Narnia that mattered, all the dear creatures, have been drawn into the real Narnia through the Door. And of course it is different; as different as a real thing is from a shadow or as waking life is from a dream.' His voice stirred everyone like a trumpet as he spoke these words: but when he added under his breath 'It's all in Plato, all in Plato: bless me, what do they teach at these schools!' the older ones laughed.[42]

Lewis's other source was someone whom he regarded as his spiritual and literary master, the nineteenth-century Scottish novelist and children's writer, George MacDonald. MacDonald's fairy stories are powerful allegories of good and evil and, in a way comparable to *The Chronicles of Narnia*, they combine Christian symbolism and mystical imagination. Lewis was especially moved by their sense of another world. At the start of his conversion back to Christianity, in October 1929, Lewis read MacDonald's *The Diary of an Old Soul* (1880), 366 poems for devotional reflection. Thirty-three years later he presented Joy Davidman with a copy of this work, inscribed by the author and himself, for Christmas. But it was MacDonald's short story 'The Golden Key', first published in 1867 in *Dealings with the Fairies,* that influenced Lewis's understanding and depiction of the Shadowlands. Like Bunyan's *The Pilgrim's Progress,* 'The Golden Key' is an extended apologue of the individual's spiritual quest through life. The story follows two children's search for the 'land from whence the shadows fall', the primary theme being that death is not an end but a transformation.

The idea of the Shadowlands, then, is laden with meaning. William Nicholson has adroitly and sensitively structured his play around it; he uses the Shadowlands as a metaphor for the personal journey Lewis completes and the profound changes his journey entails. At the beginning of Act One, Lewis, alone on stage, assures his audience:

God loves us, so He makes us the gift of suffering. Through suffering, we release our hold on the toys of this world, and know that our true good lies in another world. [...]

For believe me, this world that seems to us so substantial, is no more than the shadowlands. Real life has not begun yet.

It is a lesson he recites with the ivory-towered detachment of a well-rehearsed high-table rhetorician. But when he revisits this image at the close of the play, he speaks with the authority of one who has suffered 'the torments of the damned' at the prospect, and indeed the reality, of losing his wife, and all his late-found happiness, to cancer. He is no longer armed with ready answers:

No shadows here. Only darkness, and silence, and the pain that cries like a child.

It ends, like all affairs of the heart, with exhaustion. Only so much pain is possible. Then, rest. [...]

So you can say if you like that Jack Lewis has no answer to the question after all, except this: I have been given the choice twice in my life. The boy chose safety. The man chooses suffering. [...]

I find I can live with the pain after all. The pain, now, is part of the happiness, then. That's the deal.

Only shadows, Joy.

In his period of complacency Lewis painted God as the Cosmic dispenser of tough love, and in his grief he lashes out at 'God the vivisectionist'. His final speech begins where his first speech ended. This time, however, it is not a lecture but a soliloquy in which he contemplates and, perhaps for the first time, fully absorbs the truth and the immense difficulty of his own precepts. His words are 'transformed by his own suffering'.

The challenge of recreating this epic emotional and spiritual journey on stage was what attracted Nigel to the play. 'The joy of it,' he said, 'is that [Lewis's] beliefs are turned topsy-turvy and he's made to reassess.'[43] In accepting this challenge he underwent a catharsis strikingly similar to his character's. One of the many books Nigel read, as part of his research for the role, was *A Grief Observed*, Lewis's moving and honest dissection of his grief at his wife's death. Originally published in 1961 under the pseudonym N. W. Clerk,[44] the book is a collection of notes composed as a way of surviving 'the mad midnight moments'.[45] In it Lewis says:

Your bid – for God or no God, for a good God or the Cosmic Sadist, for eternal life or nonentity – will not be serious if nothing much is staked on it. And you will never discover how serious it was until the stakes are raised horribly high; until you find that you are playing not for counters or for sixpences but for every penny you have in the world. Nothing less will shake a man – or at any rate a man like me – out of his merely verbal thinking and his merely notional beliefs. He has to be knocked silly before he comes to his senses. Only torture will bring out the truth. Only under torture does he discover it himself.[46]

Towards the end of Nicholson's play, Lewis, in the depths of his own grief, tries to talk to his young stepson Douglas, who is 'profoundly hurt by his mother's death, but is refusing to show it.' The stage directions at this point call for a monumental release of emotion:

> *Douglas can't take any more. He reaches out for comfort, pressing himself*
> *against Lewis. Lewis wraps his arms round the boy, and at last his own tears*
> *break through, in heart-breaking sobs, unloosing the grief of a lifetime. His*
> *emotion releases the tears that have been waiting in the boy.*

Nicholson was, at first, sceptical about Nigel's ability to manage this crucial scene: 'Lewis is a role that rips you apart. The actor has to tear himself in pieces on the stage in front of us. I didn't know if Nigel could do it.' But during the final rehearsal in Plymouth something extraordinary happened which cancelled completely any doubts the playwright had. Nigel had previously avoided playing out the climax of the scene in rehearsal but, on this particular day, he responded to the dramatic situation purely by instinct and in a manner beyond his control:

> *We got to the end of the play and the boy's mother had just died. I had to say*
> *to him something like, 'You can't just hold in your emotions; you have to let*
> *go.' And he suddenly ran to me and threw his arms around me, and I could*
> *feel this huge reservoir of emotion about to explode. I fought it. I remember*
> *putting my hand on my head to try and stop it leaking out. But it just went*
> *and I began to cry. I must have cried for twenty minutes. And after that, I*
> *could always recreate that moment, and I was no longer afraid of emotion.*[47]

His co-star Jane Lapotaire, realising that it was not C. S. Lewis but Nigel who was crying, also stepped out of character and held him in her arms, while the director, Elijah Moshinsky, stood by in embarrassed silence. Nicholson recalled, 'Nigel broke down and just went on crying. He couldn't stop himself and couldn't finish the play. I was in tears myself. I said to the director, "If he can keep doing that every night, the play's going to be a sensation".'[48] When Nigel did reproduce this reaction every night in the theatre, it broke the hearts of the audience. Trevor Bentham remembers that, at that moment, 'you could hear people's collective intake of breath.' The brief lull of exhaustion between Nigel's sobs of agony and his final soliloquy was equally memorable. In the sermon he gave at Nigel's funeral, the Right Revd Christopher Herbert, Bishop of St Albans, spoke of 'the silence that followed his roar of grief in *Shadowlands'* as 'a silence which is eloquent of the mystery and the beauty of God, the Word made flesh.'

This most naked expression of pain came from deep within him and each night left him emotionally drained. 'You can't really fake that sort of thing,' he explained at the time. 'You have to take the journey the character takes. Sometimes I cry in the wings afterwards, and people come up and wrap their arms around me. It's always very hard to smile during curtain call.'[49] Nigel's experience in that final rehearsal was parallel in significance to the experience of both his stage character and the real Jack Lewis: a lifetime's hurt and turmoil, carefully stored away, suddenly erupted with a vengeance. It was as though he had a gaping wound and could not staunch the bleeding. In the midst of this emotional explosion, Nigel the actor made a mental note of precisely how he felt and behaved during those twenty minutes, which became integral to his performance process. 'As in any role,' he said, 'you have to make it as much of you as possible: if the part contains a lot of you – and I wouldn't do one if it didn't – then you draw on your own experience of how to behave in certain circumstances.'[50]

The release of emotion at the play's conclusion was the powerful culmination of Nigel's sympathetic and well-developed portrait of the man before, during and after his crisis of faith. Several people noted that this portrait made Lewis a softer, more appealing character than the intellectual bully he actually was. But neither Nigel nor Nicholson purported to be presenting photographic or historical reality. The playwright made clear his intention to Allan Wallach of *Newsday:*

> *What I'm actually creating are characters who are kind of parallel to the real people. Of course they're not the real people. They are a kind of dramatized construct, which gives you, I hope, some of the feeling of the real people, but more important, makes characters that live on the stage for those two hours.*
>
> *And that's what I really care about. I want people to come out of the theater not saying, 'Now I know more about C. S. Lewis' but, 'Now I know more about myself.'*[51]

Throughout the first half of the play Nigel created illuminating public and private personae for Lewis – the unfaltering Christian apologist with his captive public; the combative scholar comfortably ensconced amid the Senior Common Room badinage; the affectionate, if laconic, brother; and the shy, artless suitor. He thus demonstrated the character's emotional insularity as well as his latent vulnerability, preparing the way for the emancipation of his feelings.

Interestingly, the real Douglas Gresham (the younger of Joy's two sons, and the only one depicted in the play) saw the production in New York and 'thought Nigel's portrayal to be very good except for one criticism which was that I felt that he overplayed the humorous aspects of the character to the extent that at times he (the character) came across as almost a buffoon.' Nigel certainly exploited the comedy and eccentricity of his character, but he had always maintained that humour was an appropriate and effective prelude to tragic exposition and serious reflection, a philosophy that Lewis himself seemed to embrace. In a letter (dated 7 March 1960) to his friend Peter Milward, a newly ordained Jesuit priest, Lewis offered the young man some advice on preaching: 'If you want people to weep by the end, make them laugh in the beginning.'[52] William Nicholson, for one, believed Nigel's interpretation had achieved the perfect balance between comedy and tragedy:

> *What he does on stage is amazing. You take somebody who you start off thinking is a bit of a joke, this uptight, comic man, and by the end he's breaking your heart with what he's feeling on stage, night after night, eight times a week.*[53]

Following its world premiere at the Theatre Royal in Plymouth, *Shadowlands* opened at London's Queen's Theatre on 23 October 1989. If not all the critics were enamoured of, or convinced by, the play's theological propositions, the production was sufficiently impressive to be judged Best Play of 1990 in the *Evening Standard* Drama Awards. Nigel was nominated for the Olivier Award for Best Actor in a New Play but lost to Oliver Ford Davies, the star of David Hare's *Racing Demon*. There was little disagreement, however, about the outstanding quality of his performance. To many people Nigel's compelling expression of raw, overwhelming suffering was a revelation:

> *Hawthorne's metamorphosis from bookish, corduroy-clad academic to a bleeding human being in touch with his own emotions for the first time since the childhood death of his mother, is deeply affecting. (Clive Hirschhorn,* Sunday Express*)* [54]

> *Lewis' turmoil as he makes his soul-searing pilgrimage from intellectual perception to emotional involvement is superbly reflected by Nigel Hawthorne. One by one the barriers of education, training, class and natural reserve fall and the naked need of the man is revealed. It is a magnificent performance. (David Nathan,* Jewish Chronicle*)* [55]

> *Nigel Hawthorne's depiction of the growing dependence of Lewis upon Joy, his overflowing happiness at discovering love for the first time and his agonising despair at losing it, is unbearably moving. It is a performance that threads nuances between great joy and utter misery. (Milton Shulman,* Evening Standard*)* [56]

Hawthorne reminds us in particular of Lewis's gift for humanising the abstract; his ideas were as lived-in as his worn corduroy coat. But the particular pleasure of this performance is in its dramatising of inhibition and exposure: here we have a man who can anatomise the heart but is almost too shy to invite a woman to tea. (Kate Kellaway, Observer) [57]

When Mr Hawthorne's self-imposed barriers of bracing intellectual bonhomie are finally swept aside by the prospect of losing her and by the heroic good grace with which Miss Lapotaire grasps her brief but miraculous spell of remission, we indeed are watching a man made whole through adversity. (Jack Tinker, Daily Mail) [58]

The climactic confrontation of the piece is not [...] with Joy or with God, but with Douglas after her death. Presented with an image of himself motherless at eight, Hawthorne recoils and writhes as though this were a vision to be dreaded. Then, in a burst of grief, that has all the naked violence of a child's, he at once hugs his step-son and re-embraces, salutarily, his damaged childhood self. (Paul Taylor, Independent) [59]

In terms of appearance there was not much similarity between Nigel and C. S. Lewis, who had the look of a cumbersome rustic encased in rumpled tweed and pipe smoke. But Nigel's study of the man was comprehensive; he inhabited Lewis intellectually, emotionally and corporeally, conveying both the inhibition and liberation of all aspects of his character. Michael Billington extolled the performance as the latest demonstration of Nigel's gift for physical comedy and tragedy, his ability to infiltrate the essence and history of a character through his invention of eloquent non-verbal peculiarities:

Nigel Hawthorne does not naturally possess the ruddy-complexioned, country-farmer look of the real C. S. Lewis but he is excellent at conveying the faint embarrassment of an intellectual surprised by passion. He is forever staring at his shoes, twitching his raincoat, thrusting his hands deep into his pockets as if taking evasive action against the promptings of his heart. He is also very good in his snappish, inconsolable desolation immediately after his wife's death. [60]

A notable feature of his physical interpretation of Lewis was that once again the memory of Nigel's hero was invoked. Charles Osborne in the *Daily Telegraph* remarked: 'Nigel Hawthorne, who is beginning to acquire the personality and mannerisms of the late Ralph Richardson, presents Lewis as a churchy, donnish character, which sounds just about right.'[61]

C. S. Lewis in *Shadowlands,* New York 1990. *(Martha Swope)*

In August 1990 the American actress Jane Alexander replaced Jane Lapotaire in the role of Joy. She recalls Nigel's hospitality and helpfulness:

Nigel was a remarkable actor to work with – 'present' at all times, never giving less than 100%. It was not easy welcoming a new actress into the part of Joy Davidman when Jane Lapotaire had played it so well with him prior to my taking over the role, but welcome me he did and went that extra step to ensure my comfort. Nigel also taught me that napping before a performance was absolutely vital for actors and that I had better teach myself how immediately, which of course I did. I continue the practice to this day and am grateful for his sound advice. I miss his smile, his laughter, and his huge talent.

Three months later the play transferred to Broadway where it opened at the Brooks Atkinson Theatre on 256W. 47th Street, the first theatre to be named after a critic.[62] Nigel and Alexander retained their parts in an otherwise new and chiefly American cast.

Before settling into an enormously successful run, the company's immediate challenge was to survive the slings and arrows of Frank Rich, the trenchant and apparently omnipotent *New York Times* drama critic, who had the aura and sway of a Roman emperor at a gladiatorial contest. During his reign of terror in the 1980s and early 1990s Rich was one of the most powerful and potentially prejudicial journalistic voices in the city, earning himself the epithet 'The Butcher of Broadway'. His review of *Shadowlands* was by no means his deadliest fusillade and was, in fact, relatively restrained, but it did deliver a few stinging blows:

How you will feel about Shadowlands *depends a great deal on your degree of Anglophilia. The play, by William Nicholson, has little more intellectual or emotional depth than a tear-jerker set in two-car-garage suburbia, but it does boast a certain rarefied British atmosphere. This is the kind of work that is often described as 'literate', especially by nonreaders, because its characters frequently mention works of literature. As at 84* Charing Cross Road, *its London theatrical prototype, no visitor to* Shadowlands *need worry that anyone on stage will be so boorish as to discuss the actual substance of the books and authors whose names are bandied about.*[63]

Nicholson and Alexander sustained the brunt of the attack, being accused of superficiality, while Rich reserved most of his praise for Nigel's performance:

Mr Hawthorne migrates from absent-mindedness to passion. His performance reaches an exquisite peak of comic turmoil when he finds himself torn between the gesture he always uses to put off Joy's affection – a random, reflexive search of his many pockets for some unspecified object – and his ravenous hunger for a kiss.

When suffering overwhelms his spirit, Mr Hawthorne goes further still, spitting out his grief in pink-faced rage. The actor makes one see how

Shadowlands *might have been as moving as Lewis's own memoir,* A Grief Observed. *But Mr Nicholson and Ms Alexander undercut the actor by refusing to bring his romantic partner to life.*[64]

Other heavyweight New York critics were also greatly impressed with the range and depth of Nigel's characterisation. Rich's predecessor on the *New York Times,* Clive Barnes, now writing for the *New York Post,* enthused:

Looking like a remarkable amalgam of Lewis himself and Ralph Richardson, Hawthorne magnificently plays the drama as if it were a church organ. Larger than life, yet smaller than death, Hawthorne runs from flippant profundity to the extremity of pain with the pace of a champion. What a performance![65]

In *Time* magazine William A. Henry III continued the Richardson analogy:

[Nicholson] prospers [...] by Nigel Hawthorne's epic performance, reminiscent of Ralph Richardson at his finest, as Lewis. Shuffling and shambling, looking as if forever surrounded by muddy acres and faithful hounds, Hawthorne is the embodiment of an older, surer England coming to grips with a new world that is not so much brave as demanding of bravery. He makes theological abstractions breathe – and weep.[66]

Nigel was duly honoured with Broadway's most prestigious accolade, the Tony Award for Best Performance by a Leading Actor in a Play, as well as the New York Outer Critics' Circle Award for the Outstanding Actor in a Play on or off Broadway. He now enjoyed the highest respect and recognition on both sides of the Atlantic and, as film producer Sam Goldwyn Jnr perceived, 'he became in America the actor's actor.' In his Tony acceptance speech Nigel thanked 'the producers for steering us through some difficult times, like the long winter, the Gulf War, a recession and Frank Rich.'

In 1993 a film version of *Shadowlands* was produced. Richard Attenborough had secured the screen rights and already had in mind Anthony Hopkins to play the lead. Inevitably the film was packaged as a romantic drama and much of the play's meaning lost. This was the second time Nigel had successfully created a role on stage only to be denied the opportunity of recreating it on film. It was a cruel, though not unexpected, disappointment, but Nigel's moment of movie stardom, for which he had waited long and patiently, was a good deal closer than he could possibly have imagined. One night in New York, director Nicholas Hytner, the wunderkind of British theatre, came to see *Shadowlands* and, although neither he nor Nigel was aware of the fact, back in North London, Alan Bennett was working on a new play about the madness of King George III, which was to provide them both with the chance of a lifetime. Hytner says:

I'd always thought Nigel was a marvellous actor, particularly a marvellous comic actor. I thought his performance in Privates on Parade *was absolutely wonderful. But I hadn't known quite how huge his range was and the emotional depth that he was capable of until I saw* Shadowlands. *And I have to admit that I didn't see* Shadowlands *in London. I was in New York doing a show on Broadway with Jonathan Pryce in it* [Miss Saigon], *and Jonathan said we had to go and see* Shadowlands *and I said, 'Oh, do we have to? It sounds exactly like the kind of play I'm not going to like.' In fact I thought the play was terrific. I remember we were sitting there, Jonathan and I, both of us weeping like babies. We went and said hello to Nigel afterwards, in fact we had a meal with him. I think maybe I'd met him just to say hello to before. And at that time I didn't even know that Alan was working on this George III play – he kept his cards very close to his chest. But when the play arrived, it occurred to me immediately that Nigel would be the actor who could do everything that this part required, and in the event he did a lot more. He found things in the part which, I think, nobody was expecting.*

Notes to Chapter 8

1 Interview with Blake Green, 'Playing C. S. Lewis Flat Out', *Newsday,* November 1990.
2 *Guardian,* 14 October 1977.
3 *Observer,* 16 October 1977.
4 *Evening Standard,* 14 October 1977.
5 'Play that makes no concessions', *Times,* 14 October 1977.
6 *Guardian,* 14 October 1977.
7 *Theatre Newsletter,* November 1977.
8 *Sunday Times,* 23 October 1977.
9 *Sunday Telegraph,* 16 October 1977.
10 The play was first produced in German at the Akademie Theater in Vienna in January 1936. Two months later it had its first English-language premiere in Melbourne, Australia. In September 1936 it received its first production in England when it was performed by the Matthew Forsyth Repertory Company in Bexhill. After an aborted wartime attempt to stage the play at the Globe (now the Gielgud), *The Millionairess* finally had its West End premiere at the New Theatre (now the Albery) in June 1952, with a cast headed by Katherine Hepburn and Robert Helpmann.
11 'Russian Gems', *Punch,* 12 December 1979.
12 Gems (1979) 58-59.
13 Ibid 58.
14 *Lady,* 20 December 1979.
15 This production in July 1963 also featured Sybil Thorndike, Lewis Casson, Fay Compton, and Rosemary Harris.
16 'Russian Gems', *Punch,* 12 December 1979.
17 Interview with Charles Spencer, 'Chamber Chekhov', *Evening Standard,* 16 November 1979.
18 *Evening Standard,* 16 November 1979.
19 Gems (1979) 59.
20 *Plays and Players,* February 1980, 29.
21 Gems (1979) 60.
22 *Sunday Times,* 2 December 1979.
23 Interview with Charles Spencer, 'Chamber Chekhov', *Evening Standard,* 16 November 1979.
24 Francis King, *Sunday Telegraph,* 9 March 1986.
25 Introduction to Wood (1997) 7.
26 *Daily Telegraph,* 28 February 1986.
27 *Plays and Players,* April 1986, 22.
28 'Tom Stoppard gets physical', *Daily Telegraph,* 10 March 1988.
29 Michael Ratcliffe, *Observer,* 13 March 1988.
30 Michael Billington, *Guardian,* 9 March 1988.
31 Irving Wardle, *Times,* 9 March 1988.
32 J. Wilders, *Times Literary Supplement,* 18-24 March 1988.
33 Charles Osborne, *Daily Telegraph,* 10 March 1988.
34 Peter Kemp, *Independent,* 10 March 1988.
35 *Plays and Players,* April 1986, 23.
36 Nadel (2002) 376.

37 Interview with Sheridan Morley, 'Life's equation solved', *Times,* 7 March 1988.

38 Nadel erroneously refers to Roger Rees (the actor who played Kerner) as Roger Lewis.

39 Nadel (2002) 374.

40 'Playing C. S. Lewis Flat Out', *Newsday,* November 1990.

41 Lewis (1980) 171-72.

42 Ibid 159-60.

43 'Playing C. S. Lewis Flat Out', *Newsday,* 1990.

44 'N. W.' stood for Nat Whilk (Anglo-Saxon for 'I know not whom'), a pseudonym under which Lewis had previously published poems in *Punch.*

45 Lewis (1966) 31.

46 Ibid 33.

47 Interview with Andrew Billen, 'Lear Crowns Hawthorne's Career', *Evening Standard,* 8 October 1999.

48 Interview with Kim Hubbard and Tony Kahn in New York City.

49 Interview with Kim Hubbard and Tony Kahn in New York City.

50 Interview with Blake Green, 'Playing C. S. Lewis Flat Out', *Newsday,* November 1990.

51 Interview with Allan Wallach, 'C. S. Lewis Revealed', *Newsday,* 11 November 1990.

52 See Griffin (1988) 380.

53 Interview with Allan Wallach, 'C. S. Lewis Revealed', *Newsday,* 11 November 1990.

54 *Sunday Express,* 29 October 1989.

55 *Jewish Chronicle,* 27 October 1989.

56 *Evening Standard,* 24 October 1989.

57 *Observer,* 5 November 1989.

58 *Daily Mail,* 24 October 1989.

59 *Independent,* 25 October 1989.

60 *Guardian,* 25 October 1989.

61 *Daily Telegraph,* 25 October 1989.

62 Brooks Atkinson had been the drama critic of the *New York Times* since 1926. On his retirement in 1960 the Mansfield Theatre was rechristened the Brooks Atkinson.

63 *New York Times,* 12 November 1990.

64 Ibid.

65 *New York Post,* 12 November 1990.

66 'In Search of a Healing Magic', *Time,* 19 November 1990.

Chapter 9

Every Inch a King

THE MADNESS OF GEORGE III

ὁ δ' οὐκέτ' αὐτὸς ἦν
(But he was no longer himself.)

(Euripides, *The Madness of Heracles,* 931)

What's madness but nobility of soul
At odds with circumstance?

(Theodore Roethke, 'In a Dark Time', ll. 7-8)

In the last decade of his life Nigel presented on stage two portraits of royal madness. The first was in Alan Bennett's *The Madness of George III* which opened at the Royal National Theatre in November 1991. Over the next three years this production toured Great Britain, the United States, Greece and Israel and ran for several seasons in repertoire on the Lyttelton stage. Nigel's towering performance in the title role received unanimous and lavish accolades from the critics and won him the 1992 Olivier and Evening Standard Awards for Best Actor. When he repeated the role on film in the summer of 1994 he earned an Academy Award nomination, preparing the way, at the age of sixty-five, for a successful international film career. His perfect realisation of each stage of the King's descent into madness confirmed what *Shadowlands* had already revealed: his powers as a modern tragedian.

In August 1991 a reading of *The Madness of George III,* which Alan Bennett had already twice rewritten, was organised at the National Theatre Studio. Nigel, fresh from his New York triumph in *Shadowlands,* was the only actor who, at that stage, had been cast. The remaining parts were assumed by current members of the Company, including Simon Russell Beale as Fox and Robin Bailey as Thurlow. When it came to his turn to read, with great apprehension and no pre-rehearsed strategy for the part, Nigel brought the character of King George to life by means of an intuitive understanding and with a spontaneous dynamism:

I was very nervous because there were a lot actors that I respected, and also I'd been cast and suddenly we were doing the reading of the thing. And so when my first entrance came up, I just went for it. I hadn't really discussed how I was going to do it or anything with anybody, but I came to bits and I just did them as I thought that they could possibly be, and quite violently, quite aggressively.

While director Nicholas Hytner was aware of Nigel's emotional depth and dramatic range from his performance in *Shadowlands*, to Alan Bennett, who had first seen Nigel in *West of Suez* at the Royal Court in 1972, the choice of lead actor was not immediately obvious:

I hadn't seen him in Shadowlands. *I obviously knew him as an actor but I'd not seen him playing, as it were, heavier roles. So when Nick suggested him I was a bit dubious, as much really on his physique as anything else. I could see that his face and his geniality would work, but I didn't know that he was as solid as he was. In my eyes he'd always been rather a lissom actor, which he was when he was younger. So that was one of the reasons and, of course, I was totally wrong. But, fortunately, Nick persuaded me and he had seen him in* Shadowlands, *so I just deferred to his judgement. There wasn't any fight about it. Then we had a read-through in August 1991 and as soon as I saw him I was convinced.*

The script the actors read was a daunting and cumbersome entity, and, according to Nigel, assembled in somewhat unruly fashion:

[Alan Bennett] had used about eight different typewriters, all of the most ancient variety – an old Royal, an old Olivetti, and the o's were up there, and the a's were down there, and the t's were everywhere, and then when he got a little bit that he thought he liked, he would snip it out of the page, and stick it on there, and build up a sort of collage, and that's what we got. And then they were put into the photocopier, and we got these pages of strange happenings.

But as Hytner witnessed, from these 'strange happenings' something completely unexpected emerged:

Alan always delivers a first draft that is very baggy and it's quite deliberate. It's what he likes to do. He wants to hear from the director, producer, the few people he sends it to, feedback. Alan is completely open to the opinions of the people around him that he trusts. It was a very long play and it was as much about the political manipulations around the Regency Crisis as it was about everything else. I don't think it was obvious off the page how wrenching an emotional journey there was in the play ready to be pulled out by an actor like Nigel.

Between the initial read-through and the first performance the play underwent substantial reconstruction, some of this only two weeks before it went on stage. The abnormal delay in finalising the working script, Bennett maintains, was surprisingly not resented by the company:

Rewrites often mean crisis time in the theatre. There wasn't any sense of that and even when the rewriting got quite complicated, the cast weren't fazed by it or worried by it. One of the good things about Nick Hytner is that he does go on working at a play right up until the last minute. Directors, in my experience, are quite lazy and once it's on and doing previews they tend to leave it all and not still be looking at it, trying to find ways to improve it.

Originally the play's focus, as envisaged by Bennett, was the political manoeuvring and medical incompetence surrounding the demented monarch which received a satirical treatment. However, Nigel recalled that the focus very quickly began to shift:

Alan Bennett thought he'd written a satirical play about the conflict between the politicians and the doctors over the man who happened to be the king of the country. But, at the end of the read-through the director rang me up and said, 'Alan has just realised, by listening to what you were doing with George, that he's got to make it the story of the King.' Alan then started to chip away everything that didn't actually relate to the journey that the king was making. And that's what it became. So then when we got into the rehearsal room the journey was something which had become an obsession with me.

In order to make central the King's journey and resolve difficulties of structure and dramatic tension, which were evident from the read-through and rehearsal period,[1] Bennett, with Hytner as patient collaborator, completed two further rewrites:

I realised from Nigel's reading that the King was magnetic and that it was his story you were interested in. The other thing I realised was that when he was mad there was a limit to what you could take. You weren't as interested in him mad as you were when he was sane or going mad. Once he was mad he was in a place the audience couldn't reach or didn't want to be in, because it didn't make sense. A little went a long way.

In dramatising the King's madness, Alan Bennett subscribed to the theory, first proposed by the mother and son physicians Ida Macalpine and Richard Hunter,[2] that George III was suffering from porphyria, a metabolic disturbance affecting the nervous system and creating symptoms similar to dementia and dermatitis.[3] The play's temporal setting was the period from October 1788 to March 1789, believed to be the first in which the illness affected the King's mind. Occurring five years after the American War of Independence and immediately before the French Revolution, it also precipitated the Regency Crisis,[4] which in turn resulted in the permanent curtailment of the work and influence of the Crown. Bennett was thus able to exploit the inherently dramatic nature of these historical and political circumstances.

Superficially, King George seemed an unusual subject for Bennett, who is commonly acclaimed as the eloquent chronicler of the quiet desperation of the ordinary and marginalised, and of the parameters of tragedy and comedy which define their daily existence. It was also a boldly chosen subject in view of the late twentieth century's preoccupation with the socially relevant and anti-heroic in drama. In terms of his position and the height from which he falls, George III, 'urban, metropolitan and royal', more closely resembles the great heroes of Greek and Shakespearean tragedy than the familiar figures who populate Bennett's fictional and real worlds such as Midgley, Graham Whittaker and Miss Shepherd. The nearest in stature to George III among Bennett's other stage characters, apart from HMQ, are the Cambridge spies Guy Burgess and Anthony Blunt. Yet, what made *The Madness of George III* accessible to a modern audience was the emergence in the course of Nigel's performance of the King's simple and suffering humanity. Moreover, by reason of his kingship, no less than his madness, George III's world was as circumscribed as that of Bennett's more ordinary characters. The playwright, in fact, sees a kinship between George in his madness and Miss Shepherd:

She was mad in a different way, but they were alike in this sense, that they were utterly without self-consciousness, either of them. In that sense Miss Shepherd was monarch of her own world. The two are also connected in that they don't listen a lot to other characters on stage. The Lady in the Van was criticised in exactly the same way as George III as being a one-character piece, because of the sort of towering central performance. But that was how it was here. [...] The absolute self-centredness of kingship is like the absolute self-centredness of madness and you don't have far to go from one to the other. The modes of address and the way of talking about oneself in the third person are the kind of things you associate with madness, but they're the accepted form of kings.

Nicholas Hytner also believes that George III is a more typical Bennettesque creation than he first appears:

Nigel's George was a character that just said everything. Nothing was held in. There were no secrets. [...] On the one hand, you could say, Alan writes spies, who are, by definition, people with secrets. On the other hand, he writes people who are so naked. Miss Shepherd has a huge secret, which is who she was before she went into the van, but she has something in common with George III in that she just says everything.

Rehearsals began in September. As was usual in his approach to a biographical role, Nigel's research into the period and the man was thorough, but when he had assimilated sufficient biographical, political and medical detail, he then stored this away in order to give his imagination and love of experimentation free reign. In his process of discovery he was encouraged by Nicholas Hytner who, he said, 'let me find my own world with George, he gave me my head, and let me find my own horizons. And that was the way to do it because it meant that I could then imaginatively explore the world this man lived in.' The relationship between actor and director, Hytner states, was characterised by an easy reciprocity of ideas:

Nigel prefers it when there is an absolutely free give and take between him and the director. He wants suggestions; he doesn't like to keep it all to himself. Different actors want different things and need different ways of collaborating, and, personally as a director, I'm very happy to tune into whatever an actor wants, but it's more enjoyable to work with someone like Nigel who lets you become part of his process. It's great fun.

Bennett observed that Nigel's exploration of his character combined a respect for historical accuracy with invention and intuition:

He would ask me things about George III, but he wasn't fussy in the way that, say, Alec Guinness would be. He trusts his own instincts, I think, and wasn't over-literal. He has a lot of theatrical flair and actors tend to trust that rather than any over-meticulous sticking to fact or to research. And, after all, it is a character he's created. It's not George III. Of course, some of the things George III did were intensely theatrical – the 'what-whatting' and all that – and they were a gift.

One of the first and most useful aids Nigel found to realising his character, and representing the course of his journey, was costume. In the rehearsal room he compiled a list of costume essentials with which he could suggest, in a very visual way, George's decline and recovery:

I asked at the very first rehearsal for an assortment of clothes. I said 'I want some slippers, and some stockings, and a dressing gown, and nightshirt and a cap, and something to simulate a uniform and a sash. And as we went from day to day to day, I'd start to think what I would be wearing. I'd start off wearing the uniform and then start stripping bits off.

In rehearsal as George III at the National Theatre, 1991. *(Donald Cooper / Photostage)*

In the final production the King's mental deterioration was reflected in the stripping away of his regal and public exterior and the subsequent exposure of a broken and abased private self. Nigel's use of costume did not, however, record a steady decline, but rather the fluctuations which were characteristic of George III's illness:

> *He was sometimes better and sometimes worse and the clothes indicated that. I just had an old cotton wool wig in rehearsal, but the way he wore the wig was on one side or back to front, and then I'd pick it up and throw it at somebody. All those things were all part of the madness that people saw in him. Whether the stockings were wrinkled or whether they were down round his ankles or pulled up tight, and whether his trousers were unbuttoned, all these things indicated very much the way the King was moving.*

In a nice piece of ring composition the play opened and closed with the King dressed in full regalia, his family and ministers in obedient attendance. In between he appeared as an increasingly isolated figure in nightshirt or small clothes, with one stocking rolled down and his wig askew, with his legs bandaged, and in a nappy, but still wearing the ribbon of the Garter as a last, mocking vestige of his august person. He was also seen in a strait waistcoat and gagged.

The most compelling piece of staging devised by Hytner, and one that highlighted the humiliating incongruity between illusion and reality, was the close of Act I where for the first time the King was shown the restraining chair into which he was unceremoniously bundled and fastened. As the King was being manhandled, the audience heard Handel's Coronation Anthem, 'Zadok the Priest'. This powerful image of the sovereign helplessly enthroned in a restraining chair brutally parodied the pomp and procession associated with the sovereign's coronation.[5] It was a striking and critical scene, but also, as Alan Bennett remembers, extremely hard to achieve:

> *That was very difficult to rehearse because it had to be synchronised very, very carefully. Charlie Kay, who played Willis, had to be able to say, 'No, sir. You are the patient' in a pause in the music, and then the music had to come in. So it had to be absolutely as if he were an instrument in an orchestra. Now Charlie was less sure on his words than Nigel was and so time and again this went wrong in rehearsal, and that would make Nigel very frustrated and cross, which then made Charlie more and more nervous. That always, even in performance, could be a dodgy and difficult moment.*

The Madness of George III opened in the Lyttelton Theatre at the National on 28 November. The original cast[6] included Janet Dale (Queen Charlotte), Julian Wadham (Pitt), James Villiers (Thurlow), Harold Innocent (Baker), Cyril Shaps (Pepys), Michael Fitzgerald (Prince of Wales), Charles Kay (Willis), Richenda Carey (Lady Pembroke) and Anthony Calf (Fitzroy). The play itself was well received by the London critics, although many believed the central performance eclipsed the text. *The Sunday Express,* for example, pronounced, 'It is a great performance in a very good play.'[7] A few thought the work a mediocre offering from Bennett, others his finest hour. Several of the major reviewers described Nigel's George as 'the performance of his life'[8] and to most of them the emotional range he executed within this single character seemed a revelation: 'In a performance of prodigious physical intensity, he switches between shuddering, bandaged wreck and stocky confident monarch' *(Tribune)*;[9] 'Nigel Hawthorne's performance shines out as (the play's) focal point like the light and dark sides of the Moon. [...] He takes us on a painful and piteous journey to the other side of human endurance' *(Daily Mail)*;[10] 'Nigel Hawthorne [...] makes of the king not only a clinically mesmeric subject, but also a man tragically alienated from his people, his wife, his children and his own spiritual resources. He moves from inquisitive testiness to gibbering panic and a state of benign, becalmed wisdom; Lear's journey exactly' *(Observer)*;[11] 'The part essentially demands playing King Lear, Ubu Roi and The Elephant Man on the same stage in random rotation. Hawthorne is, to order, vulgar, witty, pompous, humble, pathetic, raving, razor-sharp' *(Independent)*;[12] 'We knew Mr Hawthorne to be a deft comedian but he here gives us the king's tyrannical humours, surreal babblings, unconscious desires and helpless vulnerability' *(Guardian)*;[13] 'This portrayal is an imaginative feat. These days, there is no one remotely like George III. Here is a man who is massively confident but neither arrogant nor self-regarding. Hawthorne plays the sane man with absolute precision in his opening scenes and thereby makes his collapse into howling vulnerability as pitiful and shocking as possible. It's a colossal performance, never to be forgotten' *(Plays and Players)*.[14]

In marvelling at this acting feat, Michael Billington recognised quite rightly that Alan Bennett had 'created in the "mad" king one of the richest roles in post-war drama.'[15] It was a role that called upon all of Nigel's resources as a stage actor and stretched him further than any role previously had. The sheer logistics of the role, entailing thirty-nine costume changes, demanded singular stamina. He was seldom off stage during the play's running time of three hours and, whenever he was on, he was required as the anchor for all the other performances. He said at the time of the American tour, 'the exhausting thing isn't playing the 'madness'. It's the energy required to keep all the other performances going. George is central. And his illness goes through stages of deterioration, then recovery – all of which has to be shown dramatically. I'm busy, *very* busy.'[16] In its progression from sanity to insanity the part also necessitated a good deal of extreme acting, a style from which Hytner and Bennett normally recoil and which, in the hands of a different actor, might have approached histrionics. Hytner pointed out:

> *A lot of it, on the page, looked exactly like the kind of acting neither Alan nor I can stand – show-off mad acting. It's absolutely not one of those awful seventies plays with authority figures going mad and challenging the world order – I won't mention any names – but it's not one of those. That kind of acting would have completely destroyed it.*

As it was, Bennett explained, the delicacy and complexity with which Nigel endowed the role meant that the extreme moments were never less than totally believable:

> *A lot of it had to be extreme, but he was also very domestic and very affecting in his affection for the Queen, for instance, and in the little things he did. There was bravura acting, obviously there had to be, but it wasn't all like that, otherwise I think then you do lose the audience. […] He surprised me, not merely by the individual, the particular things he did, but also by the general impression he made. He gave a very detailed performance. There's a broad sweep there, but he's very delicate within that frame.*

The physical journey on which Nigel's King embarked transported him from a state of robust health and inexhaustible, almost violent, energy, to the point where his body was tortured by the workings of his illness and his physicians' over-zealous application of blisterings and purgatives. Nigel said that physically his George was:

> *an amalgam of characters in my life. My father first, because I saw him when he had had a few strokes, very ill, incontinent, all those things described in the play. My father's illness made a vivid impression of great horror on me: what I saw, the way he walked, everything, everything. And it's all part of George on stage. And there's a certain amount of Alastair Sim and Ralph Richardson.*[17]

At a deeper level, however, the interpretation relied on self-awareness and self-exposure:

When you come down to it, I suppose it's really all me, what I've become. The layers of influence. What has happened going through life. All those people, experiences, corners, dark places that have left their mark. When you get a part as enormously rich as George, it gives you licence to extend your horizons, to find out how far you can take it.[18]

The most graphic aspect of Nigel's physical characterisation of George was the rawness with which he exposed the King's harrowing regression to the condition of a helpless child who babbled noisily and indiscreetly, soiled his clothes and demanded attention and the security of the familiar. In the early part of the play Nigel's movements caught the King's authoritative presence, his intimidating formality and impatience, as well as his bluffness and vigour, thus providing a clear portrait of the sane George against which the audience could gauge his physical metamorphosis and register the external signals of his recovery.

Equally enlightening was Nigel's mastery of George III's verbal quirks. Alan Bennett took advantage of the wealth of information concerning the progress of the King's malady, contained in courtiers' diaries, physicians' reports and other eighteenth-century accounts of patients with mental illness. He noted down phrases and sometimes whole passages from these sources so that he could reproduce accurately the King's sane speech, which was iterative, insistent, slightly obsessive and nervously punctuated by 'What? What?' or 'Hey? Hey?', and his insane idiom, his accelerated, incessant and often circumlocutory monologues. Nigel had thus to contend with both types of discourse and to show the gradual transition between the two. At the beginning of the play he adopted the King's idiosyncratic staccato delivery and his self-consciously hearty manner of address. When the King became deranged, and all his normal inhibitions disappeared, he gave a verbal *tour de force,* impeccably capturing the flurried pace at which George took his words; his tendency compulsively to repeat a single word, and to run words together in a rapid, asyndetic confluence of ideas ('Not mad-mad-mad-mad. Madjesty majesty. Majust just nerves nerves nerves sss', 'Can't see can't see mist mist missed Queen missed her, oh missed her Queen, gone gone gone'); his eccentric word associations ('I am the subordinate clause, the insubordinate George') and his frenzied use of alliteration and assonance ('Morning is the matter. Not being attended to is the matter. And don't mutter. Or mutter will be the matter', 'Insults. Assaults. And salts besides rubbed into these wounds.'). Nicholas Hytner maintains, 'A lot of the mad stuff, Alan would be the first to admit, is made up of brilliant patterns of words on the page. It's entirely up to an actor to find what's going on underneath all that.' Of the actor's handling of the quantity of the King's mad speech, Bennett himself insisted, 'without Nigel Hawthorne's transcendent performance the King could have been just a gabbling bore and his fate a matter of indifference. As it is, the performance made him such a human and sympathetic figure the audience saw the whole play through his eyes.'[19]

In addition to the physical and verbal feats of the performance, Nigel was required, in the course of the play, to traverse a vast emotional plane in which he was by turns wrathful, obstreperous, playful, tender, remorseful, despairing and afraid. Nicholas Hytner declared, 'He's meticulous, Nigel, in the way he researches, but the most remarkable thing about him is his complete emotional availability, his rawness. There is an enormous emotional life that he can convey because he's so truthful as an actor.' While Nigel extracted a great amount of comedy from the character, his performance was most memorable for the way it movingly underscored the private tragedy of the mad King whose temporary fall from greatness was caused not through any *hamartia* (a failure or error), but through the external agent of a misdiagnosed disease. Early in the play, when the distraught Prime Minister attempted to secure the King's signature on an urgent warrant, the King was convinced that the paper before him concerned America. His usual obsession with the loss of the American colonies had been aggravated by his delirium and what began as an angry rebuke to Pitt developed into a soliloquy, of elegiac proportions, on loss of a very personal kind:

> *Peace of mind! I have no peace of mind. I have had no peace of mind since we lost America. Forests, old as the world itself, meadows, plains, strange delicate flowers, immense solitudes. And all nature new to art. All ours. Mine. Gone. A paradise lost. The trumpet of sedition has sounded. We have lost America. Soon we shall lose India, the Indies, Ireland even, our feathers plucked one by one, this island reduced to itself alone, a great state mouldered into rottenness and decay. And they will lay it at my door.*

Nigel spoke these lines with such pathos, investing them with a plaintive beauty as well as a genuine horror, that he made palpable the analogy between this lost paradise and the King's lost self. The condition of precipitate and humiliating decline predicted for the body politic was made incarnate in the sovereign's body.

What Nigel succeeded, above all, in portraying was George III's painful awareness, throughout his illness, of his physical deterioration, dislocated reason and irresistible prolixity. He discovered that the key to playing the King was to believe that he was not mad and that he knew his physical malady was being wrongly treated. Hytner locates the genius of the performance in the actor's extraordinary ability to communicate this awareness to an audience.

By being so human, truthful, emotional, by being so unrestrained about revealing the pain of the man, Nigel enabled the audience to identify completely with the King. At a very simple and basic level, what you're seeing is a fellow man in enormous pain, a form of pain that, I think, affected people as deeply as pain can on the stage because it involved a consciousness of how the world must be misreading him. That was what was so marvellous about that performance, that, however mad he got, he always knew he wasn't mad, but always knew he must seem to the rest of the world completely desperate.

At one point, when the Queen tried to compose the King, who was violently babbling obscenities, she asked him whether he thought he was mad. As Nigel gave his answer he brilliantly conveyed the King's tragically acute apprehension that something was horribly amiss and that he was utterly helpless in its grip:

I don't know. I don't know. Madness isn't such torment. Madness is not half-blind. Madmen can stand. They skip! They dance! And I talk. I talk. I hear the words so I have to speak them. I have to empty my head of the words. Something *has happened.* Something *is not right.*

The King's self-awareness was most movingly expressed in the play's rehabilitation scene for which Bennett deliberately borrowed from Act IV, scene vii of *King Lear*. The scene did not appear in Bennett's original draft, but was, Hytner explains, one of the additions made after the read-through:

The place where the whole play landed we found out at that read-through. Robin Bailey did Thurlow and was hilariously funny. It was a combination of seeing emotionally that that was what the play needed from Nigel and also thinking how funny it would be to have Thurlow playing Cordelia, and, of course, accurate that George III was obsessed by King Lear.

Historically Dr Willis did read Shakespeare's tragedy with the King, although whether Thurlow was actually co-opted into the reading and took the part of Cordelia is merely a delightful hypothesis. George III always identified strongly with Lear. During the last ten years of his life, having been declared insane and confined to Windsor Castle, he assumed the appearance of Lear with his wild hair and long white beard. His last words were reputed to be 'Poor Tom's a-cold' from Act III, scene iv of *King Lear*.

Deviating from his Shakespearean prototype, the context, which Bennett constructed for George III's rehabilitation, was that of a play-within-a-play, and the King's awakening in the aftermath of madness was part of the internal performance. Since George III had remained conscious of his condition throughout each stage of his 'madness' and was now simply acting the symptoms of *dusgnoia* (perplexity or disorientation), this device allowed him to engage in a form of therapeutic introspection. Nigel, as George, assumed with relish the part of Lear, announcing, 'It's my story.' The way in which he delivered the King's interjectory remarks on the appositeness of Shakespeare's words to his own recent experience ('"child-changed father"'s very good' and [of the wheel-of-fire metaphor] 'Oh it's so true!') revealed a depth of understanding and empathy agonisingly achieved. Nigel said, 'This rather jokey reading of *King Lear* becomes very poignant because you realise that Lear's restoration is what's happening to him as well.' Nicholas Hytner claims, 'Nobody realised, until Nigel got hold of it, how emotional that restoration to health would be.' This included Alan Bennett, who says, 'The audience were on his side, so they were willing him to recover and that's what made his recovery, when it came, such a good scene, with a lot more power to it than I had imagined when writing it.' Nigel's execution of this scene was fascinating because, in its beautifully understated emotion, it gave a beguiling glimpse of the Lear the actor might one day perform and, at the same time, remained entirely true to the character of George III, not only in the impatience he showed with his doctor's incompetent acting, his tyrannical choreography of the scene, and old ham's curtain call, but also in the King's compassionate rendering of the lines and his quiet contemplation of the importance of remembering how to seem. It was, in fact, an enthralling union of realism and the metatheatrical. Moreover, as Hytner perceived, because it was 'so specifically and particularly human,' Nigel's reading of the restoration scene made accessible the mythic element of the story, whereby the king experiences a *katabasis* (a descent into Hell), dies, and is brought back to life:

> *There has to be mythic resonance to a story about a king dying and coming back to life. The king dies and comes back to life and the nation rejoices. And*

that's what happened in the theatre. That's why it works. I didn't realise this until well after the play opened, but if you presented it as a myth … that form of theatre is interesting, effective and sometimes impressive, but it was the truthfulness and the humanity of the performance that, I think, enabled the huge audience that it got to tune into that cycle of death and rebirth. That's one of the dramatic archetypes.

At the end of the restoration scene the King addressed one of his equerries with 'What? What?', a verbal tick which had vanished with the onset of his madness and which at this point alerted those on stage and in the audience to his return to normalcy. What happened in the theatre each night after this point was extraordinary. With the plot and dramatic suspense effectively concluded, the audience, having earlier felt the King's humiliations as their own, were overcome with relief and joy at his recovery and spent the remainder of the play in celebratory mood, delighting in, and even cheering at, the sight of the newly sane King brusquely sending his doctors packing and mischievously tormenting his eldest son. This reaction continues to astound Hytner who says:

The play could have gone on forever. There were twenty-five minutes between "What? What?" and the end of the play. It's amazing. It defies all the laws of theatrical narrative. When he says, 'I have remembered how to seem. What? What?', that's the end of the play. He's better.

In the summer of 1992 *The Madness of George III* toured Britain, returning between sections of the tour to the Lyttelton. The following year in autumn the production was taken on a nine-week tour of the United States, beginning in Stamford, Connecticut, and ending in Boston. In America the play enjoyed respectable, rather than electrifying, success. Nigel was delighted by, and the press swift to highlight, the irony of the King being brought to the colonies which, over 200 years earlier, had disowned him and which he had never visited in his lifetime. In fact, Nigel revealed, 'I really wanted to do a film about an imaginary visit that the King made to the colonies and how history would have been altered possibly by his visit.'

The text engendered minor problems of translation. A few jokes, which hinged on very British terms of reference, such as the government's five-year term of office and the Piccadilly store Fortnum and Mason's, invariably fell flat. American audiences also found discomfiting the rawness and realism with which George III's medical condition was depicted, particularly the play's preoccupation with the King's urine and stools, which they interpreted as typical of the obsessive scatological tendencies of the British. Their reaction to the character of Willis revealed an interesting cultural disjunction between the United States and Britain. In the play Bennett never suggests that Willis was the agent of the King's recovery, yet, as Nicholas Hytner observed:

> *American audiences, certainly critics, were tremendously impressed by Willis because he's very much a part of a certain American metropolitan culture – the shrink. And what a lot of them thought they saw was the King being cured by Willis, quite specifically.*

One advantage, which these national peculiarities gave American audiences, was that they heightened the suspense and made the play a medical and historical thriller. Since, for many Americans, British history comes to a halt in 1776, and the chronological details of the Regency Crisis are less familiar, the King's recovery at the end of the play was unexpected. This was, of course, not infrequently the case for audiences in England, who could easily confuse the events of 1788 with those of 1810.

One night, after the company's return from America, eighteenth-century history was rewritten, fortunately out of Alan Bennett's earshot. What appeared to be a momentary lapse of concentration by Julian Wadham triggered an on-stage contest in ad libbing between himself and Nigel. In his desperate attempt to retrieve the situation, Wadham had unwillingly and dangerously thrown down a gauntlet to the Theatre Workshop veteran and virtuoso of improvisation. The few minutes that ensued have had an interesting afterlife. On Nigel's death, Nicholas Hytner recorded the incident in an article for the *Daily Telegraph*:

> *Nigel's wit and the King's merged. On stage, his first big scene with Mr Pitt, the Prime Minister, would start: 'Married yet, Mr Pitt, what, what?' To which Julian Wadham, as Pitt, would reply wearily and superciliously: 'No, Your Majesty.' And the King would launch into a hymn of praise to married life, twinkling with malicious merriment at the distaste on Pitt's face.*
>
> *One night, Nigel asked, as usual: 'Married yet, Mr Pitt?' and Julian, his mind God knows where, answered: 'Yes, Your Majesty.'*
>
> *Short pause, and a mischievous flash in Nigel's eye. 'Who to, Mr Pitt? What, what.'*
>
> *Blind panic from Julian. Who the hell to? 'The Duchess of Bedfordshire, Your Majesty,' thus altering history at a single, terrified stroke. But the King wasn't through. 'What's she like, Mr Pitt?' This was too much for Julian, who grabbed one of his red boxes and blustered his way back to business.*[20]

At a celebration of Nigel's life held in the National's Olivier Theatre in June 2002, Hytner, who directed the occasion, reprised the story and brought the house down. According to Hytner's version of events, Julian Wadham's deviation from the text was unintentional. In fact, it was a small but very deliberate act of rebellion against Nigel's infuriating practice of changing his performance each night and expecting those around him to keep pace mentally and physically. A few months after the National celebration Sheridan Morley purloined the anecdote, retelling it in a slightly different version towards the end of his memoirs (the 'Duchess of Bedfordshire' became 'a sister of the Duchess of Marlborough') and claiming that a few nights later Nigel confided to him, 'I rather suspect your late father [Robert Morley] was with me that night, too.'[21]

Like their British counterparts, what American critics and audiences responded to most enthusiastically was Nigel's star performance. One reviewer of the United States premiere in Rich Forum asked, 'Is there another actor alive who could bring George III so vividly to life?',[22] while in Boston Nigel's interpretation was hailed as 'one of the great performances of our time'[23] and 'an acting feat that erupts into one of the theatre's great, volatile, star turns.'[24] The review that appeared in the *Westport News* in Stamford could not be outdone in exuberance and extravagance:

> *His towering performance dominates the evening and rocks the stage. Hawthorne literally climbs inside the skin of the feisty, vulnerable king. We felt as if we were discovering the power of theatre for the first time. We may live in an age of mediocrity but occasionally an actor such as Hawthorne comes on stage to remind us of what theatre is all about.*[25]

In February 1994 the company embarked on a second overseas tour to Greece and Israel. In Jerusalem, where the play opened on 16 February, the cast was assigned an ambassadorial role as the visit coincided with British Week, a programme organised by the British Overseas Trade Group for Israel, in association with the British Council.

The production finally closed back in London on 5 March 1994, after an extraordinarily extended residence at the National and having earned Nigel an enviable collection of plaudits and prestigious awards. This marked the end of one of the play's lives and the beginning of another. In July 1994 shooting began in Oxfordshire on the film version of *The Madness of George III*. The way in which the film came to be produced is a remarkable tale of artistic vision and integrity displacing commercial conservatism, and one that has been, to a certain extent, mythologised in the retelling. That the play might be transformed into a film did not immediately occur to its author who, according to Hytner, applied himself to this possibility strictly at his own pace and on his own terms:

> *Quite early on there were people interested in the film rights. Alan Bennett doesn't deal in film rights. He just doesn't do it. He isn't for* The Lady in the Van *either. It's great because it drives them all crazy, all those people whose only job is to buy and sell and say they have the rights. He just sits down one day and writes the film. So he did just that. The film rights were not for sale, which drove them all nuts. He could have got a lot of money for the film rights. He could have got more money, probably, for selling the rights to that film than he eventually got for making the movie in the way we did. What could have happened then is the film could have stayed on a shelf somewhere gathering dust, but he just wrote the screenplay and then made it very clear that the only way he would sell the screenplay, the only way he would allow the screenplay to be made into a film, was if Nigel played the King.*

Bennett himself insists that the intransigence he displayed in demanding that both Nigel and Nicholas Hytner (who had never directed a film) be retained for the project, has been magnified and incorrectly represented as an act of great piety and loyalty:

> *That has been portrayed as me being very, as it were, self-denying and turning down huge offers from Hollywood for scripts. That's a myth. There weren't any huge offers. I'm sure if Anthony Hopkins had played it, I would have got more money – that's absolutely true. But it never got to that stage and we never even thought about anyone else really. I knew at the time that he was nervous that we would, but it was just inconceivable.*

What is more, by presenting the original creative team as a package deal, Bennett preserved the integrity of his script and ensured for himself a degree of artistic control rarely enjoyed by Hollywood screenwriters.

Nigel's anxiety, based on his experience with *Privates on Parade* and *Shadowlands,* about losing the film role to a more commercially viable star like Hopkins, induced him, in the interim, to try to raise his profile in Hollywood by accepting from Joel Silver the role of the villain in *Demolition Man,* a forgettable action movie starring Sylvester Stallone and Wesley Snipes. Aside from being an unhappy and alien experience, which did nothing at all to invest him with the requisite box-office might in middle America, Nigel's participation in *Demolition Man* was unnecessary.

The British press made much of Bennett's noble stand against recasting the title role, but another, largely unsung, hero of the story of the film's creation, who also had more to lose, was the producer Samuel Goldwyn Jnr. What is not generally known, or, at any rate, acknowledged, is the history of Goldwyn's support for Nigel and Alan Bennett. He had seen *Shadowlands* in the West End and on Broadway and bid on the rights to the film version, which he wanted to produce with Nigel as C. S. Lewis, but Richard Attenborough, who had already decided on Anthony Hopkins for the lead role, outbid him. 'I blame myself,' Goldwyn says, 'for not having been a little more aggressive about it. It's actually what made me be aggressive about *George.*' After seeing *The Madness of George III* at the National in 1992, Sam Goldwyn visited Alan Bennett backstage at the Comedy Theatre, where the playwright was starring with Patricia Routledge in his own production of a double bill of his *Talking Heads.* Goldwyn recalls telling Bennett:

> *'This is mine. I want to do the picture and he's got to do the part.' Everyone kept talking about Hopkins again and I said, 'No, this guy's going to do it and he's going to get nominated [for an Academy Award].' And sure enough it all happened.*

It was not the first time Goldwyn had been involved in a project with Alan Bennett, whom he regards as 'one of the greatest playwrights in the English language.' Always a nonconformist and risk-taking Hollywood producer, in 1987 he had secured the distribution rights to the film made from Bennett's second screenplay *Prick Up Your Ears,* which had been adapted from John Lahr's biography of Joe Orton. The manner in which he safeguarded the interests of the writer, director and leading actor in translating *The Madness of George III* to the screen is virtually without precedent. Far from needing to be won round, Goldwyn's confidence in these three men never faltered and his vision and certainty were the initiating force behind the movie. He supplied 80 per cent of the film's budget; the other 20 per cent came from Channel Four Films.

Apart from Nigel, a good handful of the stage cast (Julian Wadham, Anthony Calf, Cyril Shaps, Roger Hammond, Matthew Lloyd Davies and Paul Corrigan) repeated their roles on film, while many of the others appeared in small cameo parts. The principal replacements were Helen Mirren as Queen Charlotte, Rupert Everett as the Prince of Wales, Ian Holm as Willis, Amanda Donohoe as Lady Pembroke and Rupert Graves as Greville. A couple of the recasting decisions, intended to glamorise the picture, were resented by Bennett:

I didn't want Rupert Everett and I didn't want Amanda Donohoe, and those parts could have been better cast. That was not Nick's fault. It's just that's the box office. Having thought they'd been very brave about having Nigel, they then felt they had to bolster him up with other people. That was a shame.

Despite his lack of experience in film directing, Hytner understood the perils involved in adapting the play to the big screen and was careful to avoid making, from the original ingredients, a stagy costume drama on film. He was, however, momentarily nonplussed when, at the first rehearsal for the film, Nigel, who had honed his performance over the last three years on stage, said to him, 'Of course you know I'll have to give a totally different performance for the film. I realise that very easily what worked on the stage could be very much over the top and disconcerting.' Sam Goldwyn was in awe of Nigel's innate understanding of how to adapt his performance to the camera, his mastery of the role and his concentration: 'He had that whole performance thought out – the underplaying of the madness. He was under it all the time, except for that moment when he collapsed by the wall and one of the torture sequences.'

Early on in the shooting it was clear that the play's running time of three hours would have to be reduced and much of the court and parliamentary intrigue pared away, with the result that, to an even greater degree than the play, the film centred on the journey of the King. The increased dramatic licence, which the requirements of the different medium afforded Bennett, was not something the playwright, and former junior lecturer in history at Oxford, relished:

Beginning my career as an historian, I find it harder to take liberties with the truth than someone whose upbringing has been less factually inhibited. I have to be forced into departures from history by the exigencies of the drama, the insistence of the director and sheer desperation. Had Nicholas Hytner at the outset suggested bringing the King from Kew to Westminster to confront the MPs, I would have been outraged at this adjustment to what had actually happened. By the time I was plodding through the third draft I would have taken the King to Blackpool if I thought it would have helped.'[26]

Hytner is proud of the fact that, in spite of Bennett's reservations, the film attained an exceptional standard of historical accuracy:

There are details which I kick myself that we could have got right if they had been fully researched – just little details of costume and ritual which should be right but aren't. But very little that happens in the film didn't or couldn't have happened. The main lie the film tells is the King's arrival in the yard at Westminster on the day of the Regency debate. That didn't really happen. He got better a couple of weeks or ten days before the Regency debate, or before the final Bill was about to be passed, but that seems to me to be totally allowable.

He further indicates that one aspect of the film's truthfulness, which rightly gained enormous respect, was its depiction of the madness:

One of the incredibly honest things about Alan as a writer is that he will not speculate further than where he knows and what he knows. People who know about mental illness, by and large, despise its depiction in films because it's almost always so sentimental and simplistic. There's always a tremendously sentimental 'get out' clause. The Madness of King George is one of the few films that are honest about mental illness, which is ironic because it's not really about mental illness; his restoration to health is inexplicable. The film tentatively puts forward, in a caption at the end, that, maybe, what was wrong with him was, in fact, the physical disease porphyria that produces symptoms similar to madness, and Alan doesn't do anything other than tentatively repeat that speculation. Otherwise he simply puts it down like it was. There's nothing more riveting than the truth and nothing more convincing than it. And Nigel goes no further than that either.

In researching the King's madness Bennett had read accounts of the symptoms of porphyria, particularly that by Macalpine and Hunter, and he consulted friends like Jonathan Miller, Roy Porter and Michael Neve, but he remains uncertain whether his observations from real life had influenced him:

My mother suffered from severe depression towards the end of her life and so I saw the inside of several mental hospitals, but I don't know whether that had anything to do with it because it's a totally different kind of thing. George III was manic, whereas Mam was very passive.

Although convinced that in the film he had hold of a winner, Sam Goldwyn was unsure how best to market the finished product in order to capture the interest of American audiences. He secured an agreement, which he believed very worthwhile, from *The New Yorker* for a photo layout to publicise the film. In an effort to exploit the concept of royalty and connections to the British royal family, Lord Snowdon was commissioned to do the layout. On the afternoon of the photo shoot Goldwyn received a telephone call from Nigel:

> He said, 'I see rocky seas ahead.' I said, 'Well, what are the rocky seas, Nigel?' He said, 'This business of your marketing this picture about royalty is not going to work. This is a play about human beings; it's not about royalty. And the whole challenge of doing this part – and Helen and I have talked about this – is that anybody could be George, not that it's about a king. I don't think Americans are as preoccupied with kings as we are here in Britain, and the American market is far more important to you than the British market.' Which is true. He said, 'The play's well known, I'm well known, Alan Bennett's well known. I think the film will do well here for what it is, but your bigger challenge is going to be America and other parts of the world. And the only way, I think, it's going to work is if you humanise this man. You've got to humanise this story in your marketing, so that it's not a portrait of royalty and stately homes.' He said, 'I hope you don't mind,' and there was a lot of mumbling about him stepping over the line and all of that, which he was doing, and he knew damn well, and he was going to do it anyway. And he said, 'There's another thing. This business of calling it The Madness of George III *is a terrible idea. Most people in America will think it's like* Rambo *I, II, and III. They'll say they didn't see* George *I and II. I'd just call it* The Madness of King George.*'

The proposed new title still needed to be put to Alan Bennett for approval, a responsibility firmly declined by Nicholas Hytner and Bennett's agent, Anthony Jones, who both feared the playwright's wrathful response. Goldwyn himself then contacted Bennett, who, to everyone's astonishment and relief, embraced the change at once. Goldwyn realised that Nigel's suggestions were, in fact, the result of a great amount of careful thinking and that his initial diffidence masked an astute appreciation of the entire film-making process. He was surprised at having been taught by the stage veteran a valuable lesson in American movie-marketing: 'I'm always amazed at how many lessons I learn late and I think this was one of the greatest pieces of advice I'd ever been given, and it applies to so many other things.'

The Madness of King George was released in the United States at Christmas time in 1994, just prior to the end-of-year deadline to qualify for the Academy Awards. It opened in a modest way in only one cinema in New York and one in Los Angeles, but it was given excellent reviews and soon moved into the top ten list of the US box office. At the time of the film's American release Nigel was directing and starring in *The Clandestine Marriage* at the Queen's Theatre in London. When it seemed that he might be in contention for an Oscar nomination, Sam Goldwyn bought out the theatre for two nights and on 15 January 1995 flew Hawthorne to New York to head an intensive publicity campaign in advance of the nominations on 14 February. The film received four nominations, including Best Actor and Best Adapted Screenplay. It won just one award for Art Direction, while the Best Actor Oscar was presented to Tom Hanks for his performance in the saccharine American fairytale *Forrest Gump*. Goldwyn was impressed by Nigel's gracious and imperturbable handling of the pre-Oscars ballyhoo and his subsequent disappointment:

> *He seems to project many things, but not bitterness about some of the bad breaks, and he enjoys the good things. When he didn't get the Academy Award he said, 'But it was a wonderful experience. I shall probably never have this again.'*

The experience was, however, spoiled by a vicious and idiotic outing campaign at both the tabloid and broadsheet ends of the British press. Nigel's long and happy relationship with Trevor was suddenly 'exposed' and held up to ridicule for no other reason than a malicious delight on the part of editors in trying to cut down to size a revered public figure in his moment of triumph. His friend Jonathan Lynn branded the behaviour of the press 'completely despicable':

> *They managed to ruin for him what should have been a really great time in his life and they managed to disgrace themselves, really. Why would they set out to humiliate a great British actor who has been nominated for an Oscar against the odds in a little British movie? They should have been proud of him. They're always beating the drum about the Brits in Hollywood and when it actually happens they still can't get it right. They can't resist being brutal.*

The following year, at the BAFTAs ceremony in London, Nigel collected a British Academy Award for Best Actor, while *The Madness of King George* collected the Alexander Korda Award for Best British Film. A gratifying corollary of the national and international recognition Nigel achieved for his performance in *The Madness of King George* was the opportunity to work more regularly in film, a medium he enjoyed and which suited his talents, and to take larger roles in movies of quality and substance. In the remaining years of his life he had a brief but distinguished movie career, which spanned the independent and big-budget sectors in the United Kingdom and America, and included projects as diverse as adaptations of Shakespeare's *Richard III* and *Twelfth Night*, the Spielberg epic *Amistad*, and a remake of Rattigan's *The Winslow Boy*, scripted and directed by David Mamet. During this period of the mid to late 1990s Nigel also returned to work in South Africa for the first time in over thirty years, starring in the films *Inside* and *A Reasonable Man*, which each dealt with different aspects of the troubled post-apartheid South Africa. Conforming to the pattern of his professional existence, film stardom had arrived late. Sam Goldwyn speculated on what might have been had fortune smiled on Nigel as a young actor:

> *He became in America the actor's actor, the way Alec Guinness was. If he'd had the parts, if he'd had David Lean, when Guinness and Lean met up and made* Great Expectations, *Nigel would have had that career. That's where he was cheated in some respects. Both Nigel and Guinness have this ability to step from the common man into something else and to invest that something with qualities of the common man.*

On the day Nigel left London to spearhead *The Madness of King George*'s two-day publicity blitz on New York, a profile appeared in the *Sunday Times* which reflected on his belated screen stardom and concluded, 'Hawthorne, at age sixty-five, could well feel that the world, at last, is his oyster, even if it is irritated by the sands of time. Will he now attempt Lear or will he succumb to the glitter of Hollywood?'[27]

Alan Bennett had given Nigel what all actors dream of, but seldom encounter – the great part which nobody else has played. The stage and film versions of *The Madness of George III* combined represent the pinnacle of his acting career and, as Goldwyn illustrates, best exemplify the theme 'the readiness is all':

> *There are two defining moments that seem to sum up what Nigel is about. We were coming back from Castle Howard where we shot* The Madness of King George *one Saturday afternoon. It had been a hot day and Nick Hytner was a little bit depressed about this and about that, and he said to me, 'I'm supposed to know so much. Don't people realise this is my first picture?' We sat for a moment and I said, 'You know the amazing thing is that, if you're ever lost, Nigel seems to know where to go.' And he said, 'Yes, this is his moment and he's ready for it.' Fade out. I go to* The Clandestine Marriage *and I go backstage afterwards to pick him up to have dinner and I said, 'I feel very pleased about being with you because it's very exciting to be with somebody at that moment in their life.' I knew it was going to be a*

good picture. Sometimes you don't know and think 'How did I get into this?'
Other times you just know you've got a hold of something wonderful. And I
told him what Nick had said and he said, 'Yes, he's quite right. You know
what Baden Powell said, "Be prepared".'

Nigel unveiling Turnerelli's bust of George III at the British Library in November 1999.
(J. Caddock/ Courtesy of The British Library Board)

The fact that Nigel's portrayal of the King on stage and film generated a
phenomenal degree of audience identification and sympathy had much to do
with the actor's own empathy for the real George III: 'I was very admiring of
George and sort of got to understand a bit about him and got quite close to
him.' His admiration was for a good and moral man, a patron of printers,
artists and dramatists, who had both a scientific and a rural mind, and was not

without humour or wit, but who is too frequently dismissed as a Hanoverian tyrant or a buffoon. It was fitting then that when the new British Library was given a bust of George III to sit in front of its six-storey centrepiece of the King's personal library (a 17-metre glass-walled tower comprising 65,000 volumes, 20,000 pamphlets, and over 400 manuscripts), it was not a member of royalty, but instead Nigel who was invited to unveil it.[28] The unveiling on 23 November 1999 also provided Nigel with a wonderful link between George III and the character he was currently playing on stage. He was shown inside the collection and allowed to handle a first edition of the King's favourite Shakespearean tragedy. The play was *King Lear.*

That year Nigel's abilities as an interpreter of Shakespearean tragedy underwent their most difficult test with his second exploration of a king's lost self in the Royal Shakespeare Company's Anglo-Japanese production of *King Lear,* under the direction of Yukio Ninagawa. It was one of the most anticipated theatrical events of the decade, but ultimately it was the weight of expectation that denied Nigel the critical reception he deserved.

Notes to Chapter 9

1 In his introduction to the play text (1992) x-xx, Bennett discusses the problems encountered during the play's early development and the considerable rewriting and reconstruction on which he embarked.

2 See Macalpine & Hunter (1991) chs 1-11.

3 In his introduction to the play text (1992), xi, Alan Bennett remarks, 'From a dramatist's point of view it is obviously useful if the King's malady was a toxic condition, traceable to a metabolic disturbance rather than due to schizophrenia or manic depression. Thus afflicted, he becomes the victim of his doctors and a tragic hero.'

4 For a comprehensive treatment of this crisis, see Trench (1964). For descriptions of the King's illness of 1788-89 as an extensive public crisis, see Macalpine & Hunter (1991) xv and 22 and Ingram (1991) 1 and 5.

5 For a discussion of this scene and its staging, see Duncan Wu's interviews with Alan Bennett and Nicholas Hytner (2000) 84, 104 and 107.

6 Between 1991 and 1994 there were three separate casts for the production. Nigel Hawthorne and several other actors remained in their roles throughout.

7 Clive Hirschhorn, *Sunday Express,* 1 December 1991.

8 Among them were Tony Dunn (*Tribune,* 6.12.91), Kenneth Hurren (*Mail on Sunday,* 1.12.91), Michael Coveney (*Observer,* 1.12.91) and Christopher Edwards (*Spectator,* 7.12.91).

9 Tony Dunn, *Tribune,* 6 December 1991.

10 Jack Tinker, *Daily Mail,* 29 November 1991.

11 Michael Coveney, *Observer,* 1 December 1991.

12 Mark Lawson, *Independent,* 30 November 1991.

13 Michael Billington, *Guardian,* 30 November 1991.

14 Gwyn Morgan, *Plays and Players,* February 1992, 35.

15 *Guardian* 30 November 1991.

16 Interview with Kevin Kelly, 'Nigel Hawthorne retakes the colonies', *Boston Sunday Globe,* 24 October 1993.

17 Ibid.

18 Ibid.

19 (1992) xix.

20 'We were so slow to recognise his worth', *Daily Telegraph,* 28 December 2001.

21 Morley (2002) 321.

22 *The Hour* (Norwalk, CT), 17 September 1993.

23 *Boston Journal,* 11 November 1993.

24 *Boston Globe,* 3 November 1993.

25 *Westport News* (Stamford, CT), 17 September 1993.

26 Bennett (1995) xxi.

27 'By George, Hollywood will be mad about him', *Sunday Times,* 15 January 1995.

28 The bust was sculpted by Peter Turnerelli in 1812 and had only recently been discovered in the United States. Turnerelli was a teacher of modelling to the daughters of George III and was later appointed Sculptor-in-Ordinary at the Court. The bust depicts the King as a Roman Emperor, wearing laurel wreath and toga. The King's Library was donated by his son George IV in 1823.

Chapter 10

Reason in Madness

KING LEAR

Let us sit upon the ground
And tell sad stories of the death of kings.

(*Richard II*, III.ii.155-56)

Inevitably, after the triumph of *The Madness of George III* and the play's tantalising Shakespearean parallels, there was an expectation, among both the public and the theatre establishment, that Nigel might soon take up the challenge of *King Lear*. One of the people who exerted the most pressure on him was director Declan Donnellan, co-founder with designer Nick Ormerod of *Cheek By Jowl* and an associate of the National Theatre with an impressive record of classical and modern productions. Nigel, however, disclaimed any ambition to join the illustrious roll-call of actors who had attempted the most formidable part in the Shakespearean canon. His resistance is explained by two important facets of his character which, at first sight, appear contradictory: his humility and his determination not to follow a path defined by others' achievements, but to go where none had gone before him.

Nigel never believed himself to be an actor with the vocal power and commanding personality of Wolfit, Gielgud or Scofield, which are commonly held to be pre-requisites for the part of Lear. As a performer of Shakespeare he was, like Alec Guinness, more of a miniaturist, capable of constructing a complex heroism through reason, accuracy and the illumination of subtle levels of irony and pathos, but to whom the grand flourish and declamatory technique were alien and false. Sheridan Morley believes 'He is not a natural Lear. He's a Gloucester or a Kent.' But, as a reason for Nigel's reluctance to play Lear, more profound than his consciousness of his limitations was his independence. In an interview with Carole Zucker in October 1997, six months after Ian Holm's Lear for Richard Eyre at the National had been acclaimed 'one of the best King Lears London's stage has ever seen,' Nigel reiterated his disinclination to undertake the role himself:

I need to make my mark in my own way. And when I did King George, *that was a sort of* King Lear, *although it wasn't* King Lear. *And perhaps, without being conceited about it, that's really the way things should be. I should do things that are unexpected, rather than follow a familiar path.*[1]

His last assertion is the clue to his finally agreeing, a year later, to perform *King Lear* for Japan's foremost and internationally renowned theatre director Yukio Ninagawa.

Ninagawa made an extraordinary impact on British audiences when he brought to the 1985 Edinburgh Festival his famous Samurai production of *Macbeth,* set amid the civil strife of sixteenth-century Japan, and again when he returned to the Festival the following year with his open-air production of Euripides' *Medea,* which was staged in the quadrangle of Old College at Edinburgh University. Both plays incorporated elements of *kabuki* and were memorable for their visual power and beauty. They were staged in England in 1987, earning Olivier Award nominations and establishing Ninagawa's reputation in Britain as an inspired interpreter of classical and Renaissance drama.

In the last decade Ninagawa consolidated this reputation by presenting on the London stage productions of *The Tempest, A Midsummer Night's Dream, Hamlet* and *Peer Gynt.* His *King Lear* with Nigel was to be the fourth production in an ambitious project, conceived by Makoto Moroi, President and General Director of Arts at the Saitama Arts Foundation, to direct all thirty-seven of Shakespeare's plays at the publicly funded Saitama Arts Theatre, north of Tokyo. The first three plays in the Saitama cycle, *Romeo and Juliet, Twelfth Night* and *Richard III,* as with Ninagawa's previous Shakespearean productions in Britain, were performed in Japanese translation. *King Lear* was to be Ninagawa's first experience of directing Shakespeare in English with a British company. It was, moreover, to be a conscious fusion of the traditions of Eastern and Western theatre, a collaboration between the Royal Shakespeare Company and West End impresario Thelma Holt (Ninagawa's British Producer since 1987), with the Sainokuni Shakespeare Company. Ninagawa thus offered the sort of atypical theatrical challenge Nigel typically sought. Sheridan Morley declares:

With Nigel you know you're going to get something special that isn't available anywhere else, the way actors nowadays are interchangeable; Nigel is not. He is very much sui generis, *his own type. He invented himself. He's never the same twice. What he plays isn't familiar, it isn't safe, it isn't reliable; it's quirky and strange.*

In a BBC *Omnibus* documentary on his life filmed in 1999, Nigel commented, in relation to the unpredictable route his career had taken and, specifically, his belated undertaking of Lear, 'I never wanted an easy ride; I always wanted an interesting ride.' His choice of Ninagawa as his guide to realising the notoriously difficult character of Lear was not only unexpected, but also promised a degree of danger, not least because Ninagawa's direction would need to be conveyed to the actors through an interpreter, and questions of verse and textual interpretation left largely to the associate director, David Hunt. Morley observes, 'It's very typical of Nigel that he went that route, because it is very challenging. It was a brave thing to do and certainly was original.'

The cast gathered for *King Lear* included stalwart members of the Royal Shakespeare Company such as John Carlisle and Christopher Benjamin, who played respectively Gloucester and Kent, and able younger performers like Siân Thomas as Goneril and Michael Maloney as Edgar. The sole Japanese member of the company, playing his first English-language role, was Hiroyuki Sanada, Japan's most popular movie actor. Although a seasoned star of action and martial arts films, Sanada's range also encompassed musical comedy and Shakespearean tragedy. He had played Hamlet in Ninagawa's production at the Barbican in 1998 where he was spotted by Nigel. Impressed by the fact that 'this Hamlet had an extraordinary athleticism but also a gentleness and a vulnerability,' Nigel immediately suggested to Thelma Holt that Sanada play the role of Lear's Fool. The casting of the thirty-eight-year-old Sanada was a conscious departure from the recent convention of a Fool comparable in age to Lear. His relative youth made him a surrogate son to Lear, and the gentle development of this relationship enhanced the humorous and human dimensions of the King. Thelma Holt maintains:

> I have never seen that relationship before and part of it was based on what was happening off stage. The relationship between these two men was quite beautiful. Here we had this megastar in his own country and here he was just a Japanese actor given no quarter. People were very nice to him, but they didn't treat him any better because he had come all that way and was a stranger. It could have been very lonely for him. He was under Nigel's wing from day one, and then you gradually saw how the relationship progressed, that there were times when Nigel was under his wing. You didn't know when Lear and the Fool ended and when Nigel and Hiroyuki Sanada began.

Sanada was a slightly androgynous Fool of acrobatic litheness as well as lyricism, and brought to the part an Eastern wisdom and an otherness that were entirely apposite, as Nigel explained:

He has a wisdom that is acquired from the East or from some other such strange world that the King can't quite fathom. The King has to keep going to him for his advice, this boy – 'Teach me', he says. A lot of people objected to the Fool being Japanese and said his English was fractured. Well, why not? Why should his English be perfect? A lot of things that the Fool says are incomprehensible today and so the foreignness with which he says them seems only to emphasise the oddness. But people are so used to one particular way of doing things. It became fashionable for the Fool to be played by an older man, but the King calls him 'boy' all the way through. Why shouldn't he be a boy or a young man? That seemed to be right. And an older Fool would only vie for attention with the King, but a younger man would be playful and cheeky, and the King would like that. There would be a strain between them sometimes, as there would between lovers, but that's quickly over, it's forgotten.

In his own working script of the text Nigel has written opposite the Fool's entry in Act I, scene iv, 'The Fool is an outsider. He's the only person in the Court who can tell the King what he doesn't want to hear. He's Jiminy Cricket – the King's conscience. The choice of Sanada is a good one as it is the perfect bridge between East and West.' As the outsider in the play as well as the company, Sanada found in Nigel an invaluable mentor who was both friend and teacher. He recalls:

I had four coaches for language. In Japan the British teacher was there and in the UK my own dialogue coach and from the Company the assistant director taught me about the text, the voice coach from the RSC taught me verse speaking and rhythm and Shakespearean speaking, but I think the best coach was Nigel. He knows everything about the stage, about Shakespeare, about acting. Every day he taught me – in rehearsal, on stage, backstage. Every day just two or three little pieces of advice he gave me. He knows acting.

King Lear officially opened in Japan on 23 September 1999 at the Saitama Arts Theatre. As audiences had come to expect from Ninagawa, there was in the production an emphasis on the aesthetic and on sensory effect. The stage design by Yukio Horio incorporated many features of Noh theatre. Most notably, the set was dominated by two huge doors on which was depicted in relief an ancient pine tree symbolising eternal life. Ryudo Uzaki's music, which made use of traditional Japanese instruments, had an unearthly percussive quality. The costumes, designed by Lily Komine, included elaborate and richly coloured kimonos, and in the opening scene the King wore a cloak that combined classical Japanese design with swathes of fur that suggested an ancient British majesty. Similarly, in the battle scenes the combatants had the simultaneous appearance of Celtic and Samurai warriors.

Like its subsequent seasons in London and Stratford, the Japanese run of sixteen performances was sold out. At each of these performances the famously undemonstrative Japanese audience gave the company a standing ovation. Both the production and Nigel's interpretation of Lear were greeted enthusiastically by the Japanese critics. The *Japan Times* said of Nigel, 'At age seventy, he brings power, subtlety and intelligence to the human hurricane that is Lear. […] Hawthorne achieves the most difficult and important aspect of *King Lear*, more than portraying a character, he reveals Shakespeare's archetypal truth.'[2] When the production transferred to London in October its reception was very different.

In the preceding months great expectations of the last significant Lear of the millennium were fostered by the British press who, at that stage, declared their approval of, and excitement at, the unusual Anglo-Japanese collaboration. Opening night at the Barbican on 22 October, however, was met by a reactionary and, in some quarters, xenophobic furore. The London critics, almost with one voice, panned the production and condemned Nigel as egregiously miscast. The hyperbolic tone of disappointment struck in several reviews, and the unworthy form of *ad hominem* criticism descended to in a few, ensured that the publicity attending the play's critical reception superseded that which was generated in anticipation of its opening. 'High theatrical hopes came tumbling down last night,'[3] trumpeted the *Evening Standard*, while the *Mail on Sunday* declaimed, 'The disappointment is huge, because we all expected so much from a great play, a great actor and a great theatrical company.'[4] The reviews themselves became a major news story in the daily papers, ensuring a stressful time for Nigel:

> It was really disturbing for me to have people coming round to the house from the press and saying 'How are you reacting to the bad reviews?' and being smuggled into the theatre. And I just thought, 'What have I done that is so wrong? I think I've done it right. Why do they think – not all of them, but some of them – not that I've just missed a little bit, but gone wildly, wildly wrong?'

The critics' main complaint was that Nigel was underpowered in the role. This was generally conveyed by means of facile, and sometimes nonsensical, comparisons: 'More like Worzel Gummidge than a mighty monarch';[5]

'When he calls on darkness and devils he might just as well be ordering a nice cup of tea';[6] 'He pleads, "Oh let me not be mad" with the docility of a child asking Father Christmas for a train set.'[7] Dissatisfaction with Nigel's reading of the part centred on the storm scene in Act III, usually played violently and at high volume. Benedict Nightingale in *The Times* queried whether 'so essentially benign an actor as Hawthorne [was] the right chap to play Lear,'[8] and, similarly, Charles Spencer in the *Daily Telegraph* had wondered whether 'such a master of poignancy would also be capable of the capricious majesty and titanic rage which the role demands.'[9] Not only did these musings conveniently overlook the emotional extremes Nigel had acted in *The Madness of George III,* and the transition from tyrannical aggression to childlike vulnerability which he expertly effected in this earlier role, but they also neglected the possibility that his quieter reading of the part of Lear was the product not of his limitations, but of his imagination; that Lear was not beyond his range, but rather he was deliberately breaking new ground.

Although Nigel was generally given credit for realising the pathos and humour of the character, his overall interpretation was denied legitimacy because, in his 'failure' to deliver an epic rage, he did not conform to the critics' preconceptions of how the role should be played, which were based on an entrenched Anglocentric tradition of playing Lear. This is certainly the feeling of Thelma Holt, who comments, 'I think that we suffered from people coming to review the play with baggage. They expected a certain sort of Lear.' Similarly, Jonathan Lynn says that some critics:

seemed to miss a big, declamatory, old-fashioned version of Lear. *Critics go and review what they think they want to see, not what they're actually seeing. I thought Nigel's was a performance of enormous subtlety, and very touching, but the critics seemed to want Donald Wolfit and there's no way you're going to get that from Nigel. I'd rather watch Nigel any time. People get fixed in wanting to see things a certain way. It seems to me the interest in going to see Shakespeare over and over again is to see what's new in the way it's being thought about because you don't really want to see the same things as you saw last time.*

You would think from the way the critics behaved that Nigel was a kind of master criminal or that anybody was who gave a performance that they didn't like. I think the press has essentially driven Nigel out of the theatre and I think they ought to be very ashamed of themselves. Nigel's performance was superb but, whether it was or not, that's not the point. The point is they shouldn't write that way if they want to keep great actors coming to work.

Nicholas Hytner's explanation for the critics' reaction to *King Lear* is another damning indictment of the current state of theatre criticism in Britain:

The reason King Lear *got a drubbing was because now everything is news. Theatre criticism is just another branch of the news industry, and the news industry is just another branch of the entertainment industry. And to say 'this is what's good', 'this is what disappointed me' or 'this' – never mind good or bad – 'is what the performance is', is now absolutely beyond the remit of theatre critics. They all work for thoroughly disreputable entertainment organisations. There were two things they could have said about that* King Lear *– 'the best ever' or 'the worst ever'. They happened to plump for 'the worst'. That's now how it operates and it's really depressing.*

Nigel took a similarly pessimistic view of the way in which the viability of serious and inventive theatre was being undermined by the inimical agenda of powerful critics:

Look at what it's doing to the theatre. You speak to somebody like Thelma who invests not just other people's money, but sometimes her own money in things which she wants to do and believes in and does with integrity and honesty, and they [the critics] jump up and down on her. Sooner or later she's not going to be able to do that anymore, and so her name will be wiped off the West End list of people that really care about what they're doing. We'll become more and more like Broadway, there will be more and more musicals because they'll have to fill the theatres, and people will be scared to do straight plays because that barrage of attack means that they can't survive in an open market, there's just no way. The critics have been given so much power. It's quite interesting if you look at theatre critiques of the Edwardian period, say, and you'll very often find a review and at the bottom will be: 'From our theatre critic'. Now it's 'Benedict Nightingale' or 'Nicholas de Jongh' and a picture of the critic smiling in a benign way, and you think, 'Well, that's really quite a change.' They always talk about actors being vain and self-centred, but, God, critics!

You have no redress as an actor because they either get you at the same time or they get you next time. I know that's the world we enter; you walk onto a stage and there will be people there who want to criticise what you're doing. But we're there to tell a story. We don't set ourselves up to be admired. We set ourselves up to tell a tale, at least I've always done that, and you find the best way of telling it.

The attitude towards success in England is quite nasty. We've started really to resent people who are successful.

Yukio Ninagawa and Hiroyuki Sanada also came under fire from the London critics. Paul Taylor of the *Independent* denounced Nigel's alliance with Ninagawa instead of Declan Donnellan as perverse,[10] and Michael Coveney ruled, 'The director, Yukio Ninagawa, represents everything that is anathema to how Adrian Noble defines the RSC.'[11] In a comparable display of chauvinism, Benedict Nightingale denigrated Sanada's Fool as 'an inarticulate intruder from another culture.'[12] A particularly vitriolic and gratuitously offensive group attack was launched on BBC2's *Late Review*,[13] where the host Mark Lawson blamed Ninagawa for what, with a stunning lack of logic, he saw as the production's greatest shortcoming: 'The director doesn't speak English, so it hasn't been directed at the level of text at all.' One member of the programme's panel of reviewers, Germaine Greer, dismissed Sanada's performance with equally alarming fatuity, complaining, 'I don't really want to see a Chinese opera tumbler,' while another, Natasha Walter, summed up the production as 'a bog standard RSC interpretation of the play with some Japanese accessories.' This sort of antipathy towards the Japanese influence in the production was reminiscent of the critical response to John Gielgud's fourth and final stage Lear, which closed the 1955 season of the Shakespeare Memorial Theatre and for which the Japanese-American sculptor Isamu Noguchi designed highly controversial sets and costumes. In both cases the critics gave little credit to the daring experimentation of the production.

So condemnatory were the majority of critics in their assessment of the production and what they regarded as Nigel's overly restrained interpretation, that they prompted two revisionist critiques from Michael Billington of the *Guardian* and Sheridan Morley of the *Spectator*. Billington countered the impression given in many reviews that this *Lear* was a disaster commensurate to Peter O'Toole's Macbeth in 1980 for the Old Vic Company, by proclaiming Nigel merely the latest in a long line of great actors, stretching from Edmund Kean, who had failed to realise the tragic heights and cosmic suffering of the character. He also dissented from the majority in his liking for the production's 'oriental beauty.'[14] Morley, who thought 'the general tenor of the reviews was so personally rude to Nigel', went further in challenging his colleagues' offended Western sensibilities by protesting the value of an unfamiliar rendering of a familiar classic:

I have to object that the wonder of this Lear is precisely that it does not correspond to anything we currently think we know about the play. [...]

What this King Lear *usefully reminds us is that we don't hold the patent on Shakespeare, and that Japanese conventions and traditions, both social and theatrical, can give us insights into the play we would never otherwise have learnt.*[15]

Robert Gore-Langton of the *Express,* responding to the public attention given to the criticism of *Lear* and the particular drubbing administered to Nigel, felt it necessary to submit an *apologia* defending his fellow critics from the charge of malice:

Why should a respected actor have to suffer the slings and arrows of a bunch of hacks who couldn't tie their own shoelaces without help? Well I'm afraid the answer is because it's our job. [...] We are kind, nice and stagestruck and we want the very best. Hawthorne's Lear was judged lacking. [...] The critics had not duffed up Sir Nigel – by and large he was let off.[16]

There were those, among the London critics, who did applaud Nigel's unorthodox Lear and appreciate his interpretation as an imaginative and innovative essay on old age and mental disease. John Peter of the *Sunday Times* said:

Lear does not whinge or prattle in his mad scenes: he is in a world of a private, visionary sanity, where things look newborn and translucent [...] The great Greek scholar E.R. Dodds has written about the way ancient Greek civilisation passed from a shame culture to a guilt culture. Something similar happens to Hawthorne's Lear. This magnificently gnarled performance shows how the king passes from shame, the public stigma of losing power, to a sense of guilt, which is man's moral judgement over himself.[17]

Similarly, Alastair Macauley of the *Financial Times* commended the depth and appropriateness of Nigel's portrayal of a non-raging Lear:

Nigel Hawthorne gives an impressive, hot-blooded, changeable, touching account of the title role. He is not one of your roaring, leonine Lears. But he never feels like a comedian spluttering out of his depth; and he never forces any artificial kind of power. Hawthorne's Lear has natural authority, within which he shows us the heart that suffers, the spirit that smiles, the mind that learns.[18]

John Stokes, writing in the *Times Literary Supplement,* viewed Nigel's Lear as the metaphysical creation of a scholar clown:

Nigel Hawthorne's extraordinarily temperate Lear is, from first to last, an ironist, though the depth of his perceptions changes greatly in the course of his journey. Cloaked at first like a moulting hawk, he begins with whimsicality, puts Cordelia on the throne even before he questions her, arbitrarily draws lines on the map of England, smiles and shrugs at the inadequacy of all his daughters, enjoys his own jokes. He progresses to mock bewilderment and then, more interested in riddles than protests, turns, as the crisis darkens, less to passion than to philosophical speculation, offering 'Let copulation thrive' as no more than an absurd proposition. Keen to resist madness, self-aware even as he succumbs to its inevitability, he is witness to his own ageing. When he complains that he is not in his 'perfect mind', he stresses 'perfect' as if to suggest other levels of spiritual possibility.[19]

He believed that this performance 'of rare and [...] quite un-English sensitivity' was consonant with the soul of the production: 'It is Ninagawa's unremitting feeling for what Yeats called the "continual presence of reality", above all in the face of death, that gives his production its strange and alien beauty.'

Stokes raised an important point about Nigel's performance when he said: 'Hawthorne gives his movements the precision, the allusive subtlety, that is paradoxically available only to actors steeped in comic technique.' It is a point on which Jonathan Lynn has elaborated:

We all know that comedy is more difficult because it needs a kind of precision that tragedy, or at least drama, doesn't need. When you're doing a great tragedy you run the risk of becoming ludicrous. We've all seen examples of that, of big tragic performances that don't work and then they're funny, like Peter O'Toole's Macbeth years ago at the Old Vic which brought the house down. From a purely technical point of view the skill is the same: in comedy you have to organise your performance to get the laughs in and in tragedy you have to organise it to get the laughs out. You don't want anyone to laugh when you're staggering on crying 'Howl, howl, howl' with Cordelia in your arms. And from a point of pure acting technique the skill that you learn in comedy of maximising the laughs is exactly what you need in reverse when you do tragedy, when you have to minimise them or, in fact, remove them. And that's all to do with the rhythm of the performance and the way you control the audience. An unsuccessful King Lear *would be a* King Lear *where the audience is laughing at the wrong times. Nobody was laughing at the wrong time when we saw Nigel's Lear. Everybody was moved by it. So I think that the technique you acquire in comedy is crucial. It's why there are a lot of dramatic actors who are not very good at comedy but very few comedy actors who can't do tragedy. Comedy requires greater technical skill.*

At the time Nigel's own response to the adverse criticism levelled at him was chiefly to ignore it. But in an interview I had with him during the Stratford run of *Lear,* he spoke candidly about his resentment of the critics' myopic reaction to his efforts:

As a senior actor I reckon I'm entitled to my interpretation. I think that that should be allowed me and that critics shouldn't arrive with a preconception. They should have an open mind and see what I'm doing and understand it. [Their failure to do so] diminishes the critic because it does mean that there was a sort of campaign to get at me and to get at the Japanese. I don't know whether they got together, but it was like a cabal. Yet, the production has been sold out every night. We are sold out till the end of the run. That's gratifying of course, although we don't make any money out of it. We work for very little money at the RSC. So you're really doing it for the love of doing it, and you do it for the audience and that's been the great balm. The audience has been hugely enthusiastic every night. They give us this wonderful reception, they cheer, they stand and they queue for returns. So word of mouth has got round that it's interesting and people are coming to see it because of that, not because of what the critics have said.

An example of Nigel's enormous dedication, which must have made the savagery of some of the reviews doubly hard to endure, was the fact that during the Barbican run his cab fare home to Hertfordshire each night was more than his week's salary. Six months before he died, his anguish at the critical pounding had scarcely subsided:

It haunts me and always will, I suppose, all my life, because I believed what I was doing in King Lear *was right, and still believe it was right, for the part. I understood that man as well as I've understood any character I've ever played in my life and so to have the press, or some of the press, be so vitriolic about it – although I didn't read them, it was communicated to me – has always been very, very hurtful and puzzling to me and made me not want to do theatre anymore. I just thought, 'Well, if that's really what they want, then I don't want to be a part of it; if I do my best and they sneer at it, then there's no point in continuing.' [...] That was the zenith of my acting career playing* King Lear *over the Millennium at Stratford, the first time I'd ever played Stratford. I was really so honoured and felt that it had come at the right time; and then to have those tables turned on me was just puzzling and off-putting.*

When reading through Nigel's original working script for *King Lear,* which is housed at the Shakespeare Institute Library in Stratford, I discovered the following note, dated February 2000, which he had handwritten and signed:

Although this production by Yukio Ninagawa, and my performance in the leading role, were sneered at by the daily critics, it would seem that they had come with a preconception rather than an open mind.

There is no doubt in <u>my</u> mind that what we are doing is totally right for the play, and I have been immensely proud to be part of the production.

It has played – first in Tokyo, then at the Barbican in London and finally over the Millennium here in Shakespeare's home town – to large audiences who nightly stand and cheer at the curtain calls.

We must have been doing something right.

Also included with the script was a short poem by Dominic Dobbin, 'the peasants' poet', from which Nigel obviously derived some consolation:

> *When reading drama notices*
> *And noting what they say*
> *We learn much more about the critic*
> *Than we do about the play.*
> *And furthermore, the actor's job,*
> *I think you will agree,*
> *Is that of pleasing customers*
> *Not those who get in free.*

While performing in Stratford, Nigel asserted, 'Every single word I say in the play I have a good reason for saying the way I do. I may say it differently from night to night, but the thought process behind it is the same.' During rehearsals he applied the same kind of diligence and inventiveness to the process of discovering his character, and to mapping his dramatic journey, that he had shown in the development of George III. This was observed by Hiroyuki Sanada who remembers, 'Every day Nigel was the first man on stage at rehearsal. He was standing alone on stage trying out, repeating and finding things.' His preparation for the role included extensive research into the literary and even textual criticism of the play:

> *I'd been working on that play every day for a year. [...] I bought as many editions of* Lear *as I could find and then I started to work very slowly through the play, making sure that I knew what each word meant. That was before it was cut or anything. I studied the play daily, worked at speeches, found rhythms, found ways of interpretation. It was something that I had taken an inordinate amount of time preparing for.*

Among the company he was the undisputed authority on the text, and it was Nigel who was largely responsible for the final pre-rehearsal cut.

He was especially eager to work out an emotional framework for the play's beginning in order to elucidate aspects of the King's condition and of his relationships with other characters. Revealing his director's eye, he theorised about the importance to the first scene, and a number of subsequent scenes, of the figure of Queen Lear, and whether the context of the first scene was mourning at the Queen's death or celebration at the betrothal of Cordelia:

> *That first scene is very difficult. There's not enough written to make it really plausible. For example, you don't have enough of him and Cordelia to really understand the warmth there is between them. And for him to get so angry on such a slender premise makes you think, 'Well, why does he behave like that?' It's not because he's an irate, impossible autocrat, a tyrant. [...]*
>
> *When I was in Japan, no, even before we went to Japan, I met Ninagawa and I said, 'If you take that first scene, what you, as a member of the audience watching, have to say is "Why does the King behave like that to Cordelia, why is he so angry, when it doesn't seem to be all that terrible what she says?" Supposing we take Queen Lear. Who was Queen Lear? Let's imagine that there is a catafalque on the stage, or it is brought on, and everybody's in mourning, and the King is sitting somewhere apart in grief.' But also, there's a line in the scene with Cornwall and Regan, the one where they come in wearing the kimonos, where she says, 'I'm glad to see your highness', and the King says 'If thou shouldst not be glad, / I would divorce me from thy mother's tomb, / Sepulchring an adultress.' Now, okay, he's maybe saying that in a jokey way, but he could be saying it with anger. If she'd been an adulteress, there would have been a mixture of grief at her passing and rage at what she'd done. So when the daughters arrive in their mourning gear, the row should take place over the wife's coffin, and that*

would seem to me to be the right sort of mood. But then our associate director said, 'But, what about the wedding and the betrothal of Cordelia. I think it's a celebration, the mood is one of celebration and not of mourning, because out of celebration comes anger.' And I'm still in two minds about it. I still think that perhaps Queen Lear might have been the key. I mentioned it to Ian Holm and he said, 'Oh, I wish I'd had that idea myself.' It's another scenario, and everything the King did in that first scene would have been tempered by that coffin. It is interesting when you start to unfold it all and there are so many different ways you can go. You always need a springboard.

When I was talking about doing a production of Lear *about four or five years ago to another director – and I eventually pulled out because it was too near* George *and there were too many resonances – I had the idea of the King pushing Cordelia on a swing. So that the play starts with Gloucester, Kent and Edmund down at the front talking, and in the back you see this joyful man and daughter, and she's dressed almost in bridal gear, and there could be lanterns everywhere, because it's a celebration of this wedding. So you would already get an idea of the proximity between the King and Cordelia. But there are all sorts of different ways of going into it. Finding the authority of the King is very important because that's what he's giving up.*

It was Nigel's idea to place Cordelia on the throne during the competition, thereby establishing her pre-eminence in his affections and creating unease among her sisters, a move he remembered was vigorously resisted in rehearsal by Robin Weaver who played Cordelia:

I said to Ninagawa, 'I'm going to put her on the throne,' and he liked the idea. She hated it. I said, 'Come on, I'm going to put you on the throne.' She froze and said, 'But why, why?' 'Because he wants to elevate you to the highest place that he can possibly imagine,' I said. And she wouldn't do it. Eventually she very reluctantly did it and slumped down into the throne. I said, 'Don't slump. Sit up straight and don't cross your legs.' This was in rehearsal. She burst into tears and there was a terrible scene and she thought I was Public Enemy No.1. What she didn't realise was that I was putting her in the best position she could ever, ever imagine. It unnerves the others. They've had sections of the kingdom given to them, but they don't know what Cordelia's going to get. Suddenly he puts her on the throne – is she going to be Queen, is he going to make her Queen, what's going on in this man's mind? It unravels a whole thing of doubt about what is going to happen.

In the opening scene the imposing presence of the actor helped to establish the commanding presence of the King and the height from which he fell. The massive doors at the rear of the stage opened to reveal a venerable warrior king, who was still physically august, striding purposefully towards his throne, flanked by his daughters and courtiers. His attitude upon the throne was formidable and instantly authoritative. This initial image of the King seated upon his throne in full regalia and command contrasted powerfully with the final image of him dressed in a simple robe, sitting on the ground, and cradling in his arms the lifeless form of his daughter Cordelia, his tragic fall complete.

Owing to the fact that the play begins *in medias res* and the act of abdication and the competition, which Lear initiates between his three daughters, are beset with inconsistencies, the opening scene presents the players and audience alike with considerable difficulties in terms of dramatic plausibility. Nigel was, for a great number of people, the first actor successfully to confront, and make sense of, these difficulties. Unlike many of his famous predecessors in the role, whose histrionic excesses tended to override any attempts to explain or make plausible Lear's madness, Nigel acted out a sensitive and compelling thesis on the deterioration of the King's mind. He did not portray Lear as either a ranting tyrant or a savage monster redeemed only in the penultimate act. His emphasis on the pathos, absurdity and simple humanity of the King was certainly very different from the interpretation critics and audiences had clearly come to expect, but his was a subtler, more interesting and ultimately more enlightening creation:

> *Whatever Lear ended up as, which was probably mad, or possibly mad, in my mind, was more akin to something like Alzheimer's today or senile dementia. A man of eighty years of age who starts to disintegrate and becomes lucid, becomes confused, becomes panicky, becomes angry and becomes wretched in quick succession.*

Throughout the play the audience was taken along on a 'journey of doubt' and shown periods of lucidity and reason cleft by behaviour that was not only irrational but also clearly uncharacteristic. Nigel explained:

> *As in Alzheimer's, the mind just goes dead for a second. So everybody thinks, 'What's he going to do?' It makes the King unpredictable. There were all those sort of inconsistencies [in the first scene], which started me to think that there was an irrational man there. So we started to put these gaps where nothing happened, where the atmosphere just died. And then*

out of that he'd say something like, 'Give me the map.' So he had the authority but he was also behaving in an odd way.

To this process of hinting at the King's condition the first scene was crucial: 'If you can already start to see the disintegration of the mind in the first scene, then there seems to be a reason for his behaviour.' Nigel's insertion of uncomfortably long pauses during his announcement of the competition made the King an unnerving and volatile figure, as was evident from the bewildered reaction of the assembled court. Further expounding his thinking behind this interpretation, he said:

If you go through King Lear *you cannot find a single reference to the fact that he booms, you cannot find a single reference to the fact that he's an unpleasant man, a cruel man, an autocrat in any way. He has such loyalty from people around him such as Gloucester and Kent. The more I studied it, the more I thought, 'Well, what is it about him. It's not just royalty that they're being loyal to. It's something about the man; and why can't he be a gentle man? Isn't it more interesting that he is at a confused time of his life when, perhaps, he's got the beginnings of Alzheimer's?' Madness was always put as a label on people who were behaving in an uncharacteristic way. But he didn't seem to be mad at the beginning; it was puzzling the way he treated Cordelia and Kent. And why did he do it? It came out of nowhere and I thought it was much more interesting, therefore, to play a man who was behaving in a way that nobody expected, that was uncharacteristic. So these waves of sanity or clarity or disturbance that came across him were only transitory. They weren't things that stayed with him all the time; they came and they went.*

Nigel's most heavily criticised break with convention occurred during the storm scene where he was said to lack the necessary 'convulsive tumult'[20] Ninagawa's use of falling lumps of rock and shafts of sand in the staging of the storm also drew a scornful response for its distracting, almost bathetic effect, which one critic branded 'one of the most risibly disastrous sequences ever seen on the London stage.' In defence of his lack of naked violence, his refusal to out-Herod Herod, Nigel argued:

The words do so much for you. In the storm scene, you don't need storm effects because Shakespeare has written the words and he paints the picture for the audience. Now you'll always get a director who'll want to put his directorial stamp on the storm scene, and here we've got the rocks and the sand and everything. When Robert Stephens played it here [in Stratford], he actually had rain, he had to stand in pouring rain, which must have been miserable to do, apart from anything else, but also unnecessary because, as I say, it's all in the words. And so I think that when it comes to the big moments, if they're played with intensity, it's almost better than if they're played at high volume because they have a reality to them then. I was criticised very much by the press for not ranting and raving, but I can find no evidence in the text that he rants and raves. Through the centuries actors have seized on these moments like the storm scene and wanted to display their histrionic ability, and so they've let loose, but it seems to me to say much more about the actor than it does about the King.

King Lear, with Christopher Benjamin, Michael Maloney and Hiroyuki Sanada, RSC 1999.
(Donald Cooper/Photostage)

At the heart of his reading of the storm scene were two lines spoken by one of Lear's knights and seized upon by Nigel in his close study of the text. At lines 10-11 of Act III, scene i, the Knight informs Kent that the King 'Strives in his little world of man to out-scorn/ The to-and-fro conflicting wind and rain'. In his working script, Nigel has quoted these lines opposite Act II, scene iv and noted, 'The storm dominates Lear. Not the other way round. His rage is impotent.' His performance thus illuminated an important aspect of Lear's behaviour during the tempest that is often overlooked by directors and editors. Much of his interpretation hinged on Lear's desperate attempts to contain emotion and to conceal weakness.

When moments of unrestrained emotion did occur, therefore, they were all the more powerful and persuasive, as, for example, in his passionate 'O, reason not the need!' speech in Act II, scene iv:

A lot of Lear is to do with crying, with holding back the tears. And I think sometimes when you're saying 'don't cry', that's probably when you're crying the most, because you're trying to stop crying. I've done that in the 'Reason not the need speech': 'let not women's weapons, water-drops, / Stain my man's cheeks' – they are already stained.

Interestingly, at the 2002 Festival of Canada in Stratford, Ontario, Christopher Plummer performed the role of Lear under Jonathan Miller's direction and there were important points of resemblance between his interpretation and that of Nigel's, with the marked difference that the North American critics responded warmly to Plummer's departure from tradition. Miller located in *King Lear* 'moments of great clinical accuracy'[21] which he saw as evidence of Shakespeare's knowledge of conditions like senile dementia, and he deemed it 'the perfect play to try out some of the new developments in psycholinguistics.'[22] Like Nigel, Miller and the seventy-four-year-old Plummer sought to make sense of the madness and to map out a persuasive psychological journey. The result, according to Ben Brantley of the *New York Times,* was a more restrained, human and accessible Lear:

The production's greatest pleasure [...] comes from Mr Plummer's taking you step by step through his Lear's enormous changes in temperament and insight and justifying every turn on both an intellectual and gut level. This is true when Lear is talking to the elements in the storm, and not in Promethean defiance but with a conversational ardor that finds the sense in his insanity. [...]

Though Mr Plummer can be the grandest of grandstanders, he tends to play down his actorly magnificence here in favor of a Lear with whom everyone must identify. It's a bold choice, and there may be those who object that Lear has been too domesticated. On the other hand, I have never seen an audience so saturated in tears at the end of King Lear *as this one was.*[23]

In Act IV, scene vi, when Nigel's Lear met the blinded Gloucester, he seemed at first not to know him – 'Ha! Goneril, with a white beard!' But as Gloucester's delight at hearing the King's voice, and his amusement at the King's distracted antics, gave way to uncontrollable weeping, Lear suddenly took him in his arms and said, 'If thou wilt weep my fortunes, take my eyes. / I know thee well enough, thy name is Gloucester.' Lear's recognition of Gloucester, whereby the mad man gave comfort to the blind man, was one of the most affecting parts of Nigel's performance. In his working script he has contemptuously crossed out all stage directions in the scene that refer to a fey and fantastically dressed King intermittently distributing wild flowers, and his annotations record the intelligence and sensitivity of his reading as well as the richness of his characterisation. Throughout the scene he brilliantly interwove contrasting emotions and personae: he imitated and mocked the sycophancy of his court; affected the demeanour of a ham actor; moralised in the fashion of an evangelist preacher; and fought imaginary battles with his sons-in-law. At first he was mercurial, absurd and childlike. He then ricocheted from lewdness to savage anger and from anger to ruefulness, and in the midst of madness, sitting beside Gloucester, he suddenly exposed a clarity of vision, an empathy and a self-awareness that were almost unbearably moving. Thelma Holt believes the scene on the beach at Dover to be the defining moment of Nigel's performance and the production:

> *If you take a play like* Lear *or* Julius Caesar *— the big ones — I have never seen an unflawed production of any of these plays. There's always got be a flaw and there's always got to be special things. But there are moments in plays, like, for instance* Albert Speer, *a deeply flawed play in my view, but there is a scene in* Albert Speer *when Speer comes home and dines with his family for the first time, which, if the production had been bad, — and it wasn't — would have made it worthwhile. Just to see that scene, to isolate that scene, was acting at its best, when you appreciate why it's a major art form and not a minor one. And, in my view, there were those moments in* Lear. *And the one that was absolutely priceless was Dover. The Dover scene was the best Dover scene I've ever seen in my life, and I suppose I've seen more* Lears *than I've had hot dinners. It was the finest.*

The scene was given added pathos by its consistency with Nigel's reading of the madness not as a passionate, short-lived *furor*, but as a variable mental affliction:

> *I think what you've got to see is an irrational rage. It's not that the King is in a huge temper for a long period; it just comes and it's gone, and he's something else then. He even tries to adjust himself to the change. He says to the Fool, 'I did her wrong', as though it's something that's been worrying him and he's got to tell somebody. And it's really the first time*

he's ever admitted doing anything wrong to anybody, so that the Fool is sort of thrown by the King's confession.

Similarly, Nigel's momentary expressions of remorse towards the end of the first scene; the impression he created, in the presence of Regan and Goneril, of a gravely distressed man addressing himself and fearful for his own sanity; and his belated recognition of the loyal and ever-present Kent demonstrated the volatility, disorientation and isolation that can be symptomatic of Alzheimer's disease. In Stratford he said:

I've tried to find moments in the play where he talks obliquely to people, as though he's talking to himself. For example, in the scene with Goneril, which ends with the dreadful curse invoking sterility on her, his mind is already flittering about. He's not actually talking to anybody except to himself, which is a sign of the mind starting to wander, as though people are not there. Then he comes back to lucidity and then goes again and becomes angry. It comes and goes; it's not something that's consistent.

His characterisation provided the audience with insights into each stage of the terrifying journey of a man 'Fourscore and upward' towards the dark chaos that replaces reason:

I chose to unfold, if you like, or take the audience along on a journey with the King. So you see him, even in the very first scene, starting to regret what he's done. When he banishes Kent and Kent goes, I deliberately look after Kent with regret, thinking I've gone too far. I then go back to Cordelia, look at her, 'What have I done to this relationship?' And when he says to Kent, 'Away! By Jupiter,/ This shall not be revoked', as I say it, I hesitate as if I'm about to revoke it. But because it's in a court and because it's in public, he can't pull back, so he has to go ahead with it, and it's his undoing and everybody else's undoing. So I've taken him on that journey of doubt and it manifests itself in all sorts of different ways.

Testimony both to the meticulous research he had undertaken for the role, and to the empathy he had for Lear, was the fact that Nigel received a significant amount of correspondence from medical practitioners, among them specialists in psychiatry and in Alzheimer's disease, remarking on the extraordinary accuracy and observation with which he communicated the various stages of Lear's madness. Thelma Holt comments, 'Having a couple of doctors write nice letters to you is one thing, but having the amount of letters that he received is quite another, and saying, to a man, that he must have considerable knowledge of this situation. He hadn't; he'd just done his homework very, very thoroughly indeed.' One person who was particularly impressed by Nigel's interpretation of Lear's madness was the distinguished psychiatrist Dr Anthony Storr, whom the actor had consulted in Oxford as part of his research for the role. In addition to his ample research, Nigel drew on his personal experience of witnessing the deterioration of his grandfather and friends who had been afflicted by Alzheimer's and mental illnesses such as depression:

> *I knew a very, very gentle man. He was an actor. I worked with him at one stage, and he made quite a lot of films in Hollywood as well as in England. And when he got elderly he went to a retirement home and became violent. Now there was no violence in the man. So what steers some gentle creature, ordinary person, into this state? Somebody went to see him and he had a black eye. He'd tried to attack someone and they'd fought back. I think we're all scared, and the older we get the more scared we are, of madness, of slipping into something that isn't predictable. And the people that I know who have Alzheimer's, it's dreadfully tragic to watch because they seem lucid. A lady I know came and saw* Lear, *and when she came into my room (and she's in her eighties), she had with her a minder, a helper, who had to keep reminding her of the play that she'd just seen, because she just got bewildered. Although she'd clearly enjoyed it, she was already starting to lose track of having seen it at all. Madness affects people in so many different ways and I had a grandfather who went mad. When you're putting it in dramatic terms, obviously you've got to heighten it, otherwise it would be very boring if you just played somebody who was constantly being distracted and forgetful. So you've got to have your climaxes.*

The restoration scene at the end of Act IV, in which Lear is reconciled with Cordelia, was played by Nigel at an appropriately muted pitch, and the King's private world of suffering in which he is 'mightily abused' was poignantly evoked. In complete contrast, Ian Holm had played the scene as an agonising awakening into Hellish torment, with the emphasis on the 'wheel-of-fire' metaphor, but it seemed to Nigel that 'playing the anger still in the man was wrong, because the Gentleman says, "the great rage/ You see is killed in him".' Just as in his portrayal of George III, Nigel made us see King Lear in his madness reduced to his humanity; against the machinations of his eldest daughters and Edmund, he set in stark relief the vulnerability of the 'child-changed father'. According to Jonathan Lynn's wife Rita, Nigel also ensured that 'the intrinsic goodness of the man in the end came out in spite of his earlier appalling behaviour. It's hard for an actor to play goodness unless they're a good man. It's easier to play evil.'

Identifying Nigel's gift for small-scale but powerful effect and the emotional and psychological depth he was able to convey in the subtlest gesture or facial expression, Thelma Holt said:

We couldn't have filmed that Lear. *It wasn't staged for film, but his performance could have actually been filmed. What you saw in his face, the terror you saw in his face, the confusion, was really quite beautiful and very moving. I was moved by it night after night after night. Now you're always moved on the first night because you're frightened. You're always moved with relief by the time you get through the previews and get through the press night. There are all kinds of other things that contribute to your emotional reaction, but when you see a play night after night after night, month after month after month, if you still find a lump in your throat there has to be something emotionally terribly twenty-four carat gold about it. And Nigel never ever sells you cheap; he's worth the price of the ticket.*

Indicative of this 'golden' quality was Nigel's heartbreaking rendering of the line 'Cordelia, Cordelia, stay a little' (Act V, scene iii, 269). In these few simple words he encapsulated the tragedy of King Lear who discovers late the way to reconciliation and redemption only to have the happiness promised by that discovery brutally annulled. In his sermon at Nigel's funeral, Bishop Herbert declared:

Those of us who saw Nigel's King Lear *will have recognised in a way that the too-talkative and too-knowing critics did not seem able to, that this was a magisterial performance based on tenacious self-awareness and tenacious vulnerability, an exploration of age and failing powers, and done with the disciplined, selfless attention to the beauty of the text and the power of the pattern that can only come from a courageous and aching awareness of all human weakness.*

King Lear is a play that has many parallels with ancient tragedy and Nigel's thoughtful and sympathetic interpretation of the central role helped to underline these. In his 'Come, let's away to prison' speech in Act V, scene iii he exhibited a heroism and defiance built on gentleness, calling to my mind William Arrowsmith's description of Euripides' tragedy on another mad king, namely Heracles: '[it] is a play which imposes suffering upon men as their tragic condition, but it also discovers a courage equal to that necessity, a courage founded on love.'[24] When Nigel made his final entry carrying the body of Cordelia, the aching intensity of his howls of grief recalled the figure of King Creon at the end of Sophocles' *Antigone,* bearing in his arms the body of his son Haemon whom he has fatally wronged.

In *The Madness of George III* and *King Lear* Nigel took his audience on a journey, which he charted with bravery and compassion, and in which his identification with his character was supreme. His achievement in both roles was the revelation of the private tragedy engendered by the public loss of self. *George III* is Nigel's unassailable monument in the chronicles of British theatre. Regrettably, his *Lear* may be remembered more for the critical storm it provoked than its originality and power, although not, I suspect, by those to whom for the first time the plight of this 'foolish, fond old man' made absolute sense. Whatever the case, these two performances equally demonstrated Nigel's capacity as a stage actor both to challenge and to be challenged, to provoke the intellect, enlighten the soul and move the heart – precisely the vocation of the actor at its noblest.

Notes to Chapter 10

1   In Zucker (1999) 68.
2   Linda Inoki, *Japan Times,* 5 October 1999.
3   Nicholas de Jongh, *Evening Standard,* 29 October 1999.
4   Peter Hillmore, *Mail on Sunday,* 31 October 1999.
5   Michael Coveney, *Daily Mail,* 5 November 1999.
6   Charles Spencer, *Daily Telegraph,* 20 October 1999.
7   Susannah Clapp, *Observer,* 31 October 1999.
8   *Times,* 20 October 1999.
9   *Daily Telegraph,* 29 October 1999.
10 *Independent,* 30 October 1999.
11 *Daily Mail,* 5 November 1999.
12 *Times,* 29 October 1999.
13 28 October 1999.
14 *Guardian,* 30 November 1999.
15 *Spectator,* 6 November 1999.
16 *Express,* 2 November 1999.
17 *Sunday Times,* 31 October 1999.
18 *Financial Times,* 1 November 1999.
19 'The ironist at the gates', *Times Literary Supplement,* 5 November 1999.
20 Michael Coveney, *Daily Mail,* 5 November 1999.
21 Miller in an interview with Lawrence B. Johnson, *Detroit News,* 22 August 2002.
22 Miller in an interview with Ray Conlogue, *The Globe and Mail,* 21 August 2002.
23 'Every Inch a King, Every Moment a Revelation', *New York Times,* 12 September 2002.
24 Arrowsmith (1969) 44-59, at 53.

ACT THREE:
Chronologies

CHRONOLOGY I: STAGE

Year	Play *Author*	Director	Company/ Theatre	Opening Performance	Role
1947	Juno and the Paycock *Sean O' Casey* (a dramatic reading)	Rosalie van der Gucht	Cape Town Repertory Theatre Society, Members' Evening, Little Theatre, Cape Town	2 September	Johnnie Boyle
	The Merchant of Venice *William Shakespeare*	Rosalie van der Gucht	The Speech-Training Department, University of Cape Town, Little Theatre, Cape Town	September	Tubal
	Tobias and the Angel *James Bridie*	Joyce Burch	Cape Town Repertory Theatre Society Little Theatre, Cape Town	10 November	Bandit / Sam / Asmoday
1948	She Stoops to Conquer *Oliver Goldsmith*	Joyce Burch	The Speech-Training Department, Universityof Cape Town, Little Theatre, Cape Town	21 June	Sir Charles Marlow / Yokel
	St Simeon Stylites Splatterdashes: An Evening of One-Act Plays *F. Sladen-Smith*	Cecil Jubber & Helen Houghton	University of Cape Town Dramatic Society, Little Theatre, Cape Town	21 August	St Simeon
1949	St Simeon Stylites *F. Sladen-Smith*	Cecil Jubber	The Players Muizenberg Pavilion, Muizenberg	17 February	St Simeon
	Puppet Show *Sidney Box*	Nigel Hawthorne	The Players Muizenberg Pavilion, Muizenberg	17 February	Puppet-Master
	The Proposal *Anton Chekhov*	Jobie Stewart	The Players Muizenberg Pavilion, Muizenberg	17 February	Stepan Stepanovitch
	The Match Girls *Robert Mitchell*	Rosalie van der Gucht	The Speech-Training Department, Universityof Cape Town, Little Theatre, Cape Town	9 March	Edward / Foreman
	The Western Chamber *Wang Shih-Fu / trans.* *Prof. S. I. Hsiung Shih-i*	Matine Harman	The Speech-Training Department, Universityof Cape Town, Little Theatre, Cape Town	25 March	Sun Flying-Tiger
	Cockpit *Bridget Boland*	Leonard Schach	University of Cape Town Dramatic Society Little Theatre, Cape Town	3 May	Sergeant Barnes

Year	Play *Author*	Director	Company/ Theatre	Opening Performance	Role
	Mr Sleeman is Coming *Hjalmar Bergman*	Arnold Pearce	University of Cape Town Dramatic Society Cape Peninsula District Drama Festival of FATSSA Labia Theatre, Cape Town	7 July	The Hunter (Walter)
			11th Annual National Festival of FATSSA (Finals) Town Hall, Benoni	30 July	
	A Phoenix Too Frequent *Christopher Fry*	Leonard Schach	The Speech-Training Department, University of Cape Town Season of Comedy Little Theatre, Cape Town	12 September	Tegeus- Chromis
	Mr Sleeman is Coming *Hjalmar Bergman*	Arnold Pearce	University of Cape Town Dramatic Society, Little Theatre, Cape Town	29 September	The Hunter (Walter)
	Love and How to Cure It *Thornton Wilder*	Jobie Stewart	Little Theatre, Cape Town	2 December	Arthur Warburton
1950	The Western Chamber *Wang Shih-Fu / trans.* *Prof. S. I. Hsiung Shih-i*	Matine Harman	The Speech-Training Department, University of Cape Town Little Theatre, Cape Town	28 March	Sun Flying-Tiger
	Home of the Brave *Arthur Laurents*	Leonard Schach	Cockpit Players Labia Theatre, Cape Town	4 April	Finch
	Professional Debut: The Shop at Sly Corner *Edward Percy*	Gabriel Toyne	The Brian Brooke Company Hofmeyr Theatre, Cape Town	19 April	Archie Fellowes
	Travellers' Joy *Arthur Macrae*	Gabriel Toyne	The Brian Brooke Company Hofmeyr Theatre, Cape Town (+ tour of Union and Southern Rhodesia)	10 May	Mr Olson
	Edward, My Son *Noel Langley &* *Robert Morle*	Gabriel Toyne & Shaun Sutton	The Brian Brooke Company Hofmeyr Theatre, Cape Town (+ tour of Union and Southern Rhodesia)	31 May	Mr Prothero
	Travellers' Joy *Arthur Macrae*	Gabriel Toyne	The Brian Brooke Company His Majesty's Theatre, Johannesburg	16 June	Mr Olson

Year	Play *Author*	Director	Company/ Theatre	Opening Performance	Role
	Edward, My Son *Noel Langley &* *Robert Morley*	Gabriel Toyne & Shaun Sutton	The Brian Brooke Company His Majesty's Theatre, Johannesburg	30 June	Mr Prothero
	See How They Run *Philip King*	Shaun Sutton	The Brian Brooke Company His Majesty's Theatre, Johannesburg (+ tour of Union and Southern Rhodesia)	10 July	The Rev. Arthur Humphrey
	Travellers' Joy *Arthur Macrae*	Gabriel Toyne	The Brian Brooke Company, Opera House, Pretoria	17 July	Mr Olson
	See How They Run *Philip King*	Shaun Sutton	The Brian Brooke Company Opera House, Pretoria	20 July	The Rev. Arthur Humphrey
	Present Laughter *Noël Coward*	Brian Brooke & Petrina Fry	The Brian Brooke Company Tour of Union and Southern Rhodesia		Fred
	See How They Run *Philip King*	Shaun Sutton	The Brian Brooke Company Hofmeyr Theatre, Cape Town	22 September	The Rev. Arthur Humphrey
	Rain *John Cotton &* *Clemence Randolph/* *adapted from* *Somerset Maugham's* *short story* *'Sadie Thompson'*	Shaun Sutton	The Brian Brooke Company, Hofmeyr Theatre, Cape Town	17 October	Private Griggs
	Thark *Ben Travers*	Shaun Sutton	The Brian Brooke Company, Hofmeyr Theatre, Cape Town	31 October	Lionel Frush
	The Case of the Frightened Lady *Edgar Wallace*	Shaun Sutton	The Brian Brooke Company, Hofmeyr Theatre, Cape Town	28 November	Lord Lebanon
	Present Laughter *Noël Coward*	Petrina Fry	The Brian Brooke Company, Hofmeyr Theatre, Cape Town	12 December	Roland Maule
	Charley's Aunt *Brandon Thomas*	Mary Byron with Peter Drew	The Brian Brooke Company, Hofmeyr Theatre, Cape Town	20 December	Charles Wykeham
1951	Bonaventure *Charlotte Hastings*	Mary Byron	The Brian Brooke Company, Hofmeyr Theatre, Cape Town	30 January	Willy Pentridge
	The Bird Cage *Arthur Laurents*	Brian Brooke	The Brian Brooke Company, Hofmeyr Theatre, Cape Town	13 February	Cork

Year	Play Author	Director	Company/ Theatre	Opening Performance	Role
	On Monday Next *Philip King*	Petrina Fry	The Brian Brooke Company, Hofmeyr Theatre, Cape Town	22 February	Jackson Harley
	The Little Foxes *Lillian Hellman*	Mary Byron	The Brian Brooke Company, Hofmeyr Theatre, Cape Town	8 March	Leo Hubbard
	Murder at the Vicarage *Agatha Christie/* *dramatised by Moie* *Charles & Barbara Toy*	Shaun Sutton	Anthony Hawtrey's Company, Playhouse Theatre, Buxton	4 June	Ronald Hawes
	High Temperature *Avery Hopwood*	Shaun Sutton	Anthony Hawtrey's Company, Playhouse Theatre, Buxton	11 June	Joe
	Bonaventure *Charlotte Hastings*	Shaun Sutton	Anthony Hawtrey's Company, Playhouse Theatre, Buxton	18 June	Willy Pentridge
	The Ghost Train *Arnold Ridley*	Shaun Sutton	Anthony Hawtrey's Company, Playhouse Theatre, Buxton	25 June	John Sterling
	Travellers' Joy *Arthur Macrae*	Shaun Sutton	Anthony Hawtrey's Company, Playhouse Theatre, Buxton	2 July	Mr Olson
	A Murder Has Been Arranged *Emlyn Williams*	Shaun Sutton	Anthony Hawtrey's Company, Playhouse Theatre, Buxton	9 July	Jimmy North
	The Holly and the Ivy *Wynyard Browne*	Shaun Sutton	Anthony Hawtrey's Company, Playhouse Theatre, Buxton	16 July	Mick Gregory
	Queen Elizabeth Slept Here *Talbot Rothwell*	Shaun Sutton	Anthony Hawtrey's Company, Playhouse Theatre, Buxton	23 July	Steve Hadlett
	Pick-Up Girl *Elsa Shelley*	Shaun Sutton	Anthony Hawtrey's Company, Playhouse Theatre, Buxton	30 July	Policeman Owens
	Charley's Aunt *Brandon Thomas*	Shaun Sutton	Anthony Hawtrey's Company, Playhouse Theatre, Buxton	6 August	Charles Wykeham
	Tovarich *Jacques Deval/adapted* *by Robert E. Sherwood*	Shaun Sutton	The Playhouse Theatre Festival (part of the Festival of Britain) Anthony Hawtrey's Company, Playhouse Theatre, Buxton	20 August	Chauffourier- Dubieff
	Poison in Jest *Val Gielgud*	Anthony Hawtrey & Shaun Sutton	The Playhouse Theatre Festival (part of the Festival of Britain) Anthony Hawtrey's Company, Playhouse Theatre, Buxton	3 September	Nigel Bathurst

Year	Play *Author*	Director	Company/ Theatre	Opening Performance	Role
	School for Spinsters *Roland Pertwee*	Shaun Sutton	Anthony Hawtrey's Company, Playhouse Theatre, Buxton	10 September	Tom Harding
	Fresh Fields *Ivor Novello*	Shaun Sutton	Anthony Hawtrey's Company, Playhouse Theatre, Buxton	17 September	Tim Crabbe
	Black Chiffon *Lesley Storm*	Shaun Sutton	Anthony Hawtrey's Company, Playhouse Theatre, Buxton	24 September	Roy
	Rope *Patrick Hamilton*	Shaun Sutton	Anthony Hawtrey's Company, Playhouse Theatre, Buxton	1 October	Charles Granillo
	Captain Carvallo *Denis Cannan*	Shaun Sutton	Anthony Hawtrey's Company, Playhouse Theatre, Buxton	8 October	Professor Winke
	See How They Run *Philip King*	Shaun Sutton	Anthony Hawtrey's Company, Playhouse Theatre, Buxton	15 October	The Bishop of Lax
	London Debut: Magnolia Street Story *Emmanuel Litvinoff /* *based on the novel* *by Louis Golding*	Terence De Marney	Anthony Hawtrey's Company, Embassy Theatre, Swiss Cottage	7 November	A Sailor
	You Can't Take It With You *Moss Hart &* *George S. Kaufman*	Shaun Sutton	Anthony Hawtrey's Company, Embassy Theatre, Swiss Cottage	27 November	Donald
	The Merchant of Yonkers *Thornton Wilder*	André Van Gyseghem	Anthony Hawtrey's Company, Embassy Theatre, Swiss Cottage	26 December	Rudolph, a waiter
1952	The Cat and the Canary *John Willard*	Shaun Sutton	Anthony Hawtrey's Company, Playhouse Theatre, Buxton	30 June	Roger Crosby
	Deep are the Roots *Arnaud D' Usseau* *& James Gow*	Shaun Sutton	Anthony Hawtrey's Company, Playhouse Theatre, Buxton	7 July	Roy Maxwell
	Home at Seven *R. C. Sherriff*	Shaun Sutton	Anthony Hawtrey's Company, Playhouse Theatre, Buxton	14 July	Mr Petherbridge
	George and Margaret *Gerald Savory*	Anthony Pelly	Anthony Hawtrey's Company, Playhouse Theatre, Buxton	21 July	Dudley
	Dr Morelle *Ernest Dudley* *& Arthur Watkyn*	Raymond Lovell	Anthony Hawtrey's Company, Playhouse Theatre, Buxton	28 July	Guthrie
	One Wild Oat *Vernon Sylvaine*	Raymond Lovell	Anthony Hawtrey's Company, Playhouse Theatre, Buxton	4 August	Fred Gilbey

Year	Play *Author*	Director	Company/ Theatre	Opening Performance	Role
	Outward Bound *Sutton Vane*	Raymond Lovell	Anthony Hawtrey's Company, Playhouse Theatre, Buxton	11 August	Henry
	The Hollow *Agatha Christie*	Raymond Lovell	Anthony Hawtrey's Company, Playhouse Theatre, Buxton	18 August	Gudgeon
	Who Goes There? *John Dighton*	Raymond Lovell	Anthony Hawtrey's Company, Playhouse Theatre, Buxton	25 August	Guardsman Arthur Crisp
	The White Sheep of the Family *L. du Garde Peach & Ian Hay*	Raymond Lovell	Anthony Hawtrey's Company, Playhouse Theatre, Buxton	1 September	Peter Winter
	Away From It All *Val Gielgud*	Raymond Lovell	Anthony Hawtrey's Company, Playhouse Theatre, Buxton	8 September	Johnny Quayle
	The Family Upstairs *Harry Delf*	Raymond Lovell	Anthony Hawtrey's Company, Playhouse Theatre, Buxton	15 September	Willie Heller
	The Barretts of Wimpole Street *Rudolf Besier*	Raymond Lovell	Anthony Hawtrey's Company, Playhouse Theatre, Buxton	22 September	Captain Surtees Cook
	Poison Pen *Richard Llewellyn*	Peter Rosser	The London Players Grand Theatre, Southampton	27 October	Malcolm McCleod
	Laburnum Grove *J. B. Priestley*	Peter Rosser	The London Players Grand Theatre, Southampton	10 November	Harold Russ
	Rope *Patrick Hamilton*	Frederick Tripp	The Savoy Players Palace Theatre, Walthamstow	1 December	Kenneth Raglan
1953	**West End Debut:** Red Herring *Dan Sutherland*	Leslie Phillips	The Repertory Players Strand Theatre, London	18 January	Plain Clothes Man
	The King's Son *Thomas Browne & Malcolm Stewart*	Nigel Stock	The Repertory Players New Theatre, London	22 February	Police Sergeant
1954	The Sultan's Turret *James Doran*	André Morell	The Repertory Players Wyndham's Theatre, London	4 April	Attendant
	The Sport of Kings *Ian Hay*	Alex Reeve	Northampton Repertory Players Royal Theatre, Northampton	2 August	Algernon Sprigge
	Rain *John Colton & Clemence Randolph / based on the story of 'Miss Thompson' by Somerset Maugham*	Alex Reeve	Northampton Repertory Players Royal Theatre, Northampton	9 August	Sergeant O'Hara

Year	Play *Author*	Director	Company/ Theatre	Opening Performance	Role
	Quiet Weekend *Esther McCracken*	Alex Reeve	Northampton Repertory Players Royal Theatre, Northampton	16 August	Jim Brent
	Escapade *Roger MacDougall*	Alex Reeve	Northampton Repertory Players Royal Theatre, Northampton	23 August	Sir Harold Cookham
	For Better, For Worse *Arthur Watkyn*	Alex Reeve	Northampton Repertory Players Royal Theatre, Northampton	30 August	Tony
	Beyond the Horizon *Eugene O' Neill*	Alex Reeve	Northampton Repertory Players Royal Theatre, Northampton	20 September	Andrew Mayo
	A Spell of Virtue *C. Neilson &* *Z. Bramley-Moore*	Alex Reeve	Northampton Repertory Players Royal Theatre, Northampton	27 September	Sir Launcelot Du Lae
	Spring Model *Alex Atkinson*	Alex Reeve	Northampton Repertory Players Royal Theatre, Northampton	4 October	Charlie
	Vanity Fair *William Makepeace* *Thackeray / adapted* *by Constance Cox*	Alex Reeve	Northampton Repertory Players Royal Theatre, Northampton	11 October	Captain Dobbin
	Let's Talk Turkey *Dudley Leslie &* *Audrey A. Erskine-Lindop*	Alex Reeve	Northampton Repertory Players Royal Theatre, Northampton	18 October	Russell MacColl
	The Letter *Somerset Maugham*	Alex Reeve	Northampton Repertory Players Royal Theatre, Northampton	25 October	John Withers
	The Flashing Stream *Charles Morgan*	Lionel Hamilton	Northampton Repertory Players Royal Theatre, Northampton	8 November	Lieut.- Commander Peter Brissing, R. N.
	The Man in Grey *Barbara Toy &* *Moie Charles*	Alex Reeve	Northampton Repertory Players Royal Theatre, Northampton	15 November	Swinton Rokeby
	Off the Road *Ian Hay &* *Stephen King-Hall*	Alex Reeve	Northampton Repertory Players Royal Theatre, Northampton	22 November	Tom D'Arcy, MP

Year	Play *Author*	Director	Company/ Theatre	Opening Performance	Role
	Dear Charles *Marc-Gilbert Sauvajon* *& Frederick Jackson* *(Les Enfants d'Edouard) /* *adapted by Alan Melville*	Alex Reeve	Northampton Repertory Players Royal Theatre, Northampton	13 December	Walter
	Dick Whittington *Book by Alex Reeve /* *new music by* *Stephen Sylvester /* *lyrics by Stephen Sylvester* *& Alex Reeve*	Alex Reeve	Northampton Repertory Players Royal Theatre, Northampton	27 December	Joe, Second Mate
1955	The Sleeping Prince *Terence Rattigan*	Alex Reeve	Northampton Repertory Players Royal Theatre, Northampton	24 January	The Second Footman
	Peril at End House *Agatha Christie /* *adapted by Arnold Ridley*	Lionel Hamilton	Northampton Repertory Players Royal Theatre, Northampton	31 January	Charles Vyse
	Cut for Partners *Barry Phelps*	Alex Reeve	Northampton Repertory Players Royal Theatre, Northampton	7 February	George
	As Long as They're Happy *Vernon Sylvaine*	Alex Reeve	Northampton Repertory Players Royal Theatre, Northampton	14 February	Peter Pember
	Stolen Waters *Lionel Brown*	Alex Reeve	Northampton Repertory Players Royal Theatre, Northampton	21 February	George Lawrence
	Angels in Love *Hugh Mills*	Alex Reeve	Northampton Repertory Players Royal Theatre, Northampton	28 February	Cedric, Lord Fauntleroy
	As You Like It *William Shakespeare*	Alex Reeve	Northampton Repertory Players Royal Theatre, Northampton	15 March	Orlando
	The Gay Dog *Joseph Colton*	Alex Reeve	Northampton Repertory Players Royal Theatre, Northampton	28 March	Leslie Gowland
	The Archers *Edward J. Mason &* *Geoffrey Webb*	Alex Reeve	Northampton Repertory Players Royal Theatre, Northampton	4 April	Phil Archer
	See How They Run *Philip King*	Alex Reeve	Northampton Repertory Players Royal Theatre, Northampton	11 April	The Intruder

Year	Play Author	Director	Company/ Theatre	Opening Performance	Role
	Dial 'M' for Murder *Frederick Knott*	Alex Reeve	Northampton Repertory Players Royal Theatre, Northampton	18 April	Max Halliday
	Happy Memories *Gertrude Jennings*	Alex Reeve	Northampton Repertory Players Royal Theatre, Northampton	25 April	Vivian
	The Little Hut *Andre Roussin /* *adapted by Nancy Mitford*	Alex Reeve	Northampton Repertory Players Royal Theatre, Northampton	3 May	First Stranger
	Sabrina Fair *Samuel Taylor*	Alex Reeve	Northampton Repertory Players Royal Theatre, Northampton	9 May	David Larrabee
	When We are Married *J. B. Priestley*	Alex Reeve	Northampton Repertory Players Royal Theatre, Northampton	16 May	Gerald Forbes
	Indoor Sport *Jack Perry*	Alex Reeve	Northampton Repertory Players Royal Theatre, Northampton	23 May	Jefferson Connolly III
	Flare Path *Terence Rattigan*	Alex Reeve	Northampton Repertory Players Royal Theatre, Northampton	30 May	Flt Lieut Graham
	Rookery Nook *Ben Travers*	Alex Reeve	Northampton Repertory Players Royal Theatre, Northampton	6 June	Clive Popkiss
	Born Yesterday *Garson Kanin*	Alex Reeve	Northampton Repertory Players Royal Theatre, Northampton	20 June	Senator Norval Hedges
	The Confidential Clerk *T. S. Eliot*	Alex Reeve	Northampton Repertory Players Royal Theatre, Northampton	27 June	Colby Simpkins
	The Lady of the Camellias *Alexandre Dumas, Fils /* *trans. and adapted by* *Phyllis Hartnoll*	Alex Reeve	Northampton Repertory Players Royal Theatre, Northampton	25 July	Varville
	Witness for the Prosecution *Agatha Christie*	Alex Reeve	Northampton Repertory Players Royal Theatre, Northampton	8 August	Leonard Vole

Year	Play Author	Director	Company/ Theatre	Opening Performance	Role
	Come Back Peter *A. P. Dearsley*	William Sellars	Northampton Repertory Players Royal Theatre, Northampton	15 August	George (Pie face)
	The Manor of Northstead *William Douglas Home*	Lionel Hamilton	Northampton Repertory Players Royal Theatre, Northampton	22 August	Lord Pym (Tony)
	Meet Mr Callaghan *Gerald Verner /* *from the novel of* *The Urgent Hangman* *by Peter Cheyney*	Alex Reeve	Northampton Repertory Players Royal Theatre, Northampton	29 August	Bellamy Meraulton
	Daddy Long Legs *Jean Webster*	Alex Reeve	Northampton Repertory Players Royal Theatre, Northampton	5 September	John Codman / Griggs
	The Cat and the Canary *John Willard*	Alex Reeve	Northampton Repertory Players Royal Theatre, Northampton	12 September	Paul Jones
	Book of the Month *Basil Thomas*	Alex Reeve	Northampton Repertory Players Royal Theatre, Northampton	19 September	Nicholas Barnes-Bradley
	The Secret Tent *Elizabeth Addyman*	Alex Reeve	Northampton Repertory Players Royal Theatre, Northampton	10 October	Christopher Martyn
	The Rivals *Richard Brinsley Sheridan*	Alex Reeve	Northampton Repertory Players Royal Theatre, Northampton	18 October	Captain Absolute
	Both Ends Meet *Arthur Macrae*	William Sellars	Northampton Repertory Players Royal Theatre, Northampton	24 October	Mr Wilson
	The Heiress of Rosings *Cedric Wallis /* *after Jane Austen*	Alex Reeve	Northampton Repertory Players Royal Theatre, Northampton	7 November	The Marquess of Chippenham
	Seagulls Over Sorrento *Hugh Hastings*	Lionel Hamilton	Northampton Repertory Players Royal Theatre, Northampton	14 November	Able Seaman McIntosh ('Haggis')
	I am a Camera *John van Druten*	Alex Reeve	Northampton Repertory Players Royal Theatre, Northampton	21 November	Fritz Wendel

Year	Play *Author*	Director	Company/ Theatre	Opening Performance	Role
	Come on Jeeves *P. G. Wodehouse &* *Guy Bolton*	Alex Reeve	Northampton Repertory Players Royal Theatre, Northampton	28 November	Colonel Meredith, Chief Constable
	The Running Man *Anthony Armstrong &* *Arnold Ridley*	Alex Reeve	Northampton Repertory Players Royal Theatre, Northampton	5 December	Frank
	The Moon is Blue *F. Hugh Herbert*	Alex Reeve	Northampton Repertory Players Royal Theatre, Northampton	12 December	Donald Gresham
	Babes in the Wood *Alex Reeve*	Alex Reeve	Northampton Repertory Players Royal Theatre, Northampton	26 December	Will Scarlet
1956	Ring Round the Moon *Jean Anouilh / adapted by* *Christopher Fry*	Alex Reeve	Northampton Repertory Players Royal Theatre, Northampton	23 January	Hugo / Frederic
	You and Your Wife *Denis Cannan*	Alex Reeve	Northampton Repertory Players Royal Theatre, Northampton	30 January	Ellis
	Late Love *Rosemary Casey*	Lionel Hamilton	Northampton Repertory Players Royal Theatre, Northampton	13 February	Matthew Anderson
	Where There's a Will *R. F. Delderfield*	William Sellars	Northampton Repertory Players Royal Theatre, Northampton	20 February	Ralph Stokes
	The Barretts of Wimpole Street *Rudolf Besier*	Alex Reeve	Northampton Repertory Players Royal Theatre, Northampton	27 February	Henry Bevan
	A Midsummer Night's Dream *William Shakespeare*	Alex Reeve	Northampton Repertory Players Royal Theatre, Northampton	13 March	Lysander
	The Hasty Heart *John Patrick*	Alex Reeve	Northampton Repertory Players Royal Theatre, Northampton	26 March	Lachlen
	Tons of Money *Will Evans & Valentine*	David Poulson	The Bromley Repertory Company New Theatre, Bromley	17 September	George Maitland

Year	Play *Author*	Director	Company/ Theatre	Opening Performance	Role
	Cinderella (pantomime) *music & lyrics by* *Lionel Bart &* *Jack Grossman / book by* *Una Brandon-Jones,* *John Gold & Roger Woddis*		The Bromley Repertory Company New Theatre, Bromley	26 December	Old 'Enery
1957	Night of the Fourth *Gordon Harbord &* *Jack Roffey*	Arnold Fry	The Bromley Repertory Company New Theatre, Bromley	28 January	Dallas
	Seagulls Over Sorrento *Hugh Hasting*	Lionel Hamilton	Northampton Repertory Players Royal Theatre, Northampton	11 February	Able Seaman McIntosh ('Haggis')
	Look Back in Anger *John Osborne*	Leonard Schach	Cockpit Players Hofmeyr Theatre, Cape Town	20 November	Cliff Lewis
	Summer of the Seventeenth Doll *Ray Lawler*	Leonard Schach	National Theatre Organisation National tour, beginning Reps Theatre, Johannesburg	31 December	Johnnie Dowd
1958	The Waltz of the Toreadors *Jean Anouilh*	Leonard Schach	Cockpit Players Hofmeyr Theatre, Cape Town	25 March	Doctor Bonfant
	Professional **Directorial Debut:** Doctor in the House *Ted Willis / based on* *the novel by* *Richard Gordon*	Nigel Hawthorne	The Eagle Players Hofmeyr Theatre, Cape Town	22 April	Tony Grimsdyke
	The School for Scandal *Richard Brinsley* *Sheridan*	Leon Gluckman	National Theatre Organisation National tour, beginning Reps Theatre, Johannesburg	2 July	Crabtree / Charles Surface
			Hofmeyr Theatre, Cape Town	12 August	
	The Male Animal *James Thurber &* *Elliot Nugent*	John McKelvey	Cockpit Players Hofmeyr Theatre, Cape Town	8 October	Joe Ferguson
	Long Day's Journey into Night *Eugene O' Neill*	Leonard Schach	Cockpit Players Hofmeyr Theatre, Cape Town	30 October	Edmund Tyrone
	Separate Tables *Terence Rattigan*	Leonard Schach	Cockpit Players Hofmeyr Theatre, Cape Town	19 November	Charles Stratton

Year	Play *Author*	Director	Company/ Theatre	Opening Performance	Role
	The Matchmaker (Der Shadchen) *Thornton Wilder*	Leonard Schach	Cockpit Players Hofmeyr Theatre, Cape Town	18 December	Cornelius Hackl
1959	Try for White *Basil Warner*	Leonard Schach	Cockpit Players Hofmeyr Theatre, Cape Town (+ tour of Southern Africa)	27 January	Robert Matthews
	Long Day's Journey into Night *Eugene O' Neill*	Leonard Schach	Cockpit Players Intimate Theatre, Johannesburg	9 February	Edmund Tyrone
	Try For White *Basil Warner*	Leonard Schach	Cockpit Players Intimate Theatre, Johannesburg	2 March	Robert Matthews
	The Matchmaker (Der Shadchen) *Thornton Wilder*	Leonard Schach	Cockpit Players Brooke Theatre, Johannesburg	31 March	Cornelius Hackl
	The Grass is Greener *Hugh & Margaret Williams*	Petrina Fry	Brooke Theatre, Johannesburg	16 June	Sellars
	Under Milk Wood *Dylan Thomas*	Hugh Goldie	Johannesburg Repertory Society Reps Theatre, Johannesburg	12 August	Three Parts
	Sabrina Fair *Samuel Taylor*	Hugh Goldie	Johannesburg Repertory Society Reps Theatre, Johannesburg	15 September	David Larrabee
1960	The Cave Dwellers *William Saroyan*	Victor Melleney	National Theatre Organisation National tour, including Benoni Main Town Hall	10 February	The Duke
			Brakpan Town Hall	11 February	
			Nigel Town Hall	12 February	
			Modderfontein Club Hall	13 February	
			Germiston Town Hall	15 February	
			Boksburg Hennie Basson School Hall	16 February	
			The Playhouse, Johannesburg	2 May	
	The Puppet Prince *Michael Drin*	Richard Daneel	Children's Theatre Library Theatre, Johannesburg	8 July	Marko
	Intimate Relations (Les Parents Terribles) *Jean Cocteau*	Hugh Goldie	Johannesburg Repertory Society Alexander Theatre, Johannesburg	28 September	Michel

Year	Play *Author*	Director	Company/ Theatre	Opening Performance	Role
	The Caretaker *Harold Pinter*	Leonard Schach	Cockpit Players Hofmeyr Theatre, Cape Town (+ tour of Southern Africa)	30 November	Aston
	Rookery Nook *Ben Travers*	Nigel Hawthorne & Aubrey Louw	Cockpit Players Hofmeyr Theatre, Cape Town	20 December	Gerald Popkiss
1961	The Unexpected Guest *Agatha Christie*	Leonard Schach	Cockpit Players Hofmeyr Theatre, Cape Town	9 March	Michael Starkwedder
	The Tenth Man *Paddy Chayefsky*	Leonard Schach	Cockpit Players Hofmeyr Theatre, Cape Town	10 April	The Rabbi
			Playhouse Theatre, Johannesburg	8 May	
	Beyond the Fringe *Alan Bennett,* *Peter Cook,* *Jonathan Miller* *& Dudley Moore*	Leonard Schach	Cockpit Players Hofmeyr Theatre, Cape Town (+ tour of Southern Africa)	11 October	Various (principally the parts originally performed by Jonathan Miller)
1962	Saint Joan *George Bernard Shaw*	Guy Vaesen	Connaught Theatre, Worthing	30 April	Gilles de Rais (Bluebeard) / English Soldier
	Something to Hide *Leslie Sands*	Guy Vaesen	Connaught Theatre, Worthing	7 May	Inspector Davies
	The Caretaker *Harold Pinter*	Robert David McDonald	The Bromley Repertory Company New Theatre, Bromley	4 June	Aston
	Talking to You *William Saroyan*	Arthur Storch	Royal Court Theatre, Liverpool	17 September	Fancy Dan
			Duke of York's Theatre, London	4 October	
	Across the Board on Tomorrow Morning *William Saroyan*	Arthur Storch	Royal Court Theatre, Liverpool	17 September	Sammy
			Duke of York's Theatre, London	4 October	
1963	A Doll's House *Henrik Ibsen*	James Roose-Evans	Theatre West Tour of south-west England		
	Squaring the Circle *Valentin Kataev*	James Roose-Evans	Theatre West Tour of south-west England		
	The Albatross *Howard Koch*	Ilya Chamberlain	Theatre Royal, Stratford East	4 November	Samuel Coleridge

Year	Play *Author*	Director	Company/ Theatre	Opening Performance	Role
1964	Oh, What a Lovely War! *Charles Chilton &* *The Company*	Joan Littlewood & Kevin Palmer	Theatre Workshop Golders Green, Hippodrome	31 August	Pierrot / Various
			Wimbledon Theatre	14 September	
			The Hippodrome, Brighton	5 October	
			Theatre Royal, Nottingham	30 November	
			(+ two European tours)		
1965	The Rivals *Richard Brinsley* *Sheridan*	Willard Stoker	Connaught Theatre, Worthing	15 March	Faulkland
	Summer's Ending *Jean-Louis Roncoroni /* *English version by Gillian* *& Campbell Singer*	Malcolm Farquar	Connaught Theatre, Worthing	29 March	Valentin
	Nymphs & Satires *Leon Gluckman &* *Jerome Kilty /* *words & music by* *Stanley Glasser,* *Adolf Wood, et al.*	Leon Gluckman	Apollo Theatre, London	25 May	Various
1966	Are You Normal, Mr Norman? *David Wilson*	Ian Watt-Smith	Hampstead Theatre Club, London	27 February (Sunday night performance)	Mr Lugg
	Blithe Spirit *Noël Coward*	Willard Stoker	Northampton Repertory Players Royal Theatre, Northampton	30 July	Charles Condomine
	The Winslow Boy *Terence Rattigan*	Willard Stoker	Northampton Repertory Players Royal Theatre, Northampton	16 August	Arthur Winslow
	The Ghost Train *Arthur Ridley*	Willard Stoker	Northampton Repertory Players Royal Theatre, Northampton	29 August	Teddie Deakin
	The Home Front *Arthur Watkyn*	Willard Stoker	Northampton Repertory Players Royal Theatre, Northampton	13 September	Colonel Bourne
	Man and Superman *George Bernard Shaw*	Willard Stoker	Northampton Repertory Players Royal Theatre, Northampton	27 September	Octavius Robinson
	The Creeper *Pauline Macauley*	Willard Stoker	Northampton Repertory Players Royal Theatre, Northampton	11 October	Edward Kimberley

Year	Play Author	Director	Company/ Theatre	Opening Performance	Role
1967	In At the Death *Duncan Greenwood & Robert King*	Ray Cooney	Phoenix Theatre, London	21 April	The Angry Neighbour
	The Marie Lloyd Story *Daniel Farson & Harry Moore / original lyrics by Daniel Farson & original music by Norman Kay*	Joan Littlewood	Theatre Workshop Theatre Royal, Stratford East	25 November	Sir Oswald Stoll / Various
1968	Mrs Wilson's Diary *Richard Ingrams & John Wells / lyrics by John Wells & music by Jeremy Taylor*	Joan Littlewood	Theatre Workshop Criterion Theatre, London	This production opened at the Theatre Royal, Stratford East on 21 September 1967 and transferred to the Criterion on 24 October. NH's part was written after Roy Jenkins became Chancellor on 29 November 1967. He appears in the programme from January 1968.	Roy Jenkins
	Early Morning *Edward Bond*	William Gaskill	English Stage Society Royal Court Theatre, London	31 March ('Sunday night production without décor')	Prince Albert
				7 April ('Critics' Dress Rehearsal' matinée)	
	Narrow Road to the Deep North *Edward Bond*	Jane Howell	Belgrade Theatre, Coventry (Part of the 'People and Cities' conference)	24 June	Commodore
	Total Eclipse *Christopher Hampton*	Robert Kidd	English Stage Company Royal Court Theatre, London	11 September	M. Mauté de Fleurville / Étienne Carjat / Judge Théodore T'Serstevens
	The Tutor *Jakob Lenz / adapted Bertolt Brecht & trans. Richard Grunberger*	Barry Hanson	English Stage Society Royal Court Theatre, London	13 October ('Sunday night production without décor')	Count Wermuth
1969	Narrow Road to the Deep North *Edward Bond*	Jane Howell	English Stage Company Royal Court Theatre, London	19 February	Commodore
	Early Morning *Edward Bond*	William Gaskill	English Stage Company Royal Court Theatre, London	13 March	Prince Albert

Year	Play *Author*	Director	Company/ Theatre	Opening Performance	Role
	The Double Dealer *William Congreve*	William Gaskill	English Stage Company Royal Court Theatre, London	22 July	Lord Touchwood
	Narrow Road to the Deep North *Edward Bond*	Jane Howell	English Stage Company Royal Court Theatre, London	8 September	Commodore
			European tour (with Edward Bond's *Saved*) Palazzo Grassi, Venice	18 September	
			Wolkra Theatre, Prague	25 September	
			State Theatre, Lublin	30 September	
			Dramatcyzny Theatre, Warsaw	3 October	
	Insideout *Frank Norman*	Ken Campbell	English Stage Company Royal Court Theatre, London	26 November	Commander Pemberton
1970	Henry IV, Part I *William Shakespeare*	Michael Rudman	Sheffield Repertory Company Sheffield Playhouse	4 March	Falstaff
	A Day in the Death of Joe Egg *Peter Nichols*	Paul Hellyer	Sheffield Repertory Company Sheffield Playhouse	25 March	Bri
	Strip Jack Naked *Christopher Wilkinson*	Colin George	Sheffield Repertory Company Sheffield Playhouse	29 April	Wyngate
			Royal Court Theatre, London	10 May (Sunday night production without décor')	
	Stand For My Father *an adaptation of* *Shakespeare's* *Henry IV, Parts I and II* *Mike Gwilym &* *Nigel Hawthorne* *(under the pennames* *of Francis Coleridge* *& John Hudson)*	Michael Rudman	Traverse Theatre, Edinburgh	4 June	Bolingbroke, afterwards King Henry IV /Sir John Falstaff
	Curtains *Tom Mallin*	Michael Rudman	Traverse Theatre, Edinburgh	9 July	Niall
	Ubu and Ubu are Dead *devised by Jules* *Boardman & Kevin Sim /* *music by Bread,* *Love and Dreams* *& Michael Garrett*	Kevin Sim	Traverse Theatre, Edinburgh	9 September	Ubu

Year	Play *Author*	Director	Company/ Theatre	Opening Performance	Role
	Macbeth *William Shakespeare*	Colin George	Sheffield Repertory Company Sheffield Playhouse	21 October	Macbeth
	The Ruling Class *Peter Barnes*	Frank Hatherley	Sheffield Repertory Company Sheffield Playhouse	18 November	14th Earl of Gurney
	Black Mass *Edward Bond*	Nigel Hawthorne	Sheffield Repertory Company Sheffield Playhouse	4 December (lunchtime show)	N /A
1971	Curtains *Tom Mallin*	Michael Rudman	Open Space, London	19 January	Niall
	Rosencrantz and Guildenstern are Dead *Tom Stoppard*	Kenny McBain	Cambridge Theatre Company Arts Theatre, Cambridge	12 February	The Player
	West of Suez *John Osborne*	Anthony Page	English Stage Company Royal Court Theatre, London	17 August	Christopher
			Cambridge Theatre, London	6 October	
1972	The Trial of St George *Colin Spencer*	Frederick Proud	Soho Poly, London	8 March	Judge
	The Taming of the Shrew *William Shakespeare*	Frank Dunlop	Young Vic Theatre Company Young Vic, London	2 May	Baptista
	An Alchemist *'an entertainment mainly by Ben Jonson'*	Frank Dunlop	Young Vic Theatre Company Young Vic, London	8 June	Face, a butler
	The Taming of the Shrew *William Shakespeare*	Frank Dunlop	Young Vic Theatre Company Festival Canada Theatre of the National Arts Centre, Ottawa	3 July	Baptista
	An Alchemist *'an entertainment mainly by Ben Jonson'*	Frank Dunlop	Young Vic Theatre Company Festival Canada Theatre of the National Arts Centre, Ottawa	6 July	Face, a butler
	Julius Caesar *William Shakespeare*	Peter James	Young Vic Theatre Company Young Vic, London	16 August	Marcus Brutus
	The Comedy of Errors *William Shakespeare*	Frank Dunlop with Peter James	Young Vic Theatre Company Edinburgh Festival Haymarket Ice Rink, Edinburgh	25 August	The Duke
			Young Vic, London	5 October	

Year	Play *Author*	Director	Company/ Theatre	Opening Performance	Role
	A Sense of Detachment *John Osborne*	Frank Dunlop	English Stage Company Royal Court Theatre, London	4 December	Chairman
1973	The Philanthropist *Christopher Hampton*	Robert Kidd	Mayfair Theatre, London	This production opened at the Royal Court Theatre, London on 3 August 1970 with Alec McCowen in the title role and at the Mayfair Theatre on 7 September 1970. NH took over the lead from George Cole on 19 March 1973.	Philip
	The Ride Across Lake Constance *Peter Handke / trans.* *Michael Roloff*	Michael Rudman	Hampstead Theatre Club, London	12 November	Nigel
			Mayfair Theatre, London	12 December	
1974	How The Other Half Loves *Alan Ayckbourn*	John Neville	Citadel Theatre, Edmonton, Alberta	9 February	Frank Foster
	Bird Child *David Lan*	Nicholas Wright	Theatre Upstairs, Royal Court Theatre, London	24 April	Colonel Krou
	As You Like It *William Shakespeare*	Clifford Williams	By arrangement with the National Theatre of Britain Tour of North American cities Geary Theatre, San Francisco	16 July	Touchstone
			Greek Theatre, Los Angeles	5 August	
			Lewiston Artpark, Lewiston, New York	14 August	
			Theatre of the Stars, Atlanta Civic Centre, Atlanta Georgia	20 August	
			Ravinia Park, Chicago	27 August	
			Wolf Trap Farm Park, Vienna, Virginia	4 September	
			Théâtre Maisonneuve, Place des Arts, Montreal	9 September	
			National Arts Centre, Ottawa	16 September	

Year	Play *Author*	Director	Company/ Theatre	Opening Performance	Role
	As You Like It *(continued)*		Mechanic Theatre, Charles Centre, Baltimore	26 September	
			Clowes Memorial Hall, Butler University, Indianapolis	30 September	
			Uihlein Hall, Performing Arts Centre, Milwaukee	3 October	
			Hancher Auditorium, Iowa City	7 October	
			American Theatre, St Louis, Missouri	10 October	
			Music Hall Centre, Detroit	17 October	
			O'Keefe Centre, Toronto	21 October	
			Shubert Theatre, Philadelphia	4 November	
			Shubert Theatre, Boston	18 November	
			Broadway Debut: Mark Hellinger Theatre, New York	3 December	
1975	The Doctor's Dilemma *George Bernard Shaw*	Robert Chetwyn	Mermaid Theatre, London	21 April	Cutler Walpole
	Otherwise Engaged *Simon Gray*	Harold Pinter	The Oxford Playhouse, Oxford	8 July	Stephen
			Richmond Theatre, Surrey	21 July	
			Queen's Theatre, London	30 July	
1976	Sitting Ducks: 'Prompt!' *Nigel Hawthorne*	Andrew Carr	Soho Poly, London	29 March (lunchtime performance)	Harry Figdore
	Sitting Ducks: 'Mummy' *Nigel Hawthorne*	Andrew Carr	Soho Poly, London	29 March (lunchtime performance)	Man
	As You Like It *William Shakespeare*	Peter Gill	Riverside Studios, London	30 May	Touchstone
	Clouds *Michael Frayn*	Michael Rudman	Hampstead Theatre, London	16 August	Owen
1977	Privates on Parade *Peter Nichols /* *music by Denis King*	Michael Blakemore	Royal Shakespeare Company Aldwych Theatre, London	22 February	Major Giles Flack

Year	Play / Author	Director	Company/ Theatre	Opening Performance	Role
	Blind Date *Frank Marcus*	David Proudfoot	King's Head Theatre Club, London	7 March	Brian
	The Fire That Consumes (La Ville dont le Prince est un Enfant) *Henri de Montherlant / English version by Vivian Cox with Bernard Miles*	Bernard Miles	Mermaid Theatre, London	13 October	M. L' Abbé de Pradts
1978	A Miserable and Lonely Death *(a dramatised reading based on the transcript of the inquest into the death of Stephen Bilko)*	Walter Donohue	Royal Shakespeare Company The Warehouse, Covent Garden, London	5 February (Sunday performance)	Prins
	Privates on Parade *Peter Nichols / music by Denis King*	Michael Blakemore	Royal Shakespeare Company Piccadilly Theatre, London	8 February	Major Giles Flack
	The Millionairess *George Bernard Shaw*	Michael Lindsay-Hogg	Theatre Royal Haymarket, London	14 December	Julius Sagamore
1979	Uncle Vanya *Anton Chekhov / a new version by Pam Gems*	Nancy Meckler	Hampstead Theatre, London	22 November	Ivan Petrovich Voynitsky, Uncle Vanya
1980	The Heiress *Ruth & Augustus Goetz after Henry James*	Geoffrey Reeves	Theatre Royal, Nottingham	17 April	Dr Austin Sloper
			Richmond Theatre, Surrey	5 May	
			Theatre Royal, Brighton	12 May	
1981	Smash! *Jack Rosenthal*	Barry Davis	University of Warwick Arts Centre, Coventry	29 April	Theo
			Cambridge Theatre Company, Arts Theatre, Cambridge	11 May	
1982	John Mortimer's Casebook: 'Interlude' *John Mortimer*	Denise Coffey	Young Vic, London	6 January	J. Brownhill
	John Mortimer's Casebook: 'The Dock Brief' *John Mortimer*	Denise Coffey	Young Vic, London	6 January	Morgenhall
	John Mortimer's Casebook: 'The Prince of Darkness' *John Mortimer*	Denise Coffey	Young Vic, London	6 January	A. K. Bulstrode

Year	Play *Author*	Director	Company/ Theatre	Opening Performance	Role
1983	Peer Gynt *Henrik Ibsen / trans.* *David Rudkin*	Ron Daniels	Royal Shakespeare Company The Pit, London	9 June (This production opened on 9 June 1982 at The Other Place, Stratford- upon-Avon. NH took over the characters originally played by Derek Godfrey.)	Solveig's father / von Eberkopf / The Strange Passenger / The Buttonmoulder
	Tartuffe *Molière / trans.* *Christopher Hampton*	Bill Alexander	Royal Shakespeare Company The Pit, London	28 July	Orgon
1986	Across from the Garden of Allah *Charles Wood*	Ron Daniels	Yvonne Arnaud Theatre, Guilford	29 January	Douglas
			Theatre Royal, Bath	17 February	
			Comedy Theatre, London	27 February	
	Jacobowsky and the Colonel *Franz Werfel /* *English version by* *S. N. Behrman*	Jonathan Lynn	National Theatre Company Royal National Theatre, London (Olivier Theatre)	22 July	Colonel Tadeusz Stjerbinsky
	The Magistrate *Arthur Wing Pinero*	Michael Rudman	National Theatre Company Royal National Theatre, London (Lyttelton Theatre)	24 September	Mr Posket, Magistrate of the Mulberry Street Police Court
1988	Hapgood *Tom Stoppard*	Peter Wood	Wimbledon Theatre, London	12 February	Blair
			Aldwych Theatre, London	8 March	
1989	Shadowlands *William Nicholson*	Elijah Moshinsky	Theatre Royal, Plymouth	5 October	C. S. Lewis
			Queen's Theatre, London	23 October	
1990			Brooks Atkinson Theatre, New York	11 November	
1991	The Madness of George III *Alan Bennett*	Nicholas Hytner	National Theatre Company Royal National Theatre, London (Lyttelton Theatre)	28 November	King George III
1992			Theatre Royal, Newcastle	21 April	
			Lyceum Theatre, Sheffield	27 April	

Year	Play *Author*	Director	Company/ Theatre	Opening Performance	Role
			Royal National Theatre, London (Lyttelton Theatre)	11 May	
			Theatre Royal, Bath	18 May	
			Alhambra Theatre, Bradford	25 May	
			Royal National Theatre, London (Lyttelton Theatre)	4 June	
			King's Theatre, Edinburgh	7 September	
			Royal National Theatre, London (Lyttelton Theatre)	17 September	
1993			Royal National Theatre, London (Lyttelton Theatre)	17 July	
			Truglia Theatre, Rich Forum, Stamford, Connecticut	11 September	
			Brooklyn Academy of Music, New York City	28 September	
			Morris A. Mechanic Theatre, Baltimore	12 October	
			Colonial Theatre, Boston	2 November	
			Royal National Theatre, London (Lyttelton Theatre)	29 November	
1994			National Theatre of Greece, Athens	2 February	
			State Theatre of Northern Greece, Thessaloniki	10 February	
			Sherover Theatre, Jerusalem	16 February	
			Royal National Theatre, London (Lyttelton Theatre)	2 March	
	The Clandestine Marriage *George Colman, The Elder & David Garrick*	Nigel Hawthorne	Theatre Royal, Newcastle	2 November	Lord Ogleby
			Festival Theatre, Malvern	7 November	

327

Year	Play *Author*	Director	Company/ Theatre	Opening Performance	Role
			Yvonne Arnaud Theatre, Guilford	14 November	
			Theatre Royal, Bath	21 November	
			Queen's Theatre, London	5 December	
1999	King Lear *William Shakespeare*	Yukio Ninagawa	Royal Shakespeare Company Saitama Arts Theatre, Japan	22 September	King Lear
			Barbican Theatre, London	23 October	
			Royal Shakespeare Theatre, Stratford-upon-Avon	4 December	

CHRONOLOGY II: SCREEN

Year	TV/Film	Title	Author	Role	Director
1956	TV play	Cry Wolf	Shaun Sutton	P. C. Bray	Shaun Sutton
1963	TV serial	The Desperate People	Francis Durbridge		Alan Bromly
	TV series	Death in Ecstasy	Ngaio Marsh	Temple Doorkeeper	Shaun Sutton
1969	TV (11 Sept.)	Dad's Army, episode 3.1: 'The Armoured Might of Lance-Corporal Jones'	Jimmy Perry & David Croft	Angry Man	David Croft
1972	Film	Young Winston	Winston Churchill (book), Carl Foreman	Boer Sentry	Richard Attenborough
1974	Film	S*P*Y*S	Lawrence J. Cohen, Fred Freeman, Malcolm Marmorstein	Croft	Irvin Kershner
1975	Film	The Hiding Place	Corrie Ten Boom (book), Lawrence Holben, Allan Sloane	Pastor De Ruiter	James F. Collier
1977	TV mini series	Marie Curie	Elaine Morgan	Pierre Curie	John Glenister
1978	Film	Watership Down	Richard Adams (novel), Martin Rosen	Campion (voice)	Martin Rosen
	TV serial	Going Straight	Dick Clement & Ian La Frenais	Wellings	
	TV mini series	Holocaust	Gerald Green	Oldendorf	Martin J. Chomsky
	TV mini series	Warrior Queen	Martin Mellet	Catus Decianus	Neville Green & Michael Custance
	TV movie	The Sailor's Return	David Garnett (novel), James Saunders	Mr Fosse	Jack Gold
	TV mini series	Edward and Mrs Simpson	Simon Raven	Walter Monkton	Waris Hussein
1979	TV	The Knowledge	Jack Rosenthal	Mr Burgess, 'The Vampire'	Bob Brooks
1980	TV series (25 Feb-7 Apr.)	Yes, Minister (1st season)	Antony Jay & Jonathan Lynn	Sir Humphrey Appleby	Sydney Lotterby (and Peter Whitmore)
	TV	A Tale of Two Cities	Charles Dickens / adapted by John Gay	Stryver	Jim Goddard
	TV	The Tempest	William Shakespeare	Stephano	John Gorrie
1981	TV series (23 Feb.-6 Apr.)	Yes, Minister (2nd season)	Antony Jay & Jonathan Lynn	Sir Humphrey Appleby	Sydney Lotterby (and Peter Whitmore)
	Film	Memoirs of a Survivor	Doris Lessing / adapted by Kerry Crabbe & David Gladwell	Victorian Father	David Gladwell
1982	TV	The Hunchback of Notre Dame	Victor Hugo / adapted by John Gay	Magistrate at Esmeralda's Trial	Michael Tuchner

Year	TV/Film	Title	Author	Role	Director
	TV movie	A Woman Called Golda	Harold Gast & Steve Gethers	King Abdullah	Alan Gibson
	Film	Firefox	Alex Lasker & Wendell Wellman	Pyotr Baranovich	Clint Eastwood
	Film	Gandhi	John Briley	Kinnoch	Richard Attenborough
	TV mini-series	The Barchester Chronicles	Anthony Trollope / dramatised by Alan Plater	Archdeacon Grantly	David Giles
	TV play	The Critic	Richard Brinsley Sheridan	Mr Sneer	Don Taylor
	TV series (1 Nov.-23 Dec.)	Yes, Minister (3rd season)	Antony Jay & Jonathan Lynn	Sir Humphrey Appleby	Sydney Lotterby (and Peter Whitmore)
1983	TV movie	Pope John Paul II	Christopher Knopf	Cardinal Stefan Wyszynski	Herbert Wise
1984	TV series	Mapp and Lucia (1st series)	Gerald Savory / based on the stories of E. F. Benson	Georgie Pillson	Donald McWhinnie
	TV Play	Tartuffe	Molière / translated by Christopher Hampton	Orgon	Bill Alexander
	TV series (17 Dec.)	Yes, Minister: 'Party Games'	Antony Jay & Jonathan Lynn	Sir Humphrey Appleby	Peter Whitmore
1985	Film	The Chain	Jack Rosenthal	Mr Thorn	Jack Gold
	Film	The Black Cauldron	Lloyd Alexander (novel), Ted Berman et al.	Fflewddur Fflam (voice)	Ted Berman & Richard Rich
	TV	Jenny's War	Jack Stoneley (book), Steve Gethers	Colonel	Steve Gethers
1986	TV series (9 Jan.-27 Feb.)	Yes, Prime Minister (1st season)	Antony Jay & Jonathan Lynn	Sir Humphrey Appleby	Sydney Lotterby (and Peter Whitmore)
	TV series	Mapp and Lucia (2nd series)	Gerald Savory / based on the stories of E. F. Benson	Georgie Pillson	Donald McWhinnie
1987	TV series (3 Dec.-27 Jan. '88)	Yes, Prime Minister (2nd season)	Antony Jay & Jonathan Lynn	Sir Humphrey Appleby	Sydney Lotterby (and Peter Whitmore)
1988	TV play	The Miser	Molière / translated by Alan Drury	Harpagon	Michael Simpson
1989	TV play	The Shawl	David Mamet	John	Bill Bryden
	TV	Spirit of Man	Peter Barnes	Rev. Jonathan Guerdon	Peter Barnes
	TV movie	King of the Wind	Phil Frey & Leslie Sayle	Achmet	Peter Duffell
	Film	En Handfull Tid	Erik Borge	Ted Walker	Martin Asphaug
1990	TV play	Relatively Speaking	Alan Ayckbourn	Philip Carter	Michael Simpson
1991	TV	The Trials of OZ	Geoffrey Robertson	Brian Leary	Sheree Folkson
1992	TV movie	Flea Bites	Stephen Lowe	Kryst	Alan Dossor

Year	TV/Film	Title	Author	Role	Director
1993	Film	Demolition Man	Daniel Waters, Robert Reneau, Peter M. Lenkov	Dr Raymond Cocteau	Marco Brambilla
1994	TV	Late Flowering Lust	Based on an original concept by Trevor Bentham and using the poetry of John Betjeman	Cousin John	David Hinton
	Film	The Madness of King George	Alan Bennett	King George III	Nicholas Hytner
1995	Film	Richard III	William Shakespeare / screenplay by Ian McKellen & Richard Loncraine	Clarence	Richard Loncraine
1996	TV mini-series	The Fragile Heart	Paula Milne	Edgar Pascoe	Patrick Lau
	Film	Twelfth Night	William Shakespeare / screenplay by Trevor Nunn	Malvolio	Trevor Nunn
	Film	Inside	Bima Stagg	Colonel Kruger	Arthur Penn
	Film	Murder in Mind	Michael Cooney	Dr. Ellis (& Assoc. Producer)	Andrew Morahan
1997	Film	Amistad	David Franzoni	Martin van Buren	Steven Spielberg
	TV	Forbidden Territory: Stanley's Search for Livingstone	John Pielmeier	David Livingstone	Simon Langton
1998	Film	The Object of My Affection	Wendy Wasserstein	Rodney Fraser	Nicholas Hytner
	Film	Madeline	Ludwig Bemelmans & Malia Scotch Marmo	Lord Covington	Daisy von Scherle Mayer
	Film	At Sachem Farm	John Huddles	Uncle Cullen (& Exec. Producer)	John Huddles
	Film	The Winslow Boy	Terence Rattigan / screenplay by David Mamet	Arthur Winslow	David Mamet
1999	Film	Big Brass Ring	F. X. Feeney & George Hickenlooper / based on a screenplay by Orson Welles & Ojar Kodar	Kim Menaker	George Hickenlooper
	Film	Tarzan	Edgar Rice Burroughs (novel), Tab Murphy et al.	Professor Archimedes Q. Porter (voice)	Chris Buck & Kevin Lima
	Film	A Reasonable Man	Gavin Hood	Judge Wendon	Gavin Hood
	Film	The Clandestine Marriage	George Colman the Elder & David Garrick / screenplay by Trevor Bentham	Lord Ogleby (& Assoc. Producer)	Christopher Miles
	TV	BBC Omnibus: 'Yes, Sir Nigel'		Himself	Ian Leese

Year	TV/Film	Title	Author	Role	Director
2001	TV	Victoria & Albert	John Goldsmith	Lord Melbourne	John Erman
	TV	Call Me Claus	Paul Mooney, Sara Bernstein, Gregory Bernstein, Brian Bird	Nick	Peter Werner

CHRONOLOGY III: EVENTS IN BRITISH THEATRE 1950-2000

Year	Event	London Premieres
1950	(14 Nov.) The repaired Old Vic opens.	(Jan.) Fry, *Venus Observed* (Jan.) Fry, *Ring Round the Moon*
1951		(Apr.) Hunter, *Waters of the Moon*
1952		(Mar.) Rattigan, *The Deep Blue Sea* (Jun.) Ackland, *The Pink Room* (Nov.) Christie, *The Mousetrap*
1953	(Feb.) Joan Littlewood's Theatre Workshop takes up the lease of the Theatre Royal, Stratford East.	(Nov.) Rattigan, *The Sleeping Prince*
1954	(Sept.) Kenneth Tynan becomes theatre critic of the *Observer*.	(Apr.) Whiting, *Marching Song* (Sept.) Rattigan, *Separate Tables*
1955	Actor and director Stephen Joseph founds a company with the express purpose of presenting plays 'in the round'.	(Aug.) Beckett, *Waiting for Godot*
1956	(April) Opening season of the English Stage Company at the Royal Court under the artistic direction of George Devine (1st production Angus Wilson's *The Mulberry Bush,* 2 April). (Aug.) Peter Daubeney invites the Berliner Ensemble under the direction of Bertolt Brecht to the Palace Theatre, London. Foundation of the National Youth Theatre by Michael Croft.	(8 May) Osborne, *Look Back in Anger* (May) Behan, *The Quare Fellow*
1957	The British Theatre Museum Association is founded.	(Apr.) Beckett, *Fin de Partie* (Apr.) Osborne, *The Entertainer*
1958	(27 Mar.) Belgrade Theatre, Coventry (First of Britain's post-war theatres) opens.	(Apr.) Lerner & Lowe, *My Fair Lady* (May) Pinter, *The Birthday Party* (May) Delaney, *A Taste of Honey* (Oct.) Behan, *The Hostage*
1959	(28 May) Mermaid Theatre, London opens.	(Jul.) Wesker, *Roots* (Sept.) Wesker, *The Kitchen* (Oct.) Arden, *Serjeant Musgrove's Dance*
1960		(Apr.) Pinter, *The Caretaker* (Jul.) Bolt, *A Man for All Seasons* (Sept.) Waterhouse & Hall, *Billy Liar*
1961	The Royal Shakespeare Company created in Stratford-upon-Avon and at Aldwych Theatre, London under the direction of Peter Hall. The Round House taken over by Arnold Wesker to serve as the home of his Centre 42.	(May) Bennett, Cook, Miller, Moore, *Beyond the Fringe*
1962	(3 July) The Chichester Festival Theatre opens under Laurence Olivier. Formation of the National Theatre Company at the Old Vic under the direction of Olivier. Stephen Joseph founds the Victoria Theatre in Stoke-on-Trent, Britain's 1st permanent, full-time theatre-in-the-round.	(Apr.) Wesker, *Chips with Everything* (Dec.) Bond, *The Pope's Wedding*
1963	(Jan.) Traverse Theatre, Edinburgh opens. (11 Dec.) New Nottingham Playhouse opens.	(Mar.) Chilton & Theatre Workshop, *Oh, What A Lovely War!*

Year	Event	London Premieres
1964	(12 Jan.) The RSC begins a Theatre of Cruelty season at LAMDA. Director Peter Brook is inspired by the writings of Antonin Artaud, particularly *Le Théâtre et son double*. (17 Mar.) The first World Theatre Season opens with the Comédie Française in Molière's *Tartuffe*. Seven foreign companies are invited by Peter Daubeney to perform at the Aldwych while the RSC is on tour.	(May) Orton, *Entertaining Mr Sloane* (Sept.) Osborne, *Inadmissible Evidence*
1965	Theatre in Education Movement founded at the Belgrade Theatre, Coventry. (Sept.) William Gaskill takes over as Artistic Director of the Royal Court.	(Jun.) Pinter, *The Homecoming* (Nov.) Bond, *Saved*
1966		(Sept.) Orton, *Loot*
1967		(Apr.) Stoppard, *Rosencrantz and Guildenstern are Dead* (Jul.) Nichols, *A Day in the Death of Joe Egg* (Aug.) Terson, *Zigger Zagger*
1968	(Jan.) The Arts Laboratory opens in a disused warehouse in Drury Lane. The Open Space is founded by Charles Marowitz and Thelma Holt. (28 Sept.) George Strauss's bill, *The Theatres Act of 1968*, becomes law, removing the power of the Lord Chamberlain to censor plays and vesting theatre licensing in local authorities. Trevor Nunn succeeds Peter Hall as Director of the RSC. American Ed Berman founds Inter-Action, England's leading community theatre group.	(Jun.) Stoppard, *The Real Inspector Hound* (Oct.) Bennett, *Forty Years On*
1969	(17 Feb.) The Round House officially opens as a new London theatre with the Free Theatre's production of *Hamlet*. (24 Feb.) The Theatre Upstairs opens at the Royal Court (intended for experimental and low budget works).	(Feb.) Barnes, *The Ruling Class* (Oct.) Nichols, *The National Health* (Oct.) Storey, *The Contractor*
1970	A second Young Vic is founded by Frank Dunlop under the auspices of the National Theatre. Sam Wanamaker establishes the Globe Playhouse Trust with the central objective of raising funds to rebuild the Globe. Southwark Council offers the Trust a 1.2-acre site beside the Thames, approx. 200 yards from the site of the original Globe.	(Jun.) Storey, *Home* (Aug.) Hampton, *The Philanthropist*
1971	Crucible Theatre, Sheffield opens.	(Sept.) Bond, *Lear* (Nov.) Storey, *The Changing Room*
1972	(Jul.) Oscar Lewenstein becomes Artistic Director of the Royal Court.	(Feb.) Stoppard, *Jumpers* (Mar.) Wood, *Veterans* (Aug.) Lloyd Webber & Rice, *Jesus Christ Superstar*
1973	(1 Jan.) The New Theatre, London is renamed the Albery after Sir Bronson Albery. Ed Berman hosts a 'Women's Festival' at the Almost Free. (Nov.) Peter Hall succeeds Olivier as Director of the National Theatre.	(May) Bennett, *Habeas Corpus* (Jul.) Ayckbourn, *Absurd Person Singular* (Jul.) Shaffer, *Equus*
1974	Women's Theatre Group founded. The Young Vic becomes an independent body. Joint Stock company formed. The Other Place opens in Stratford.	(Jun.) Stoppard, *Travesties* (Aug.) Ayckbourn, *The Norman Conquests*

Year	Event	London Premieres
1975	Ed Berman presents a lunchtime season of homosexual plays at the Almost Free. Gay Sweatshop company formed.	(Apr.) Pinter, *No Man's Land* (Jul.) Ayckbourn, *Absent Friends*
1976	The National Theatre opens in its new home on the South Bank. (16 Mar.) The National's first theatre, the Lyttleton gives its opening performance. (30 May) Riverside Studios opens on a part time basis with *As You Like It*. (9 Jun.) Dame Sybil Thorndike dies. (4 Oct.) The National's second theatre, the Olivier gives its opening performance. (14 Oct.) Dame Edith Evans dies.	(Sept.) Churchill, *Light Shining in Buckinghamshire*
1977	(4 Mar.) The National's third theatre, the Cottesloe gives its opening performance. RSC opens a studio theatre, The Warehouse, in Covent Garden.	(Sept.) Bennett, *The Old Country*
1978	(12 Jan.) Riverside Studios formally opens its theatre full time. Terry Hands appointed Joint Artistic Director with Nunn of the RSC.	(Apr.) Hare, *Plenty* (Nov.) Pinter, *Betrayal*
1979	Max Stafford-Clark becomes Artistic Director of the Royal Court.	(Mar.) Churchill, *Cloud Nine* (May) Sherman, *Bent*
1980	Brenton's *The Romans in Britain* is prosecuted.	(Apr.) Harwood, *The Dresser*
1981		(Jan.) Nichols, *Passion Play* (May) Lloyd Webber, *Cats* (Jul.) Gray, *Quartermaine's Terms*
1982	(3 March) The Barbican Centre, the RSC's new London home, opens.	(Feb.) Frayn, *Noises Off* (Nov.) Stoppard, *The Real Thing*
1983	(10 Oct.) Sir Ralph Richardson dies.	(Sept.) Hampton, *Tales from Hollywood*
1984	National Theatre Studio founded.	(Apr.) Frayn, *Benefactors*
1985		(May) Hare & Brenton, *Pravda* (Oct.) Schönberg & Boublil, *Les Misérables*
1986	RSC's Swan Theatre opens. Nunn resigns his post at the RSC. Renaissance Theatre Company founded by Kenneth Branagh and David Parfitt.	(Oct.) Lloyd Webber, *The Phantom of the Opera* (Oct.) Whitemore, *Breaking the Code*
1987	The Theatre Museum (a branch of the Victoria and Albert Museum) opens in Covent Garden.	(Mar.) Churchill, *Serious Money* (Oct.) Shaffer, *Lettice and Lovage*
1988	Adrian Noble succeeds Hands as Director of the RSC.	(Sept.) Wertenbaker, *Our Country's Good* (Dec.) Bennett, *Single Spies*
1989	Richard Eyre succeeds Hall as Artistic Director of the National Theatre. (Feb.) Remains of the Rose discovered. (11 July) Lord (Laurence) Olivier dies. (Oct.) Remains of the Globe discovered.	(Sept.) Schönberg & Boublil/ Maltby, *Miss Saigon*
1990	Stephen Dalrdy takes over the Gate Theatre, Notting Hill.	(Feb.) Hare, *Racing Demon* (Mar.) Harrison, *The Trackers of Oxyrhynchus*
1991	(14 Jun.) Dame Peggy Ashcroft dies.	(Oct.) Hare, *Murmuring Judges*

Year	Event	London Premieres
1992	(Oct.) The Donmar Warehouse opens under the artistic direction of Sam Mendes.	(Jan.) Kushner, *Angels in America Part I: Millennium Approaches*
1993		(Nov.) Kushner, *Angels in America Part II: Perestroika*
1994	Stephen Daldry succeeds Stafford-Clark as Artistic Director of the Royal Court. (Nov.) The Globe Theatre on Shaftesbury Avenue is officially renamed the Gielgud.	(Apr.) Elyot, *My Night With Reg*
1995	(Jun.) Mark Rylance appointed Artistic Director of the Globe (as of Jan. 1996).	(Feb.) Marber, *Dealer's Choice* (May) Hare, *Skylight* (Sept.) Barry, *The Steward of Christendom*
1996	Peter Hall opens a season of 12 plays at the Old Vic.	(Feb.) Gems, *Stanley* (Mar.) McDonagh, *The Beauty Queen of Leenane* (Oct.) Reza/ Hampton, *Art*
1997	Trevor Nunn succeeds Eyre as Artistic Director of the National Theatre. (12 Jun.) Rebuilt Globe Theatre officially inaugurated by HM Queen Elizabeth II. (29 May-21 Sept.) Opening season of the Globe.	(May) Marber, *Closer* (Jul.) McPherson, *The Weir* (Sept.) Stoppard, *The Invention of Love* (Oct.) Whitemore, *A Letter of Resignation*
1998	(Mar.) The National Theatre buys the Old Vic Annexe. (Jul.) Canadian entrepreneurs Ed and David Mirvish sell the Old Vic to a non-profit trust specially set up to preserve it for serious drama.	(Apr.) Reza / Hampton, *The Unexpected Man* (Apr.) Barry, *Our Lady of Sligo* (May) Frayn, *Copenhagen*
1999		(Sept.) Harwood, *Quartet* (Dec.) Bennett, *The Lady in the Van*
2000	(Jan.) Andrew Lloyd Webber buys Stoll Moss's 10 West End theatres, making him the single biggest West End theatre owner (22 Feb.) The Royal Court Theatre in Sloane Square reopens after a £25 million refurbishment (opening production Conor McPherson's *Dublin Carol*). (21 May) Sir John Gielgud dies. (5 Aug.) Sir Alec Guinness dies.	(Apr.) Wright, *Cressida* (May) McGuinness, *Dolly West's Kitchen*. (Aug.) Ayckbourn, *House/ Garden*

Epilogue

A Most Ingenious Paradox

He nothing common did nor mean
Upon that memorable scene.
(Andrew Marvell, 'An Horatian Ode upon
Cromwell's Return from Ireland', ll. 57-58)

In the late nineteenth century the great German classical scholar Ulrich von Wilamowitz-Moellendorff, expounding what he held to be the ideal of tragic exegesis, compared the task of the philologist to that of the actor. In making this radical comparison he drew an illuminating distinction:

> *We must carry in us something of the actor* (Schauspieler), *not of the virtuoso, who stamps his own image onto a role, but of the true artist* (echten Künstler), *who gives life to the dead words through his own heart's blood.*[1]

The true artist, according to Wilamowitz, is one who is able to submerge his own personality, to inhabit wholly, and thus animate immediately and credibly, a given character. But at the same time, and paradoxically, the actor's concealment or even cancellation of self rests on his capacity to bring to a role his very essence as a person, his heart's blood.

This ideal of hermeneutic and histrionic elucidation, and the paradox it contains, have particular relevance to the career of Nigel Hawthorne, whose versatility as a performer was uncommonly matched by the depth of his characterisations. Nigel had an extraordinary ability to vanish into a role. 'I just wanted to be accurate,' he said, 'to get as near the truth as possible.' His objective was 'a more honest approach rather than a demonstration of one's talent.' In his youth he viewed acting as a means of disguise, of masking his shyness and insecurity and 'as a way of not having to be me'. Crucial to his development, however, was the discovery that, in building a character and getting to the truth, what mattered was 'finding out what was going on underneath', and that to do this he had to lay bare his own doubts and vulnerabilities:

> *I realised that instead of putting on funny noses and funny voices and 'acting', the more I was myself the more I understood who I was and the more*

I presented this fallible absurd being that we all are, the more successful I would be.[2]

Such an approach required self-knowledge and self-exposure without self-absorption, and emotional and spiritual nakedness devoid of narcissism. It was an individualistic methodology with inclusive results.

In an epilogue to Nigel's autobiography, Trevor Bentham spoke movingly of the many paradoxes that defined his partner as a man. As an actor Nigel was a similarly paradoxical figure. His status as a pre-eminent theatre knight owed more to his creation of roles in contemporary plays than to his reinterpretation of the classics or his association with one of the established classical companies. He was not a heroic actor in any conventional sense, yet his greatest stage role, George III, belonged unmistakably to the tragic-heroic tradition. Not unlike his idol Alastair Sim, he combined the skills of a gifted character actor with the charisma of a personality actor. As Alan Bennett remarked, 'He has such a winning quality about him. You're just happy to see him.'

When the leonine actor-manager Donald Wolfit played Lord Ogleby (Nigel's penultimate stage character) in *The Clandestine Marriage* at the Old Vic in 1951, Kenneth Tynan described him as 'an actor with a comedian's face and a tragedian's soul.' Nigel, although a very different actor from Wolfit, embodied something of this amalgam. He was able with his humour and honesty, and his powerful gift for pathos, to transform comedy into tragedy and tragedy into comedy. Giles Flack, Mr Posket and Lord Ogleby (on stage), Georgie Pillson and Malvolio (on screen) were all examples of his sad clowns, absurd characters whom he gave unexpected richness and dimension.

'Scholar clown', the term Joan Littlewood applied to her actors, is, as I have noted, an especially apposite description of Nigel's genius, encapsulating as it does the Littlewoodian philosophy of profound and reasoned buffoonery, controlled chaos, and the interdependence of the physical and the cerebral, ribaldry and refinement. Deriving from the same source was what Bishop Christopher Herbert identified as Nigel's 'tenacious vulnerability' and his 'attentive, hard-crafted, hard-disciplined lightness'. Always behind the discipline and professionalism lurked danger, anarchy and mischief. His meticulous research and diligent preparation did not inhibit his spontaneity and inventiveness on stage or reduce his love of improvisation. In his recent biography of Alec Guinness, Gary O' Connor stated:

Guinness was never an actor who relaxed at heart *and could therefore allow an unpredictable inspiration to take over and change a performance. Pre-planning and calculation: they were supremely in control.*[3]

Nigel, who was in some respects Guinness's natural successor, represented the antithesis of this psychology. With him instinct, good taste, sound judgement and imaginative flair typically prevailed over design and technique. Every aspect of a play and a character would be analysed and constantly re-analysed. The freedom to explore and to change was his guiding aesthetic.

He loved language and literature but rebelled against textual rigidity, the notion of words, and the ideas behind them, being set and sacred, preserved in lifeless form. He had the stout heart of an actor and the critical eye of a director. Often to the exasperation of his colleagues he would leap ahead with suggestions, endlessly and indefatigably experimenting, rethinking, revising, with the bigger picture permanently in sight.

The paradoxical nature of Nigel's creative power is borne out by the contradictory assessments of the director Nicholas Hytner and the critic Sheridan Morley. Equating him with such fictional characters as T. S. Eliot's confidential clerk, Graham Greene's whisky priest and John le Carré's George Smiley, Morley maintains that Nigel was 'very good at the invisible men, at secretiveness, and at suggesting emptiness,' that he projected 'a kind of secrecy, a gay sort of separateness, a closeted sense of secrecy.' In stark contrast, Hytner said in relation to Nigel's performance as George III, 'Nothing was held in. There were no secrets'; he was 'so unrestrained about revealing the pain of the man.' Speaking more generally of Nigel's qualities as an actor, Hytner continued:

> The most remarkable thing about him is his complete emotional availability, his rawness. There is an enormous emotional life that he can convey because he's so truthful as an actor.

He also regarded Nigel as 'one of the few British actors who can completely let rip emotionally, completely let go.'

These apparently opposing perceptions of Nigel's talents are illustrative of the two essential elements of Wilamowitz's ideal paradox – submersion and revelation – and of Nigel's mastery of both. It is important to stress that the enormous emotional life that Nigel could convey, his rawness and emotional availability were not about grand effects; they were tempered by subtle thinking and sensitivity. The key was, as Hytner indicates, his truthfulness, his accuracy. Witness Nigel's controversial Lear, which was not a performance of visceral rage and elemental fury but a humane and finely detailed portrait of a mind dissolving into fearful confusion.

Nicholas Hytner pointed to another paradox when he said Nigel's 'veins were full of professional steel'.[4] Beneath the innate gentleness, unfailing courtesy and lingering self-doubt were a toughness, pride and resilience that go some way towards explaining the length of his stage career and his progression from juvenile character actor in weekly rep to international star. These attributes sometimes made him a difficult and intimidating force as he demanded the best from himself and from those around him.

It is a sad fact that in the end his professional toughness deserted him. The critical overreaction to his Lear wounded him deeply and shook from him the confidence he had struggled for so many years to achieve. He vowed he would never again set foot on stage. In the last six months of his life, at a time when his health seemed to be improving, his old confidence and enthusiasm were partially restored and he had plans to direct a West End play in 2002. Whether he would have returned to the theatre to act we cannot say, but I suspect that, had he lived, his natural resilience would eventually have triumphed over his own misgivings and the fickle acerbity of the critics.

What has indisputably triumphed is his outstanding legacy of imagination, truthfulness, dignity and humanity.

Notes to Epilogue

1 Wilamowitz (1959) Vol. I, 257: *'müssen wir etwas vom Schauspieler in uns tragen, nicht vom Virtuosen, der seiner Rolle eigene Lichter aufsetzt, sondern vom echten Künstler, der dem totem Worte durch das eigene Herzblut Leben gibt.'*
2 Interview with Luaine Lee for *Scripps Howard News Service*, 'Nigel Hawthorne is More Than He Seems', 5 May 1999.
3 O' Connor (2002) 405.
4 *Guardian,* 27 December 2001.

Theatre Awards

1977   SWET (Society of West End Theatres) Actor of the Year in a
Supporting Role *(Privates on Parade)*

Clarence Derwent Award, Best Supporting Actor
(Privates on Parade)

1991   Tony Award, Best Performance by a Leading Actor in a Play
(Shadowlands)

New York Outer Critics' Circle Award, Outstanding Actor in a
Play on or off Broadway *(Shadowlands)*

London Critics' Circle Theatre Award, Best Actor *(The Madness
of George III)*

1992   Olivier Award, Best Actor *(The Madness of George III)*

Evening Standard Award, Best Actor *(The Madness of George III)*

Plays and Players Award, Best Actor *(The Madness of George III)*

Time Out's Readers Award, Best Actor *(The Madness of George III)*

Appendix

Nigel Hawthorne's working script of *King Lear:* Act I, scene I; Act IV, scene vi; Act V, scene iii.

"KING LEAR"

STRATFORD-UPON-AVON
FEBRUARY 2000

Although this production by Yukio Ninagawa, and my performance in the leading rôle, were sneered at by the daily critics, it would seem that they had come with a preconception rather than an open mind.

There is no doubt in my mind that what we are doing is totally right for the play, and I have been immensely proud to be part of the production.

It has played—first in Tokyo, then at the Barbican in London and finally over the Millenium here in Shakespeare's home town—to huge audiences who rightly stand and cheer at the curtain calls.

We must have been doing something right.

Nigel Hawthorne

Nigel

KING LEAR

BY

WILLIAM SHAKESPEARE

Edited and cut by Yukio Ninagawa / David Hunt *and N. H.*

Third cut – 8th of July 1999 (3b)

<u>Final Pre-rehearsal cut</u>

**ROYAL
SHAKESPEARE
COMPANY**

**Royal
Shakespeare
Theatre**
Tel: **01789 296655**

Barbican Theatre
Tel: **0171 628 3351**

Please return to:
Thelma Holt Ltd.
Waldorf Chambers
11 Aldwych
London WC2B 4DA

Take your time this scene
Don't rush this scene
Make him good-natured Kent
and jokey. Check with Kent
when he makes a funny

I. 1

The most difficult scene to make convincing
The King must show authority above everything
The Court must kneel to him. Jump when
he commands. By the next scene he no
longer has power.

The King has decided to retire. This is serious
Divide the Kingdom — very worrying for the
whole country despite King's faith in his
family's keeping the peace

"Tell me my daughters". Make disquieting
PAUSE first. What's gone wrong? Is the
King well?

Insane competition: Having told daughters
the one who loves him most will get the
largest portion, he straightway gives the
first section to Goneril.
                              The same with Regan.
Now it's Cordelia's turn. There is only a
third left. It's already decided. Their
declarations make no difference to the
outcome. Besides he knows who loves
him best __ Cordelia

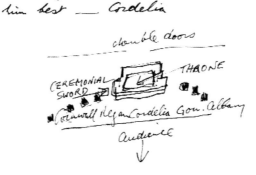

double doors

CEREMONIAL
SWORD   THRONE

Cornwall Regan Cordelia Gon. Albany

audience

Enter with huge energy. Get onto the throne and sit. Keep them waiting on their knees.

4

I.i

KING LEAR   Attend the lords of France and Burgundy, Gloucester.

GLOUCESTER   I shall, my liege.

[Exeunt GLOUCESTER and EDMUND] *Lackeys race in indicate their seats.* *Place MAP on floor*

KING LEAR   Meantime we shall express our darker purpose.
Give me the map there. Know that we have divided
In three our kingdom; and 'tis our fast intent
To shake all cares and business from our age,
Conferring them on younger strengths, while we
Unburdened crawl toward death. Our son of Cornwall
And you, our no less loving son of Albany -
We have this hour a constant will to publish
Our daughters' several dowers, that future strife
May be prevented now. The princes, France and
Burgundy,
Great rivals in our youngest daughter's love,
Long in our court have made their amorous sojourn,
And here are to be answer'd. Tell me, my daughters
Which of you shall we say doth love us most
That we our largest bounty may extend
Where nature doth with merit challenge. Gonerill,
Our eldest-born, speak first.

command no charm
Authority.
playful
(mean for too long)
favourite
check with heaven. Smile a little then LONG SILENCE before
relish the wo
Regan offers to ope Cut her down angrily
When they laugh unstable them. Make them uncomfortable

GONERILL   Sir, I love you more than word can wield the matter,
Dearer than eyesight, space, and liberty,
Beyond what can be valued, rich or rare,
No less than life, with grace, health, beauty,
honour,
As much as child e'er loved, or father found;
A love that makes breath poor and speech unable;
Beyond all manner of 'so much.' I love you.

Bored; She's over the top and not sincere
As she sinks to her Reground keep her waiting. No applause

CORDELIA [*Aside*]   What shall Cordelia speak? Love, and be silent

LEAR   *Take sword*
X Of all these bounds, even from this line to (this)? *tease*
With shadowy forests and with champains rich'd,
With plenteous rivers and wide-skirted meads,
We make thee lady. To thine and Albany's issues
Be this perpetual. - What says our second daughter,
Our dearest Regan, wife to Cornwall?

indicate to Lord this is official

REGAN   I am made of that self mettle as my sister
And price me at her worth. In my true heart
I find she names my very deed of love;
Only she comes too short, that I profess
Myself an enemy to all other joys
And find I am alone felicitate
In your dear highness' love. *applause*

X react to gonerill. "What do you say to that?"

The King is suffering from a form
of senile dementia. His moods come
and go as does his concentration.
Angry, hurt, frightened, lucid,
bewildered. Have I made the wrong
decision?

Make the Count aware that he's
behaving oddly. What's he going to say
next. Make him jumpy. His flashes
of rage sudden. Unnerving. Suddenly
normal again. Jokey. Then hurt — and
so on

I.i

CORDELIA [*Aside*]   Then poor Cordelia!
And yet not so, since I am sure my love's
More ponderous than my tongue.

KING LEAR   To thee and thine hereditary ever   *she looks disappointed*
             Remain this ample third of our fair kingdom,
 angrily   No less in space, validity, and pleasure———   *Go to Cordelia.*
             Than that conferr'd on Gonerill. —Now, our joy, *Bring her to*
             Although our last and least, to whose young love   *centre*
             The vines of France and milk of Burgundy
             Strive to be interess'd: what can you say to draw
             A third more opulent than your sisters'?/Speak!

CORDELIA   Nothing, my lord.   *offer Cordelia the seat of*
                                                          honour - the throne. She
KING LEAR   Nothing?/(*not wanting others to hear*)   *sits in embarrassment*
                                               this.

CORDELIA   Nothing. *trying to make light of it*   /*they laugh. Cut them*
                                                           with a look.
KING LEAR   ⑧· Nothing will come of nothing/ Speak again.(*gentle*)
             trying to make light of it

CORDELIA   Unhappy that I am, I cannot heave
   angry. My heart into my mouth. I love your majesty
 Move away According to my bond, no more nor less.

KING LEAR   How, how, Cordelia! Mend your speech a little
             Lest it may mar your fortunes.

CORDELIA   Good my lord,
             You have begot me, bred me, loved me.
             I return those duties back as are right fit,
             Obey you, love you, and most honour you.
             Why have my sisters husbands, if they say
             They love you all? Haply when I shall wed,
             That lord whose hand must take my plight shall carry
             Half my love with him, half my care and duty.
             Sure I shall never marry like my sisters,
             To love my father all.
                                      (*VERY*
KING LEAR   But goes thy heart with this? (*upset*)

CORDELIA   Ay, good my lord.

KING LEAR   So young, and so untender?

CORDELIA   So young, my lord, and true.

KING LEAR *Decision* Let it be so! Thy truth then be thy dower!
             For by the sacred radiance of the sun,   *Lear has not*
             The mysteries of Hecat and the night,   *lived to the Gods*
             By all the operation of the orbs   *Use wherever*
                                                              poss.

I loved her most. echo competition
"Which of you shall we say doth love us most?"
"Thought to set my rest"   I was going to
spend my retirement with her & Burgundy.

I.i

From whom we do exist, and cease to be, *note the "PS"*
Here I disclaim all my paternal care,
Propinquity and property of blood,
And as a stranger to my heart and me   *⊗ Loses control to end of speech*
Hold thee from this for ever. (X) The barbarous Scythian,
Or he that makes his generation messes
To gorge his appetite, shall to my bosom
Be as well neighbour'd, pitied, and relieved,
As thou my <u>sometime</u> daughter.

KENT   Good my Liege, –

KING LEAR   Peace, Kent! (*TRY TO GET CONTROL OF HIMSELF*)
              Come not between the dragon and his wrath.
which of you <u>I loved her most</u>, and thought to set my rest (*hurt*)
shall we say On her kind nursery. Hence and avoid my sight!
doth love, So be my grave my peace as here I give *to Gods* *⊗ stark*
us most? <s>Her father's heart from her.</s> Call France! (X) Who stirs?   *angril*
              Call Burgundy! <u>Cornwall and Albany</u>, *wait for them to settle*
              With my two daughters' dowers digest the third.
              Let <u>pride</u>, which she calls <u>plainness</u>, marry her.
              I do invest you jointly with my power,
              Pre-eminence, and all the large effects   *singly out for later*
              That troop with majesty. Ourself <u>by monthly course</u>,
              With reservation of an hundred (knights,)   *look at Cordelia. He*
make sure <u>By you</u> to be sustain'd, shall our <u>abode</u>   *expected to spend*
they know this Make with you by due turn. Only we shall retain   *his retirement*
              The name and all th'addition to a king; the sway,   *with her.*
              Revenue, execution of the rest,
              Beloved sons, be yours; which to confirm,
              This coronet/part between you.   *a very difficult moment.*
              remove crown   *Painful to give up. Relinquish*
              [*Giving the crown*]   *his duty, his life.*

KENT   (Royal Lear,) *giving round to*
              Whom I have ever honour'd as my king,   *his friend. He'll*
              Loved as my father, as my master follow'd –   *help*
              Come on. get on with it.

KING LEAR X   The bow is bent and drawn; make from the shaft.

KENT   Let it fall rather, though the fork invade
              The region of my heart. Be Kent unmannerly,
X furious When Lear is mad X What wouldst thou do, old man?
move away from Think'st thou that duty shall have dread to speak
the Court When power to <u>flattery</u> bows? To plainness honour's
Kent follows bound   *angry*
              When majesty stoops to folly. Reserve thy state,
              And in thy best consideration check
glance at Court This hideous rashness. (X) Answer my life my judgment,
              Thy youngest daughter does not love thee least,
              Nor are those empty-hearted whose low sounds
              Reverb no hollowness.   (X) *look how dare you?*

I.i

KING LEAR   Kent, on thy life, no more! *dangerous*

KENT   My life I never held but as a pawn
To wage against thine enemies; nor fear to lose it,
Thy safety being motive.

KING LEAR   Out of my sight!

KENT   See better, Lear, and let me still remain
The true blank of thine eye.

KING LEAR   *moving away* Now by Apollo, -

KENT   Now by Apollo, King,
Thou swear'st thy gods in vain.

KING LEAR   *take sword. threaten him* O, vassal! Miscreant!   *sword high over right shoulder*
[*He makes to strike him*]

ALBANY   )
) Dear sir, forbear!
CORNWALL   )

KENT   Do;   *retract sword*
Kill thy physician and thy fee bestow
Upon the foul disease. Revoke thy gift,
Or whilst I can vent clamour from my throat
I'll tell thee thou dost evil.

KING LEAR   Hear me, recreant,   *He should kneel to the King*
On thine allegiance hear me! *(point.*
That thou hast sought to make us break our vow,
Which we durst never yet - take thy reward. *THINK OF HIS SENTENCE*
make sure Cordelia knows he won't change his mind Five days we do allot thee for provision
To shield thee from disasters of the world, *use the map*
And on the sixth to turn thy hated back
Upon our kingdom. If on the next day following   *use the map*
Thy banish'd trunk be found in our dominions
The moment is thy death. Away! By Jupiter,
This shall not be revoked!! *But be uncertain. Then sit on throne. Confused and disturbed*
LOOK UP THE ROBE

KENT   Fare thee well, King, sith thus thou wilt appear, *relations between France and England were seldom worse.*
Freedom lives hence and banishment is here.
KENT MOVES TO CORDELIA
[*To CORDELIA*]

Try to hear their conversation The gods to their dear shelter take thee, maid,
That justly think'st and hast most rightly said.

I.i

[*To REGAN and GONERILL*]

And your large speeches may your deeds approve   *What's he done.*
That good effects may spring from words of love.
Thus Kent, O princes, bids you all adieu;
He'll shape his old course in a country new.   *Then look*

[*Exit*]   *Watch Kent go. Unable to retract. at Cordelia with fear because of what he's done. It has escalated out of all pro-*

[*Flourish. Enter GLOUCESTER, with KING OF FRANCE, portion.*
BURGUNDY, and Attendants]

GLOUCESTER   Here's France and Burgundy, my noble lord.   *X Brush Gloucester aside impatiently*

KING LEAR   *make show of getting off throne with difficulty* My lord of Burgundy, *Play for time*   *"Can't you see? Sir, try in to think".*
We first address toward you, who with this king
Hath rivall'd for our daughter. What in the least
Will you require in present dower with her
Or cease your quest of love? *practical*

BURGUNDY   Most royal majesty,
I crave no more than what your highness offer'd,
Nor will you tender less.

KING LEAR   Right noble Burgundy, *smooth, diplomatic*
When she was dear to us we did hold her so;
But now her price is fall'n. Sir, there she stands; *and ruthless*
If aught within that little-seeming substance,
Or all of it, may fitly like your grace,
She's there and she is yours.

BURGUNDY   I know no answer.

KING LEAR   *reasonable*   *heaven again*
Then leave her, sir, for, by the power that made me,
I tell you all her wealth. *(turn back corner of map to show her portion is nil.)*

[*To KING OF FRANCE*]

           For you, great king,
I would not from your love make such a stray,
To match you where I hate; therefore beseech you
T'avert your liking a more worthier way
as/to Cordelia Than on a wretch whom Nature is ashamed
Almost t'acknowledge hers. *spiteful*

KING OF FRANCE   This is most strange,
That she whom even but now was your best object,
The argument of your praise, balm of your age,
The best, the dearest, should in this trice of time
Commit a thing so monstrous to dismantle
So many folds of favour. Sure her offence

CORDELIA   I yet beseech your majesty –
                    If for I want that glib and oily art
Not what   To speak and purpose not – that you make known
you think   It is no vicious blot, murder or foulness,
                    No unchaste action or dishonour'd step
                    That hath deprived me of your grace and favour.

KING LEAR   Better thou
Savage   Hadst not been born than not t'have pleased me
                   better.

KING OF FRANCE Is it but this, a tardiness in nature
                    Which often leaves the history unspoke
                    That it intends to do? My lord of Burgundy,
                    What say you to the lady? Love's not love
                    When it is mingled with regards that stands
                    Aloof from th'entire point. Will you have her?
                    She is herself a dowry.

BURGUNDY   Royal Lear,   *Shake her*
                    Give but that portion which yourself proposed,   *NO WAY*
                    And here I take Cordelia by the hand,
                    Duchess of Burgundy. *Catch onto the "N" – extend it*
Have fun with the word. Mock Cordelia.
KING LEAR   Nothing! I have sworn; I am firm. *(indicate map)*

BURGUNDY   I am sorry then you have so lost a father
                    That you must lose a husband.

CORDELIA   Peace be with Burgundy!
                    Since that respect of fortunes are his love,
            King   I shall not be his wife.
                    Starts to leave the Court.
KING OF FRANCE Fairest Cordelia, that art most rich, being poor,
The King stops   Most choice, forsaken, and most loved, despised,
on his way out   Thee and thy virtues here I seize upon.
Furious at   Be it lawful I take up what's cast away.
leaving France   Gods, gods! 'Tis strange that from their cold'st
take over   neglect *(get nearer to hear what he's saying)*
                    My love should kindle to inflamed respect.
                    Thy dowerless daughter, King, thrown to my chance,
                    Is queen of us, of ours, and our fair France. *Okay then, I*
                    Not all the dukes of waterish Burgundy *took at Burgundy*
                    Can buy this unprized-precious maid of me. *He's got you*
                    Bid them farewell, Cordelia, though unkind. *summoned up*
                    Thou losest here, a better where to find.

KING LEAR   Thou hast her, France; let her be thine, for we
Ruthless   Have no such daughter, nor shall ever see
                    That face of hers again. Therefore begone
                    Without our grace, our love, our benison!
for Burgundy's   Come noble Burgundy.
benefit   [Flourish. Exeunt all but KING OF FRANCE, GONERILL,
                    REGAN, and CORDELIA]

The fool is the outsider

He's the only person in the Court
who can tell the King what he doesn't want
to hear. He's Jiminy Cricket — the King's
conscience. The choice of Sanada is a good
one as it is the perfect bridge between East
and West. Also he's a brilliant tumbler
and will do back flips and double
somersaults.

He's the King's surrogate son.
After all, there are three daughters and the Queen
is only referred to once. The King needs someone
in whom he can confide who is not part of
the Court sycophancy he criticizes in IV Scene 6

IV.vi

I took it for a man; often 'twould say
'The fiend, the fiend'; he led me to that place.

EDGAR   Bear free and patient thoughts.

[*Enter KING LEAR, fantastically dressed with wild
flowers*]   *ZIG ZAG IN*

KING LEAR   No, they cannot touch me for coining. I am the
King himself.

EDGAR   O thou side-piercing sight!

KING LEAR   Nature's above art in that respect. There's your   *ⓧ take it*
press-money. - That fellow handles his bow like a   *from*
fearful crow-keeper. - Draw me a clothier's yard. - Look,   *mouth*
left up look, a <u>mouse</u>! - Peace, peace! This piece of toasted   *throw*
shirts cheese will do 't ⓧ There's my gauntlet; I'll prove   *it, it*
it on a giant. ⓧ Bring up the brown bills. - O, well   *becomes*
flown, bird! I' the clout, i' the clout! Hewgh!   *me gauntlet*
- Give the word.

EDGAR   Sweet marjoram.   *ⓧ give the signal*

KING LEAR   Pass.

GLOUCESTER   I know that voice.   *mock the court. Imitate*
them

KING LEAR   Ha! Gonerill, with a white beard ⓧ They flattered
me like a dog and told me I had white hairs in my
beard ere the black ones were there. To say 'ay'
and 'no' to everything that I said! 'Ay' and 'no'   *ⓧ He's back i*
too was no good divinity ⓧ When the rain came to   *the storm.*
wet me once and the wind to make me chatter; when   *shiver.*
the thunder would not peace at my bidding; there I
found 'em, there I smelt 'em out. Go to, they are
not men o' their words. They told me I was every
thing. 'Tis a lie: I am not ague-proof.

GLOUCESTER   Is 't not the King?

KING LEAR   Ay, every inch a king:
<u>When I do stare see how the subject quakes</u>. *HAM ACTOR*
to
Gloucester ⓧ I pardon that man's life. What was thy cause?
Adultery? *accusing*   *cross to Edgar*
vulgar Thou shalt not die. Die for adultery? No.   *indicate size*
gesture <u>The wren goes to 't</u>, and the small gilded fly   *with fingers*
Does lecher in my sight.
Let copulation thrive; for Gloucester's bastard son
Was kinder to his father than my daughters   *See his "men" have deserted*
Got 'tween the lawful sheets. *him*
<u>To 't, luxury, pell-mell, for I lack soldiers.</u>

IV.vi

Behold yon simpering dame
Whose face between her forks presages snow,
That minces virtue and does shake the head *imitate*
To hear of pleasure's name – *and mock*
The fitchew nor the soilèd horse goes to 't SAVAGE
With a more riotous appetite.
Down from the waist they are centaurs, *Think of*
Though women all above; *daughters*
But to the girdle do the gods inherit,
Beneath is all the fiends' –
There's hell, there's darkness, there is the
sulphurous pit, burning,/ scalding,/ stench/
consumption.
~~Fie, fie, fie! Pah,~~ *spit* ~~pah!~~ Give me an ounce of civet,
good apothecary, sweeten my imagination.
There's money for thee.

[~~He gives flowers~~]

GLOUCESTER   O, let me kiss that hand! *quick sniff and a wipe on robes*

KING LEAR   Let me wipe it first;/ it smells of mortality.

GLOUCESTER   O ruin'd piece of nature! This great world
             Shall so wear out to nought. Dost thou know me? *Gloucester removes the bandage*

KING LEAR *Examine him* I remember thine eyes well enough. Dost thou squiny
             at me? No, do thy worst, blind Cupid; I'll not
             love. Read thou this challenge; mark but the
             penning of it. *extend palm of hand*

GLOUCESTER   Were all the letters suns, I could not see *move it in and out perhaps the hand will get into focus for him?*

EDGAR   [Aside] I would not take this from report. It is
             And my heart breaks at it.

KING LEAR   Read. *Come on. Surely you can.*

GLOUCESTER   What, with the case of eyes?

KING LEAR   O, ho, are you there with me? No eyes in your
             head, nor no money in your purse? Your eyes are in
             a heavy case, your purse in a light; yet you see how
             this world goes.

GLOUCESTER   I see it feelingly.

KING LEAR   What, art mad? A man may see how this world goes *Cover his own*
             with no eyes. Look with thine ears. See how yon *eyes.*
             justice rails upon yon simple thief. Hark in
             thine ear change places and, handy-dandy, which
             is the justice, which is the thief? Thou hast seen
appeal to Edgar not to let on. Go to other side of Gloucester. *Game. Laugh with him*   *Big pause. a silence on the beach at Dover*

IV.vi   a farmer's dog bark at a beggar?

GLOUCESTER   Ay, sir.

KING LEAR   And the creature run from the cur? There thou
               mightst behold the great image of authority: a
               dog's obeyed in office. *wrap cloak around him like lear actor*
               Thou rascal beadle, hold thy bloody hand
① Find someone   Why dost thou lash that whore? Strip thy own back.
in the audience.   Thou hotly lusts to use her in that kind
Back of the   For which thou whipp'st her. The usurer hangs the *(Lear's)*
stalls   cozener. *Get next to Gloucester. Arrange his*   *cloak*
               Through tatter'd clothes great vices do appear;   *neatly around*
               Robes and furr'd gowns hide all. Plate sins with   *him*
               gold,
Pick up stick   And the strong lance of justice hurtless breaks;
and drop it   Arm it in rags, a pygmy's straw does pierce it.
               None does offend, none, I say, none; I'll able 'em:
               Take that of me, my friend, *(know that of me)*

               [Giving flowers] *his note is rubbish!*
                              who have the power
               To seal th' accuser's lips. Get thee glass eyes, *(impatient)*
               And like a scurvy politician seem *stress the word*
               To see the things thou dost not. Now, now, now, now! *Pat him*
               Pull off my boots. Harder, harder – so.   *on the arm*
               Start to laugh. Become helpless. The two old men on a beach
EDGAR   O matter and impertinency mix'd! *one mad one blind, in*
               Reason in madness! *(A starts to cry (Gloucester)*   *unison*

KING LEAR   *(X)* If thou wilt weep my fortunes, take my eyes.
① embrace   I know thee well enough; thy name is Gloucester.
Gloucester   Thou must be patient; we came crying hither.   *smell the*
               Thou know'st the first time that we smell the air   *sea air*
               We wawl and cry. I will preach to thee – mark.

               [He takes off his coronet of flowers] *(no, he doesn't)*

GLOUCESTER   Alack, alack the day!   *he refers to his head.*
               First line as bible thumper   *This is a good idea!*
KING LEAR   When we are born we cry that we are come
               To this great stage of fools. *(X)* This's a good block.
               It were a delicate stratagem to shoe
X his   A troop of horse with felt *(X)* I'll put 't in proof;
stockinged   And when I have stol'n upon these son-in-laws,
feet   Then, kill, kill, kill, kill, kill, kill!
               attacks imaginary son-in-laws with his stick
               [He throws down flowers and stamps on them] *no he doesn't*

               [Enter a GENTLEMAN, with Attendants]

GENTLEMAN   O, here he is. Lay hand upon him. – Sir,

IV.vi

Your most dear daughter – *I present his stick in surrender*

Rhiets the Cleavens

KING LEAR No rescue? What, a prisoner? I am even
The natural fool of fortune. Use me well; *Cries out*
You shall have ransom. Let me have surgeons; *He indicates Edgar. Hell pay!*
I am cut to the brains.

GENTLEMAN   You shall have anything.

KING LEAR *back to normal* No seconds? All myself?
Why, this would make a man a man of salt,
To use his eyes for garden water-pots,
Ay, and laying autumn's dust. I will die bravely, *comic dance*
Like a smug bridegroom. What! I will be jovial.
official Come, come; I am a king; masters, know you that? *point to grooms*
                                                           X Rather they should kneel to him

GENTLEMAN You are a royal one, and we obey you.

KING LEAR *Lot line to the Gods* Then there's life in't. Come, *to the men* and you get it you
shall get it with running. Sa, sa, sa, sa. *escapes laughing followed by men*

[*Exit running; Attendants follow*]

GENTLEMAN A sight most pitiful in the meanest wretch,
Past speaking of in a king. – Thou hast one daughter
Who redeems nature from the general curse
Which twain have brought her to.

EDGAR Hail, gentle sir.

GENTLEMAN   Sir, speed you: what's your will?

EDGAR Do you hear aught, sir, of a battle toward?

GENTLEMAN Everyone hears that,
Which can distinguish sound.

EDGAR   But, by your favour,
How near's the other army?

GENTLEMAN   Near, and on speedy foot.
Though that the Queen on special cause is here,
Her army is moved on.

EDGAR   I thank you, sir.

[*Exit GENTLEMAN*]

GLOUCESTER You ever-gentle gods, take my breath from me.
Let not my worser spirit tempt me again
To die before you please.

Act V, scene ii - *A field between the two camps*

[*Enter EDGAR and GLOUCESTER*]

EDGAR   Here, father, take the shadow of this tree
                For your good host. Pray that the right may thrive.
                If ever I return to you again
                I'll bring you comfort.

GLOUCESTER   Grace go with you, sir!

        [*Exit EDGAR*]

[*Alarum within. Enter, with drum and colours, KING LEAR, CORDELIA, and Soldiers, over the stage; and exeunt*]

              [A battle]

              [*Alarum and retreat within. Re-enter EDGAR*]

EDGAR   Away, old man! Give me thy hand; away!
                King Lear hath lost, he and his daughter ta'en.
                Give me thy hand; come on.

GLOUCESTER   No further, sir; a man may rot even here.

EDGAR   What, in ill thoughts again? Men must endure
                Their going hence, even as their coming hither;
                Ripeness is all. Come on.

GLOUCESTER   And that's true too.

        [*Exeunt*]

Act V, scene iii - *The British camp near Dover*

[*Enter, in conquest, with drum and colours, EDMUND, KING LEAR and CORDELIA, prisoners; Captain, Soldiers, etc*]

EDMUND   Some officers take them away.

CORDELIA   We are not the first
              Who with best meaning have incurr'd the worst.
              For thee, oppressèd King, I am cast down;
              Myself could else out-frown false Fortune's frown.
              Shall we not see these daughters and these sisters?

[handwritten margin note:] Be weak. Find climbing stairs difficult in the A soldier pushes the king roughly. He stumbles and nearly falls.

V.iii

re-energised giving her strength

KING LEAR   No, no, no, no! Come, let's away to prison.
We two alone will sing like birds i'the cage;
When thou dost ask me blessing I'll kneel down,
And ask of thee forgiveness; so we'll live,
And pray, and sing, and tell old tales, and laugh
At gilded butterflies, and hear poor rogues
Talk of court news; and we'll talk with them too —
Who loses and who wins, who's in, who's out —   *unselfish*
And take upon's the mystery of things
As if we were God's spies; and we'll wear out,
In a wall'd prison, packs and sects of great ones
That ebb and flow by the moon.

EDMUND   Take them away.

KING LEAR   Upon such sacrifices, my Cordelia, *(hold her face tenderly)*
The gods themselves throw incense. Have I caught
    thee?
embrace   ⊗He that parts us shall bring a brand from heaven
her   And fire us hence like foxes. Wipe thine eyes;
The good-years shall devour them, flesh and fell,
Ere they shall make us weep. We'll see 'em starv'd
    first. *(laugh)*   *Be brave Cordelia*
Come.

   [*Exeunt KING LEAR and CORDELIA, guarded*]

EDMUND   Come hither, captain. Hark.
Take thou this note;

   [*Giving a paper*]

                          go follow them to prison.
One step I have advanced thee; if thou dost
As this instructs thee, thou dost make thy way
To noble fortunes. Know thou this, that men
Are as the time is; to be tender-minded
Does not become a sword; thy great employment
Will not bear question; either say thou'lt do 't,
Or thrive by other means.

CAPTAIN   I'll do 't, my lord.

EDMUND   About it; and write happy when thou hast done.
Mark, I say, instantly; and carry it so
As I have set it down.

CAPTAIN   If it be man's work, I'll do 't.

   [*Exit*]

Calm feather

V.iii

ALBANY   The gods defend her. Bear him hence awhile.

     [*EDMUND is borne off*] *at back*

     [*Re-enter KING LEAR, with CORDELIA dead in his arms;*
     EDGAR, Captain, and others following]
     Come down between the armed men.

KING LEAR   Howl, howl, howl! O, you are men of stones!
     Had I your tongues and eyes I'd use them so
     That heaven's vault should crack. She's gone for
        ever.
     I know when one is dead and when one lives;

set her down   She's dead as earth. Lend me a looking-glass;   *an unlikely*
     If that her breath will mist or stain the stone,   *request from*
     Why then she lives.   *a group of soldiers*

KENT   Is this the promised end

EDGAR   Or image of that horror?

ALBANY   Fall, and cease!   *"find" feather on on the floor.*

KING LEAR   This feather stirs - she lives! If it be so,
kneel beside her   It is a <u>chance</u> which does redeem all sorrows
     That ever I have felt. *lift her up in his arms*

KENT   [*Kneeling*]   O my good master!

KING LEAR   Prithee away. (*not now*)

EDGAR   'Tis noble Kent, your friend.

KING LEAR   A plague upon you, murderers, traitors all! (*test her breath*)
accusing   I might have saved her; now she's gone for ever.   PAUSE
     Cordelia, Cordelia stay a little. Ha!
     What is't thou say'st? Her voice was ever soft,
     Gentle and low - an excellent thing in woman.
     I kill'd the slave that was a-hanging thee.

CAPTAIN   'Tis true, my lords, he did.

KING LEAR   Did I not, fellow?
     I have seen the day, with my good biting falchion
     I would have made him skip. I am old now
     And these same crosses spoil me. Who are you?   *x Kent*
     Mine eyes are not o' the best, I'll tell you
        straight.

~~KENT~~   ~~If Fortune brag of two she loved and hated~~
     ~~One of them we behold.~~

V.iii

KING LEAR This is a dull sight. Are-you-not Kent?

KENT The same –
Your servant Kent. Where is your servant Caius?

KING LEAR He's a good fellow, I can tell you that;
He'll strike, and quickly too. He's dead and rotten.

KENT No, my good lord; I am the very man, –
That from your first of difference and decay
Have follow'd your sad steps –

KING LEAR *vague* You are welcome hither.
extend hand to be ~~been~~ kissed

KENT Nor no man else. All's cheerless, dark, and deadly.
Your eldest daughters have fordone themselves,
And desperately are dead.

KING LEAR *vague* x Ay, so I think.

ALBANY He knows not what he says, and vain is it
That we present us to him.

[Enter a Captain]

CAPTAIN Edmund is dead, my lord.

ALBANY That's but a trifle here.
You lords and noble friends, know our intent:
What comfort to this great decay may come
Shall be applied. For us, we will resign
During the life of this old majesty
To him our absolute power.

[To EDGAR and KENT]
All friends shall taste
The wages of their virtue, and all foes
The cup of their deservings. - O, see, see!

all stops out   *Breathing*

KING LEAR x And my poor fool is hang'd! No, / no / no / life!
Why should a dog, a horse, a rat have life,
And thou no breath at all? Thou'lt come no more x
SLOW Never / never / never / never / never ⓧ *on final*
to Edgar Pray you undo this button. Thank you, sir.
Do you see this? Look on her! Look, her lips,
Look there! Look there! *Falls to the*
to all the soldiers   *ground.*

x put her down gently. Begin to rise. "never" clutch left arm as though heart attack / PAIN!

[Dies]

EDGAR He faints. My lord, my lord!

Works Cited

Adams, John (1993) '*Yes, Prime Minister:* The Ministerial Broadcast (Jonathan Lynn and Antony Jay), social reality and comic realism in popular television drama', in G. W. Brandt, ed., *British Television Drama in the 1980s,* 62-85. Cambridge

Agate, James (1945), *Immoment Toys: A Survey of Light Entertainment on the London Stage, 1920-1943.* London

Arrowsmith, William (1969) 'Introduction to *Heracles*', in D. Greene & R. Lattimore, eds., *Euripides II,* 44-59. Chicago & London (originally published 1956)

Bennett, Alan (1992) *The Madness of George III.* London

(1994) *Writing Home.* London

(1995) *The Madness of King George.* London

Carpenter, Humphrey (2000) *That Was Satire That Was: The Satire Boom of the 1960s.* London

Davies, Russell, ed. (1994) *The Kenneth Williams Diaries.* London (originally published 1993)

Doty, Gresdna A., & Billy J. Harbin, eds. (1990) *Inside the Royal Court Theatre, 1956-1981: Artists Talk.* Baton Rouge

Dunn, Kate (1998) *Exit Through the Fireplace: The Great Days of Rep.* London

Eddington, Paul (1995) *So Far, So Good: The Autobiography.* London

Eliot, T. S. (1951) *Selected Essays,* 3rd edn. London

Eyre, Richard, & Nicholas Wright (2000) *Changing Stages: A View of the British Theatre in the Twentieth Century.* London

Findlater, Richard, ed. (1981) *At the Royal Court: Twenty-Five Years of the English Stage Company.* Ambergate (Derbyshire)

Foulkes, Richard (1992) *Repertory at The Royal: Sixty-Five Years of Theatre in Northampton* 1927-92. Northampton

Gaskill, William (1988) *A Sense of Direction: Life at the Royal Court*. London

Gems, Pam (1979) *Uncle Vanya* (A new version). London

Goorney, Howard (1981) *The Theatre Workshop Story*. London

Gray, Simon (1985) *An Unnatural Pursuit and Other Pieces*. London

Griffin, William (1988) *C. S. Lewis: The Authentic Voice*. Tring, Hertfordshire (originally published 1986)

Guinness, Alec (1996) *Blessings in Disguise*. London (originally published 1985)

Harwood, Ronald, ed. (1984) *The Ages of Gielgud: An Actor at Eighty*. London

Hay, Malcolm, & Philip Roberts (1980) *Bond, a study of his plays*. London

Hobson, Harold (1978) *Indirect Journey: An Autobiography*. London

Holdsworth, Nadine (1999) "'They'd Have Pissed on My Grave": The Arts Council and Theatre Workshop', *New Theatre Quarterly* 57: 3-16

Ingram, Allan (1991) *The Madhouse of Language: Writing and Reading Madness in the Eighteenth Century*. London & New York

Inskip, Donald (1977) *Stage by Stage: The Leonard Schach Story*. Cape Town

Johnston, John (1990) *The Lord Chamberlain's Blue Pencil*. London

Lewis, C. S. (1966) *A Grief Observed*. London (originally published 1961)

(1980) *The Last Battle*. London (originally published 1956)

Littlewood, Joan (1994) *Joan's Book: Joan Littlewood's Peculiar History As She Tells It*. London

Lynn, Jonathan, & Antony Jay (1986) *Yes, Prime Minister: The Diaries of the Right Hon. James Hacker*, vol. I. London

Macalpine, Ida, & Richard Hunter (1991) *George III and the Mad-Business*. London (originally published 1969)

Morley, Sheridan (2002) *Asking for Trouble: The Memoirs of Sheridan Morley*. London

Nadel, Ira Bruce (2002) *Double Act: A Life of Tom Stoppard*. London

Nichols, Peter (2000) *Diaries 1969-1977*. London

O'Connor, Gary (2002) *Alec Guinness The Unknown: A Life*. London

Rebellato, Dan (1999) *1956 And All That: The Making of Modern British Drama.* London & New York

Roberts, Philip (1999) *The Royal Court Theatre and the Modern Stage.* Cambridge

Schach, Leonard (1996) *The Flag is Flying: A Very Personal History of Theatre in the Old South Africa.* Cape Town

Stuart, Ian, ed. (2000) *Selections from the Notebooks of Edward Bond.* London

Trench, Charles Chenevix (1964) *The Royal Malady.* London

Tucker, Percy (1997) *Just the Ticket! My Fifty Years in Show Business.* Johannesburg

Tynan, Kenneth (1975) *A View of the English Stage, 1944-1965.* London

(1989) *Profiles.* London

Wherrett, Richard (2000) *The Floor of Heaven: My Life in Theatre.* Sydney

Wilamowitz-Moellendorff, Ulrich (1959) *Herakles,* vol. I. Darmstadt (reprint of 2nd edn of 1895/ 1st edn 1889)

Willmer, John (1999) *Full Circle: The Story of Worthing's Connaught Theatre.* Worthing

Wood, Charles (1997) *Plays One.* London

Wu, Duncan (2000) *Making Plays: Interviews with Contemporary British Dramatists and Directors.* London

Zucker, Carole (1999) *In the Company of Actors: Reflections on the Craft of Acting.* London

Index